THE NONCONFORMISTS

7/12

280.
m4n

Please renew/return items by last date
shown. Please call the number below:

Renewals and enquiries: 0300 123 4049

Textphone for hearing or
speech impaired users: 0300 123 4041

www.hertsdirect.org/librarycatalogue
L32

Hertfordshire

James Munson

THE
NONCONFORMISTS

In search of a lost culture

First published in Great Britain 1991
SPCK
Holy Trinity Church
Marylebone Road
London NW1 4DU

British Library Cataloguing in Publication Data

Munson, James
The nonconformists.
1. England. Nonconformist churches. History
I. Title
280.40942

ISBN 0–281–04495–3

Typeset by Pioneer Associates, Perthshire
Printed in Great Britain at
the University Press, Cambridge

CONTENTS

To
my mother,
Vera Susan Elizabeth Bradbury Munson

FOREWORD

This book grew out of an essay on Nonconformity's reaction to the 1902 Education Act which was awarded the Thomas Arnold Historical Essay Prize in the University of Oxford. It was then transformed into a doctoral thesis on that exotic attempt by Edwardian Nonconformists to attack the 1902 Education Act in the name of conscience – the 'Passive Resister' movement. Afterwards and over the years it has been expanded into its present form.

My first duty is to thank H.M. the Queen for her gracious permission to examine and quote from material held in the Royal Archives or under Crown copyright. My second is to acknowledge the debt I owe Dr Eric Stone of Keble College, Oxford for his friendship, support and teaching. I wish to thank Lord Dacre, then Professor Hugh Trevor-Roper, who encouraged me in my research, the Committee of Graduate Studies and the Arnold, Bryce and Read Funds for their generous support, Dr K. O. Morgan who guided my work and gave me copies of manuscript letters he had uncovered, Dr Clyde Binfield of Sheffield University who helped and shared his extraordinary knowledge of English Nonconformity with me, Dr Paul Hayes, who helped me in my original research, Dr John Walsh who exemplifies in his unostentatious way some of the most sterling traits in the English Nonconformist character and the many people, too numerous to list here, who, as descendants of Passive Resisters, answered my many questions.

I also wish to thank the Duke of Devonshire, the Marquess of Salisbury, the Viscount Harcourt, the Earl of Selborne, the Archbishop of Canterbury and the Trustees of Lambeth Palace Library for permission to cite manuscripts owned by them and the Viscount Furness for his help. I must also thank the Archbishop for permission to see the address quoted in the Afterword and the late Dr E. A. Payne, CH, Mr Denis Duncan, Mr Edward England,

Mr Rayner Unwin, Miss Tabitha Driver, the Rev. Graham James, Chaplain to the Archbishop of Canterbury, Mr K. T. Payne, MBE, the Rev. Arthur Hughes, Mr F. Charrett, the Minister and Deacons of Queen's Road Baptist Church, Coventry, the Rev. J. Dalby, Mrs Linda Shaw, Assistant Keeper of Manuscripts, University of Nottingham, Mr L. H. Brown, Mr C. Stirzaker, the late Mr Kenneth Young, and the Minister and Deacons of Milton-under-Wychwood Baptist Church, Oxfordshire.

In my research I was greatly aided by the staffs of the following libraries: Duke Humfrey Library, the Bodleian Library, Oxford, the House of Lords Record Office, the House of Commons Library, the Public Record Office, the British Library and the Newspaper Library at Colindale, Christ Church College, Oxford, Dr Williams's Library, the Greater London Record Office, Lambeth Palace Library, Nuffield College, Oxford, the National Libraries of Scotland and Wales, the Society of Friends, the Sheffield Central Reference Library, Newcastle upon Tyne University Library, the Berg Collection in the New York Public Library, the University of Nottingham, University College, London and the University of Birmingham Library.

I would like to thank the staffs of Baptist Church House, the Methodist Archives (now transferred to the John Rylands Library), the Free Church Federal Council, whose Free Church Council manuscripts are in the process of being transferred to Dr Williams's Library, Chatsworth House and the County Record Offices of Buckinghamshire, Dorset, County Durham, Gloucester, Kent, Norfolk, Northamptonshire and Warwickshire. Finally I would like to record my gratitude to my late father who helped me in my research and, as a Presbyterian, joyfully noted the shortcomings of his wife's Baptist ancestors, Dr R. J. Carwardine who gave me the benefit of his wide knowledge of American religion, Mr T. D. Gebbels of The Queen's College, Oxford, for his enthusiasm and support, Dr R. F. Mullen for his invaluable help, friendship and encouragement over the years, Mr A. F. Kerr for his help with the Society of Friends, and Judith Longman of SPCK for her assistance and understanding.

5 September 1990.   *James Munson*
                                                        Oxford

INTRODUCTION

The decline of English Nonconformity as a major part of English culture in the twentieth century may well be seen as being as profound a change in English history as the suppression of the monasteries under Henry VIII. Unlike the monasteries' disappearance, Nonconformity's decline has been gradual and may well be seen as having come from within, not imposed from without. The very causes which brought about Nonconformity's great strength may also have brought about its decline. Like the monasteries some of its 'ruins' still bear testimony to its lost influence: the chapels turned into bicycle shops and off-licences, the great suburban churches in which a handful of the faithful gather where once thousands sat entranced under great preachers. However, unlike the monasteries, Nonconformity's influence has survived its institutional decline. Indeed, it has so permeated English life in the twentieth century that the Nonconformist legacy has affected millions who have never set foot inside a chapel.

One of its most important contributions, at least in popular speech, is 'The Nonconformist Conscience'. To the historically minded, this is remembered as a legacy of late nineteenth century political history, a product of the Parnell divorce case of 1890. To the majority it is seen, if anything, as an essentially middle-class moral crusade against Sunday concerts and the evils of the drink trade. It is a hangover from the nineteenth century, a Victorian Aunt Sally 'flanked by the Albert Memorial and the "Idylls of the King"'.[1] Yet behind this term lies a vast hinterland, something of a lost culture, that gave it meaning and power. It is the object of this book to explore that land.

Victorian Nonconformity has, perhaps, been more attacked than any other expression of English Christianity. 'Theirs', the novelist, Hugh Walpole, wrote of some of his characters, 'was the Nonconformist mind and vision: grey

1

stone, drab clothes, un-coloured minds.'[2] Nonconformity was many things but its stones were not grey, its clothes were not drab and its minds were never un-coloured. Victorian Nonconformity has also been called narrow yet it was as much, if not more, internationally minded than the Church of England and played a far more vital role in the creation of the English-speaking world, both in America and in the colonies, than the Established Church did or ever could do.

The period on which this book concentrates (1890–1914) was the hey-day of Nonconformist power and English Nonconformity was as powerful and influential a force in national life as any organized religious minority has ever been. It was vibrant, even by the standards of an England that had yet to discover a stiff upper lip and it rejoiced in its own strength: the laws of historical development told them that the twentieth century would actually see them surpass the Church of England to become the real church of the English nation. The laws of nature and of social evolution meant that the new century of the common man would belong to the churches of the common man. It was as inevitable as progress itself. A democratic England, like democratic America, would be a Nonconformist England.

One President of the Baptist Union, who started life as a butcher before entering the ministry, said in the last year of the old century:

> We are leaving behind us a century of the most colossal progress the world has ever witnessed . . . There are locks now for which there are no keys, but the keys will be made that will fit the locks, and the doors will be opened, and more amazing treasures will be found.[3]

This was based, he added, not on dreams, but on the 'solid facts of the past'. A perceptive critic who looked at Nonconformity from the outside at this same period wrote in the Anglican *Church Quarterly Review* that it presented a 'spectacle of vast religious organisations throughout the whole Anglo-Saxon world consolidating their machinery, utterly uncommitted to their past declarations, and cheerfully ready to adapt themselves to whatever the future may stipulate'. 'Life' he added, 'is a Triumph, not a Tragedy.'[4]

Thirteen years later the Great War began and the self-confident Victorian liberalism of which Nonconformity had become such an expression received a shock from which some argue it never recovered. In looking at what may be called Nonconformist England I concentrate on its four largest denominations – Congregationalists, Baptists, Wesleyan and Primitive Methodists. Seventy-seven out of every one hundred English Nonconformists belonged to one of these four denominations and with the exceptions of small groups, like the Quakers or Unitarians, whose influence far exceeded their numerical strength, they broadly represented the development of Nonconformity as a whole and reflected the basic divisions as to organization and beliefs.

The Wesleyan 'Connexion' was governed by a clerical conference which met yearly and which owned all denominational property. The Connexion was a tightly organized structure, ruled from the top. It was not until 1877 that laymen were allowed to sit in Conference and in the 1890s, led by the Rev. Hugh Price Hughes, they pressed for more power. The country was divided into districts and the districts were divided into circuits within which ministers 'travelled' among various 'stations' which were, in most cases, chapels. These ministers, who were ordained at the annual conference after a probationary period, moved circuits every three years and were assisted by lay or local preachers who often presided over smaller 'stations'. In theory the basic unit of Methodism was not the chapel with its Sunday services but the 'class meeting' to which admittance was gained by possessing a 'class ticket' although much of this antiquated structure was ignored by the 1890s for a greater concentration on the chapel and its activities. In doctrine they were close to Low Church Evangelicals in the Church of England. The Primitive Methodists, who dated from 1811, were the largest of the four Methodist bodies to have separated from Wesley's 'Connexion'. They gave more power to laymen and to the Districts. By the closing decades of the nineteenth century their basic difference from Wesleyanism lay in what they were rather than in how they were organized or what they believed: they were more rural and working class.

The Baptists and Congregationalists had much looser national unions or confederations, based on county associations or unions, which were in turn made up of self-governing chapels. These were, in law, charities ruled by trustees under a trust deed. They could join the local body and through it the national union or they could stay outside: both Joseph Parker's City Temple and Spurgeon's Metropolitan Tabernacle were, for some years, outside the official national union even though they were among the denomination's most famous churches. Local chapels were governed by deacons, elected by the members; 'the church', which met in 'the chapel' was made up of believers immersed after a profession of faith, in the case of Baptists, or of believers who had been baptized as infants and later professed salvation, in the case of Congregationalists. Congregationalists and, to a lesser degree, Baptists had survived a fundamental change in the nineteenth century, a change which saw the old 'High Calvinism' of the seventeenth and eighteenth centuries gradually replaced by a more 'Arminian' or traditional Christian understanding of evangelism. It was only in the early 1890s that the two strands within English Baptists – Arminians and Calvinists – were united into the Baptist Union. There was still a wide range of beliefs and strictly speaking the individual chapel's creed when spelled out was done so in the Trust Deed.

Methodists, however, stood largely aside from these developments. Methodism as descended from John Wesley had never been Calvinist; only in Wales was there a 'Calvinistic Methodist Church'. Regarding scripture they remained conservative. There had been, however, two fundamental changes which affected Wesleyans. The first was the altered way in which Anglicans saw their own Church due to the increasing power of the High Church movement and especially of the Anglo Catholics in the 1880s onwards. There had traditionally been a deep-seated reluctance among Methodists to attack the Church of England because such an attack made them sound like Radicals, with their cry for disestablishment and because Methodists continued to share the same basic outlook; it was also 'vulgar'. The second change had begun within Methodism itself. In 1883 Conference decided by a vote of

266 to 134 to end the use of the *Prayer Book* and substitute a new *Book of Public Prayers and Services*. Conference removed the collect, epistle and gospel readings for saints' days and changed the wording of Holy Communion and Baptism to transform these sacraments into protestant commemorative ordinances. Wesleyans were in effect saying that they would define their own doctrine and services because they were a church in their own right, without reference to the Established Church. It was a victory of 'Dissenting Methodists' over 'Church Methodists'. Even so, many Wesleyans still turned to the Church for great occasions. As the novelist, Arnold Bennett, quipped, 'all good Wesleyan Methodists marry themselves in church' and ecclesiastical assertions were another matter altogether.[5]

My aim in this book is to show the influence Non-conformity had on English society, literature, education, architecture, religion and politics – the culture behind the phrase, 'the Nonconformist Conscience'. It may be that historians will say that Nonconformity was like the monasteries, developing slowly from small beginnings, in this case in the seventeenth century, and flowering as a great power in its heyday. Ultimately, however, if its twentieth-century decline carries on and proves permanent, it will survive in small communities, perhaps revived on a local level from time to time. It will then take its assigned part as yet one more part of this island's long history, a relic not a power, like those monastic communities revived by Anglicans and Roman Catholics. More perceptive historians may see that despite its decline, English Nonconformity has left, unlike the monasteries, an indelible mark on the national character which will long outlive its institutional strength. This book is intended for those who are interested in the culture that once throve behind those now closed chapel doors and for those who want to understand something of English Nonconformity's lasting influence.

1

THE NONCONFORMIST IMPACT ON VICTORIAN LIFE

In the last year of the nineteenth century the President of the National Free Church Council, the Rev. Charles Kelly, a leading Wesleyan Methodist, bade farewell to a century which had arguably seen the greatest changes in English religious life since the Reformation: 'For the Free Churches the nineteenth century has been a great century. It has been rich in splendid opportunities . . . The nineteenth century will die soon, but Free Churches will not – they will live and flourish.' A visitor to England in 1900 would have been amazed at the impact Nonconformity now had on English life: throughout the country, in villages and towns, in the great cities and expanding suburbs, Nonconformist chapels helped to fashion the Victorian townscape and, through their multiplying clubs and organizations, to form the substance of social life for millions. The most working-class denomination, the Primitive Methodists, could boast in June 1901: 'It is a source of much satisfaction that our people are everywhere participating in the social and intellectual advance of the times.' A symbol of this change in English life arrived in 1899 when, after a somewhat bizarre and involved history, Hamo Thornycroft's statue of a pensive Oliver Cromwell was secretly unveiled early one November morning outside the Palace of Westminster. He was perhaps as perplexed as his enemies as to why he had been placed outside the very institution he had once disbanded.[1]

Nonconformists had established their position as the greatest single power behind the Liberal Party as once the landed gentry had been behind the Tories, aristocrats had been behind the Whigs and Trade Unions would in turn be behind the Labour Party. Much attention has been paid to the number of Nonconformists returned in the Liberal landslide of 1906 but little to those in the Liberal remnant that survived the Tory victory six years earlier. However, of the 186 Liberal MPs returned in 1900, 129 were Nonconformist. Among the 'new men' from whom the next generation of leaders was expected to emerge, Asquith, Lloyd George and Haldane were Nonconformists. The much reviled leader of the Liberal Unionists and Colonial Secretary, Joseph Chamberlain, was a Unitarian. In 1902 *The British Weekly* reported some forty Nonconformist mayors in England and Wales and they were not confined to traditional strongholds like Birmingham or Norwich or the North of England but extended throughout the country. In industry, trade, charity, intellectual life, architecture, town planning, social work and research Nonconformists had an influence, and in some cases a lead, which belied the fact that by the end of Victoria's reign they made up no more than some fifteen per cent of the population of England and Wales. Among social reformers Nonconformists had made their mark: General Booth with his Salvation Army, Dr Barnado with his homes and George Cadbury, who pioneered the 'garden suburb' and town planning. The YMCA had largely been the creation of Nonconformists. The Congregational minister, Benjamin Waugh, was the main founder of the National Society for the Prevention of Cruelty to Children. It was he who pressed for legislation to allow courts to remove abused children from parents, thereby laying the foundation for much of the work done by the twentieth century's army of social workers.

Some of the leading researchers into the new urban civilization which had sprung up, men like Seebohm Rowntree and Charles Booth, were Nonconformists. In literature, journalism, publishing and academic life not just in the new civic universities like Birmingham, Liverpool or Manchester but even at Oxford and Cambridge, Nonconformists were playing an increasing role. The most influential lexicographer of the age and editor of the first *Oxford English Dictionary*, James Murray, was a Nonconformist as were some of the leading historians, men like Firth, Stoughton and Gardiner. The wealth earned by industrialists and merchants like John Ryland, Charles Booth, Frederick Horniman, Sir Richard Tangye, W. H. Lever, Sir Henry Tate and Samuel Courtauld went into public service, building up major centres of scholarly research or collecting art treasures for the enjoyment of all. In music it was a Congregational minister, John Curwen, who is credited with inventing the Tonic-sol-fa system which greatly increased the spread of popular music. In the law, England had her first Nonconformist-born Lord Chancellor in Farrer Herschell; in the civil service the most famous civil servant of the century, Sir Rowland Hill, was a Nonconformist; in scientific research some of the leading names included men like Joseph Lister and Sir Michael Faraday and in natural science, Philip Gosse and Henry Seebohm. The Wesleyan Methodist minister, W. H. Dallinger, was four times President of the Royal Microscopical Society and was elected to the Royal Society in 1880. In industrial innovation families like the Tangyes in Birmingham, the Crossleys in Halifax, the Wills in Bristol or the Levers in Port Sunlight not only led the way but helped to create a new economy based on cheap production for an ever-expanding market. In industrial research, Sir John Brunner's firm, Brunner, Mond & Co., laid the foundation for what later became Imperial Chemical Industries. When it came to improving the lot of working families it was Nonconformist industrialists like Salt, Lever, Rowntree, Cory, Reckitt and especially George and Richard Cadbury who showed the role decent housing could play.

In the mission field the greatest missionary of the century, David Livingstone, had been sent out by the London Missionary Society, essentially a Congregational body; even in the army one of the great heroes of the Indian Mutiny had been Sir Henry Havelock who led the relief of Lucknow in 1857; in the theatre, once a forbidden field, Nonconformists had given Victorian England her greatest actor and actress, Henry Irving and Ellen Terry. In poetry it was the Nonconformists Elizabeth Barrett and Robert Browning who gave the language some of its most beautiful verses and one of its most moving love-stories: in all these fields Nonconformists were to be found making sizeable contributions to Victorian culture. Denominations were cooperating to a degree never known before and there was an exchange of views and a ferment of new ideas fully the equal of what was going on in the Church of England if not greater. Increasingly, Nonconformist ministers were among the most notable figures in provincial towns, men like R. W. Dale in Birmingham, J. B. Paton in Nottingham or Alexander Maclaren in Manchester. In the capital, preachers like the Baptists, Spurgeon, F. B. Meyer and John Clifford, Congregationalists like C. Silvester Horne, R. F. Horton and Joseph Parker and Wesleyan Methodists like Hugh Price Hughes drew audiences in the tens of thousands. Parker's City Temple in Holborn, Spurgeon's Metropolitan Tabernacle near the Elephant and Castle, Meyer's Christ Church on Westminster Bridge Road, Clifford's Westbourne Park Chapel in Paddington and Horne's Tabernacle on the Tottenham Court Road were as much tourist sights as were the Crystal Palace, Madame Tussauds or Buckingham Palace.

Those blessed with the gift of hindsight can point out that Nonconformist progress was beset by problems and that the increase in membership was not as promising as it looked. These will be discussed in due course although most of the problems were recognized at the time: overlapping between competing denominations, especially in villages; the decay of town centre chapels due to the members' migration into the expanding suburbs; the fear by some of too great an involvement in political activity by the churches and especially by younger ministers and, finally, the need to improve the education of those ministers. Even so, an acute observer of religion wrote at the time that 'all other considerations are swallowed up in the overwhelming discovery that the Free Churches are at last beginning to get on'.[2]

This note of triumphalism was supported by statistics which were seen by Victorians in general and Nonconformists in particular as irrefutable indices of progress. While these have to be handled with the greatest of care they do, at the end of the day, provide us with at least an indication of strength and are impressive. Figures published for the first year of the twentieth century (1901) showed that over half the active membership of all non-Roman Catholic churches in England and Wales was Nonconformist. (The figures, which included the Salvation Army and Wales, were published by a Nonconformist body and were biased towards Nonconformity: active members, not baptised, are counted. In that case the Church of England would manifestly have surpassed their rivals because the Anglican figures were only for Easter communicants.) Great stress was also placed on the predominance of 'Nonconformity' within the Anglo-Saxon world. There the supremacy of the descendants of the Dissenters was obvious. The 1902 *Free Church Year Book* boasted that throughout the Empire and America there were but 3,367,052 Anglican as opposed to 18,231,688 Methodist, Baptist, Presbyterian and Congregational 'communicants'. In addition there were just over fourteen million Sunday School students. Again, because the figures were based on active membership the Anglican position looked worse than it was.[3]

All of the four leading denominations had increased their membership during the last third of the nineteenth century. Baptists had increased by 51 per cent and stood at 243,534. Wesleyan Methodists had grown by 27 per cent, to 404,890. Primitive Methodists had grown by 23 per cent, to 183,505. Accurate figures for 1870, the year of comparison, are not available for Congregationalists but by 1901 they numbered 258,434 in England. It is not unreasonable to assume that their membership had increased by about the same percentage as the Wesleyans. Again we are looking at membership and even though the Wesleyan and Primitive Methodists and the Congregationalists used infant baptism, membership among the latter was based on a profession of religious belief. Methodists only became full members after a period of probation and through admission to the Class Meeting. (The 1909 official *History of Methodism* felt that membership totals should be multiplied by four to take account of children, 'probationers' and 'hearers' who did not hold a Class Ticket.) Admittedly the increases had not kept pace with the rise in population. In 1870 Wesleyan membership formed 1.7 per cent of the English population while Baptists formed .85 and Primitive Methodists, .79. By 1901, after a population increase of 43.23 per cent, the Wesleyan percentage had fallen to 1.33 while the Baptists had fallen to .79 and the Primitive Methodists to .60. Congregationalists, for whom no comparison can be made, constituted .84 per cent in 1901. Baptists had proved the healthiest group: their absolute numbers had increased more rapidly and their relative percentage of the population had declined less markedly. One Baptist leader did recognize in 1898: 'For though we advance, we are receding relatively to the ever-increasing population.'[4]

If we take the advice in the Methodists' official history and multiply by four, Nonconformist numbers rise to 4,361,452 or 14.24 per cent of the population in 1901 and this, of course, is only for the four major denominations. This does not include the three small Methodist denominations, the Salvation Army, smaller groups such as the Society of Friends and Unitarians and various unaffiliated chapels. Indeed, the number of 'adherents' could grow while the number of actual members declined and Wesleyan Methodists did complain of a decreasing sense of denominational loyalty in cities, where most of the growth took place. This applied to other denominations as well. Therefore, it is not unreasonable to argue that the real Nonconformist 'presence' in Victorian life would have exceeded four and a half million people. As impressive as this sounds we should remember that these millions still constituted only fifteen out of every 100 people in England and Wales and the proportion was falling, not rising.

There were also statistics of growth from another quarter where Nonconformists had not expected to find it. This was the 1902–1903 survey of religious life in London conducted by Richard Mudie-Smith for the *Daily News*. Smith was a member of John Clifford's Westbourne Park Baptist Church. Surprisingly, given traditional Nonconformist weakness in the capital, the survey showed that of 1,252,433 'worshippers' surveyed, the largest group, 545,477, was Nonconformist. Anglicans numbered 538,477, Roman Catholics 96,281 and 'others' 72,358. The marked decline in Londoners' church-going since the great religious census of 1851 had mainly affected the Established Church. London Nonconformity had been saved by the Baptists: they had actually increased their membership and their percentage of London's population. Although some argued that the creation of large 'Central Halls' by Wesleyans mitigated their decline, the fact was that all the major Nonconformist denominations had declined with the exception of the Baptists. Their growth was put down to the dynamism of Spurgeon's disciples with their Tabernacles but it was mainly due to the expansion of London into the suburbs, especially to the north. This was the area where the lower-middle classes went and these were the people from whom Baptists largely drew their strength.[5]

There were other statistics which encouraged Nonconformists. One favourite Victorian pastime was counting the number of sittings provided in a church or chapel and in 1901 observers counted 8,140,767 seats in Nonconformist churches in England and Wales. There were, in addition, 384,175 Sunday School teachers with 3,276,895 students, 10,097 fully employed ministers and 52,341 local or lay preachers. It was a vast religious network and it was also a wealthy one: Victorian Nonconformists spent an incredible amount of money in their work and this extended back for a large part of the century. In the 1870s, for example, Primitive Methodists, perhaps the poorest of the four largest denominations, spent £1,057,511 on 897 new chapels. On 19 January 1875 Congregationalists opened their Memorial Hall, the first of the Nonconformist denominational headquarters in London, and built on the site of the old Fleet Prison which had once held Protestant martyrs. It cost £75,520 of which a third was contributed by four of their wealthiest members – Samuel Morley, John Crossley, Sir Titus Salt and J. R. Mills. The five major Congregational societies which aided local chapels in erecting new buildings had spent by 1885 some £3,628,300. Andrew Mearns, who compiled these records, asserted as a 'low calculation' that by 1885 Congregational churches were raising just over one million pounds a year. When we remember that these figures should be multiplied by about thirty-three to approach the pound's value in 1990 we see their real importance: the Congregational societies' spending on buildings before 1885 becomes £117,000,000 while their annual spending rises from £1m to £32,500,000.[6]

In the last decade of the century Baptists, Wesleyan and Primitive Methodists spent just under £11m on home missions, ministerial education, repayment of loans, repairs, building, and foreign missions – £357m in today's currency. (There are no fully reliable figures for Congregationalists.) All this expenditure does not include the mammoth efforts put forward by all leading denominations at the turn of the century to raise 'Twentieth Century' funds. A new era called for a new effort and Wesleyans, Baptists and Congregationalists all had funds to raise, respectively, one million guineas, £250,000 and 500,000 guineas. Primitive Methodists had raised a Jubilee Fund between 1893 and 1900 of £50,048 and Baptist women had a Million Shillings fund: this made a grand total among the four for the new century of £1,967,000 or just under £64m.[7] In 1908 Baptists and Congregationalists went on to raise a further £250,000 in 'Sustentation Funds' to supplement the stipends of their worst paid ministers. While there were criticisms of the Twentieth Century funds because of the allocation of the money, they still stand as one of the greatest religious fund-raising efforts in English history.

In some cases individual chapels had become famous for the amounts they raised and spent in their work. In 1872, for example, land was bought in Lambeth on the Westminster Bridge Road at the corner of Kennington Road for a new building to house Rowland Hill's famous Surrey Chapel founded in 1782. For neighbours the new Congregational church, to be called Christ Church, had Spurgeon's Metropolitan Tabernacle, St George's Roman Catholic Cathedral and Lambeth Palace. The appeal for funds was supported by prominent people outside the Congregational fold such as the Duchess of Argyll, whose son had married Queen Victoria's daughter, Princess Louise, the year before, the Duke of Westminster, the Marchioness of Exeter, Earl Russell, the Earl of Shaftesbury, the Countess of Gainsborough, Lady Augusta Stanley, a close friend of Queen Victoria and wife of the 'little Dean' of Westminster – Arthur Stanley, Florence Nightingale, by various wealthy Congregational laymen and by fourteen MPs. A copy of the Appeal was sent to the Prime Minister, William Gladstone. The buildings cost £25,000 (over £800,000 today) because the church was only the centre of a vast operation: there were thirteen Sunday Schools for 5,000 children and 400 teachers; there was a mission to working men, a Benevolent Society to help the poor, a Nursing Auxiliary to visit poor invalids, various missions, clothing societies, a School of Industry to train fifty girls for domestic service, almshouses for twenty-three old women, and a day school. The church had forty services each week for the poor of Lambeth and spent an average of £3,000 a year in social work.[8]

Christ Church was not unique for there were many other famous London churches which equalled it. During the pastorate of Alfred Rowland (1875 to 1911), Park Congregational Chapel, Crouch End, Hornsey raised £131,000. John Clifford's Westbourne Park Chapel raised £160,657 between 1877 and 1906 and R. F. Horton's Congregational chapel, Lyndhurst Road, in Hampstead raised a quarter of a million between 1879 and 1909. Charles Brown's Ferme Park Baptist Chapel, Hornsey, had by 1906 an annual income of £5,000 (£162,500).

Victorian England also saw a blossoming of Nonconformist mercantile princes, products of that industrial and urban civilization which had brought about the transformation in England's religious practices. These Nonconformist businessmen permeated every aspect of national life and helped to change the business, cultural and social life of the nation. As we shall see, many were and still are household names even though the original family businesses have long since given way to limited companies, holding companies and multinational conglomerates. Nonconformity was proud of its new aristocracy and wanted it to play its full part in the new pluralist society the twentieth century would inevitably introduce. At the same time it was afraid of the attractions of 'the establishment' to lure wealthy families into its nets before Nonconformity's increasing strength had got rid of those nets. In 1897 the Reverend Joseph Parker, minister of the influential City Temple in Holborn, and a man never at a loss for words, admitted that 'of course, it is very tempting to become anything but a Dissenter, if you can be invited to dine late in the suburbs'. He undoubtedly spoke from experience as he lived in some state in Lyndhurst Gardens, NW3, one of the wealthiest parts of Hampstead. Because he was himself able to resist the temptation he warned those who converted to the Church of England 'for social reasons' that 'a gentility bought is the coarsest vulgarity'.[9]

Such is the English character that a yearning for gentility is inevitably combined with a desire to remove oneself from the taint of trade. Undoubtedly the desire to hide one's origins among those anxious to enter the portals of the Establishment affected Nonconformists as much or as little as anyone else. Equally, however, there was a legitimate desire to play one's part in English society, especially if one believed that the world's riches were given by God in trust to help others. There was a refusal to accept that Nonconformists must forever live in the shop's back parlour when progress had converted the shop into a multi-million pound industry. The list of these mercantile princes is a long one and we can only look at a few to illustrate the changes that were taking place.

In Bolton W. H. Lever developed the giant Lever Brothers: he launched his Sunlight soap tablets in 1884 designed for a working-class market. He hit on the trick of using vegetable oil to give a better lather and by 1887 his Warrington factory was producing 450 tons. (A new factory opened by the Queen in 1988 would produce 70,000 metric tons a year.) Lever became famous for the building of a model housing estate for his workers, Port Sunlight, adjoining the works. He was a liturgically-minded Congregationalist and built Blackburn Road Congregational Chapel in Bolton in memory of his parents. According to the journalist, A. G. Gardiner, Lever was 'Stiff, and a little challenging, with something of the watchful reserve of the self-made man, he goes his way, a plain simple citizen, proud with the pride of conscious justice – a real russet-coated captain of industry.' He served as a Liberal MP, bought Stafford House (now Lancaster House) from the Duke of Sutherland and gave it to the nation. By 1912 his annual income was £250,000 (£8,125,000); not surprisingly he made many gifts to Port Sunlight.

One of the most lasting of these was The Lady Lever Art Gallery which Lever began in 1913 and meant to be the central attraction of his new development. It was the last great private gallery built in England and cost £156,436. Lever gave paintings by Reynolds, Constable, Turner, Gainsborough and Stubbs as well as by the great Victorian painters, Holman Hunt, Rossetti, Leighton and Burne-Jones. He donated furniture and furnishings of the sixteenth, seventeenth and eighteenth centuries as well as his collection of oriental porcelain. (Lever loathed Victorian furniture.) He had one of the largest collections of Wedgwood not just because he liked it but because he admired the eighteenth-century Nonconformist, Josiah Wedgwood. (The other great Wedgwood collection was owned by the Quaker industrialist, Sir Richard Tangye and was given to the Birmingham Art Gallery.) The gallery was not finally opened until 1922 when it began drawing an annual attendance of 150,000, fulfilling Lever's belief that art could refine and broaden the mind of working people. By the 1980s the annual attendance had fallen to about 40,000. He died in 1925 with an estate proved at £1,625,000 – over fifty million pounds.[10]

Lever had been made a baronet in 1911 and a baron in 1917; in 1922 he was created Viscount Leverhulme. The social advance of this 'plain simple citizen' is amusingly reflected in his copy of Eleanor Rathbone's biography of her father, William. He was a wealthy Unitarian Liverpool grain merchant, though not in Lever's league, and did much to help his city's University College as well as the North Wales college in Bangor. Lever's copy contains three book plates. The first is a standard printed plate purchased at a stationer's shop with 'W. H. Lever, Thornton Manor, Thornton Hough, Cheshire' inserted by a printer across the bottom. The Manor was one of his thirteen homes. The second plate, especially printed, has the arms of 'Sir W. Hesketh Lever, Bart' and the motto, '*Mutare vel timere sperno*' which may be rendered 'I reject the need to change or to fear'. The following page contains his third book-plate with his much more elaborate arms as Baron Leverhulme of Bolton-le-Moors.[11]

Samuel Morley, who died in 1886, expanded the family hosiery firm of I. & R. Morley to make it the largest hosiers in the country: two of his sons died millionaires. The firm counted among its customers Queen Victoria, whose stockings they had woven in 1837. Morley, an active Congregationalist, 'proved the possibility', his biographer claimed, 'of carrying on business to an unprecedented success, in accordance with the letter, as well as the spirit, of the gospel'. However his understanding of the spirit of the gospel did not allow him to employ Roman Catholics, because, he said, they would proselytize other employees. Those non-Catholics whom he did employ were given a non-contributory pension scheme. He sat in Parliament and on the London School Board, was a keen philanthropist, gave money towards the completion of Bristol Cathedral, supported the temperance crusade and helped Lord Shaftesbury's work for the poor. In 1877 he was part of a triumverate who bought the *Contemporary Review*, one of the great Victorian monthly magazines. The rumour soon went round the literary world that he was looking for an editor 'sufficiently sound' in his theological views. He was part of the Royal Commission on housing the poor and in 1870 took on a country seat in Kent where he became the local squire. His four sons went to Cambridge and one, Arnold, became Liberal Chief Whip from 1886 to 1892. Gladstone had offered to recommend Morley for a peerage in 1869 to balance that which he wanted to offer to Sir Nathan Rothschild. John Bright, however, had already told Lord Granville, Liberal leader in the House of Lords, who passed the information on to Gladstone, that although Morley was 'first rate for our purposes – has wealth, brains and a great hold on Dissenters – He doubts whether he would be foolish enough to accept'. He did not but Rothschild did sixteen years later in 1885. The manufacturer's son, S. H. Morley, became Baron Hollenden of Leigh in 1912.[12]

In Bristol the Wills family had carved for themselves a niche in English life after three generations in the tobacco business. Like Morley and Lever they were Congregationalists; in politics the family split after the Home Rule crisis of 1886. Frederick Wills, one of the three sons of H. O. Wills Jnr stood unsuccessfully as a Liberal Unionist candidate for Launceston in 1895. The following year the Liberal Unionist leader in the Commons, Joseph Chamberlain, wrote to the Prime Minister, Lord Salisbury, about selecting names to submit to the Queen for the New Year's Honours List, a chore Salisbury loathed:

F. Wills wants a Baronetcy. He is brother [*sic*] to Sir W. Wills, who was made a Baronet by the Gladstonians . . . He

belongs to a great Nonconformist family & his influence as a
Unionist is of great importance in the West. He has been a
liberal contributor to the party funds.

Wills got his baronetcy, stood again for Launceston in a
by-election in 1898 and was again defeated. He was finally
elected, for Bristol North, in the Khaki Election of 1900.
He only sat for one Parliament and did not stand for re-
election in 1905. He died four years later, leaving an estate
proved at just over three million pounds, or £100m at
today's prices. His unsuccessful candidature in the 1898
by-election for the North-East division of Cornwall shows
in microcosm the role Nonconformists were playing in
English life. Wills was defeated by the Liberal candidate,
J. F. Moulton QC, a Wesleyan Methodist. Moulton was
the son of a Methodist minister and Senior Wrangler at
Cambridge: for many years he was famous for having
scored the highest total of marks in the University's
history. He became a Fellow of Christ's, was called to the
bar and in 1906 was made a Privy Councillor, given a
knighthood and made Lord Justice of Appeal. Six years
later he was made Lord of Appeal in Ordinary. His brother,
William, was a Wesleyan minister, first headmaster of
The Leys School, the denomination's public school for
boys established in 1875 at Cambridge. He was also a
Biblical scholar, part of the committee which worked on
the New Testament for the Revised Version of the Bible
and President of the Wesleyan Methodist Connexion in
1890.

Sir Frederick Wills's Liberal cousin, William, whom
Chamberlain mistook for his brother, did better out of the
Liberals than Frederick had done out of the Liberal
Unionists: his baronetcy dated from 1893, between his
terms in the Commons as MP for Coventry (1880–85) and
Bristol East (1895–1900). He was a great benefactor to
Bristol: he built the art gallery, erected the statue of
Edmund Burke, built a branch library and gave large
sums to the University where an imposing tower bears the
family's name. He also helped the Congregational college
in Oxford, Mansfield, and the denomination's boys public
school at Mill Hill in north London. In 1906 he was raised
to the peerage as Baron Winterstoke only to die without
issue in 1911. By the third generation the four grandsons

of the first H. O. Wills, had collected two baronetcies and one barony. Millionaire members of the family who died between 1883 and 1949 left estates proved at a total of almost £42m.[13]

In Sheffield the two Firth brothers, Thomas and Mark, developed the steel works founded by their father. The Firths belonged to one of the smallest of the Methodists groups, the Methodist New Connexion. In 1879 the brothers used their wealth to establish Firth College, at a cost of £20,000: an endowment was provided as well as a chair in chemistry. This later became the nucleus of the University of Sheffield. Four years earlier, in 1875, when Mark Firth was Mayor, a thirty-six acre park was given to the borough and was opened by the Prince and Princess of Wales who stayed at the Firth's home. In Hull, Joseph Rank, a Wesleyan Methodist, transformed the family's milling business into the largest firm of flour millers and grain importers in Britain. His son, J. Arthur, carried on his father's charitable work, went into the film business in the twentieth century and was eventually ennobled.[14]

In Halifax the sweets manufacturer, H. V. Mackintosh, was also a member of the Methodist New Connexion. He inherited and expanded a business begun by his parents. When he went through his mother's papers after her death he found two envelopes: one contained a letter from her Sunday School superintendent given on her retirement as a teacher and the other, her original recipe for the toffee which was the basis for his growing wealth. He was recommended for a Viscountcy by Harold Macmillan in 1958.[15] However, the Nonconformist family which really dominated Halifax was not the Mackintoshes but the Crossleys whose wealth lay on their carpets. The firm was started by John Crossley, a weaver, in 1802. It is said that when Mrs Craik wrote her famous novel, *John Halifax, Gentleman*, published in 1857, she patterned her hero, one of 'nature's gentlemen', after John Crossley although she set the story in Tewkesbury. After his death in 1837 his three sons were responsible for the business and they harnessed steam power to drive their looms. By 1869, eighteen years after a patent was taken out on their new loom, the brothers were employing 4,400 men and their factories covered twenty-seven acres. Two of the brothers became active in politics, one at the local level and one in Parliament.

The brothers were generous to their native town: in addition to building the oddly named Square Congregational Chapel (the name referred to its location, not its shape) the brothers provided an orphanage, almshouses, hotel, baths, a park laid out by Sir Joseph Paxton, a lodging house and some model houses. When the Prince of Wales came to open the new town hall, built on land given by the family, he was the guest of the Mayor who was, naturally, one of the Crossley brothers. There were also the great houses built by and for the family: when one brother, Frank, built his new house, Belle Vue, he arranged for it to have a view of the spire of his chapel, much as a squire would have had his house look out on the village church. Frank, who was a Radical MP for Halifax and then for the West Riding until his death in 1872, was created a baronet in 1862 and, the following year, bought a country estate in Suffolk. After his death his widow, heedless of Joseph Parker's warnings, succumbed to the allurements of the Establishment, sold Belle Vue to the borough (it later became the public library) and moved to Suffolk. Her son, Sir Savile, was sent to Eton, went into the Army, became an MP – Tory, not Radical – and served in Arthur Balfour's government. In 1916 he was created Baron Somerleyton and for a while was a Lord-in-Waiting to George V. It was a long way from his grandfather's carpet loom.[16]

William Hartley began his working life in Colne with a grocer's shop and then migrated to Liverpool where he made his jam manufacturing business into one of the country's leading concerns. He was active in Liverpool's local government and a great benefactor to his own denomination, the Primitive Methodists. Like William Rathbone he made substantial gifts both to the University of Liverpool and to local charities. By the end of his life he was giving away one third of his gross income as 'the Lord's money'. He established a system of profit-sharing among his employees, provided free medical care and, like Samuel Morley, created a non-contributory pension scheme for his workers. His maxim was a simple one, 'leave the money in the bones of the worker'. He grew to become a most aristocratic looking man and was knighted in 1908, the same year in which he bought Holborn Town Hall as the location for his church's London headquarters. Four years before that his son-in-law, J. S. Higham, a wealthy Accrington cotton manufacturer and Congregationalist, was returned as Liberal MP for the Sowerby division of Yorkshire. As so often, money married money to the advantage of all concerned.[17] Also in Lancashire, but this time in St Helens, Thomas Beecham's factory was busy producing his famous medicines under the slogan, 'Worth a Guinea a Box'. Beecham's son, Joseph, expanded the business into America, was knighted in 1912 and created a baronet in 1914. The motto Joseph chose was *Nil Sine Labore*, 'Nothing Without Work'. His son, named after his grandfather, was sent to Oxford, became one of England's greatest conductors and founded both the London Philharmonic and the Royal Philharmonic orchestras. Thomas Beecham was a Congregationalist and, like Rathbone, Hartley and Lever, became a benefactor to Lancashire.[18]

Another Liverpool businessman was Henry Tate, the son of a Unitarian minister, who made his fortune by patenting a device in 1872 which would cut up the loaves in which sugar was normally bought into more manageable cubes. 'Tate's cube sugar' brought him enormous wealth and in 1880 he moved to London where, at Streatham, he began an enormous collection of works by contemporary artists. He eventually offered sixty-five paintings from his collection to the nation and promised to build a gallery if the government would find a suitable location. In 1893 the old Millbank Prison was demolished and in its stead rose, in 1897, the National Gallery of British Art which soon acquired the name, the Tate Gallery. The following year its donor was created a baronet. He also gave money to University College, Liverpool, Bedford College, London and the Unitarians' new college in Oxford, Manchester New College. Samuel Courtauld, also a Unitarian, continued the work done by Tate. He used the money gained from his family's textile firm to help Tate's new gallery. Eventually he gave not only money but his London home to the University of London to establish the art institute named after him.[19]

London also benefited from the generosity of the Quaker tea-merchant, Frederick Horniman. When travelling about in search of tea he collected specimens of native art and other natural curiosities. In 1901 an art-nouveau building was opened in south London to house the Horniman Museum of Ethnography.

Another city whose art museum benefited from Non-conformist generosity was Birmingham where Richard Tangye and his brothers had set up their tool-making firm in 1855. In the following year Brunel commissioned him to manufacture the hydraulic lifting jacks to launch his 'Great Eastern'. Eventually his 'Cornwall Works' spread over thirty acres and employed 3,000 men. He established half-day holidays on Saturdays and provided a dining hall, educational classes, concerts and lectures for his workers. He sat on the town council and on a local School Board and, in 1891, founded the *Daily Argus*. In 1880 he gave £10,000 to the city's art gallery and donated some of his own collection; the following year he gave £12,000 to the city's School of Art. When he gave his collection of Wedgwood, referred to above, he explained that he had acquired the pieces 'not as objects bought simply for their rarity, but as a series of representative specimens which could be exhibited as models to show designers, working men and others interested, beauty of form, colour and suitable application of ornament'. Tangye saw no reason why manufacturing and art should be separated. He was knighted in 1894 and in 1912 his son was created a baronet.[20]

In Hartlepool, Sir Christopher Furness, 'one of the richest men in the House of Commons', returned in the 1900 election had been baptized in the Church of England but attended a Methodist chapel. Like Hartley he offered co-partnership to his workers in the shipyards. He had sat in Parliament from 1890 to 1895 and again from 1900 to 1910 when he was succeeded by his nephew. His financial interests included both ship-building and mining and he was raised to the peerage in 1910. His family's absorption into the Establishment was secured when his son's second wife, the American-born Mrs Thelma Converse, became one of Edward VIII's mistresses. Dr Parker's fears about the lures of the Establishment, which could never have forseen the cocktail parties at Fort Belvedere, had obviously been ignored.[21] In Cardiff John Cory, a Cornishman by birth and a Methodist, was a director of the family firm of ship owners and coal exporters. Under him the company grew to include mines, railway lines and foreign depots. He was a JP, sat on the local School Board for thirteen years and gave large sums to the Salvation Army, the YMCA, University College, Cardiff, Dr Barnardo's Homes and various temperance bodies. He became Lord of the Manor of Duffryn and in 1907 was created a baronet. By his death three years later he was giving some £50,000 a year to Cardiff institutions and in his will he left over a third of his estate to charity.[22] In 1906 his son, Clifford, became Liberal MP for St Ives and was an officer in the militia, later the Territorials. Indeed, of the six MPs for Cornwall returned in the general election of that year, five were Nonconformist.

Three of the best known Nonconformist businessmen-philanthropists have been called the Quaker chocolate triumverate of Cadbury, Rowntree and Fry. The difficulty with this label is that it unfairly excludes a fourth Quaker family which made their fortune with chocolate, the Storrs, who were related to the Frys. In Bristol, J. S. Fry inherited his father's chocolate and cocoa business, established in the mid-eighteenth century. He became Clerk of the Yearly Meeting and a President of the YMCA. Even the *Dictionary of National Biography*, that most charitable of sources, admitted that his private life was 'singularly uneventful'. This was not the case in York with the Rowntree family: Joseph Rowntree II inherited his father's business and became famous for his philanthropic work, especially his concern for his workers. Seebohm Rowntree published his book, *Poverty: A Study of Town Life* in 1901 the year before Charles Booth issued a revised set of his *Life and Labour of the People in London*. Rowntree shocked people by showing that York, with its splendid Minster and mediaeval streets, contained urban poverty and destitution as severe as Booth had found in London. Between them, Rowntree and Booth, a Unitarian, had done pioneering work in investigating England's new urban civilization and had established themselves as leaders in the new discipline of sociology.

The most famous member of 'the triumvirate' was George Cadbury: like the Rowntrees, the Cadbury brothers, Richard and George, became famous for their social work and philanthropy. George Cadbury was a keen supporter of Nonconformist unity through the 'Free Church Council' movement and was President of the Birmingham Free Church Council from 1893 to 1898. He was also a keen Radical and in 1901 purchased the *Daily News*, once owned by Samuel Morley, and turned it into an anti-Boer War newspaper, later known to Tories as the 'cocoa press'. He was a regular contributor to Liberal Party funds and paid the salary of Herbert Gladstone's political secretary, Jesse Herbert. He also once gave £500 to the Independent Labour Party. He told Gladstone in 1905: 'Every ragged child I see makes my faith in Radicalism still firmer.'[23]

By the end of the nineteenth century Nonconformity's merchant princes, many now living in their splendid new country seats, with sons at Oxford or Cambridge and daughters making 'good marriages', adopted a way of life befitting their station. One such was Jeremiah Colman, Norwich's 'Mustard King'. He entered the family firm of J. & J. Colman in 1851. Although he had been raised a Baptist he married a member of the small Methodist sect, the United Methodist Free Church and he and his wife eventually compromised on Prince's Street Congregational Church, one of the city's most influential chapels. He was active in local government and sat in Parliament from 1871 to 1895. Like Samuel Morley he stood on the right wing of the Liberal Party and was to many observers the quintessential Nonconformist industrialist. Like so many other Nonconformist factory owners he established numerous benefits for his workers. Even though the offer of a baronetcy came from Gladstone's hands, Colman refused it. The weekend parties at his house in Norwich saw some of the most famous names in Victorian Nonconformity in the guest book: J. Guinness Rogers, John Stoughton, R. W. Dale and C. A. Berry, all leading Congregational ministers, were regular guests. In addition, Colman entertained Dean Hole of Rochester, famous for his roses and his volumes of memoirs, Arthur Peel, son of Sir Robert, Speaker of the House of Commons from 1884 to 1895 and the first Speaker to apply the guillotine to stop debate, Lord Rosebery and Gladstone. He let various friends in need of a rest use his yacht and he sometimes entertained at his seaside house. Had the minister of the Lower Meeting House Congregational Chapel in Amersham, whose stipend was raised to £70 a year in 1902, ever been invited, he would have been more out of place with the Colmans in Norwich than the local curate on a similar stipend would have been had he been invited to Hatfield by Lord Salisbury: at least both Salisbury and the curate would have been at Oxford.[24] If Colman had refused the offer of a baronetcy at Gladstone's hands, his son, Jeremiah II, accepted it when offered by Campbell-Bannerman in 1907. By then he had left Norwich and the works and settled in Surrey where he bought Lord Monson's house, Gatton Park, somewhat ironically given the Monsons' traditional dislike of Nonconformists. The estate was near the site of the most infamous of all pre-1832 rotten boroughs. The house is now a boarding school.

Nonconformity's mercantile princes won considerable fame in their day for the work they did to improve the living standards of their workers. The most famous were George and Richard Cadbury with their model village, Bournville, but the story began in the 1850s in Bradford where Titus Salt decided to re-locate his alpacca factory in a new town located north of Bradford on the Leeds and Liverpool Canal. He named it Saltaire because it was near the River Aire. Salt was not the first Nonconformist manufacturer to erect a model village for his workers: Josiah Wedgwood had built Etruria in the eighteenth century for this purpose. Nothing, however, had been attempted on this scale: it was proudly noted that the mill, 545 feet long, was exactly the length of St Paul's. The new town covered twenty-five acres and had 850 houses ranging from traditional 'two up-two down' to more elaborate structures. The size and style depended on one's position in the mill. The houses cost £106,562 to build or well over £3m in today's currency. There were, in addition, a hospital, schools, shops, a bank and alms houses for forty-five elderly workers receiving pensions of 7s. 6d. a week if single and 10s. if married. There was no public house. Salt, a Congregationalist, built a chapel in 1858–9 in the 'Italian' style which closely resembled S. P. and C. R. Cockerell's parish church in Banbury, put up in 1790: the family mausoleum is behind it. It was very much a Victorian equivalent to a 'squire's village' because everyone who lived in Saltaire worked for Titus Salt and was paid in tokens which could be spent in the village shops or exchanged at the bank. In 1869 Salt was given a baronetcy. Although the mill is now closed Saltaire lives on and in 1988 it was reported that a local businessman had bought the mill in order to convert it into an arts and leisure centre with one large spinning room devoted to a collection of paintings by David Hockney.[25]

Other Nonconformist industrialists followed Salt's example: in 1886 William Hartley built his new jam factory in Aintree and erected model housing nearby: a five cottage room was let for 3s. 6d. a week and twenty year mortgages were available at 3¾ per cent for workers who wanted to buy the freehold. Two years later W. H. Lever began Port Sunlight: whereas Saltaire had spread over twenty-five acres, Lever's model village covered 130. In 1901 Joseph Rowntree II opened his model houses outside York, at 'New Earswick' and let houses which cost £135 to build, at 4s. 6d. to men earning 25s. a week.[26] Sir James Reckitt, whose blueing was a standard part of any Victorian laundry, did the same outside Hull while the Wesleyan Methodist coal and shipping magnate, John Cory, erected his model estate, 'Coryville' on part of his land. Whereas the model villages of Saltaire, Port Sunlight and Aintree were built alongside new factories as part of an industrial complex, the settlements built by Rowntree, Reckitt and Cory would be patterned after the Cadbury brothers' new 'garden suburb' of Bournville, one of the most important contributions Nonconformist industrialists made to Victorian social history.

In 1879 the Cadburys had decided to move their factory from the slums of Birmingham to a plot of land outside the city. The new location, in meadow land through which flowed a trout stream called the Bourn, allowed them to build playing fields for the workers who took special trains from Birmingham to the new factory. The Cadburys also built sixteen houses for the factory foremen, conforming to Salt's pattern in Saltaire. Over the years, as the factory prospered, people were attracted to the area and the fear arose that the old pattern of cheap housing built for workers by unscrupulous developers would happen all over again. There had been talk of planned towns or villages built with more space and better housing for many years. George Cadbury began buying up the land round the factory and eventually had 842 acres: he then planned Britain's first 'garden suburb': roads had to be forty-two feet in width; houses had to be set back at least twenty feet from the pavement; only seven houses were allowed per acre; roads were not straight and long but irregular, curved and lined with trees; each house had a large garden which was stocked with fruit trees before the first residents arrived; a village institute, children's playground, local school, parks and almshouses were provided. The family built a Quaker Meeting House and gave land for a parish church which was built in due course. No public house was allowed although the restriction could be lifted. The Cadburys built 143 houses which were leased or sold at cost price on a 999 year lease. Owners could not build over or destroy the gardens. Mortgages were given at 2½ per cent if no more than half of the purchase price was borrowed and 3 per cent if over half. A cottage priced £150 would, if bought over twelve years, cost £173.

What made the scheme different and innovative was that anyone could buy or rent a house, whether or not they worked for the Cadburys; secondly, in 1901 the estate was given by the brothers to a charitable trust administered by four trustees representing the nation. Three of the trustees were appointed by local government and one, by the Society of Friends. Bournville was an experiment, not just of model houses but of a workable scheme in which working people could be housed decently for their benefit, the company's and the country's and all could be done economically. Although the Cadburys had paid for Bournville, in 1901 they gave over all control of it, having made nothing from it. By then the number of houses had grown to 370 and all rents were paid to the Trust which reinvested them in other garden suburb projects such as those in Letchworth or Hampstead Garden. Visitors from

France and Germany came to study Bournville and in both countries associations were formed to encourage similar projects. Ironically, in Germany it was the arms manufacturer, Krupp, which followed the English Quaker's vision of decent housing for working people. At home, the brothers' vision was being fulfilled in the quality of the lives led in Bournville: by 1919 the rate of infant mortality, taking the average of the period 1914–1919, was 97 per 1000 births in England and Wales. In Birmingham for the same period it was 101. In Bournville it was 51.[27]

One of the greatest social changes of the nineteenth century, a change which has formed twentieth-century life and will probably form life in the twenty-first century as well, was due to a Nonconformist Teetotaller. Although he received no honours he did establish a successful company and earned a place in history. The story began in 1841 when a Teetotal rally was scheduled in Loughborough and a young Baptist wood-turner named Thomas Cook thought it a good idea to arrange with the Midland Railway for a special train from Leicester for a day-trip to Loughborough and back. For a shilling customers got, in addition to their ticket, tea, buns and a band. This was the first advertised excursion train and led to Cook's organizing other day-trips for temperance societies and Sunday Schools. From a single teetotal acorn a mighty forest of oaks began to sprout. In 1845 he organized excursions for the same railway company and got a percentage of the ticket sales. In the same year he arranged for a pleasure trip with hotel coupons included. By 1851 some 165,000 people travelled to see the Great Exhibition on a Cook's ticket. A new English institution had been born: the day-trip and with it a new type of Englishman, the day-tripper. Whether people's mental horizons were, or are, broadened by travel remains a moot point but most decidedly their experiences and expectations have been.

Four years later Cook organized his first foreign tour, from Leicester to Calais for 31s. The following year came his first tour of Europe which included Brussels, Waterloo, Cologne, the Rhine, Mayence, Frankfort, Heidelberg, Baden-Baden, Strassburg and Paris. In 1866 he sent off his first package tour to America only one year after the end of the War Between the States. Tourism had been born. In addition to the day-trip, Cook's efforts were largely responsible for the creation of the annual holiday and the idea that what people could first afford as a luxury they should then have as an annual right. Like Lever with his soap or Crossley with his carpets, Cook tapped the increasing prosperity of the working-classes and, even more so, of the lower-middle class, the fastest growing of all Victorian social groups. Sell a lot and sell cheap was as much the key to his success as to theirs. By Cook's death in 1892 the idea of a holiday abroad had become as established among the middle classes as holidays at the seaside had become for the working classes. Cook's son, who only survived him by seven years, extended the company's operations into America, Egypt, India, and the Ottoman Empire where the Baptist tourist agent helped arrange for better treatment of Mohammedan pilgrims to Mecca. He even acquired a railway up Mount Vesuvius. Some Englishmen on the continent were not altogether delighted with the changing pattern of international travel: the Vice-Consul at Spezia told his Italian friends that the new 'tourists' were really convicts which Australia refused to take and which Cook had arranged with Her Majesty's Government to dump in various Italian cities. The difficulty was that the Italians believed him. The behaviour of some English tourists in the twentieth century might have confirmed the Italians' view.[28]

When, in 1853, Sir Titus Salt's new factory was opened at Saltaire, Mr French, on behalf of the operatives, read a poem written by Robert Storey, 'The Peerage of Industry'. Its first verse and refrain were:

To the praise of the peerage high harps have been strung
    By minstrels of note and of fame;
But a peerage we have to this moment unsung,
    And why should they not have their name?
'Tis the peerage of industry! Nobles who hold
    Their patent from Nature alone
More genuine far than if purchased with gold
    Or won, by mean arts, from a throne.[29]

Storey's radical verse was composed before Salt received his baronetcy from Queen Victoria.

While some industrialists, like the Cadbury brothers, Jeremiah Colman, Samuel Morley or William Rathbone refused honours, others, indeed the vast majority, saw no reason to refuse. Had not English history brought their prosperity about? Was not English prosperity part of a universe under Divine Providence? Could they not play an even greater role in national life if they took that place in society which society thought fit for them to occupy? Could they not add to the value of the House of Lords if they, the 'peerage of industry' took their places on the Liberal benches? If their titles and houses were new, so too had been other titles when first created and other houses when first built. Had not Hatfield House or Hever Castle been new buildings once? What of the numerous City merchants who abandoned London in the eighteenth century for the splendours of their new Palladian mansions in the country with titles to ease their transition? Was it not better to have earned a title because one had produced wealth, created jobs and improved the quality of national life than to have been the mistress of a debauched sovereign or a time-serving politician? Where lay the origins of the St Albans or Richmond titles if not in Charles II's bed? Nonconformist merchant princes were only fitting into a pattern which dated back to the middle of the century. The first 'industrial peerage' had been conferred on Edward Strutt, MP, a mill-owner, in 1856 when he became Baron Belper. The real turning point came not under the Liberals but under Lord Salisbury's first Tory government of 1885–86. Of the 222 new peerages created by the six governments of the period 1885 to 1911, roughly a third were for industrialists.[30]

Sadly these new Nonconformist peers have received short shrift: to traditional snobs they are *nouveaux riches* and could only purge their tainted pedigree by conforming to the established order and forgetting their past. Most, in time, did just that and the power of the Establishment to absorb new entrants proved greater than the power of later generations to carry on their Nonconformity. To the newer snobbery of the twentieth century's intelligentsia, many of whom ironically trace their pedigree back to

Nonconformist radicalism, the 'millocrats' were tainted not just with trade as with highly successful trade. To this generation, money spent by the state to help the poor or to improve the quality of life was good; money spent by wealthy individuals, titled or not, for the same purpose was not. Private charity became a dirty deed which could only be based on feelings of 'guilt'. To be wealthy was bad, to be a wealthy new peer was worse. When the young Quaker, Stephen Hobhouse, came away from a visit to the Cadbury family home he wrote that he was 'profoundly disturbed by their high standard of luxurious living, compared with the living conditions of most artisans and workers by whose labour we of the privileged classes were supported'. He did not explain how the Cadburys' living in a terraced cottage would help the workers nor did he say how the wealth they had earned had already helped these same workers.[31]

As we have seen, Nonconformity's merchant princes had established their right to membership in England's governing class. Many were well aware that a willingness to play their part could mask a desire to become 'Honourable' and 'Right Honourable'; many were also aware that there was a snobbery of wealth, traditionally and mistakenly associated with Calvinism, which confused bank balances and increased profits with moral worth. Jeremiah Colman, the 'mustard king', reminded his fellow 'merchants and tradesmen of England' that 'riches are not the true mark of nobility any more than title is'. There were always those who would have agreed the words of William Rathbone when, along with his fellow Unitarian, Sir Henry Tate, he was given the Freedom of the City by Liverpool Corporation in 1891:

> As we all admit, whatever we may possess of wealth, talents, station, and opportunity are not freeholds to be selfishly enjoyed by a man . . . but sacred trusts to be employed for the welfare of the community. And of all beyond what is necessary for maintenance, education, and moderate provision for his family, an increasing proportion is due as wealth and power increase to the public service, not from generosity, but as the honest payment of debt . . . Which of the sacrifices which a prosperous man makes can be considered generous when looked at with those which thousands of our men and women

make daily . . . when they share with their neighbours the means only too inadequate for the supply of the wants of . . . their families? It is easy for the prosperous to be deemed generous, difficult for them to deserve to be so called.

Of course this attitude was not confined to Nonconformists: it was, and remains, basically a Christian point of view. It was the wealthy Anglican merchant, George Moore, who wrote in his diary that 'the money belongs to God; let me give it back to Him'.[32] This belief in the stewardship of wealth was also a trait of a certain generation: many Nonconformists of later generations would have rejected it out of hand, especially as the state made philanthropy unfashionable if not impossible through taxation. In the event the new Nonconformist additions to the peerage did not fundamentally alter its nature and within a few generations the new had blended in with the old quite successfully. The economic and social changes which destroyed the great country houses and with them a way of life had no regard for the religion of the houses' owners.

Nonconformist enterprises permeated almost every aspect of Victorian life and their involvement was far greater than our discussion of its merchant princes would indicate. Wall's sausages, Cooper's Oxford marmalade, Colman's mustard, Beecham's powders, Callard's sweets, Mackintosh's toffees, Wills', Players' or Dunhill's tobacco and cigarettes, Palmer's biscuits, Tate's sugar, and Hartley's, Tiptree's or Chivers' jams were all manufactured by companies started by Nonconformists. When Bryant and May were investigated and condemned for employing women for fifty-six hours a week at 5s. 9d. for making matches, it was a Nonconformist, and in this case, a Quaker firm which was condemned. If one asked for Pickfords to send its vans to move one's furniture one was dealing with a Nonconformist company. If one slept securely at night under an Early blanket and with the door secured by a Chubb lock, one was using products made by Nonconformists. If one borrowed a book from Mudie's or Boots' circulating libraries or bought a book published by Cassell, Allen and Unwin, James Clarke or Hodder and

Stoughton, read the *News of the World*, the *Daily News*, the Birmingham *Daily Argus*, Stead's *Review of Reviews* or the *Contemporary Review* or novels by Mark Rutherford or Arnold Bennett, consulted the University of Oxford's *New English Dictionary* or purchased medicines at Boots, Howards, Allen and Hanbury or Southall and Bells chemists one was dealing in varying degrees with Nonconformist enterprises.

In every aspect of the Victorian achievement, Nonconformists had played their part. If one survived surgery it was largely because Lord Lister, born into an Essex Quaker family, had pioneered the practice of antiseptic operations. If one caught one's train on time it was because one had consulted Bradshaw, whose originator was a Nonconformist. If one went to see the works of art displayed in Birmingham, Bristol, Liverpool and London one was benefiting from the generosity of the Tangye, Wills, Lever, Tate or Courtauld families. If one bought chocolates or tins of cocoa made by Cadbury, Fry, Rowntree or Storr one was dealing with Quakers; if one's bank bore the name Lloyds, Barclays, Bevan, Tritton or Gurney one was still dealing with firms that had all been Quaker in origin. If one were horrified or pleased at the 'New Journalism' that was coming into fashion, one could blame or praise W. T. Stead. If one wished to avoid *hoi polloi* which increasingly flocked to Cooks one could book one's holiday through Lunn, which began with the Methodist, Sir Henry Lunn's 1892 tour to Rome designed for ministers and their families. If Londoners marvelled at the ingenuity involved in erecting the 186 tons of Cleopatra's Needle on the Embankment they could thank Sir Richard Tangye, the Quaker whose firm's hydraulic jacks had achieved the feat on 12 September 1878.

If foreign buyers purchased Firth's steel or, after the turn of the century, their new discovery, stainless steel, had it shipped through Cory docks and transported by Runciman, Booth or Furness ships, they were dealing with Nonconformists. To buy glass made by Pilkington, cotton thread manufactured by Clark's or Coats, carpets and velvets by Crossley, soap by Lever Brothers, blueing by Reckitts, shoes from Roger Clark's factory in Gloucestershire, hats by Christy's, wool from Salt's, hosiery from

Morley's, screws by Chamberlain, silks from Courtauld's or Joshua Wilson, tea from Horniman's or, earlier in the century, Cassell, cottons from Ashworth, Rylands or Higham or flour milled by Rank was to buy from concerns, many of which were still private and family-owned by 1900, and all of which were Nonconformist in origin. The Victorian economic miracle was to a considerable degree made possible by Nonconformist ingenuity and enterprise.

2

THE SOCIAL NATURE OF NONCONFORMITY

By the end of the nineteenth century Nonconformity had been able to establish itself as a major force in national life because of its strength in the expanding towns and cities of England. While its great merchant princes were increasingly recognized as patrons of the arts and social reformers, its base was firmly in the growing ranks of the urban middle classes. Lord George Hamilton was talking about the small number of Nonconformists who entered the Army as professional soldiers but his description applies to Nonconformity as a whole: 'Socially and financially, the great mass of Nonconformists are below the status of the officer and above that of the private.' Observers saw this: the *Church Quarterly Review* noted that 'Nonconformity has become a religion of the middle classes. It includes wealth but not aristocracy, and for the most part it excludes the poor. It has proved utterly incapable of abolishing caste distinctions.'[1] If we ignore those merchant princes who had taken titles, this article was not far from the mark.

Such observations undermined two great intertwined myths much loved by Nonconformists, myths which if true might have peculiarly equipped them to serve the religious needs of the English people in the new and democratic century. The first was that Nonconformity was still in essence a 'village religion'. One Baptist leader declared that 'our village Churches are the springs from whence the rills and rivulets arise, which, flowing together, make up the great broad river of Nonconformist opinion and life'. To Nonconformists, and indeed to many Englishmen, life in large cities, let alone in the expanding suburbs, was seen as 'something abnormal, unnatural, and as it were, accidental'. Village life, in its alleged simplicity and closeness to nature was 'real' and not artificial: the 'springs' were pure. It was not sophisticated like urban life and, by inference, like the liturgical worship of the Church of England. As we shall see, however, urban life formed the very backbone of Nonconformity's power.[2]

The second great myth was that Nonconformity was and always had been the religion of 'the people'. 'We spring from the people', one preacher told an 1895 Free Church Council meeting, 'we are in touch with the people, not as a matter of condescension, but as ourselves part and parcel of the mass.' Of course a great deal depended on what the terms meant. 'The people' had traditionally referred not so much to the new urban working classes thrown up by the Industrial Revolution as average folk, people who had no titles or inherited lands, those who had little schooling and no professional qualifications, those who had at best a trade, like joinery or tailoring and at worst, nothing but their physical strength to sell. Traditionally Congregationalists and Baptists had had great appeal to the shopkeepers and merchants of England's market and county towns and they continued to do so throughout the nineteenth century. These people were the traditional butt of novelists, the people who constituted the 'elite of the congregation' in Margaret Oliphant's *Salem Chapel* for example. These were the 'greengrocers, dealers in cheese and bacon, milkmen, with some dressmakers of inferior pretensions, and teachers of day-schools of similar humble character'.

Mrs Oliphant was not far wrong in her description. Between 1889 and 1891 the Wotton-under-Edge Congregational Tabernacle filled in the spaces under 'Rank or Profession' in their Burial Register. The deceased included servant, butcher, farmer, widow, butler, station-master and draper. Again, in 1897 the Lower Meeting House (Congregational) at Amersham decided to do something about their Trustees, the sixteen men who legally owned all chapel property under the original Trust Deed. Of the sixteen appointed in 1861 only three were left. Of the new men, two were described as 'gentlemen', but by reference to earlier records we see that this meant they were a retired maltster and a retired butter-factor. The other thirteen were the minister, two chemists, an ironmonger, a chair-maker, and a merchant, butcher, traveller, miller, farmer, surveyor, solicitor, draper and grocer.[3]

For their part, Wesleyan Methodist leaders were always wary of too close an identification with 'the people' for the fear of being defiled with the pitch of radicalism. They preferred to see their strength in witnessing to a pure and Protestant Christianity which the Established Church had lost. In 1899 the Conference Address referred to the 'ancient truisms that principle is more than taste, that character is more than culture, that without holiness it is impossible to please God'. Newer generations, inspired by men like the radical minister, Hugh Price Hughes, were prepared to throw in their lot with the Baptists, Congregationalists and even the Primitive Methodists, the lowest in social pecking order among the four leading denominations. They were on surer ground about their working-class credentials and declared in 1893 that 'God has used our church, as He has used no other . . . in caring for the poor . . . our history speaks to us, and in unmistakable language commands us to devote our attention mainly to the toiling masses'. John Wesley's Methodism had lost its more universal appeal when racked by various secessions between the end of the eighteenth century and the 1850s. This left the Wesleyans holding the middle classes and the other divisions, like the Primitive Methodists, the working classes. It also created certain regional divisions so that the Wesleyans were strong in the north of England although this was shifting to the south in the nineteenth century while the Bible Christian Methodists were strong in Cornwall and Devon and the Primitive Methodists, in the Midlands.[4]

Wits had great fun with Nonconformist claims and one classified Nonconformists in the following categories: the Congregationalist, he said, is 'the aristocrat of Dissenters'; the Wesleyan Methodist is the man 'who wants to be'; the Baptist is the man 'who is not so much concerned on the point, because he knows that his turn will come in another sphere'; the Primitive Methodist was not even considered. Some Nonconformist leaders openly bemoaned the fact that their chapels were 'run in the social and religious interests of the middle-classes, by the middle-classes'. 'A Church Member' had written in the *Nonconformist and*

Independent in the early 1880s: 'It must, I fear, be taken for granted that Congregationalism and to a great extent Wesleyanism, have come to be a middle class institution. This is as disappointing as it is true.'[5] The fact was disappointing because while chapels in small market towns might be dominated by the shop-keeping class, the congregation could still have included a wide cross-section of people. Urban life meant that the clearer class distinctions along neighbourhood lines both created and then excluded the 'working classes' and made chapel-goers feel far more 'middle class' than hitherto.

Before we have a closer look at these myths and discover the nature of Nonconformity's appeal we should look at those fundamental changes in English life which determined its growth and prosperity. Three of the greatest demographic changes in modern English history occurred between 1801 and 1901 and each benefited Nonconformity: the tremendous increase in population, the development of the world's first urban society and, finally, the massive emigration to the colonies and America.

In 1801 England's population was 8,306,000; in 1901 it was 30,813,000, an increase of just over 370 per cent. The growth in chapel membership came nowhere near this and it seems reasonable to say that the expansion in membership resulted 'chiefly from the increase in middle and lower middle-class church-going as a natural consequence of general population increase' – in other words, the class from which chapel-goers were recruited was enlarged during the nineteenth century. This enlargement was due to increasing economic prosperity, improving education, better health care and so forth; it was not due to a rise in the birth rate. This had increased from 1838 to reach a high of thirty-five per thousand of the population in 1871 but by 1901 it was down to 28.5 per thousand.[6]

Second, in the nineteenth century England became the world's first urbanized society. Estimates vary for 1801 but census figures showed that one in four Englishmen lived in an urban area, that is, a town with a population exceeding 5,000 although some later argued that it was one in every three. In either estimation it was a minority.

Fifty years later the Census showed that just over half the population of England and Wales lived either in London or in one of the sixty-two principal towns. If one had excluded Wales the percentage would have been greater. By 1901 just over six out of every ten people in England and Wales (62.5 per cent) lived in an urban area, that is a town with a population above 10,000. Third, between 1815 and 1901, over twelve million British subjects left the United Kingdom for the colonies and America in the greatest migration since the barbarian tribes over-ran the Roman Empire.[7]

One needs, of course, to remember that all statistics are to some degree misleading unless the writer bores his reader to death by listing every qualification. There were denominational differences and what applied to Congregationalists did not necessarily apply to Primitive Methodists; what applied to market towns in East Anglia did not apply to expanding conurbations in the West Midlands or the Black Country; what applied to town centres did not apply to the suburbs. The aim remains, however, to show in broad terms those factors that marked Nonconformist growth as a whole, not to examine in minute detail each denomination and region.

As we have seen, the increase in England's population was reflected in Nonconformity even if chapel membership had not kept up with the national increase. Nonconformists would have taken no comfort from knowing that their increasing membership did not come about from more successful recruiting: the proportion of people coming to chapel, when one sets the membership of the Baptist, Wesleyan and Primitive Methodist denominations against the population, actually fell during the last third of the century, i.e. between 1871 and 1901, from 3.34 per cent to 2.72 per cent. Concerning the second change, the urbanization of English life, Nonconformity had roughly kept up with the trend but in some cases was behind it. A detailed survey of the membership statistics of the four leading denominations shows that in the first year of the twentieth century sixty-seven per cent of all Baptists, sixty-six per cent of all Congregationalists, fifty-nine per cent of all Wesleyan and forty-seven per cent of all

Primitive Methodists lived in towns with a population of 10,000 and above: the percentage for the general population of England and Wales was sixty-eight. The patterns of growth for the last third of the century, when studied in detail, show that Nonconformity's strength did not lie in England's biggest cities any more than it did in the smallest towns or the villages. Despite all the rhetoric lavished on village chapels Nonconformity was a religion of England's smaller but growing provincial towns.[8]

A closer look at the available information will show this: by 1902 membership of the four leading denominations totalled 1,128,741. Of this number over half (683,411) lived in towns with a population of 10,000 and above. Despite the surprising growth of London Nonconformity referred to in Chapter 1, only 114,467 members of the four largest denominations lived in the greater London area. Likewise, only 68,893 lived in those three cities with a population over half a million – Birmingham, Liverpool and Manchester. If we look at the five cities with a population between 250,000 and half a million – Bradford, Bristol, Leeds, Newcastle and Sheffield – membership came to only 79,370. The bulk of Nonconformity's urban members lived in one of two groups of towns. The first group, towns like Bolton, Halifax or Nottingham, with populations between 100,000 and 250,000, had a total of 262,730 members. The second group, towns like Southport, Reigate or Colchester, with populations between 10,000 and 100,000 had 267,584 members.[9]

The more urbanized Nonconformity became the more Nonconformist orators waxed eloquent about village Nonconformity as 'small Christian republics' set in a sea of repression in which swarmed devouring squires and parsons. The prospect of a depopulated English countryside after the last villager had migrated to the town had become a bug-bear to late Victorians. General Booth had popularized a programme of re-colonization as a way to end urban overcrowding and slum housing. Urban growth and the rural migration which fed it seemed to be a never-ending process and a frightening one at that, especially for village chapels. So, too, might be the future of the towns: the Congregational minister, J. B. Paton, was President of the English Land Colonization Society, and addressed a conference on Congregationalism in Rural Districts in 1897. He spoke about increased urban crime and 'socialist agitators' should the village supply of constables dry up:

> It will be an evil day for England if that well-head of splendid physical energy and prowess fail to yield its supply and our towns cease to be replenished by the robust physical forces drawn from a healthful and abounding country population. How, indeed, shall order be kept in our towns if our stalwart and kindly-natured policemen, bred in the country, fail us?[10]

Nonconformists who had themselves migrated into the expanding towns or who were the first generation in their family to be born in a town looked back with fondness on rural life as somehow 'normal' and urban life in new houses on new streets as abnormal. Researchers did claim that in some villages becoming a local preacher or failing to touch one's cap to the squire was sufficient reason for being turned out of one's home and that this obviously caused a 'rankling sense of injustice'. Self interest and a genuine desire to help weaker brethren combined to demand action. The problem was not in erecting new chapels – 'hideously ugly buildings . . . with those horrid words – "New Salem" . . . legibly inscribed on a visible stone inserted above the doorway' as Trollope referred to them in *The Vicar of Bullhampton* – but in maintaining what was already there. According to one report issued in 1898 there were only some 200 villages in Great Britain which did not have a Nonconformist meeting of some sort even if only in an adherent's cottage. Indeed, one problem was 'over-lapping' or duplication where villages could have a Baptist, Congregational and at least two or three competing Methodist congregations.[11]

All the major denominations tackled the issue and held conferences, the standard religious response to any problem then as now but only one, the Primitive Methodists, ordered an investigation in 1894. They were, of course, the least urbanized of the four major denominations: over half the membership still lived in rural areas (some 53 per cent) and the number had not shrunk over the last ten years. The investigation took eighteen months to complete and was published in six volumes of information and a seventh of summary. Every chapel in the United Kingdom was surveyed and replies showed that about 70 per cent (3,453) were in rural areas. The General Committee also asked the chapels if their work was progressing, stationary or declining. Some 2,851 'stations' did not bother to reply. Of the 602 or seventeen per cent which did reply, 280 or just over 46 per cent said they were progressing; 244 or just under 40 per cent said they were stationary and seventy-eight or thirteen per cent admitted to being in decline.

The Committee asked stations if they had suffered 'discrimination' and, from the replies of those who answered, it appeared there had been ninety-nine cases where the chapel had tried to obtain land and had failed, allegedly because of discrimination: these ninety-nine were just under three per cent of the total number of stations in rural areas. The Committee also asked if 'our members or hearers have been made to suffer on account of their Methodism during the last ten years'. Those replying reported a total of forty members who had 'suffered', out of a total membership of 100,647 in Great Britain. The survey was not encouraging: even if almost nine out of every ten chapels who answered said they were at worst stationary and at best progressing, these formed but seventeen per cent of the total number of chapels. What of the other 2,851 which had not bothered to reply? Of course the picture may well have been worse for the Primitive Methodists than for the Baptists or Congregationalists if they had had such a survey. Unlike them, the Primitive Methodists could have suffered from the competition of other Methodist chapels in their district as well as from other Nonconformist churches. The simplicity of their services was as much rural as denominational and a Wesleyan chapel in the same village could have been as simple: the more sophisticated and liturgical chapels were almost totally confined to the big cities and their suburbs. Still, even if one discounts to some degree the depressing results of the survey because of facts peculiar to the denomination, the overall conclusion was hardly encouraging.[12]

Other Nonconformist churches were aware of the problem. Baptists devoted a great amount of time and rhetoric to discussing the plight of villages and allocated part of their Twentieth Century Fund for rural work including £30,000 for helping poorer chapels to pay their ministers. Their concern took literary form in a novel published in 1892 by one Baptist minister, the Rev. H. E. Stone. In *Led from Darkness: The History of a Life Struggle* a village in which most people are Nonconformist is invaded by a group of High Churchwomen, one of whom is a secret Roman Catholic. They are led by a 'black-haired, thin shaven . . . lisping vicar', Fr Shiftweight, but their machinations come to nothing. Lisping vicars, and more frequently curates, had become favourite characters to most Nonconformist orators and writers. Occasionally the voice of realism was heard and the Rev. Samuel Vincent told his fellow Baptists in 1898 that what village chapels needed was money and 'where is "a vein for the silver and a place for gold" but in our suburban churches?'. 'Does any man doubt', he asked, 'that our duty is to occupy the new suburbs of our great towns and cities . . . That there, wise efforts will give richest and quickest harvests, and furnish seed-corn for other fields. Is it not folly to let the most fertile soil lie fallow or half tilled?'[13]

Congregationalists also realized how important the village was to the success of their urban expansion. 'With a few splendid exceptions' one Chairman of the Congregational Union told his audience, 'do your missionaries and preachers not come from the villages still?'[14] There were a variety of proposals to help village churches including a programme of regular visitation, a plan of Methodist-type 'grouping' with a supervising minister assisted by lay-ministers (a scheme which Baptists also considered) and finally a grand programme of land resettlement urged by Paton which would have involved land redistribution and the encouragement of a new class of small farmers. By the time the Union was reorganized in 1904 little had been done.

Wesleyan Methodists gave less attention to the problem of rural chapels although in 1898 Conference voted £200,000 of the Twentieth Century Fund for educational work and the training of local preachers. Part of this money was rather grandly allocated for building day schools, some of which would be in villages where 'at present Nonconformists are compelled to attend either

Anglican or Roman Catholic schools'. Nothing came of this somewhat fanciful proposal. At the end of the day there was little that any of the denominations could do to redress a fundamental change in English life. The rhetoric, however, never stopped. In 1913 Lloyd George, an expert in hollow phrases and purple prose, spoke on behalf of the Baptist Sustentation Fund and soared into the stratosphere when he came to the village chapel:

> When well dressed men and women go on Sundays to a magnificent building in their carriages, it requires courage to say: 'I go to the Baptist church.' I know these little chapels – their faith, their devotion, their loyalty, their courage, and their tenacity (cheers). When I pass them, as I do sometimes when I go about, I feel like a Catholic passing a shrine, and my hand goes up. (cheers)[15]

The problem only grew worse with increased mechanization of farm work after the Great War and villages did not take on a new lease of life until the private motor car made them accessible for urban commuters. Only then was Paton and General Booth's dream of recolonization realized, albeit in ways somewhat different from those they had advocated. By that time it was too late for Nonconformity and the new settlers not infrequently set up their new home in what estate agents call 'converted chapels'.

The second great myth, that Nonconformity was a religion of 'the people', also needs closer examination. A lot depended on terms: some Nonconformists admitted this was not the case and agreed theirs was a 'middle-class' religion, but what constituted the middle class? To some, like Seebohm Rowntree, it was those people who employed at least one domestic servant – just under thirty per cent of the population. To others, it was those who paid income tax, re-instated in 1843 at 7d in the pound. By 1900 it was 8d. Those who 'suffered' the tax numbered 4,500,000 in 1880.[16] Again, since the tax was not paid unless the annual income was over £150 a clerk earning, say, £2. 17s. 6d. a week would have escaped tax with an annual income of £140. 10s. Yet on that income he could have rented a suburban house, worn a bowler hat, raised a family and been an elector while his wife could have employed at least one domestic servant. To twentieth-century readers, as to Rowntree, this man could be considered middle-class but not every Victorian would have agreed.

Some people would have defined the term in a more literal sense, as all those people who stood mid-way between those who received a weekly wage on the one extreme and the 'landed gentry' and nobility on the other. This was the sense in which William Gladstone had used the term in the 1840s: 'I, who am myself sprung from that middle class – I, who with the family of which I am a member, still claim to belong to that middle class.' This definition would have included Gladstone, a man whose father was a wealthy shipping merchant, a baronet and an MP. Gladstone himself had a country house, a carriage in town and a house on Carlton Terrace. The middle class in this sense included those whom critics described as people

> on whose foreheads it is written that they know themselves to be the salt of the earth. Their assured, curt voices, their proud carriage, their clothes, the similarity of their manners, all show that they belong to a caste and that caste has been successful in the struggle for life. It is called the middle-class, but it ought to be called the upper-class, for nearly everything is below it . . . they never look twice at twopence.

This was the class which included the 'wealthy and influential merchants whose carriages used to be drawn up in a long line, Sunday after Sunday, at the chapel gates' of the Rev. Alexander Maclaren's Union Chapel in Manchester. Indeed, under his pastorate two members died as millionaires although the effect this had on their subsequent activities is not known.[17] They were not so much middle-class as upper-middle class.

It was the Victorians who realized that urban life, by juxtaposing so many people together in such relatively small spaces, created new patterns of behaviour. Two new terms were devised to describe the new classes which dovetailed into one another. The first was the 'lower-middle class', where a Victorian observer might have placed our clerk with his bowler hat. This was the class the novelist Arnold Bennett had in mind when he described his early family life in the Potteries where his father was a solicitor: 'I was born slightly beneath it [the middle class]. But by the help of God and strict attention to business I have gained the right of entrance into it.' Bennett, however, was exaggerating for effect as most Victorians would have placed solicitors in the middle class.[18]

The second division was the upper or 'respectable' working class, the clerk who brought home 25s. to 30s. a week if he knew shorthand and 20s. if not, and the skilled artisan who could earn from 50s. to £3 and above a week by the first decade of this century. In the nineteenth century the greatest increase in wealth came among those with smaller incomes: in 1850, for example, £29,000,000 lay in deposits in Post Offices and Savings Banks. By 1907 the sum had risen to £209,500,000, well over a four-fold increase. There was likewise a great increase in skilled workers as men moved from low paid to better paid trades. Lady Bell's survey of Middlesbrough showed that of 1,274 ironworkers, 1,043 earned between 20s. and 60s. a week, 169 earned under 20s. (almost half of these were boys) and sixty-two earned over £3. (The national average weekly wage was estimated in 1901 at 27s. 6d.) The spread of this group was perhaps the most rapid of all in the nineteenth century: an 1896 survey showed that if one divided the income tax paying class into two groups of £150 to £600 and £600 to £1000, the latter group was 'nearly stationary' in the thirty years since 1850. On the other hand, those earning under £600 had increased by four per cent. This was the group which would have included Arnold Bennett's father: he was waiting for his class to catch up with his income, a not infrequent occurrence in English life. The point is that as we come down the scale of incomes the rate of growth increases. This was especially the case with those earning under £150 a year, that is the lower-middle and working classes. In 1880 this group earned £310,000,000, £10,000,000 more than the entire working population of the United Kingdom had earned in 1850. Thus the 'working classes' have 'increased in wealth more rapidly than any other class of the community'. They did not increase in numbers. That was the achievement of the middle classes for the simple reason that they absorbed the top layers of the working classes: the cloth cap was exchanged for the bowler hat.[19]

When Anthony Trollope returned from Ireland at the end of 1859 he commented on London's spreading suburbs, those endless streets of brick houses which were covering the fields of Middlesex, Surrey, Kent and Essex:

> It was a street of small new tenements, built, as yet, only on one side of the way . . . Of such streets there are thousands now round London. They are to be found in every suburb, creating wonder in all thoughtful minds as to who can be their tens of thousands of occupants. The houses are a little too good for artisans, too small and too silent to be the abode of various lodgers, and too mean for clerks who live on salaries.

Such expanding suburbs were a feature not just of London but of many English towns. In Northampton the *Northamptonshire Nonconformist* surveyed the new suburbs to the north of the town centre and realised the golden opportunity they provided. The paper urged the churches to cooperate to avoid overlapping lest 'rivalry result in a wasteful employment of power, as for instance, at Bugbrooke. But, rivalry or not, here is the land: let Nonconformists go in and possess it.'[20]

Two changes had made this growth possible. The first was the rise in wages. The average real wage, allowing for unemployment, with 1850 set at 100, was 184 in the last year of the century (1900). The second fact was the fall in prices. The overall index of vegetable, animal and principal industrial products, set at 175 in 1800 according to the Rousseaux Price Index, fell to 91 in 1900. As prices fell consumption rose: whereas the United Kingdom consumed six pounds of butter, eight pounds of sugar and twenty-two eggs per capita in 1881, by 1907 it was devouring ten pounds of butter, fifty eggs and fifty pounds of sugar. (Of no little importance to Nonconformists, tea consumption rose from four-and-a-half to six-and-a-quarter pounds per head.) It has been estimated that in the last twenty years of the nineteenth century prices fell by eight per cent while wages rose by ten. The third change was the growth of cheap, rapid transport. In London by 1892 there were 400 miles of railway lines and 391 stations within twelve miles of Charing Cross. Passengers' journeys in 1891 were estimated at 177,000,000 and tramways had no less than 200,000,000 passengers by the end of 1891. It is not surprising that social investigators reported that 'the tradesmen and middle class . . . exhibit an active religious life, mainly gathered in the larger Nonconformist bodies, especially the Baptists'. One of Charles Booth's investigators referred to such people as those 'who take to religion like "ducks to water" . . . With them prosperity and religion go hand in hand.' In Charles Booth's historic survey of London, the researcher who visited the Baptist Tabernacle in Woolwich noted its host of activities and use of a full orchestra at religious services. The congregation was made up of 'artisans' who 'save and buy their own houses at Plumstead and live comfortably; a selection, and not the ruck; men with a trade, not labourers; men who "earn good wages and spend them on their homes and wives and children".'[21]

These expanding suburbs were the result of urbanization: Victorian urban growth had depended on depopulating the countryside round the cities. Even in London it was not until 1891 that the Census showed that the capital no longer depended on the surrounding counties for its growth. Having said that, one in every three residents was still born in the country (35 per cent) although in 1851 it had stood at over half. This dependence was only confirmed by the falling birth rate which was declining faster in the suburbs. The normal course for the immigrant was to move first into the city and then to move out again into the new suburbs. As one survey noted in 1898: 'People in London are migratory to an enormous extent. They move from north to south, from south to east, and so on with astonishing rapidity. . . .' (This was exacerbated in the early years of the present century when Jews fleeing Russian pogroms started settling in parts of London and then started moving out.) Nonconformity's increase was influenced by the fact that migration into the country's expanding towns came from surrounding areas. In northeast London, which drew on East Anglia, there was a strong Nonconformist presence; in the west and southwest the suburbs drew on Surrey, Sussex and western

Middlesex which had not traditionally had a strong number of Nonconformists. Because houses were rented, moving was relatively easy if one had an adequate income. It was in these new streets, streets 'in which a considerable proportion . . . are artisans and mechanics', that the respectable working man and his family settled. Not surprisingly, these were the fastest growing areas. In London, one researcher noted that even if immigrants from the country were only one-third of the residents, the higher the percentage of immigrants in a neighbourhood, the better off the neighbourhood. Alexander Paterson observed this class of men and wrote: 'It is unfortunate, but perhaps inevitable, that the steady church-going fellow should work with greater diligence and gain promotion earlier than the rougher lad.'[22]

What was true of the respectable working man and his family was also true for the self-employed, the descendants of Mrs Oliphant's 'greengrocers' and 'dealers in cheese and bacon'. C. F. G. Masterman noted that in those suburbs with 'mixed' populations, 'the tradesmen and middle class of the poorer boroughs exhibit an active religious life, mainly gathered in the larger Nonconformist bodies, especially the Baptists'. One visitor to Spurgeon's Tabernacle in 1884 noted that the building did not hold a 'high-class congregation, and the preacher knows that its understanding can best be opened by metaphors and parables taken from the customs of the retail trade, and with similes taken from the colloquialisms of the streets'.[23] As the population moved outwards and the population began to 'go down' the churches could either take the chapel to the people in the suburbs or, if the minister was powerful enough, let the people come to him.

In 1889 the General Baptist Association built a new chapel in Ferme Park, a new suburb drawing on the exodus from Hornsey. The minister from 1890 to 1925 was the Rev. Charles Brown. The church prospered: in 1889 there were seventy-one members but by 1906 there were 1,041. On the day of the *Daily News* census 2,088 people attended the two Sunday services. A new chapel, seating 1,250, had been built. 'From the beginning', Charles Brown's biographer tells us, 'Ferme Park has been filled with devout people of the best stamp.' There was a waiting list for seats (which were rented) and the cause of the success was not hard to find:

> The neighbourhood was coming to the peak of its development, and Ferme Park reaped the benefit. People of good middle class, with substantial families, settled in Crouch End, partly because it was not too far from the city, partly because it had plenty of attractive open spaces, but still more because it had good schools and excellent churches.[24]

As we have noted before, the chapel's annual income rose to £5,000.

The problems faced by those chapels left stranded in inner city areas were tackled by all the leading denominations. In 1908 the Liverpool Free Church Council created a special commission to study the problem. It reported that between 1881 and 1908 average attendance at morning services dropped from just over forty per cent of the population to 12.5 per cent (of the seats provided). The 'broad facts show that there has been a steady decline in church attendance since 1881, and this has coincided with the exodus of the middle classes'. Of 82,903 Nonconformist worshippers surveyed at both morning and evening services, only 10,268 came from the city centre. The bulk worshipped in the suburbs, especially in Toxteth and Bootle. Poverty and Nonconformity were not suitable bed-fellows. Inner Liverpool, by which was meant the old parish of Liverpool, lost 65,000 people between 1881 and 1908. The growth was in the suburbs of Walton, Wavertree, Sefton Park and the trend was for the wealth to go to the Cheshire side and for poverty to go to the Lancashire side. The middle classes had fled the city centre for the promised land in the leafy suburbs.[25]

In the new classifications devised by Victorians there was one final class below that of the respectable wage-earner – the poor, the people who filled the town centres in properties left vacant by the fleeing middle classes. As a class 'the poor' stayed away from the chapel and this dismayed Nonconformists like John Clifford who had himself been born in poverty and worked as a boy in the mill. Yet there was a difference in the definition of poverty and it was a profound one: Clifford had been born in the Derbyshire village of Sawley where many if not most were 'poor' factory workers and therefore the term meant less. In the expanding towns and cities of late Victorian England 'the poor' had been isolated as a new class, normally and readily identified not so much by their income as by their appearance and attitudes. Clifford laid the blame squarely on the shoulders of Nonconformists themselves:

> You are so walled about by respectability and smitten by the idolatry of social rank and corrupted by the falsehoods of the world that you no longer touch human life at its heart or constrain us to think of you as the disciples of the Carpenter who knew what was in man and judged him not according to his garb and speech, but in the light of his vast possibilities of redemption and uplift.

Clifford had touched a raw nerve but Nonconformists were caught: the same social processes that were providing them with members were also ensuring that those same recruits were marked off from the mass of mankind who would never enter the chapel's doors. As Hugh McLeod has written: 'Belief in any sort of systematic doctrine tended both to arise from, and to reinforce, a self-reliant individualism, and to make its adherent an outsider.' One superintendent of district nurses noted in 1904: 'Many of the poor rarely attend church, not because they are irreligious, but because they have long since received and absorbed the truths by which they live.' They are 'not so much indifferent to the dogmas of religion as unconscious of their existence'.[26]

By the end of the century, however, the facts were that Nonconformist chapels were no more successful than the Church of England in reaching either the bulk of the working class or 'the poor' in England's sprawling new conurbations – London, Birmingham, Manchester and Liverpool. Insofar as one can be offended by a fact Nonconformists felt offended by this: had not they been among the first to point out the plight of the urban poor when the London Congregational Union issued its penny tract, *The Bitter Cry of Outcast London* in the autumn of 1883? The tract immediately won national and even international attention: the *Pall Mall Gazette* pointed out that the Viennese papers were commenting on it, presumably because Vienna itself faced an enormous problem with its own rapidly expanding population. Yet, when Charles Booth's team surveyed Newington and Walworth they pointed out that 'each religious method finds its place in London according to local conditions as to social status'. The 'outward drift of population' left the poor behind: York Street Congregational Chapel, which Robert Browning had once attended, used to have 'carriage folk' lined up from the chapel door to the Walworth Road waiting to get in for Sunday morning service. That was in the 1840s: by the 1890s the middle classes had fled. The poor's attitude to religion was summed up as 'the supreme impartiality of ignorance'. The researcher concluded that all the religious work undertaken in the area – including the enormous efforts made by Spurgeon's vast congregation at the Metropolitan Tabernacle – 'leaves practically untouched the great mass of the population whether of the poor or the working class'. Arthur Sherwell, surveying the districts immediately round Soho, concluded that 'the provision made by the Nonconformists is comparatively small', due, he said, to the exodus of the middle classes, the decline in housing and the influx of Jews from East London. The most damning indictment came from one of Booth's surveyors who introduced the survey of West Southwark and North Lambeth by quoting a local religious worker: 'The people we are told are "too poor for Dissent".'[27]

In Liverpool, Victorian England's most densely populated city, the survey conducted for the local Free Church Council showed that 'ground is continually being lost . . . in neighbourhoods that are "going down in the social scale"'. That survey had concluded that Nonconformists 'on the whole . . . have failed to secure the wage-earning classes', a failure which coincided with the flight of the middle classes to Toxteth and other suburbs. These conclusions, published in 1908 only confirmed those reached by Booth in the late 1890s. Later research showed how urban growth, by which we mean the movement of people into town centres combined with a town or city's own natural growth, affected Nonconformity in Liverpool. A religious census in 1881 showed that while Liverpool's population had almost doubled since the famous religious census of 1851, Sunday attendances had fallen from some forty-five in every hundred to some thirty-two in every hundred of the population but this was due to a sharp drop in Church of England figures. The town's four largest denominations, which included Presbyterian, increased by 28.9 per cent and this was due to movement into the suburbs. Twenty years later, the total percentage of people attending religious services remained basically the same but this time the results were mainly due to a steep rise in Roman Catholic attendances. (Due to Irish immigration, Roman Catholics had already formed a quarter of the city's population by 1831.) The number of Nonconformists who attended chapel had risen because of the suburban growth but it had not kept up with the increase in population.[28]

The solution was said to be straightforward: if the poor will not come to chapel on the chapels' terms, the chapels must go to the people on their terms. By the end of the century numerous studies, in addition to Booth or Rowland, were devoted to the problem of the inner city poor. Nonconformists were told by Mudie-Smith that the need was for 'large, handsome, central halls'. Nonconformity needed 'institutional churches', churches which provided activities and premises for a wide variety of social activities only one of which was traditional Sunday worship, roughly equivalent to late twentieth century 'leisure centres' operated by local councils or private concerns except that the twentieth century version no longer considered religion as a leisurely activity. Mudie-Smith insisted that the 'buildings we erect in the future must be the antithesis of those now in existence, if the working-classes, and those below the working classes, are to be found within them'. New voices were being heard, however, which insisted that the task was too great for the churches alone to tackle. Those within the Liberal Party who advocated a greater degree of state involvement and control under the term, 'New Liberalism', advocated a 'positive progressive policy which involves a new conception of the functions of the state', a 'positive policy of social reconstruction'.[29] The Baptists, Congregationalists and Primitive Methodists agreed in part, hence their resolutions in favour of a scheme of old aged pensions and a demand for a system of state secondary schools.

Wesleyan Methodists, although they were still frightened of such overtly 'political' demands with unforeseeable results, were also some of the greatest proponents of institutionalized churches or missions as a solution to the problem. The idea for these is usually described as a product of the 'Forward Movement' led by the Rev. Hugh Price Hughes to revitalize the Wesleyan Church, encourage more lay participation and reach areas hitherto untouched by the denomination by the use of radical and innovative methods. The first mission, however, was started in Liverpool in 1875 under Charles Garrett, ten years before the first London mission opened in the East End. It was not always an easy task: some well-to-do chapels were keen to keep their distance. The historians of Hinde Street Chapel in London referred to the opportunities in the immediate neighbourhood for a 'virile middle-class Methodism, with its special mission to the poor, the sick, the young'. That did not mean turning the chapel over to the poor. When Conference decided to open its first London 'mission' it chose a chapel which had suffered from the middle-class exodus, St George's Wesleyan Chapel. The new director found that 'those who had lived long in St George's [in the East] had been accustomed to see "carriage folk" come to the chapel' and many moved on to other chapels.[30]

The most famous of the new missions was that which Hugh Price Hughes himself undertook to manage. The West London Mission opened at St James's Hall, off Piccadilly Circus in 1887. From the beginning it was Hughes' own, just as the Metropolitan Tabernacle was uniquely the property of Spurgeon. In one sense they were a continuation of the old 'proprietary chapels'. Academic debate has raged over these Wesleyan missions. Some have seen them not so much as a response to social needs, an innovative step to reach people who would otherwise never enter a chapel and an example of a conservative body's ability to take radical action, but as a form of denominational self-advertisement: 'The context of the Forward Movement is the crisis in Methodism caused by resurgent Anglicanism, rather than the over-lapping crisis caused by awareness of a vast urban population alienated from Christianity.' Others have challenged this and said that they were genuine attempts to reach working people and that they did do so, not just through preaching a heavily politicized gospel but through the tremendous number of social, educational, nursing and welfare organizations attached to the Mission. When Booth's team visited St James's Hall they praised it for the good it did but added:

> The crowds who fill St. James's Hall come to no great extent from those residing in the neighbourhood . . . the poor are not seen there, nor the depraved, nor those who have been lifted out of those conditions . . . those who come find . . . an agreeable Sunday pastime, a pleasant change from attendance at less lively places of worship.[31]

The year before Hughes opened his mission the Central Hall in Manchester began after the old Wesleyan chapel in Oldham Street had been duly altered. By the turn of the century the mission had become the 'largest Methodist congregation in the world'. There were the usual host of activities including a men's home and 'labour yard' to give employment, a women's home, maternity home and hospital, cripples' guild, choirs, orchestras, bands, visitation schemes, Sunday Schools, Bands of Hope and so on. In 1904 Sunday attendances had soared to at least 16,000 people at all services both in the main hall itself and in various other rooms and by 1913 there were 2,500 voluntary workers. This is a remarkable achievement but the biographer of the mission's first director, S. F. Collier, admitted that the congregation was said to be too 'respectable', a charge which he went on to reject. It is not surprising, therefore, that in the official history of Methodism published in 1909 praise should have been lavished on the work done: 'It was altogether a conjunction of circumstances, of which the meaning could hardly be mistaken; and by fidelity to evangelical truth and elasticity in its expression . . . several of the silent sanctuaries have been turned into hives of Christian industry.'[32] By 1909 there were forty-one Wesleyan urban Missions and when all is said and done the scheme was a sensible use of buildings which otherwise would have gone to waste. If later generations have decided that the problems were too vast to be solved by voluntary effort it is no criticism of the churches that they, not enjoying the benefit of hindsight, tried to solve them.

The other denomination which tackled the problem of the 'unchurched millions' was the Baptists through their Tabernacles. These were established by men who were educated under C. H. Spurgeon in his Pastor's College and who followed in his footsteps. Although himself a Calvinist and conservative in theology and politics – he left the Baptist Union over their alleged liberalism and broke with the Liberals over Home Rule – his Metropolitan Tabernacle had a wide range of activities to help the poor round the Elephant and Castle. By the late 1890s the Tabernacle had twenty-one mission halls and twenty-five Sunday Schools with 8,900 students. One of Spurgeon's 'boys' was the Rev. Archibald Brown who began work at Stepney Green Tabernacle in 1867. Five years later it became the East London Tabernacle. In that same year another of Spurgeon's graduates, William Cuff, began his ministry at Providence Chapel, later Shoreditch Tabernacle. In Christmas week the chapel distributed clothes, meat and bread; for the greater part of two days, Cuff, who had trained as a butcher, cut up nearly two tons of prime beef to give to some 550 families.[33]

This type of work was by no means restricted to Spurgeon's followers. In Leicester F. B. Meyer resigned the pastorate of Victoria Road Baptist Church because of a dispute over his methods of evangelism and moved to the chapel's mission which he then developed into Melbourne Hall. Meyer began work with released prisoners, which later developed into the Discharged Prisoners' Society. In addition there were fire-wood selling and window-cleaning schemes to provide work for the unemployed. Back in London, ministers like John Clifford (Mudie-Smith's pastor and friend) and J. C. Carlile in his dockland church had begun turning their chapels into 'institutional churches' in the 1850s and 1860s respectively. Carlile later recalled one incident which occurred during the church's provision of halfpenny meals for 300–400 school children on four days in the week. One little girl, clad only in a frock (that is with no coat, boots, socks or under-clothes) turned up but without the necessary halfpenny ticket. When she was told she could have nothing to eat without the ticket she begged, 'Can't I lick the plates?'.[34]

Congregationalists' efforts at urban mission work were never as successful as those of the Baptists or Wesleyan Methodists. There were famous 'institutional churches' like C. Silvester Horne's Whitefield's Tabernacle on the Tottenham Court Road but, like Hughes' St James's Hall, this gained fame because of the minister, a 'political parson' who went on to become a Liberal MP. In Leeds the Yorkshire Congregational Union designated Belgrave Chapel as part of its own Forward Movement in 1889 and decided that 500 of the chapel's 1300 seats should be free of any annual rent. The pulpit was removed and in its stead a platform was erected to avoid too ecclesiastical an appearance. There were, in addition, the usual host of social activities. It is not surprising that Congregationalism, the most middle class of all Nonconformist denominations, had the most difficult time in working-class areas.

The Primitive Methodists came relatively late into the race, partly because most if not all of their work in the largest cities was already with working people. By the early 1890s they had some missions in London, in Clapton and Hoxton, with medical dispensaries, homes of rest and so on. They opened their first 'central mission' in Birmingham in 1896. In 1900 the Connexion established a Church Extension Fund to build churches in 'necessitous and promising localities' including inner London. This was described as a 'bold programme . . . yet not too bold'. The denomination's leading light in this work was the Rev. James Flanagan who turned his South London chapel into a Central Hall which opened at a cost of £12,000 in 1900. Visitors praised the building while the mission had the usual accessories such as mothers' meetings and Sunday Schools. Inside the hall there was a brass band, string band, large organ, trained choir and 'ardent and eloquent preacher'. Its attempts to win over the un-churched were still pronounced a failure by Charles Booth's investigator.[35]

Finally towards the end of the century Nonconformists started their own series of Settlements in imitation of those like Whitechapel's Toynbee Hall founded in 1884 by the Church of England. These were a logical extension of the idea of a Methodist Mission or a Baptist or Congregational 'Institutional Church' and were not meant to be openly religious establishments at all. The aim was to 'break free from Ecclesiasticism', to dispel fears among other religious workers at the thought of yet another stall in the religious market and, most importantly, to break down suspicion among the natives that this was yet another 'parson trap'. The first such settlement was opened by the Wesleyan Methodists in Bermondsey in 1890 and J. S. Lidgett, the first warden, was outspoken in explaining the failure of previous efforts: it was due to too close an identification with what was called the 'middle-class spirit'. Bermondsey concentrated on education, practical training as well as University Extension lectures, along with social work in the form of clubs. The identification with working-class politics was symbolized in the fact that the Dockers' Union had their South London headquarters in the Settlement.[36]

Congregationalists followed in 1890 with Mansfield House in Canning Town established by their College in Oxford. In 1895 they converted the old York Street Chapel, once one of their wealthiest chapels, into Browning Hall and named it in honour of the poet who had once worshipped there. Both Mansfield and Browning had all the clubs, lectures and classes that Bermondsey had and, in addition, a medical mission, a poor man's lawyer, a 'cripples' parlour' and a 'people's drawing room'. There was, however, a religious service called a 'People's Evening'. The Hall in its earliest days does not seem to have been as successful as Bermondsey.[37] In 1898 the Primitive Methodists' theological college in Manchester sponsored their own Settlement in Whitechapel so that by 1913 there were twenty-seven settlements in London and twelve in the rest of England. Although not all had been established by religious bodies, the bulk were Church of England, Methodist, Congregational or Roman Catholic. Baptists remained content with their own missions and Tabernacles.

The attempts by leading denominations to combat their image as churches of the middle classes which ignored the urban poor has caused some to think that at the end of the nineteenth century they were moving towards a 'social gospel', away from their traditional insistence on man's fallen nature, his need for repentance and the individualism of his response. The fact that the theologically conservative Baptists eschewed the Settlement movement and were wary of 'missions' has given support to this view. The facts are otherwise. Baptists themselves had made strenuous efforts to build 'institutional churches' under the guidance of radical ministers like Clifford, Carlile and Meyer and these were missions before their time. Secondly, men like Clifford could be very radical in politics and liberal in theology while still insisting on the reality of sin and the need for individual repentance and conversion. Thirdly, social concern was no more the sole prerogative of liberals in the period we are considering than it is now. Conservatives like the Baptists Archibald Brown, John Wilson and William Cuff devoted their lives to helping the poor of London. In Liverpool, social concern did not imply that the man was a political or theological radical: it is true that the Baptist, Charles Aked, built up Pembroke Chapel from a run-down town centre church into a highly successful chapel with over 1900 members. He was a 'pro-Boer' like Clifford and like him, a radical socialist and member of the Fabian Society until he left for New York in 1906. His departure angered socialists as much as Nonconformists. Yet it is also true that Liverpool's West Toxteth Tabernacle was opened in 1871 for W. P. Lockhart who was known as the 'Spurgeon of Liverpool' for his 'High Calvinism'. His politics had little in common with Aked's: he combined his pastorate with his career as a merchant and was a Liberal Unionist of the most orange complexion.[38] Again, much has been made of Hugh Price Hughes' 'Christian Socialism' but Hughes still insisted on individual conversions as did the bulk of those Methodists in charge of Missions, men like Garrett or Collier.

To younger generations of Nonconformists, as to their peers in the Church of England, Missions and the Settlements offered a new and concrete way in which to help those who most needed it. Sir Walter Besant, when opening Mansfield House's new residence on 5 December 1897 referred to the need to widen and enrich the lives of England's poorest classes. He told the settlement workers they were the 'new missionaries of a Christianity which makes the higher life a part of their religion'. They had a part in raising 'the level of humanity by the practical example of a teaching which the Protestant Church has always recognised and never understood', that is, orders of men and women pledged to helping the poor like the monks and nuns of the Roman Catholic and Anglican churches. It is not surprising that one of Hughes' creations at the West London Mission was an order of 'Sisters of the People' who took vows and worked according to a rule although the vows were not for life, the women did not live in community and many were married. Likewise in 1902 there was a proposal reported in the *British Weekly* for a Nonconformist religious order based on the fifteenth century Brothers of the Common Life, complete with rule, dress and community living, but nothing seems to have come of the idea.[39]

Older generations undoubtedly shook their heads, not so much at the Missions but at the Settlements, fearing that there would be so much emphasis on social improvement that the need for the gospel would be forgotten. Some, with that Victorian candour that surprises people more used to disguising their motives, saw the work as a stitch in time. The Wesleyan Mission worker, Edward Smith, insisted that the middle classes had no one but themselves to blame for their fear of revolution. He insisted that 'no portion of the English-speaking race is so much ignored by religious agencies' as the working classes. As a result working people were 'thrown into the arms of designing agitators or of social teachers who are lacking in ballast. They become truly the "dangerous class".' Hugh Price Hughes declared that if the 'common people be healthy, vigorous and free, the constitution is safe'. The Rev. Walter Walsh from Newcastle told the 1896 Free Church Congress that while they wanted working people in their chapels they must not be afraid that they would take over. Working people brought fresh ideas but 'showed a great deal of diffidence and commendable modesty'.

Even so, one must always 'keep the whip in his own hand'.[40]

The final consideration is the degree to which all this effort affected the lives of the urban poor and broadened Nonconformists' appeal. The inevitable conclusion is that the work had little effect. Visitors and reporters who investigated missions and tabernacles reported uniformly that they felt 'a pang of personal disappointment at finding the very poor to be virtually absent. There are no shabby waterproofs or battered bonnets.' At Collier's Manchester Mission we were told the congregation was too 'respectable'. Booth's investigators reported again and again that the old pattern was only reproduced in the new Missions, Tabernacles and 'institutional churches'. The working people one saw, even if technically 'poor', were 'usually sober, self-reliant and independent characters'. As such they were not of 'the poor'. Often the working men and women one saw came not as part of a family but individually, 'following their own fancy' either regarding the message or the minister. Most of the really successful Missions and Tabernacles were, just like the chapels in the prospering lower middle-class suburbs, built round a 'dynamic' preacher – Hughes, Lockhart, Clifford, Meyer, Cuff or Collier – with whom people wished to be identified. Whenever Missions or Tabernacles were in mixed areas or, like Hughes' or Aked's, in a city centre, modern transport made it possible for people to come from long distances while the poor in the immediate neighbourhood stayed away.[41]

'The Nonconformist bodies', C. F. G. Masterman wrote at the turn of the century, 'represent the ideals of the middle classes, the strenuous self-help and energy which have stamped their ideas upon the whole of Imperial Britain.' As the Chairman of the Congregational Union told his audience in the City Temple in May, 1890, 'we believe in "the survival of the fittest" [and] therefore in the immortality of our principles'.[42] This strenuous self-reliance had become in many ways the foundation of Nonconformity's appeal and to those for whom the ideal had no appeal, whether through lack of native ability, the intensity of their poverty or simple disinclination, Nonconformity would have none either. It is worth noting here that it was not until 1901 that the Primitive Methodist Conference decided that a bankrupt member could still retain his membership even though he would have to resign any church office he held. Before then he not only had to resign his office but suffer excommunication.

'Strenuous self-help' and 'survival of the fittest' presumed by the end of the century the ability to read. This was the greatest skill any child took with him from school and if he were to improve himself and rise through the ranks of the ever-expanding middle class, he would do it largely through reading. It is no coincidence that Victorian Nonconformity's growth paralleled the growth in literacy. In 1839 male illiteracy had stood at 33.7 per cent while the rate for women was 49.5; by 1900 the percentages had shrunk to 2.8 and 3.2 respectively. When Lady Bell published her study of working-class life in Middlesbrough she commented on the 900 working-class homes visited that fifty per cent of the men interviewed read only newspapers, twenty-five per cent read papers and books and twenty-five per cent read nothing at all. That seventy-five per cent who did read is the group from which Nonconformity drew its adherents, homes which the first Viscount Mackintosh recalled were 'serious, but not over-solemn' and 'emphatically . . . not joyless'. Nonconformist leaders, who had benefited from further education, recognized this fact and the dangers that accompanied it. One writer pointed out in a Congregational paper that the overriding danger was that the self-educated man would believe that 'the effort is the standard of measurement'. Self-education needed to be accompanied by self-criticism, a sense of humility to avoid overestimating oneself, and a practical application of the knowledge gained in service to others.[43]

Since the early nineteenth century there had been a succession of men, bodies and publications devoted to helping the working classes help themselves: the Society for the Diffusion of Useful Knowledge and the Working Man's Institutes, Charles Knight's *Penny Cyclopaedia*, Robert Chamber's *Encyclopaedia* and John Cassell's *Popular Educator*. Nonconformist chapels were among the leaders in providing their own form of continuing education, decades before there was talk of 'institutional churches' and 'Missions'. John Clifford's Westbourne Park Baptist Chapel established its own Mutual Improvement Society in 1861. Its membership rose to a peak of 1,300 and it received grants from the London County Council and the Exchequer. Guest speakers included leading literary lights such as Justin McCarthy, Benjamin Kidd, Edmund Gosse, Jerome K. Jerome, Prince Krapotkin, Conan Doyle and George du Maurier. Eventually the Society became part of the Paddington Technical Institute and then Paddington Polytechnic.[44] In addition there was a Young Men's Mutual Improvement Society and a debating club with an annual subscription of 4s.

In addition, Clifford also took part in the 'Pleasant Sunday Afternoons' movement. By the end of the century this was a recognized force within Nonconformity and centred on 'talks', normally by the minister or guest speaker and aimed at men only. They capitalized on Nonconformity's recognized appeal to men, something much envied by the Church of England, and concentrated on current affairs, normally seen through a Liberal viewpoint. Their motto was 'Brief, Bright and Brotherly'. At Whitefield's Tabernacle, C. S. Horne gave his own Sunday afternoon lectures at 'PSA' gatherings and it is claimed that Lenin was at one of these although our informant does not say if the future Soviet dictator benefited from the lecture.[45] Hugh Price Hughes' Sunday afternoon talks likewise centred on current affairs: as we shall see later, it was at one of these that he launched his famous attack on Charles Stewart Parnell. Suburban middle-class chapels, like R. F. Horton's in Hampstead, also had their 'Working Men's Lectures' to attract not only the men in the congregation but the unchurched male population in their district; Horton had as one speaker the future Liberal Prime Minister, Herbert Asquith. At one stage he had regularly come to 'sit under' Horton.

Since the abolition of the 'Taxes on Knowledge' the number of cheap publications aimed at working people rose steadily. Never before and never since have so many Englishmen read so many books, pamphlets, magazines, tracts and newspapers. Which to buy was the question.

Superior intellects like John Morley defined the problem: 'The reader is naturally bewildered when confronted with thousands of volumes about which he knows little or nothing. Before he can make adequate use of the treasures placed at his disposal some advice and guidance is [sic] necessary.'[46] The advice was not slow in coming. The Rev. George Jackson produced a monthly 'Reading Circle' in *Young Man* for Wesleyan Methodist youths to create 'a taste for the good things in literature' and devoted sections to scripture, biography, travel, poetry, fiction and miscellaneous. The novelist, Arnold Bennett, published a guide for 'collecting a complete library of English literature' in 1909, insisting that 'literature . . . is the fundamental *sine qua non* of complete living'. He reckoned one could have a library of 337 volumes representing 226 authors for £26. 14s. 7d. although normally one could expect a discount of 25 per cent. The Liberal politician, Sir John Lubbock, published his own guide to the best 100 books in the world, based on a lecture to the Working Men's College of London which the Congregational millionaire, Samuel Morley had helped to establish. 'Of all the privileges we enjoy in this nineteenth century', Sir John told his listeners, 'there is none, perhaps, for which we ought to be more thankful than for easier excess [sic] to books'.[47]

Nonconformist newspapers like Robertson Nicoll's *British Weekly*, which sold for a penny, specifically set out to help readers become more 'cultured'. Nicoll, who wrote much of the weekly issue himself, devoted large portions to literature and his column, 'Claudius Clear', set out to 'lead Christian thought and belief out into the spacious fields of learning and to acclimatize devout people in the atmosphere of literature'. When he eventually brought out an edition of his 'Claudius Clear' articles he promised his readers that 'every one who faithfully goes through these hundred books or so will be much more *cultured* [italics the author], much better educated, than the vast majority of men and women'. His own library, lovingly stocked with free review copies, grew to 25,000 volumes. The influence which men like Nicoll had was tremendous. One of his readers, who had an 'almost idolatrous regard' for him, told his son that 'he would rather go without his lunch in the dockyard on Fridays

than miss reading the *British Weekly*'. Another Nonconformist family passed round the paper so that 'we all
knew and read Robertson Nicoll's articles'. His own view
was basically that of Matthew Arnold, that 'Nonconformists
had too long behaved as exiles from the world of culture'.
As a Scottish dissenter he had never felt outside the
mainstream of national life and culture. His attitude
toward English Nonconformity was always that bit
different and if somewhat patronizing it also provided a
challenge to accepted views.[49]

The variety and cheapness of books which poured forth
from publishers was tremendous. 'A shilling (minus
discount)', wrote the future Archbishop of Canterbury,
Randall Davidson, 'will procure you, in a neat brown
cover, a comprehensive manual upon any subject in earth,
or sea, or sky', enabling everybody to have 'a little
knowledge'. 'Everyman' books sold at 1s. 3d. although
they went down to a shilling in 1909; Oxford's 'World's
Classics' also sold at a shilling although they, along with
the Everyman series, went up to 1s. 4d. and 1s. 2d. during
the Great War. Nelson's New Century Library sold at 2s. a
volume as did Cassell's Belle Sauvage Library; Methuen's
Little Library were priced at 1s. 6d. while the New
University Library was a shilling. There was the 'Home
University Library For Current Affairs' which produced
the 'comprehensive manuals' to which the Dean of
Windsor, Randall Davidson, referred: books on crime, the
urban poor and the rural problem. It was, therefore, not
just literature but current social problems that could be
understood by anyone who could read among what one
minister referred to as the 'upright, self-respecting but
comparatively struggling population'.[49]

The 'self-respecting but comparatively struggling population' was the group which had expanded to such a
degree in the nineteenth century. It was to them that
Nonconformity had its appeal and with them that it had
such influence. Nonconformity's great attraction, then,
was not so much to a class as to a type of person whom
the Congregational historian, Albert Peel, later described:

They were the type on whom the country's strength was built
– independent, reliable, sane. They scorned to take a day's

pay without doing a day's work; they would not be beholden to any man. They were thrifty and hated extravagance; plain-spoken and impatient of show and pretence. They were intelligent, and with few educational advantages, believed in education, and gave their lads a good start in life; they were the products of the Mechanics Institutes and Mutual Improvement Societies, of Ruskin and Carlyle, Gladstone and Bright; they took an interest in the affairs of their town and country, and were splendid citizens.

In February 1904 the President of the National Free Church Council, the Rev. F. B. Meyer, included Bristol as one of the stops on his 'motor tour' of England. His visit, the *Western Daily Press* said, was 'most successful in point of attendance and interest'. Minutes of the 'Evening Demonstration' show that Meyer, having first warned his audience of 'tableaux vivants, anything in the nature of dressing children up and teaching them to act, of everything that would savour of the theatre, [and] of kissing games as he found in the North of England', went on to spell out what was really a Nonconformist social creed. This combined the cult of respectability and individualism with a genuine concern for others. Meyer urged 'the payment of everything by cash, the living within their income, women not ordering spring bonnets until they had paid for their winter clothes . . . [for] if all the poor seamstresses who were looking for their money were to get it tomorrow, fewer would do wrong'.[50]

3

THE NONCONFORMIST CONTRIBUTION TO VICTORIAN CULTURE

In 1869, Matthew Arnold had written in *Culture and Anarchy*: 'The Nonconformist is not in contact with the main current of national life, like the member of an Establishment.' However true this might have been in the 1860s it was manifestly not the case by the 1890s. Even so, when contemporaries and some later historians came to examine the achievements of Victorian culture little room was found for Nonconformity. Arnold's strictures have stuck and remain far less 'dated' than his overblown writing. Anglo-Catholic attacks about the lack of 'valid orders' were nothing compared to the patronizing criticism of intellectuals from whom Nonconformists felt they deserved better. The chief among those appointed to guide Englishmen through the nineteenth century and into the democracy which lay ahead was, of course, Arnold himself.

In *Culture and Anarchy*, Arnold traced the effect of history on Nonconformity, 'how they have developed one side of their humanity at the expense of all others, and have become incomplete and mutilated men in consequence . . . in a word, that in what we call *provinciality* they abound, but in what we may call *totality* they fall short'. Nonconformity had never, he argued, produced any great work in literature, art, science and religion: 'The fruitful men of English Puritanism and Nonconformity are men who were trained within the pale of the Establishment – Milton, Baxter, Wesley.' (This, of course, was patent nonsense. Bunyan, Isaac Taylor, Isaac Watts, William Hazlitt, Samuel Rogers and the Brownings were all 'trained' outside the Church of England. Nonconformist achievements in science, religion and literature were far

67

from insubstantial.) Because Nonconformists stood aside the 'main current' they encouraged the national inclination to '*Hebraise*, as we call it; that is, to sacrifice all other sides of our being to the religious side'. Inevitably this left the Nonconformist with 'little leisure or inclination for culture; to which, besides, he has no great institutions not of his own making, like the Universities'. Nonconformity was made up of 'churches without great men, and without furtherance for the higher life of humanity'. In addition, Nonconformists were the 'most vital part of English Philistinism', the stiff-necked members of the middle class who 'not only do not pursue sweetness and light, but who even prefer to them that sort of machinery of business, chapels, [and] tea-meetings . . . which make up the dismal and illiberal life on which I have so often touched'.

Nonconformists were incapable, Arnold claimed, of attaining culture as he defined it, that is the 'pursuit of our total perfection by means of getting to know, on all the matters which most concern us, the best which has been thought and said in the world'. When Nonconformists like the Rev. Alex Thomson attacked Arnold they claimed his analysis of Nonconformity was an 'ingenious picture, drawn by the hand of a cunning artist . . . taken from the realm of mythology'. Yet it is ironic that both Arnold and his opponents often shared the same attitude. When Nonconformists denied that they stood outside English culture they defined that culture as '*an inward working*, a discipline and development of the intellectual side of our nature' under given moral laws. Arnold himself defined culture in the chapter on 'sweetness and light' as in 'becoming something rather than in having something, in an inward condition of the mind and spirit, not in an outward set of circumstances'.[1]

There was yet more criticism from another of the century's leading lights. This time it came from an unexpected quarter, from the one writer-philosopher respected by more Nonconformists than any other man, Ralph Waldo Emerson. His dictum in the 'Essay on Self-Reliance' that 'Whoso would be a man must be a Nonconformist' was frequently quoted by Nonconformists, normally without reference to its American context. In the chapter on religion in his collection, *English Traits*,

Emerson dismissed the unique role of the Nonconformist denominations in one sentence: 'They are only per-petuations of some private man's dissent, and are to the Established Church as cabs are to a coach, cheaper and more convenient, but really the same thing.'[2] It was a cruel and unexpected blow and it contained, as with Arnold, an element of truth hidden under a heavy varnish of over-writing and a metaphor extended too far for its own comfort.

As English Nonconformity prospered it deeply resented these criticisms. By the end of the Victorian era English Nonconformity was influencing English culture in ways which Arnold could not have foreseen. Three stand out: literature and the world of publishing, University life at Oxford and Cambridge and the diffusion of knowledge throughout English life. In all three ways Nonconformists played leading roles.

In discussing the Nonconformist contribution to English culture we need limits otherwise we might end up being as vague and discursive as Arnold. It is right we should start with the printed word because here again Arnold and Nonconformists agreed almost as much as they differed. In *Literature and Dogma* Arnold defined culture as '*reading*; but reading with a purpose to guide it, and with system. He does a good work who does anything to help this; indeed, it is the one essential service now to be rendered to education.' There was little if anything between this definition and Alex Thomson's understanding of culture as '*an inward working*, a discipline and development of the intellectual side of our nature', something which could be done through reading, study and listening. Here Nonconformists did, as Arnold urged, 'a good work'.[3]

One of the great Victorian achievements was to produce a society which was overwhelmingly literate. The impact of the printed word by the 1890s was tremendous and growing. It was something for the churches to take seriously as the Rev. Thomas Selby, a former Wesleyan missionary to China, pointed out in 1896: 'The daily press coins the commercial and political creeds of our fellow countrymen, and the successful novel-writer coins the religious creeds of equally large numbers.' This dates back to the discovery that social reformers could argue their cases through fiction and that the writers of fiction could increase sales by urging social reform. The American novelist, Harriet Beecher Stowe, made this type of fiction popular and acceptable to puritan readers with her fictionalized rendering of slavery in *Uncle Tom's Cabin*, guaranteed to give enjoyment and a comforting sense of moral outrage. Publication of *Uncle Tom* stretched over 1852 and 1853 and the book proved more popular in Britain than in America: of course, at the time Britain provided a larger book-reading and book-buying market than the United States with their smaller population. Nonconformist publishers like John Cassell were fully aware of the role of fiction in reaching audiences untouched by sermons and tracts: as he wrote to Lord Brougham, 'the province of the novelist is to show the results of certain social evils or public abuses' and he cited Dickens and Charles Reade. 'Guided by experience and observation,' he continued, 'I know what can be accomplished by fiction.' 'People will read fiction when they will read nothing else' and this natural prejudice could be used 'in elevating the moral and intellectual condition of the masses.' In addition to the 'social novel' there was the 'religious novel', a genre which was treated very seriously. As Anthony Trollope said, the novel had become the modern sermon. William Gladstone wrote a lengthy article in the *Nineteenth Century* on the most famous Victorian 'religious novel', *Robert Elsmere*, by Mrs Humphry Ward (herself a niece of Arnold), when it appeared in 1888. As we have already seen, Randall Davidson made the same point in his article, based on *Robert Elsmere*.[4]

Nonconformity itself contributed to the rise of the Victorian novel. Those whose works have survived their age include Elizabeth Gaskell, William Hale White (Mark Rutherford) and Arnold Bennett. In addition, while George Eliot was baptized into the Church of England she adopted as a teenager the Baptist views of her two schoolmistresses, views which she later rejected along with orthodox Christianity. Other Nonconformist writers famous in their day but now largely forgotten include: Arthur

Quiller-Couch ('Q'), Dinah Maria Mulock (Mrs Craik), Mrs A. Burnett Smith ('Annie S. Swan'), Ellen Thorneycroft Fowler (a daughter of a Liberal cabinet minister), F. R. Smith ('John Ackworth'), Pearl Craigie ('John Oliver Hobbes'), Mary Ann Hearn ('Marianne Farningham'), Jonathan Brierley ('J.B.') and Silas and Joseph Hocking, whom Arnold Bennett always referred to as 'The Brothers Hocking'. (Silas was the more prolific and wrote 194 novels. Between 1880 and 1900 he was selling about 1,000 copies a week, mainly to Methodists, and in 1906 and 1910 he stood unsuccessfully as a Liberal candidate for Parliament.) Although John Watson, who gained fame as 'Ian Maclaren', was a Scotsman by birth he served as a Presbyterian minister in England. Various other ministers tried their hands at being novelists including John Clifford, Joseph Parker, C. Silvester Horne, G. Holden Pike and H. E. Stone but their works are now thankfully forgotten.

Nonconformists were also involved in the production and what we might call the dissemination of literature. Publishing houses like Hodder and Stoughton, James Clarke, Allen and Unwin and Cassells were established by Nonconformists; others, like Swan and Sonnenschein, Nisbet, Isbister and Marshall, and Morgan and Scott featured Nonconformist writers. As we shall see, news-papers like the *British Weekly* and *The Christian World* played significant roles in the English literary scene. Journals like Henry Allon's *British Quarterly Review* and the Unitarians' *Hibbert Journal* were largely Nonconform-ist while the *Contemporary Review*, the *Fortnightly* and the *Nineteenth Century*, known after 1900 as the *Nineteenth Century and After*, included Nonconformist writers, usually ministers, among their most frequent contributors while the *Contemporary* was edited by a Wesleyan Methodist for many years. In 1900 Oxford University Press brought out the first in its famous series of anthologies, the 'Oxford Books'. The *Oxford Book of English Verse* has done as much as any book to diffuse English verse round the English-speaking world. It was edited by Quiller-Couch, a Cornishman from a United Methodist Free Church family. In 1910 he was knighted and two years later was appointed King Edward VII Professor of English Literature at Cambridge. In the

Preface to his collection for OUP he said his aim was 'to serve those who already love poetry and to implant that love in some young minds not yet initiated'. Before his death in 1944 his anthology had sold nearly half a million copies.[5] Although Augustine Birrell's essays are no longer read, in the fifty years between 1884, when the first of his three *Obiter Dicta* appeared, and 1930, when *Et Cetera* was published, the Liberal MP was highly respected as a critic, essayist, literary historian and biographer.

Writing and publishing books were of no value if people could not read them and in the distribution of books Nonconformists played a vital role. It is impossible to overestimate the importance of the Victorian circulating library and especially the 'Mudie Mountain', Thomas Carlyle's name for the empire built by Charles Edward Mudie, a Congregationalist. Mudie started his business life as a stationer but when only twenty-four began lending books. This was in 1842. Lending or circulating libraries had carried over from the eighteenth century but, at a guinea a year, none was as cheap as Mudie's and none influenced English literature as much as his did. His 'Select Library' established itself as a vital force in English cultural life: as Wyndham Lewis sneered, it was Mudie who gave 'the British middle-class mind those few ideas it possesses'. Mudie's Library became the most important means of distributing fiction in Britain and, as such, influenced the length, contents and style of the novel. He was also an effective censor of books he considered immoral like George Meredith's *The Ordeal of Richard Feverel*. His power, ultimately shared with his Anglican rival, W. H. Smith, lasted until the 1890s. Mudie has rightly been described as 'literature's Rowland Hill' and the great postal reformer, of course, was also a Nonconformist.[6]

Mudie catered for the middle class who had, in addition, stationers, book pedlars and, by the 1880s, the new public libraries from which to choose. What of the lower-middle class and the respectable working class, those people from whom Nonconformity predominately drew? Making literature available to these people was the achievement of yet another Nonconformist, Jesse Boot, a Methodist. As Arnold Bennett commented: 'Mr. Jesse Boot has had the singular and beautiful idea of advertising his wares by lending books to customers and non-customers at a loss of ten thousand a year. His system is simplicity and it is cheapness. He is generous.' Books were provided for two-pence so that for the lower-middle class, those people who would not use Mudie's, 'the sole point of contact with living literature is the chemist's shop. A wonderful world, this England!' (wrote Bennett in 1909). For Boots' Pure Drug Co. Ltd, it was a logical use of their national network of existing premises. For Jesse Boot, who was eventually made Lord Trent, the increased income from 'Boots Library' helped in the purchase of villas in Jersey and Cannes. While Mudie's son was noted for his work among the poor of London and died young, Boot's heir became a director of the company, a captain in the Sherwood Foresters and the second Lord Trent.[7]

It was one thing for Nonconformists to dominate the distribution of literature in England and another for them to become part of the expanding world of literature. One of the earliest efforts came in 1857 when a penny weekly, *The Christian World*, began. This was not exclusively a Nonconformist paper, however, and had an appeal to Evangelicals in the Church of England. Its first editor was a Baptist minister but in 1858 a second editor, James Clarke, a Congregationalist, was appointed and the paper began to prosper. It reached its zenith about 1880 when it had a circulation of 130,000. It was James Clarke who realized that Nonconformity could seize and hold a share in the developing 'newspaper culture' of the nineteenth century. He began to popularize the 'new learning' in Biblical scholarship; he included literary criticism and, beginning in 1868, he published a monthly supplement, *The Literary World*, which he included in his paper. He serialized novels and encouraged women writers such as Mary Ann Hearn ('Marianne Farningham') and essayists like the Rev. Jonathan Brierley ('J.B.'). Clarke's paper, however, lacked an aggressive, campaigning tone; to some it was too broad in its approach to the questions of higher criticism and the century's liberalizing tendencies generally. Its Nonconformist readership suffered when it opposed Irish Home Rule; when a new competitor appeared people realized that it was 'dated' and lacked the aggressive, campaigning tone of the new paper.[9]

The rival was the *British Weekly* which also cost a penny. It was edited by a young and unknown Scotsman named William Robertson Nicoll whom the *Daily Chronicle* eventually called the 'intellectual leader of Nonconformity'. He was the son of a Scottish Free Kirk minister and followed his father into the ministry. In 1884 he began his long literary career by editing *The Expositor* for Hodder and Stoughton. Two years later he resigned his position in Kelso and migrated to England. Within months of settling in England the thirty-five year old Scot gave up the ministry and on 5 November 1886 began publishing the *British Weekly*. The paper was specifically aimed at Nonconformists and, like its rival, included news of all the denominations. Politics were covered from a Liberal and Protestant perspective. (Covering the Westminster political scene was not unique to Nonconformist papers: the High Church weekly, *The Guardian*, established in 1846, covered political, social and Court news.) Nicoll devoted a very large section to the latest news from the worlds of literature and theology, plus numerous book reviews. In addition there were serialized novels by leading writers.

Nicoll, who wrote the bulk of the paper himself, was an arrogant and pompous man, known to *Punch* as the 'most successful Christian of his time'. He once told his children when they went up to Cambridge to be careful in making friends: they should avoid people who would not be useful in later life. As we have noted before, he basically agreed Arnold's view that English Nonconformists had stood outside the mainstream of cultural development too long. As a Scottish dissenter he had never been excluded from the main current of Scottish life because his dissent was based on a view of the relationship of church to state, not on theological grounds. In addition, because the schism which had produced the Free Church of Scotland only occurred in 1843 there was no legacy of isolation on which to draw. He quite naturally attended Aberdeen Grammar School and University. In many ways he never really became part of English Nonconformity although his influence within it was tremendous. Indeed, his aloofness from the inheritance which had shaped English Non-conformity probably helped him to assume, demand and obtain an acknowledgement from the literary and political worlds which he felt he and Nonconformity deserved. 'The importance attached to his judgments was due to the fact that they were regarded as being the expression of the Nonconformist mind.' But it was through the pages of his newspaper, whether writing as 'Claudius Clear' ('Claudius Drear' to *Punch*) or 'A Man of Kent', that he reached most people. By 1902 the *British Weekly* had a circulation of about 100,000 and a readership of up to four times that number. A 1914 survey of the British press concluded: 'This paper has exercised an influence on its contemporaries which it would be difficult to estimate . . . as a literary critic and . . . anecdotist it speaks with minute and often profound knowledge.' No 'religious' newspaper has ever had such influence in the history of modern journalism.[9]

Nicoll was well read and his own library, for which he added an upper storey to a wing of his Hampstead home, was where he mainly worked. He once claimed to read two books a day at a rate of 20,000 words every thirty minutes. (At his death 20,000 of the dog-eared and ash-filled volumes were auctioned but only fetched £1,000 or a shilling a volume.) Nicoll was a liberal in theology and therefore open to 'higher criticism'. In politics he developed, along with many Liberals, a somewhat touching devotion to Lord Rosebery and he found Liberal Imperialism attractive. He was a trenchant writer and never failed to insist that the causes of Christianity, of Protestant enlightenment and liberal progress were part and parcel with the Liberal Party. He was knighted in 1909 and invested as a Companion of Honour in 1921. Asquith included his name among those whom the government were prepared to force George V to raise to the peerage in order to pass their 1911 Parliament Act to restrict the power of the House of Lords. As we shall see later, his role as politician was on certain occasions a decisive one within Nonconformity. The American publisher, George Doran, remembered that the 'shrewd and canny Scot' was 'never happier than when waging battle'.[10]

Here we are more concerned with Nicoll as the 'grand

Panjandrum of popular literary journalism'. Although he was disliked by some writers, including Arthur Conan Doyle and G. K. Chesterton, and was singled out for attack by the novelist, T. W. H. Crosland in *The Unspeakable Scot*, his friends included Quiller-Couch, H. G. Wells, Clement Shorter, A. G. Gardiner and J. M. Barrie. In addition to the *British Weekly* Nicoll influenced public opinion through the pages of *The Bookman*, the six-penny monthly he published from 1891 to 1934 and *The Woman at Home*, another six-penny monthly which ran from 1893 to 1920. He also acted as an advisor to Hodder and Stoughton. Through his writings he was 'a course in adult education . . . Those who had no real width of literary knowledge could gain from him an introduction both to the classics and to the contemporary writers.' The intelligentsia, however, often found him wanting: while he had a first-rate knowledge of English literature, he felt it his duty in his reviews to 'recommend to the public those books which it would read with enjoyment. This he did, and the public found him a safe guide. He knew good literary work, he knew what the great public liked, and he did not confuse the two.'[11] Nicoll also compiled and edited a wide variety of books including literary biographies and theological works designed for ministers. He reviewed books for the *Contemporary Review*, *The Sketch* and the *Times Literary Supplement*, introduced numerous works and published several biographies and volumes of essays and sermons.

In 1908 he published a tribute to his father on the urging of Lord Rosebery. *My Father An Aberdeenshire Minister 1812–1891* was meant as a riposte to Edmund Gosse's classic work, *Father and Son*. The book, dedicated to Rosebery, was meant to show that an upbringing as rigid as that endured by the young Gosse did not necessarily lead to a life which was 'cabined, cribbed and confined'. His father, he wrote, 'had a Chinese reverence for printed matter' and devoted three rooms of the small manse to storing his library which eventually grew to 17,000 volumes, all bought on an average annual income of £100. As an old man he reckoned he had read a ton of periodicals, in addition to books, in twenty years. By walking from his village to the railway station, eight miles away, he was able to save 3s., enough to buy two books. Every fortnight he walked eight miles to another village where a stationer allowed him to read the latest reviews in an Edinburgh paper. His passion was buying books and sometimes purchases were taken home from the railway station in a wheelbarrow. While the elder Nicoll's views were narrow his reading was wide and, unlike the elder Gosse, he introduced his son to a cultural life outside the manse and bequeathed him a faith which endured into manhood. Unfortunately this book has never had the appeal of Gosse's. It lacks the tension brought about by the growing conflict between two powerful personalities, one young, one old, between adolescent and parent, and between an older, narrow faith and a younger, broader one which runs throughout *Father and Son*. As an author Nicoll was too detached and respectful. His is an affectionate memoir, not a penetrating story of a struggle which has an appeal to readers because it reminds them to some degree of similar struggles in their own lives.[12]

Nicoll also helped to encourage writers like John Buchan, Mark Rutherford and Arnold Bennett but his most important work was in promoting the 'Kailyard School'. This group consisted of James Barrie, S. R. Crockett and 'Ian Maclaren' – the Rev. John Watson. All three were from a Scottish Free Kirk background and all wrote stories set in Scotland, a genre that went back to Scott, was revived by Queen Victoria in the published extracts from her Journals about life in her beloved Highlands and was further popularized by George Macdonald in the 1860s and '70s. The School concentrated on simple tales of common life with heavy doses of sentiment and a liberal use of the vernacular: a kailyard was a kitchen garden. Barrie was famous for *The Little Minister*, Crockett for *The Stickett Minister* and Maclaren for *Beside the Bonnie Brier Bush*. All were successful: indeed, Maclaren's novel, his first, sold 256,000 copies in Britain and 484,000 in America by 1908. Although Nicoll did not 'discover' Barrie, who had already been published in the *St James's Gazette*, he did serialize his *Auld Licht Idylls* which started the 'school' in 1888 and, later, *A Window in Thrums*. In 1893 he persuaded John Watson to write down his stories of Scottish life for the *British*

Weekly and published the first in November. Sales of the paper soared and Watson became famous overnight. (Some insisted Barrie was the real author.) Finally, it was Nicoll who praised Crockett's first book, *The Stickit Minister*, published in 1893. Much of the group's appeal lay in their very ordinariness – their 'wholesomeness' –as a Methodist critic observed when contrasting them with Hardy's novels in 1896:[13]

> To pass from Wessex and its pits of night-soil to the sweetness of Caledonia and the kailyard, is like flitting from Purgatory to Paradise . . . Their influence upon the epidemic of fevered eroticism, fostered by much recent literature, is like that of the coming of a life-reviving wind upon the depression of a plague-stricken tropical city . . .

That the twentieth century has tended to prefer Hardy and 'fevered eroticism' over the 'sweetness of Caledonia' as described by Barrie, Crockett and Maclaren would be one of the many things to amaze the editor of the *British Weekly*.

Robertson Nicoll was likewise proud of having been one of the earliest critics to praise and defend the writings of 'Mark Rutherford', the pen-name of William Hale White. White had been expelled from the Congregational theological college in St John's Wood in 1852 for refusing to accept 'the Supreme Authority of the Sacred Scriptures', that is, divine inspiration of the words in their literal sense.[14] His first book was the *Autobiography of Mark Rutherford, Dissenting Minister*, published in 1881. Four years later he brought out *Mark Rutherford's Deliverance* and, later, volumes of essays, biographies and novels, the most famous of which was *The Revolution in Tanner's Lane* (1887). White, who had been brought up in Bunyan Meeting House, Bedford, was at his best when writing about Nonconformity. (When living in London he attended Spurgeon's Tabernacle; an unlikely but fellow attender was Ruskin.) White described provincial chapel life in towns like Bedford and the conflicts inherent in them between a young, liberal-minded minister and a conservative congregation. This world was a microcosm of that world of ideas in which an intense, intellectual struggle between a declining High Calvinism and an emerging liberal Protestantism was being fought. The battle was waged round the 'higher criticism' of scripture. On the one side was the older generation with a 'world-view' that was complete and satisfying; on the other, a younger, liberal generation which thought in terms of processes, not static assuredness, and knew more of Herbert Spencer than John Calvin.

White develops those favourite Victorian themes: the decline of faith, the rise of doubt and the construction of a new, more 'rational' faith. His world is that of the lone intellectual seeking truth regardless; his expertise in this task is seen when his work is contrasted with that by less skilful hands such as Mrs Humphry Ward in her *Robert Elsmere*. White followed the example of his friend, George Eliot, when writing about the chapel-yard, cut off from the main highways of life. His concern was with those people whose lives were, in Thomas Gray's words, 'born to blush unseen'. H. W. Massingham, brought up in one of the minor Methodist sects, referred to the events in White's novels having a 'special quality of depth in simplicity'. Rutherford himself referred to the *Autobiography* as the 'tale of a commonplace life, perplexed by many problems I have never solved'. His appeal to intellectual readers in 'search of truth' has continued although he himself warned, in the preface to the second edition of the *Autobiography*, 'we think too much of ourselves' and cautioned against 'spiritual misery'. He came to feel that 'speculations on the why and the wherefore, optimism, pessimism, freedom, necessity, causality, and so forth, are not only for the most part loss of time, but frequently ruinous'. The difficulty with the 'loss of faith' is that it cannot continue forever. It is like long division and the further one carries it the less there is to 'carry over' so that eventually there is nothing that can be divided into, nothing against which the next generation can rebel, no faith left to be lost. They are left with atheism, indifference or, as in late twentieth century Britain, a moral code which can be traced to what are called 'Christian values'. Thomas Selby, in many ways a perceptive critic, sensed this in 1896. He devoted an entire chapter to White and referred to his 'doctrinal oscillation and unsettlement'. He concluded with a caution: 'It is not impossible that the discovery may one day be made that the novel-writer who would free us from the ethical restraints of the past has been selling indulgences for gain.'[15]

If William Hale White is essentially a Victorian writer dealing with questions of faith and doubt, Arnold Bennett, whose genius Nicoll also recognized, is essentially a twentieth-century writer. He accepted and lived by White's advice in the preface to the second edition of the *Autobiography*: 'One fourth of life is intelligible, the other three fourths is unintelligible darkness; and our earliest duty is to cultivate the habit of not looking round the corner.' Bennett was brought up in a strict Wesleyan Methodist home in the Potteries but soon rejected not only Methodism but Christianity. The hero in his first novel, *A Man from the North* (1898), gave up attending Sunday School at the age of fourteen as 'awful rot' but continued to attend chapel, albeit against his will. In one of his most famous novels, *Anna of the Five Towns* (1902), which Bennett himself described in his *Journal* as 'a study of paternal authority', Nonconformist chapel life is the background against which the plot is set. The point of the novel is that 'romance is even here – the romance which, for those who have an eye to perceive it, ever dwells amid the seats of industrial manufacture, softening the coarseness, transfiguring the squalor, of these mighty alchemic operations'.[16] Nonconformity, therefore, was part of the 'squalor' of life in industrial England just as the Church of England was part of an idealized Barsetshire.

In Bennett's novels written before the Great War, Nonconformity is either laughed at, as in *A Great Man* or *The Price of Love*, or is deemed irrelevant, as in his most famous novel *The Old Wives' Tale* (1908). Here the family's Wesleyan Methodism is part of their provincial character, their unashamed acceptance and satisfaction in being provincial. To worship at Duck Bank Wesleyan Chapel in mid-century somehow fitted this provincial self-satisfaction more neatly than if his characters had worshipped in the parish church: it was essentially the world Matthew Arnold was castigating. Bennett's portrayal of a chapel service is savage in its sarcasm although he does describe the Circuit Superintendent as possessing a 'genuine mediaeval passion for souls'. Four years later, in *The Price of Love* (1912), Nonconformity is again synonymous with narrow provincialism. Great fun is had with Wesleyanism by someone who has obviously rejected it:

> No person nourished from infancy in chapel can bring himself to believe that the chief motive of churchgoers is not the snobbish motive of social propriety. And dissenters are so convinced that, if chapel means salvation in the next world, church means salvation in this, that to this day, regardless of the feelings of their pastors, they will go to church once in their lives – to get married.

Occasionally Bennett's tone is bitter, that of a man settling a score. In *Riceyman Steps* (1923) the miser is a Methodist and his brother, who inherits his fortune, is a missionary to the West Indies and a particularly loathsome creature. Between White and Bennett was a gulf fixed as wide as that between tragedy and comedy. Bennett himself explained this in his novel, *Imperial Palace* (1930):

> Comedy had replaced tragedy; and in spite of themselves, in spite of their relief, they both instinctively regretted the change. There was something magnificent in dire tragedy, in the terror of it, in the necessity which it laid upon everybody to behave nobly and efficiently. But comedy demanded naught from their higher selves. All they had to do now was to fade ingloriously away.

The 'Brothers Hocking' were Nonconformist writers because they wrote about Nonconformity for Nonconformists, a type of 'ghetto literature'. Mark Rutherford was a Nonconformist writer because he saw in Nonconformity those characters and stories of every-day life which had attracted other writers like George Eliot and because it was the world he knew best. His genius lay in seeing that in those small chapel communities the great issues of his time were being as much fought over and resolved as in the most intellectual and cosmopolitan setting. Arnold Bennett was a Nonconformist writer partly by his birth, partly because his early novels of Pottery life used Nonconformity as their background and partly because it was Nonconformity against which he reacted. In this last sense he may be considered as a provincial Nonconformist just as Hardy may be considered as a rural Anglican.

Rutherford and Bennett showed the degree to which Nonconformity had become part of the warp and woof of national life if it could thus be rebelled against and rejected.

One final Nonconformist contribution to popular English culture came ten years after Nicoll's death. Although strictly speaking it falls outside the range of this book, it should still be noticed. Just as Nicoll had urged John Watson to write down his Scottish stories, so in 1933 the *British Weekly* asked the writer, James Hilton, to contribute a Christmas story. In four days Hilton wrote 18,000 words and 'Goodbye Mr Chips!' was published on 7 December 1933. The following year, in which he also wrote 'Gerald and the Candidate' for the same paper, Hilton expanded the story of his father, headmaster of Chapel End Board School in Walthamstow, into the popular classic, *Good-Bye, Mr Chips* and gave the English-speaking world a new character to put beside Mr Pickwick, Archdeacon Grantly and Becky Sharp. The novel was put on the West End stage in 1938 and was later made into both a film and a musical.

What concerns us here is that even though Hilton was writing for a Nonconformist paper, he felt his hero could not be the organist in the local Congregational chapel nor could the story be set in a state school for working-class children. Chapel End became 'Brookfield', 'an old foundation, established in the reign of Elizabeth as a grammar school' which might 'with better luck, have become as famous as Harrow'. Hilton's own experience of public school was at The Leys School in Cambridge, founded by the Wesleyans in 1875. Its relative newness, however, did not exclude damp walls and bad sanitation: 'we were apt to find a drowned rat in the bath-tub if we left the water to stand overnight', he later recalled. If his father, a pacifist and adherent of the old, radical dissenting tradition, 'did not train aristocrats to govern the Empire or plutocrats to run their fathers' businesses' he did use 'his wise and sweetening influence just as valuably among the thousands of elementary schoolboys . . . in a London suburb'.[18] Hilton later settled in Hollywood after writing the film script for his book and gained considerable fame there.

When he wrote the film script for *Mrs Miniver* (for which he won an 'Oscar') he was said to be the highest paid script writer in Hollywood. He also wrote more novels and in his book, *Lost Horizon*, gave the English language a new word, 'Shangri-La', which might be defined as sweetness and light on a foreign shore.

This survey has been, of necessity, a cursory one but its aim has been to show that the Nonconformist contribution to English literature in the period under discussion was of sufficient quality to expunge Arnold's mid-century censures, even if James Hilton had to resort to an 'establishment' disguise for the story of a Congregational schoolmaster and a Methodist public school.

One of Matthew Arnold's most telling criticisms of Nonconformity was its tendency to 'Hebraise', that is, to 'sacrifice all other sides of our being to the religious side'. Moralizing is an inclination in the English race which seems to have become most marked in Nonconformity, at least to its critics. Insofar as this was the case it was due to Nonconformity's historic exclusion from the world of university learning. This was the more telling in a century in which the boundaries of knowledge were being pushed back and the spread of education was proceeding at a pace unknown in man's history. Were Nonconformity to retain its self-respect, let alone to increase its influence, it could not stand aside. If it did it would become either an obscurantist sect or one of those peculiar American denominations which dressed, lived and thought as if history had stopped at a certain date. Nonconformist leaders felt it an obligation to the gospel to be part of the wider world of English and imperial life. They could not preach the most sacred things from a platform of ignorance. Gibes, like that in *Truth*, regarding Spurgeon – 'It is incredible that he should ever have converted a man of anything like complete education' – hurt. This was all the more so when this weekly magazine devoted to 'exposé' added, 'tact and taste are sadly wanting in the regions of Ebenezer and Bethel'. (The magazine did not, however, 'expose' the fact that its editor, Henry Labouchere, hired his mistress off her husband for £1500 a year.)[19]

Yet, to leave the old certainties and to venture forth on Arnold's 'main current' of national life called for fundamental changes and many were frightened. Normally the debate, which continued throughout the century, centred, as Arnold had seen, on admission to the two ancient universities, especially Oxford with its High Church tradition. From 1854 Nonconformists were allowed to matriculate at Oxford and Cambridge to read for the BA degree, although it was not until 1871 that Oxford allowed them to proceed to the MA. Here we are concerned with the effect of these new opportunities on the rank and file of Nonconformists. The effect on the ministry will be discussed in Chapter 4. Almost fifty years after Oxbridge opened their doors there were still those in Nonconformity who worried about the allurements of the Establishment. In 1902 the President of the United Methodist Free Churches said he 'was not sure that the opening of the Universities . . . was so beneficial . . . as one would expect. An incessant stream of the sons of our wealthy laymen feeds the ranks of the Anglican Church, through having been educated at Oxford or Cambridge.'

Oxford, of course, with its High Church traditions was the more dangerous. In 1891 Col. J. T. Griffin, President of the Baptist Union, proposed the creation of a 'Baptist University' on the precedent of those in America. At such a university they could 'gather the sons of our wealthier and of our most cultured families'. As it was, he argued, there was only Oxford and Cambridge, and 'you know what follows'. 'In the coming conflict between the Free Church principles and those of Churches State-controlled', the Colonel warned in suitably military terms, 'the young warriors reared under the shadows of a "Trinity" or a "Balliol", amid the luxuries of a political establishment, will be emasculated ere they fight.' Nonconformity's dilemma is seen in Robertson Nicoll's recollection eleven years later that 'some of the ministers smiled' at the proposal. This fear of pollution, let alone of emasculation, from an Anglican establishment was one of the few characteristics Nonconformity shared with English Roman Catholicism. One recalls Cardinal Manning's veto of Newman's scheme for a Roman Catholic college in Oxford and the Irish hierarchy's terror at the thought of the faithful's attending Trinity College, Dublin. Yet the Colonel's was not a groundless fear: in the 1870s the Balliol philosophy don, T. H. Green, the model for the liberal tutor, Mr Grey, in Mrs Ward's *Robert Elsmere*, told R. W. Dale that opening the ancient universities had been

> an injury rather than a help to Nonconformity. You are sending up here, year after year, the sons of some of your best and wealthiest families; they are often altogether uninfluenced by the services of the [Nonconformist] Church which they find here, and they not only drift away from Nonconformity – they drift away and lose all faith.[20]

Whatever the influence on Nonconformity by the ancient universities, few doubted the influence by Nonconformity on Oxbridge. At Cambridge, for example, of the thirty-nine Senior Wranglers between 1860 and 1899, no less than twenty-one were Nonconformists and of the five Senior Wranglers between 1900 and 1904, four were Nonconformist. At Oxford the greatest and most visible achievement was the erection of Mansfield College in 1889. Mansfield was not then part of the University but a college to train Congregational ministers and therefore will be looked at in the next chapter. Yet, because it only accepted men who had already been matriculated, it did a great deal to attract Nonconformist ministerial students to Oxford. It soon created, and was meant to create, a 'Nonconformist presence' and three years after its establishment it was said that the principal and staff 'have already made themselves and their theology a felt power in the University'. To the first Principal, A. M. Fairbairn, building a Nonconformist centre was a duty placed on his generation because of the 'changed conditions and prospects of education'. Much of the college's success was due to Fairbairn, described by a Master of University College as 'the most accomplished and profound exponent of systematic theology in the University since Mozley'. Fairbairn, another of the Scottish emigrants who played such important roles in Nonconformity, had been a minister of the Scottish Evangelical Union and was regarded as a luminary by many of the late Victorian liberal intelligentsia. He was a New Testament scholar who had studied in Germany and if he was 'pompous and verbose', he was also popular.[21] He sat on the Bryce Commission on Secondary Education from 1893 to 1895 and received doctorates from Edinburgh, Yale, Manchester, Gottingen, Aberdeen, Leeds and Wales. In 1896 Oxford recognized his work and, in a roundabout way, Mansfield's existence, by making him an MA 'by incorporation'.

A second factor was Fairbairn's desire that Mansfield should mark a 'new departure' within Congregationalism: he meant for it to function as a centre of learning, not just as a theological college. In 1892, for example, Mansfield held its first Summer School of Theology when 347 participants, of whom nine came from the United States, met for eleven days. Lecturers included Canon Driver, Oxford's Professor of Hebrew, William Sanday, Professor of Exegesis, and various leading Nonconformist scholars.[22] Seven years later Fairbairn worked with Professor Sanday to convene a conference of Anglicans and Nonconformists to discuss 'Different Conceptions of Priesthood and Sacrifice', an ecumenical venture ahead of its time.

A third and not inconsiderable factor was the physical appearance of the new college. Its sponsors spent a total of £50,000 – about £1,650,000 in 1990 – and chose Basil Champneys as architect. The style adopted was fourteenth-century and stone, not brick, was used. There was a tower adorned with a statue of John Milton and a chapel containing work of a high order including a carved oak screen and stalls. The windows were filled with stained glass commemorating an eclectic group of sixty-eight scholars and saints: St Luke, Zwingli, David Livingstone, William Penn, the German Reformed philosopher, Friedrich Schleiermacher (who died in 1834), and Eusebius the fourth-century Bishop of Emesa (Homs) in Syria. For good measure, Amos and Plato were included in the south-east corner. Finally there were the coats of arms of some thirty-three universities in Britain, America and Europe as well as of some Oxford colleges. Wealthy Congregationalists made specific donations: the sons of James Clarke, founder of *The Christian World*, gave the oak canopy over the pulpit which had pride of place against the east wall, while Sir W. H. Wills, Bart., gave the organ. The message was obvious: Nonconformity was asserting its rightful place in the republic of letters. Three years after Mansfield was founded the Unitarians moved their own college from Manchester to Oxford and erected new buildings just down the road that had been created for, and named after, Mansfield.[23]

The Nonconformist invasion of Oxbridge could at best only directly affect a small number of people because of the cost. In 1892 it was estimated that an Oxford education cost about £160 p.a. and this is most decidedly a conservative estimate. Oxford was 'emphatically a place for the well-to-do, or those . . . with scholarships and exhibitions'.[24] Now a Nonconformity centred mainly in the skilled working class and the lower-middle class, whose annual income in many cases would not have surpassed or even reached £160, could hardly afford to send a son to Oxford or Cambridge. The wealthy classes and the millionaire industrialists could afford to do so but the rank and file of Nonconformists had to look to college scholarships and in this they were no different from other families. This naturally raises the question about the quality and availability of good secondary education, either at the new 'high schools' started by local authorities or the old endowed schools of England, whose reform was taken in hand after the Taunton Commission reported in 1867.

Secondary education had been expanding, albeit in a piecemeal fashion, and the fruit of the expansion was becoming evident by the 1880s. This was the underlying change affecting the two ancient universities. In 1884 Fairbairn and James Bryce noted the rising numbers at both Oxford and Cambridge and with them the rising number of Nonconformists. 'It is impossible', they wrote, 'to survey and describe the whole field of new obligations into which the changed conditions and prospects of education have introduced Nonconformity' because 'they cover the field and meet us at every point.' Two years later Fairbairn produced statistics to illustrate the trend affecting Oxbridge: between 1866 and 1884 the numbers at Oxford had increased by 34 per cent, from 7,325 to 11,050; at Cambridge the increase was slightly smaller, 31 per cent, with the numbers rising from 7,992 to 11,469. The bulk of this increase was coming from the reconstituted grammar schools. For example, before 1873 Bradford Grammar had sent no one either to Oxford or to Cambridge but between 1873 and 1886 it sent sixty-three boys. Manchester Grammar School sent 149 boys to read for honours degrees at Oxford and Cambridge between 1874 and 1886. Nonconformists, who increasingly after 1870 had become the great defenders of the Board schools, designed for the working classes, could be proud of the fact that in 'quite a number of cases' the boys had first gone to a Board school before getting a place at the local grammar school.[25]

Within this general increase in numbers going up to the two ancient universities, the Nonconformist percentage was going up as well. This was due to three causes.

The first was the increase in the numbers of boys at Nonconformist public schools. Bishop's Stortford College, for example, was known as the 'Nonconformist Rugby'. It began life as a 'Nonconformist Grammar School' in 1868 with the support of Crossley and Morley. It had forty boys in the first year but by 1877 it had 131. Fees were thirty-five to forty-five guineas a year for boarders and eight to twelve guineas for day boys.[26] Other schools included The Leys at Cambridge (where James Hilton was sent by his Congregational father), Kingswood, Mill Hill, Caterham, Taunton, Silcoats and Tettenhall. Except for The Leys and Kingswood, which were Wesleyan, all of these were Congregational in some sense.

Secondly, the schools were preparing a higher proportion to sit for university entrance examinations. The Nonconformist public schools had been established not to prepare boys for Oxford or Cambridge but to educate the sons of ministers and of the 'commercial classes' for business life. With the creation of University College in London and then the opening of Oxford and Cambridge, the schools had to adjust to a new world. Traditionally they had not shared the public school obsession with the Classics. Boys were able to study science, modern languages and even the literature and language of their own country. The Classics were taught, of course, but at some schools, pupils could substitute German for Greek. Not surprisingly, Mill Hill School in north London, founded in 1807, sent no boys to either university before 1874. Indeed in the 1860s it had to close for a brief period because of financial problems. However, between 1874 and 1886 it sent forty boys to Oxford and Cambridge. In the same period Tettenhall College, in Staffordshire, sent twelve boys to Cambridge.[27]

Thirdly, and most important of all, was the increase of Nonconformists in grammar schools. Of the 149 boys from Manchester Grammar, for example, who went up to either University to read for an honours degree between 1874 and 1886, thirty-five were Nonconformists. In 1885 and 1886 Nonconformist boys out-numbered Churchmen although this could be explained by more accurate figures. If so, this would also imply that the Nonconformist percentage had been larger throughout the period surveyed. Of the sixty-three boys from Bradford Grammar sent up in this period, the religion of forty-five was known and of these, twenty were Nonconformist.[28]

It is difficult to say how many Nonconformists there were at any one time at either Oxford or Cambridge. Horton's biographers stated that in 1882 there were at least two hundred in residence and that the numbers were increasing rapidly. In 1884 Fairbairn and Bryce suggested 'more than one hundred' at Oxford and 'a still larger number' at 'the other place'. Two years later, when the Oxford University Nonconformists' Union was dissolved, its membership numbered 102: when it began in 1881 it had thirty members. In 1899 a Wesleyan writer said that Sunday congregations at Mansfield numbered a hundred members of the University. While this number would have included some senior members it would not have included Baptists, Methodists, Unitarians and those who were back-sliding. It therefore seems reasonable to suggest that by the end of the century each of the two ancient Universities had at least 100 and perhaps double that number. J. Carvell Williams, Congregational Union Chairman in 1900, said about those Nonconformists who had gone up to Oxford and Cambridge that they had not 'flocked but have gone in considerable numbers'. The fact that their numbers were not greater was due more to economics than to religion.

While the numbers of Nonconformists were small at the end of the century their influence was still being felt. In 1902 R. F. Horton published *The Dissolution of Dissent* and claimed that Nonconformity was giving new life to a moribund Oxford: he could cite some examples to support his view. In 1893 a Nonconformist, Edward Caird, succeeded Benjamin Jowett as Master of Balliol only two years after Col. Griffin had warned of the 'young warriors' from that college. Admittedly, like Nicoll and Fairbairn, Caird was another of those Scottish immigrants who had themselves given new life, in this case, to Nonconformity. Horton himself was an Oxford man (New College) who rowed for his college, was President of the Union and founder of the Oxford Nonconformists' Union; he was also regarded as Jowett's protégé.[29] In 1879 he was elected to a fellowship at New College, only to resign it in 1883 to become minister of a new Congregational church in affluent Hampstead. (It is interesting to watch the beginning of a Nonconformist network slowly being built up within the Establishment: one of Horton's pupils was Tom Ellis who was later a Liberal MP and Chief Whip from 1894 to 1899, while one of his Hampstead congregation was Herbert Asquith. For his part Ellis was a Welsh Calvinistic Methodist.) From 1870 to 1893 the Regius Professor of Civil Law was James Bryce, who had been at Trinity and was another Scottish dissenter. Like Horton, he had been President of the Oxford Union and was, in addition, a barrister, historian, MP, cabinet minister, Ambassador to the United States and a notable mountaineer. He was believed to have been the only man since Noah to stand on the top of Mount Ararat. A. S. Peake, the distinguished Old Testament scholar and a Primitive Methodist, was an undergraduate at St John's. He won a fellowship at Merton in 1890 which he resigned two years later to teach at the Primitive Methodist theological college in Manchester. When Frederick York Powell was appointed Regius Professor of Modern History at Oxford it was only after S. R. Gardiner, the seventeenth-century historian and a lapsed 'Irvingite' or member of the exotic Catholic Apostolic Church, had refused the nomination.

At Cambridge, with its more liberal traditions, it was felt that young Nonconformists had less to fear and therefore less attention was paid to it; also, there was no Mansfield on which Nonconformist interest could concentrate. The first Nonconformist college to move to Cambridge was the Presbyterians' Westminster College which opened in October 1899, largely due to the influence of John Watson. Six years later the Congregationalists moved their theological college from Cheshunt: the foundation stone was laid by Lord Haldane, yet another Scottish dissenter, in 1913, although the opening was delayed because of the war. Like Mansfield it was confined to members of the University but, unlike Mansfield, it was residential. Despite the absence of a centre representing any of the four major denominations before 1905, Non-conformists were said to be 'both numerous and active' in Cambridge. It is, however, even more difficult to discover accurate numbers. There was a Nonconformist Union from 1883 but it folded during the First World War. Like Oxford, Cambridge had its sprinkling of Nonconformist dons: the Quaker, J. Rendel Harris; the Presbyterian, Alexander MacAlister, Professor of Anatomy; the Congregationalist, A. W. W. Dale (son of R. W. Dale) and, in the early twentieth century, the Congregationalist, B. L. Manning and, finally, the Baptist, T. R. Glover. The last was a son of the Minister of Tyndale Baptist Church in Bristol and, later, University Orator.[30]

Official Nonconformist reaction to this small but significant educational revolution was mixed. More conservative people were frightened that the current in the mainstream of national life would prove too strong for Nonconformists. As we have seen, worries over 'leakage to the Establishment' were real throughout all denominations: three years at Oxford or Cambridge could easily lead a man to think that dinner at eight was preferable to tea at five. With the discarded teapot could go an entire set of inherited social attitudes which underpinned traditional Nonconformity. From dinner at home to suburban dinner parties and evening dress was a short step and, as inevitably as cigars follow brandy, a step toward the Church of England. Official utterances were normally concerned with the changes University education was having on the ministry, not on the laity. This is not surprising when we remember that all the major denom-inational conferences and executive bodies were dominated by ministers. Even the Congregational Union, which was the least 'ecclesiastical' of the four bodies, had only three lay chairmen between 1831 and 1900. (All three were

Liberal MPs.) Wesleyan Methodists were the most conservative when it came to accepting the changes that were under way. Not surprisingly they were wary of too much diversity within an ecclesiastical order that was remarkably uniform. They did set up a committee to investigate 'Methodism in Cambridge' to see if they might not erect a centre 'worthy of Methodism and suitably near the Colleges', something along the lines of Mansfield. Their main concern was with ministerial training and they did toy with a proposal to unite all four of their theological colleges into one at Oxford, but it came to nothing.[31]

We have concentrated on Oxford and Cambridge because they held a symbolic importance beyond the numbers of Nonconformists who went up after 1854. The very fact that Nonconformists were at Oxbridge, whatever their number, showed the distance that had been covered since *Culture and Anarchy* had appeared. Despite the symbolic importance of the two ancient universities, the real advances made by Nonconformists came through the colleges of the University of London and through the new civic universities in Birmingham, Liverpool, Sheffield, Bristol and Manchester. From the start, Nonconformists were involved in these new ventures: when Manchester's Owens College was opened in 1851 it had fifty-eight students and of these fourteen were from the town's Congregational theological college. As we saw, families like the Wills in Bristol, the Firths in Sheffield, the Rathbones and Levers in Liverpool and the Cadburys in Birmingham played vital roles in establishing the new universities. In Birmingham, it was George Cadbury who gave the money for the first lectureship in town planning and the first lecturer was Raymond Unwin, from the famous Quaker family. He went on to design the 'garden city' at Hampstead although, like many architects, he preferred to live in a mediaeval farmhouse rather than in one of the new dwellings he designed. (This house, Wyldes, was preserved in the centre of the new development and still stands.) Finally, of course, there was the expanding work of London University. Here one had the advantage of doing an 'external degree' or attending one of the teaching colleges. Nonconformists had not been slow in taking advantage of London's first and 'unsectarian' college, University College.[32]

In Manchester Nonconformity was able to make a lasting contribution to English academic life through the generosity of Mrs Enriqueta Rylands, the young widow of John Rylands, the largest textile manufacturer in the United Kingdom who died in 1888. He was a shy, retiring man, a Congregationalist and very charitable. He established orphanages, homes for 'aged gentlewomen', a house of rest for poor ministers and a town hall, public baths, library and coffee house for Stretford where he lived. He developed a love of Rome – the city, not the Church – and gave money to the city's poor. He had translations of the Bible made into Italian to help a somewhat quixotic crusade to convert Italians into Protestants. In 1880 he was decorated with the Order of the Crown of Italy by the King, more for his charity than for his religious work. He was a collector of hymns and Bibles and it seemed fitting for his wife to commemorate him in Manchester by founding a library and research centre.

Mrs Rylands' chance came in June 1892 when *The Times* carried an article announcing that the fifth Earl Spencer was contemplating selling the famous Althorp Library. The most valuable part numbered 4,000 books and included many fifteenth and sixteenth-century volumes. There was a Gutenberg Bible, two copies of the Mainz Psalter, fifty-seven Caxtons and 600 works published by the Venetian, Aldus Manutius, friend of Erasmus and a prime figure in the 'new learning' of the fourteenth and fifteenth centuries. All together there were 40,000 books. In secret negotiations Mrs Rylands paid the fabulous sum of 200,000 guineas. In addition, the widow spent, it was said, a further £250,000 for the new building. The architect chosen was Basil Champneys, who had designed Mansfield College. The new Library, which now had 70,000 volumes, was opened on 5 October 1899 and on the following day Lord Spencer, as Chancellor of Victoria University (which then included what would become the University of Manchester), awarded Mrs Rylands an honorary degree. Although he was 'depressed' at losing his famous library, he desperately needed the money and was genuinely glad that 'the whole will . . . be available for the public in a better way than if at Althorp'. It was a magnificent gesture and said as much for the civic pride of England's great provincial cities as for the Nonconformist love of learning. The Library is now part of the University of Manchester.[33]

Of course the greatest amount of educational work among adults was not done in the two ancient universities, in London or even in the expanding number of new, civic universities but through self-help. With increasing literacy and decreasing costs of publishing, working men could acquire knowledge if they could only read. By 1851 the Registrar General reported that seven out of every ten working men were literate. While Nonconformity did not start the movement to educate working men, it did benefit from it. Its most famous begetters were Charles Knight and Lord Brougham. Knight, the journalist and publisher, was born in 1791, and published the tracts of Lord Brougham's Society for the Diffusion of Useful Knowledge, founded in 1827. The most popular publication was its *Penny Magazine* which ran from 1832 to 1845. At its peak in 1836 and 1837 it was selling over 200,000 copies a week. In addition there were the Mechanics' Institutes which numbered 700 by mid-century. As Knight's publications grew dated by the 1850s new ventures started: the most famous was the *Popular Educator* started in 1852 by John Cassell.

Cassell was born in 1817 in one of England's worst slums, Hunt's Bank in Manchester. Although his father was a publican young Cassell grew up a Congregationalist; he left school to work in the factory when his father died. He first made his mark as a travelling preacher for the new working-class movement, Teetotalism. After marrying a woman who brought some money with her, he turned his hand to tea and coffee merchandising in London and, after that, to radical journalism, always preaching non-violent progress and self-help by working men. Alone among the publishers of self-help tracts Cassell was born among those people who were being encouraged to help themselves. His collection of teach-yourself courses, the *Popular Educator*, proved an enormous success and six weeks after it began, circulation had reached nearly 100,000. By 1887, when a new *Educator* was started, the first series had sold over one million copies. For a penny, purchasers got lessons, for example, in English grammar, maths, French and Egyptian history, music, physiology, Latin, geometry, book-keeping, German, Hebrew and shorthand. After six months new courses were started and all courses ran for twelve months. The first six months had an almost bewildering 202 lessons under sixteen separate topics. Many of the compilers employed by Cassell were Nonconformist. Soon self-help classes were started by subscribers, often using Chapel accommodation like the Call-lane Mutual Improvement and Phonetic Society which met in Call-lane Chapel under the presidency of the Rev. Jabez Tunnicliffe. Tunnicliffe, a Baptist minister, was also a keen supporter of the Band of Hope and, in time, of the YMCA.

Some subscribers went on to sit for London University's 'Matric.' examination and this raised a problem. After matriculating they could not then sit for the actual degree as the University's statutes demanded two years' residence in one of the constituent colleges – King's or University. Cassell launched a campaign to get the Senate of the University to open examinations to non-resident students. He got the support of William Ellis, a Unitarian writer who had worked for popular education, Samuel Morley, the wealthy hosier and MP, and the five Hill brothers of whom the most famous was Rowland. The petition asked for the change because 'the middling and lower classes of the people aspire to the attainment of such honours and degrees . . . from a sincere conviction that these are truly valuable and praiseworthy, and constitute an enviable distinction among men'. Within a few years the Senate gave way and instituted the country's first 'external degrees'.

The influence publications like the *Popular Educator* could have was extraordinary. In Caernarvonshire, the young Lloyd George used it to study French for his Law Society Preliminary Examination and in Dorset, Thomas Hardy used his pocket-money to buy issues as they came out. He was one of those who dreamed, but in vain, of being one of the lucky ones to sit the London Matric. In 1853 the *Educator* published a letter from a 'farmer's boy' who had subscribed to learn Latin. At first his fellow workers thought he was speaking Gaelic but undaunted he got two ploughmen to subscribe, then a foreman and then two more men, won over by the value of the maths and penmanship lessons. Then the Master's son started the shorthand course and his two daughters took up the drawing and music lessons. A passion for learning seized the farm and the carpenter and gardener started lessons in geometry and architecture and in the gardener's case, botany. Where there had been one there were eleven students when the farmer himself sent off for 'a LIBRARY BOOK', perhaps the bound copy of past issues. In another instance a railway policeman from Leamington started the English lessons and went on to arithmetic, shorthand and the Classics. As he did his night rounds he passed the time by memorizing the stems of Greek and Latin verbs.[34]

One subscriber who did not write to the editor was a fourteen year old boy in Roxburghshire, whose father was a dissenting tailor earning an average of twelve shillings a week. The boy, James Murray, became a schoolmaster and then a bank clerk in London where he attended Camberwell Congregational Church. Murray had a natural ability with languages, especially philology, and joined the Philological Society. There he met a Baptist minister, the Rev. Richard Francis Weymouth, a graduate of University College, London, who in 1868 had been awarded the first DLitt. granted by the University of London. By 1870 he was Headmaster of Mill Hill School and in that same year invited Murray to become a master there with the understanding that he would have time to study for the London External BA degree, something that had not been possible for the original subscribers to the *Popular Educator*. Because of his expertise in languages it fell to Murray, after many complicated manoeuvrings, to be appointed editor of a new and monumental dictionary of the English language while he was teaching at Mill Hill. He erected a wooden 'scriptorium' in which to do his exhausting work.

Once the University of Oxford undertook the project Murray left Mill Hill and moved to Oxford but a fund subscribed by Old Boys secured the original scriptorium for the school. Unfortunately it was burnt down in 1902 but has since been replaced by the Murray Scriptorium or

Reading Room, attached to the school library. In Oxford Murray became a deacon at George Street Congregational Church (later pulled down to erect one of Oxford's ugliest buildings, in this case a cinema), was awarded the MA and DLitt degrees and in 1908 was knighted by George V. He became friends with Mansfield's Dr Fairbairn and before their deaths the Murrays asked to be buried beside their friend. The *Oxford English Dictionary* not only stands as one of Victorian England's greatest achievements but as a monument to its first editor, James Murray, to the involvement of Nonconformity and, indirectly, to the work of John Cassell. Like the *Dictionary of National Biography* and the *Victoria County History* it is a product of Victorian culture. Unlike those, 'Murray's Dictionary' is a tribute to Nonconformity's contribution to English letters, a contribution which if not filled with sweetness and light is still a far way from Matthew Arnold's world of the philistines.[35]

4

THE NONCONFORMIST MINISTER

In his *Autobiography*, published in 1903, J. Guinness Rogers reflected on the position of Nonconformist ministers in his youth in the 1830s:

> The general world outside knew little or nothing of them. Now and then, members of the aristocracy, perhaps even royalties, became acquainted with some Dissenting leader, and this was greatly talked about. But a Dissenting preacher who had no such exceptional distinction as this . . . was little known either to the Press or to the public. He belonged, in truth, to a different nation.

'Happily' Rogers added, 'this is changed'. Indeed it had and the Nonconformist minister stood at the very centre of the Nonconformist world we are discussing. Likewise, there is no single aspect of English Nonconformist life where the changes wrought by the nineteenth century are more obvious than in the position of ministers. An official at the Board of Education compiled a Memorandum on them in 1902: ministers were 'no longer content to be preachers and pastors for their own congregations' he wrote. They were 'now missioners to those who stand outside the pale of Church and Chapel. They are in closer contact with social problems and have a greater hold on political questions.' Nonconformists may have preached the 'priesthood of all believers' but they did not practise it. Their natural opponents, who had often been lashed for undue subservience to clerical domination, joyfully pointed this out: 'It is one of the ironies on English political life' declared *The Tablet*, the leading Roman Catholic weekly, 'that people who, when they are thinking of lies, are never tired of denouncing the influence of the clergy in politics, at the same time are quite ready to give up their political consciences to the keeping of their ministers.'[1]

By 1901 there were just over 10,000 ministers at work in England and Wales into whose hands the faithful could, if they wanted, surrender their consciences. The ministers were supported by almost 52,000 local or lay preachers: of these totals the four leading denominations we have been surveying had a total of 6,409 ministers and 44,142 lay preachers in England. The importance of these men cannot be over-estimated in any examination of English Nonconformity. The success of any chapel or Methodist circuit largely depended on the minister. He was 'virtually the general of a powerful and willing army and if he is a wise man, his opportunities for good will be as large as the sphere he occupies'. The deacons of R. F. Horton's church in Hampstead declared in 1902 that 'the Church . . . is, humanly speaking, the creation of Mr Horton'. In 1885 there had been 402 members; in 1903 there were 1,248.[2] By the end of the century some might still moan that 'it would shock many to suggest that a plain dissenting preacher might be as great a man as an Archbishop' but this was simply twaddle.[3] Nonconformist ministers, like Charles Haddon Spurgeon, Joseph Parker, Henry Allon, R. F. Horton, R. J. Campbell, John Clifford, F. B. Meyer, R. W. Dale, Alexander Maclaren, Hugh Price Hughes, C. S. Horne or Newman Hall ranked with John Keble, Cardinal Newman, Charles Kingsley, Bishop Wilberforce, E. B. Pusey or Archbishop Tait as household names to be adored or vilified, depending on one's religious loyalties.

Charles Haddon Spurgeon had been a major force in English religious life for almost forty years when he died in 1892. His published sermons on their own had a weekly circulation of 25,000 and his *John Ploughman's Talks* sold over 400,000 copies: they are still on sale today. No archbishop equalled that. His critics agreed in their analysis: to the Earl of Rosebery who heard Spurgeon in 1873 he was the 'apostle of the grocers', echoing George Eliot's view that he had 'the most superficial grocer's back-parlour view of Calvinistic Christianity'. In 1884 Baptists celebrated Spurgeon's fiftieth birthday. A writer for *Temple Bar* visited the Tabernacle and reported that the congregation dictated the style. The Tabernacle, he wrote, did not hold 'a high-class congregation', and, in a passage quoted earlier, he added that, 'the preacher knows that its understanding can best be opened by metaphors and parables taken from the customs of the retail trade, with similes taken from the colloquialisms of the streets'. To those who did not criticize, Spurgeon was virtually a demi-god: when it got out that 'the pastor', a vegetarian and total abstainer, also smoked a cigar a day – 'to the glory of God', he quipped to a visiting American – the news 'caused a terrible scandal in the dissenting world'. Of course cliques centred on ministers are not confined to Nonconformists and Spurgeon's plain speaking was in the tradition of Bunyan and before him of generations of mediaeval preachers. A similar criticism could have been made against many of Jesus's parables and sermons and some of his listeners were certainly not of the highest social class. Even those involved in Victorian retail trade needed to be saved, perhaps as much as intellectuals and aristocrats. Some critics, however, still gave praise where praise was due. Rosebery left the Tabernacle, reflecting as was his wont, and

> thinking of this vast power wielded by one man. He has raised a sort of spiritual city in the midst of London . . . Here is a great multitude, powerful, wealthy, devoted, with a perfect organization . . . with a leader of genius . . . Would it not be well for 'society' to ponder this?

Even the anonymous writer in *Temple Bar* admitted that Spurgeon had 'truly inspired eloquence' and his voice had 'the power of troubling men to the depths of their hearts'.[4]

Some, however, refused to be impressed: in 1858, when his fame was just beginning, a lady known to history only as Miss Marsh, and someone who occupied herself in converting Irish navvies, was told that the man in the railway carriage she was about to enter was Mr Spurgeon. As the diarist, Henry Greville, recorded, Spurgeon spoke to her,

> on passing a distant village, and pointing to it, he said, 'Perhaps, Madam, you are not aware that that small spot is remarkable as being the birthplace of the celebrated Mr Spurgeon.' 'Indeed!' she replied. 'Pray, sir, may I ask you, do you think that if St. Paul happened to be travelling with us and had passed the place where he was born, that he would have pointed out the fact to us?'

Apart from Miss Marsh, observers of Victorian religion acknowledged that Spurgeon was, as Bishop Boyd Carpenter of Ripon wrote, 'a recognised power in the religious life of England'. To Newman Hall he was 'the greatest Preacher of the Church of Christ'. *The Times* in an extremely complimentary lead article about Spurgeon in 1884 concluded:

> The boy who began to convert souls while our future rectors and curates were deep in criticism, history and examination subjects, and who has never had time to go to school or university since, is not impeccable in taste. He occasionally drops a phrase to provoke a smile from the soft cheeks of ladies and gentlemen, and to make them think that they could say the thing better . . . We are not sure that Latimer's and Ridley's sermons would not jar on modern refinement quite as much . . .

After his death in the south of France, which he had been visiting almost annually since the 1870s, his body was brought back and some 60,000 people filed past the coffin.[5]

More or less equal to Spurgeon in fame, and surpassing him in notoriety (for Spurgeon avoided party politics and was in many ways *sui generis*) was the Congregationalist, Joseph Parker. Like Spurgeon he had worked his way up from humble beginnings – his father had been a Northumberland stone-mason – and like Spurgeon he had had a chapel built round him. The 1886 *British Weekly* survey showed an attendance of 3,625 at his Sunday services although when his successor, R. J. Campbell, came, attendances soared to 10,589. Parker was famous for his Thursday lunchtime services designed for men, especially those working in the City, and among his guest speakers in 1877 was Gladstone. In addition to his rather rough looks and leonine hair-style Parker was famous for his unconventionality, dramatic preaching and rounded oratory: he once claimed the Church of England was based on 'a blasphemous inversion of sequence and a mischievous usurpation of prerogative'. No one was quite sure what it meant but it sounded impressive. He also described the Anglican clergyman as 'the self-conceited, pedantic, presumptuous priest . . . [who] stands between the flower and the sun . . . the soul and God.' In 1899 he was a guest at the Wesleyan Methodist Conference and caused the normally sombre gathering to explode in laughter: the speaker before him had referred to himself as 'a humble Presbyterian'. When Parker got up he told his audience that as he had heard this he had thought to himself, 'I will turn aside and see this great sight'.[6]

In that same year he spoke at the National Free Church Council's tercentenary celebration of Cromwell's birth, held in his own City Temple. The reporter from *The Times* was obviously unaware of Nonconformity's great appeal to 'the stronger sex' and noted that the audience 'consisted almost entirely of men, who interrupted the sermon again and again by enthusiastic cheering'. In the course of his address Parker attacked: the Prince of Wales and Lord Rosebery for frequenting the turf, wealthy Nonconformists who left Dissent for the Church of England, and 'shifty and superficial' political programmes (a warning against Liberal 'wire-pullers' who were tempted to down-grade issues which Nonconformists wished emphasized). He then turned his guns on Wilhelm II:

> When he heard of a Kaiser talking in an after-dinner speech about 'my friend the Sultan' he was astonished, and could have rent his garments. The Great Assassin had insulted civilization (loud cheers), and by all manner of hellish iniquities had outraged every Christian sentiment. He might be the Kaiser's friend, but he was not God's friend. In the name of God, and speaking of the Sultan, not merely as a man, but as the Great Assassin, I say 'God damn the Sultan!'

After this he wound up by attacking Anglo-Catholics and 'Nonconformist ritualism': why, he asked, should only ministers with their 'little May meeting bag' administer the Lord's Supper: why not any Christian man or woman? He finished with praise for the Free Church Council movement.[7] To his credit he, along with most Nonconformists, was among those who insisted that England as a Christian nation had an obligation to rescue fellow Christians from brutal death at the hands of fanatical Mohammedans.

The following year Parker was one of those asked by Horatio Bottomley, editor of *The Sun*, to become guest editor for a week. Parker agreed to do so 'on Christian principles' which included taking no pay and banning racing results: this was somewhat ironic, given Bottomley's links to the racing world. The paper's circulation increased by 150,000. Unlike Spurgeon, Parker was a keen and fairly radical Liberal although he did support the Boer War. In 1880 he had had a political fling and stood as a Liberal candidate for the City of London in favour of disestablishment, temperance legislation, social and political reform. The industrialist MP Samuel Morley and others persuaded him to stand down on the grounds that ministers should not directly enter the political arena and Morley paid all his expenses when he gave up the contest. The same anonymous writer who heard Spurgeon in 1884 went across the river to the City Temple but again was not complimentary: 'If you can forgive a bad delivery with occasional dropping of aspirates, and the incessant introduction of Gladstonian politics in connection with holy things, you will find in Dr Parker's sermons much that is impressive and certainly a great deal that is novel.'[9]

London did not enjoy a monopoly of famous ministers. In Birmingham, R. W. Dale was pastor of Carr's Lane Chapel from 1859 to 1891 and gained considerable fame for his theological writings, his involvement in political issues as a Liberal and his compilation in 1874 of *The English Hymn Book*. He withdrew from the Congregational Union for a while because of his opposition to Irish Home Rule but peace was restored before he died in 1895. He was succeeded at Carr's Lane by J. H. Jowett who transformed the chapel, by now surrounded by slums, into an 'institutional church' with its own 'Institute' which had a cafe, billiards room, lecture hall and cinema. When he accepted a call from Fifth Avenue Presbyterian Church in New York City in 1911 the Mayor and Corporation of Birmingham tried unsuccessfully to keep him in Birmingham. Before he left he was invited to dinner at Buckingham Palace by George V and Queen Mary. Another minister to leave for Fifth Avenue was the Rev. Charles Aked, minister of Liverpool's Pembroke Baptist Church, where he had succeeded Augustine Birrell's father. He became pastor of the Fifth Avenue Baptist Church.

In Manchester, when the Baptist minister of Union

Chapel, Alexander Maclaren celebrated his silver jubilee, his portrait was presented to Manchester Corporation. In Bristol, Augustine Birrell, MP for Bristol North, remembered that Henry Arnold Thomas, pastor of Highbury Congregational Chapel, which was home to the Wills family, was said to 'cut a greater figure on the Downs than the Bishop of the Diocese'. In London the President of the Wesleyan Conference in 1899–1900, the Rev. F. W. Macdonald, was 'presented at Court . . . [and] dined with the President and members of the Royal Academy, with the Lord Mayor of London, the Lord Mayor of Liverpool, and with two or three Cabinet Ministers.'⁹ In 1902 the President of the National Free Church Council was also presented at Court and given a seat at the Coronation. Even the fire-brand radical, John Clifford, was invited to a Garden Party at Windsor Castle in 1907 which both he and Edward VII survived intact.

Many ministers, the most famous of whom were J. Guinness Rogers and A. M. Fairbairn, wrote in the leading monthlies, at least the Liberal ones, and for many years the Congregational minister of Union Chapel, Islington, Henry Allon, edited the much respected *British Quarterly Review*. His papers show that contributors even included Thomas Trollope who lived in Rome, was Anthony's elder brother and who, like him, had been brought up thoroughly to dislike Dissenters. His contributions, however, were confined to Italian topics. Percy Bunting, a grandson of Jabez, the second founder of Wesleyan Methodism, edited the *Contemporary Review* from 1882 to 1911, although on admittedly slightly more liberal lines than his grandfather would have approved. The Unitarian, L. P. Jacks, was Principal of Manchester College, Oxford, from 1903–1931 and the first editor of *Hibbert's Journal*. He was also a friend of Lady Elcho through whom he was introduced to her special friend, A. J. Balfour, with whom he could discuss philosophy. Some ministers, like John Stoughton or Henry W. Clark, who for an inexplicable reason named his Harpenden home, 'Charisma', became respected historians. Stoughton was even a friend of Matthew Arnold, who proposed him for the Athenaeum. A. M. Fairbairn, in addition to his own works, wrote two entries for the *Cambridge Modern*

History and was a member of the first Council of the British Academy. Various ministers even attempted novels, but of these the less said the better. Others, like Clifford or J. B. Paton, were leaders in various reform movements: in Clifford's case for a national health service and the abolition of capital punishment; in Paton's, for rural colonization. In biblical scholarship Nonconformist ministers were recognized by the last third of the century for their achievements and three – the Wesleyan, W. F. Moulton, the Unitarian, Dr Vance Smith, and the Baptist, Dr Joseph Angus – worked on the Revised Authorised Version between 1870 and 1873. W. B. Glover maintains in his valuable study of Nonconformist reaction to 'higher criticism' that 'by 1900 the Nonconformists were producing biblical scholars with international reputations'. In the twentieth century they were succeeded by men like A. S. Peake (Primitive Methodist), C. H. Dodd (Congregationalist), H. Wheeler Robinson (Baptist) and P. T. Forsyth (Congregationalist) whose work was similar to Barth's and whose 'true spiritual stature was not seen or even glimpsed' until after the Second World War.[10]

Many children of leading ministers took advantage of the wider world their fathers' success had opened for them. R. W. Dale's son became a fellow of Trinity Hall, Cambridge, and one survey of leading Victorians noted, 'As the elder Dale did much to spiritualize the business men of the Midlands, the younger carries on his father's work in traditionally the most [sic] liberal of our two national seats of learning'. The younger Dale went on to become a member of the Athenaeum, a knight and Vice-Chancellor of Liverpool University. One of the Baptist J. H. Shakespeare's sons became private secretary to Lloyd George and an MP. In the Liberal landslide in 1906, there were three Nonconformist ministers returned and sixteen MPs who were sons of ministers, including Augustine Birrell, R. W. Perks, Sir Henry Fowler and Sir John Brunner, whose own son was also returned as an MP in the same election. The four daughters of the Wesleyan George Browne Macdonald, married respectively Edward Burne-Jones, Lockwood Kipling, father of Rudyard, Edward Poynter, later President of the Royal Academy and the industrialist MP Alfred Baldwin, father of the future Tory Prime Minister, Stanley. Robertson Nicoll's daughters married army officers while his son became a physician; J. H. Paton's son became High Master of Manchester Grammar School; Silvester Horne's eldest daughter went up to Oxford while one son became a barrister and the other, Kenneth, the star of BBC Radio's 'Round the Horne' series, programmes which did not always accord with the Nonconformist Conscience. The Rev. Basil Martin's son Kingsley was to become editor of *The New Statesman*. We noted in Chapter 3 that the son of Richard Glover, of Tyndale Baptist Chapel in Bristol, became a classics don at Cambridge and eventually University Orator. The conservative Wesleyan leader, J. H. Rigg, helped his son get a position at the Historical Manuscripts Commission by contacting the Prime Minister, Arthur Balfour.[11] By the end of the century Nonconformity's most famous ministers had established themselves as leaders in a wide variety of fields: biblical scholarship, local government, reform movements, journalism, history, theology, apologetics and writing. R. J. Campbell even had the honour of seeing himself in wax at Madame Tussauds.

It is, of course, very easy to pay too much attention to the famous names in Nonconformity, partially because of their importance, partially because information about them is more readily available and partially because they tended to be more involved in politics. Yet it was in the rank and file, those men known only in their own chapel and town, that Nonconformity made itself felt in English religious life. Luckily the annual *Year Books* contained small biographies of deceased ministers and these sometimes tell us much about the 'average' minister. For example, the Congregationalist Simeon Dyson was born in Hartshead, near Ashton-under-Lyne, in 1823. He went to work in the local cotton mill where his father was an 'overlooker'. His 'conversion' came early in life and he taught in the Sunday School of a local chapel. He began attending evening classes in the Mechanics' Institute and 'thereby developed the gifts of teaching and speaking, and habits of thought and reading, with so much success as to mark him out as one called of God'. He entered Lancashire

Independent College, Manchester, in 1844 to study for the ministry, and hard work made up for 'the lack of university training and degree, not then so accessible'. He spent his life in two Yorkshire pastorates, 'gaining the affection and respect of the people, and guiding the affairs of the Church with great discretion, preserving perfect harmony and living peace'. 'The pulpit' his obituary said, 'was his chosen sphere in preference to the press and the platform'. He was not 'speculative or sensational' and 'held the balance even between old and new'. He held various denominational offices, retired in 1891 and died in 1904. 'His memory will live' the obituary concluded 'and his influence will be continued, not by books written, nor by the booming paragraphs of journalists . . . nor by flattering epitaph . . . but in the honest lives . . . and manly independence of those who gratefully remember how he moulded their characters'.[12]

William Shaw was a Primitive Methodist circuit minister who was born in 1854 and died in 1931. He came from a Methodist home, made his 'supreme decision' at fourteen and became a Sunday School teacher, local preacher and eventually, in 1875, a minister. After his four year 'probation' he became a circuit superintendent and served the Connexion until he was 'superannuated' in 1919. 'It was his joyous privilege to lead many to Christ' his biography said, and 'his passion was to preach.' He was 'permitted to put in a long day's work for his Master, and it can be truly said that he gave his best'. Some ministers devoted part of their time to local affairs: S. J. Smith, for example, was born in Bedford in 1822 and became a Congregational minister in Enfield after attending a denominational college and taking the London BA. 'He was recognised by all classes as a Christian gentleman, courteous, affable, and sympathetic.' Although he 'sought to avoid public controversy' – a standard Victorian prefix to anyone who enthusiastically engaged in political warfare – he was elected as a Poor Law Guardian and a member of the Burial Board and the Public Library Committee. He was also co-secretary of the Enfield British School and chairman of the local Sunday School Union.[13]

Most ministers tended to face similar tasks: their primary work was to lead the church or, if a Methodist, to work in his assigned circuit and to supervise the 'stations' with their local preachers. His work included preparing sermons, managing a variety of organizations attached to the chapel, supervising the finances with the help of the deacons and trustees, if Baptist or Congregational, or the circuit stewards, if Methodist. Normally the financial goal was to reduce the existing debt, much of which would be due to building. Finally he would spend a great deal of time in preparing people for membership and in visiting members although here he could be helped by the deacons and stewards.

Occasionally he would have problems. Sometimes he would discover that he had not really had a 'call to the ministry'. The novelist, William Hale White, felt that some of the men he had known before being expelled from a Congregational theological college 'would have had more genuine lives if they had stood behind counters or learned some craft than they ever had in the ministry'. H. R. Williamson recalled the tension between the wealthier members of his Congregational chapel and his father, the minister, a tension produced by the power which came with money. Likewise, Kingsley Martin recalled in his autobiography how one coal-merchant 'noisily walked out of the church and slammed the door' in the middle of a sermon by his father, a Congregational minister, because the merchant felt that as an employer he had been attacked. The Rev. Richard Westrope left Belgrave Chapel in Leeds when there were complaints about the 'social gospel' topics he had chosen for his Sunday evening social addresses: of course these problems were not unique to Nonconformist ministers. In the small Essex village of Great Leighs the lord of the Manor and a Director of Barclay's Bank stormed out of Sunday Matins when the Psalm was chanted. Unlike the Rector of Great Leighs the Nonconformist minister had no security of tenure.[14] Ministers could also face congregations split over questions of finance, doctrine or politics – the last especially after 1886. At the small Wintoun Street Baptist Chapel in Leeds, for example, quarrels over finance and personalities raged for twenty-five years. Likewise it was not unusual for Congregationalists to worry about Unitarian trends in their ministers or for Baptists to bring the trust deed into debate, and sometimes into court, over the question of 'closed communion' (limiting the Lord's Supper to those attenders who had been baptized by immersion) *versus* 'open communion' (allowing non-baptized attenders to participate). Perhaps the most famous row over this took place at St Mary's Baptist Church in Norwich in the 1850s.[15]

There were constantly laments about ministerial income and the 'poverty, indifference [and] unappreciated labour' of many men. Similar complaints were heard in the Church of England about the condition of curates during the nineteenth century, a time when what pay they got came from the parish priest under whom they served or whose place they took in the parish while he lived elsewhere. In the Nonconformists' *laissez faire* way of life, ministers were frequently moving about, usually to a more advantageous and better paid position. Some ministers, like some clergymen and bishops in the Church of England, were extremely well paid: Parker appears to have received an annual salary of £1,700 (nearly £60,000 in 1990) while Spurgeon received £1,500. (He told a visiting American that £1,000 of this went to the orphanage and theological college he had founded while the rest went towards the stipends of his assistant ministers. He supported his family and himself by his writing and his dairy farm.) Both Parker and Spurgeon were able to maintain elegant homes and a carriage and pair which took them to their respective chapels. However, when the Parkers passed by, some were cruel enough to refer to the minister and his attractive wife as 'The Beauty and the Beast'. Famous ministers, like most of those who are well paid, tended to be defensive of their income: Newman Hall was very loath to talk about his £500 a year although he need not have been. John Clifford never accepted offers to increase his stipend above £600. For a comparison we should note that a headmaster of an average Board school in 1901 received £170. 10s. 9d.; the stenographer who took down Parker's sermons received £100 per annum; the average annual wage for manual workers in 1896 was £64 while the highest yearly wage for agricultural workers in 1902 was £53. 4s.[16]

Ministers' remuneration had improved with the century:

in 1851 a Primitive Methodist minister with three children received £71 a year and Baptists generally received less than £80; within Congregationalism the divergence was too great to allow for any average figure. In the 1860s Wesleyan ministers received £120 p.a. Stipends were generally better in town churches: when Joseph Parker began his ministry in Banbury in 1853 he received 50s. a week or £130 p.a. although when he left Banbury for the affluent Cavendish Street Chapel in Manchester in 1858 his income jumped to £1,700. By the 1870s matters had improved for some: a survey of Nonconformist ministers in the city of Oxford in 1875 showed stipends ranging from £60 p.a. plus house and allowances for a Primitive Methodist minister to about £300 p.a. for the Wesleyan Superintendent of the Oxford Circuit.[17] In the same decade Peter Thompson was sent to an impoverished Wesleyan circuit in Broughton-in-Furness with six members and no chapel: he lived on sixpence a day. In 1882 the Congregational Union studied the problem of low stipends and reported that of 1,527 ministers in charge of chapels in England and Wales, 668 or over 43 per cent received under £150 p.a. Four years later the Union admitted that an annual minimum salary of £150 was still a goal but it was one which was never reached in the nineteenth century. In Stroud, the minister of the Old Meeting House in 1897 was promised all revenue from seat rents, all weekly offerings and £75 or a total of £180 p.a. In the same period the pastor of Aylesbury's Congregational chapel got £200 p.a. plus £9. 1s. for supplies. The pastor of Nottingham's Broad Street Chapel had his salary raised in 1892 from £250 to £300.[18]

Of course ministers, like everyone else, were helped by the increase in the purchasing power of the pound from 20s. in the pound in 1873 to 23s. 1d. in 1900. In addition there were various 'perks' such as the NFCC's free lending library, the 'J. A. Spurgeon Home of Rest for Ministers' opened by the Baptists in 1900, and denominational pension funds. Retired Baptist ministers, for example, were getting an average of £32. 15s. a year in 1889 from their Society for Aged or Infirm Baptist Ministers; Wesleyan retired ministers, after thirty years' work, got £44 p.a. In some cases there was help towards the cost of educating minister's children and towards a retirement home. In addition, since the vast majority of people rented their homes, retiring ministers were not faced with the late twentieth–century dilemma of buying a house when one's income ceased. Frequently congregations made free gifts to their ministers but as these were often wealthy congregations which could also afford a high salary the bonus served as icing to an already rich cake: Joseph Parker, for example, got £1,000 to mark the twenty-fifth anniversary of his ministry and John Clifford was given a round-the-world trip when his health failed in 1897. In this case the money came from a single, wealthy shipowner who attended his chapel. On the other hand, there were gifts in kind: when Alfred Rowland was in Frome in the 1860s and 1870s he got free milk, and sometimes game and fowls. It was fairly standard practice for retiring ministers to receive a departing gift: John Stoughton, for example, received a magnificent gift of £4,000 when he resigned as pastor of the Congregational church in Kensington in 1874. Fourteen years later the minister of Nottingham's Mansfield Road Baptist Church got a more typical £75 when he left.[19]

Throughout the century the basic problem remained the same: a wide divergence meant that while some men were extremely well paid, others, no less devoted or hard working, lived in straitened circumstances. Secondly, there was no agreed minimum. If it was any consolation the same basic problems existed in the Church of England, while among Roman Catholics few if any clergy were well paid. By the end of the century things had at last begun to change: in 1899 Primitive Methodists agreed a minimum of £100 while Congregationalists and Baptists set aside part of their Twentieth Century Funds for salaries. In 1908 the Congregational Union agreed a minimum of £120 (£30 less than that recommended by Mearns in 1886). Baptists began raising a Sustentation Fund in 1908 and set a minimum salary of £160 in 1912. There was less real poverty among ministers by the end of the century than there had been, but for men who insisted on their professional status and were increasingly better educated, the dilemma was always present. The education and social status of the minister had risen notably during the century while his income had not. His dilemma lay 'in always having rather less than you need by the standards to which you are brought up'.[20]

For the Nonconformist minister as well as for the man in the pew, preaching lay at the heart of chapel life. In his reflections on the religious census of London, Mudie-Smith insisted that 'the outstanding lesson of the Census is that the power of preaching is undiminished'. C. F. G. Masterman in his contribution to Smith's report observed the 'manifest tendency of the Nonconformist worshippers to collect together into strong centres . . . which is inevitable where preaching is so emphasised and the stimulus and guidance of the pulpit so much desired'. To an American observer, preachers were 'the very mouth-pieces of their congregations, expressing for them their better selves, the very voice of their inmost hearts so that the whole congregation found itself raised above its ordinary self'. There were, inevitably, undesirable aspects in this emphasis on preaching: congregations shopped about and when a preacher died the congregation dwindled: after Spurgeon's death the attendance at the Tabernacle fell from over ten thousand to just over 3,500. R. J. Campbell was himself a highly successful, because dramatic and controversial, preacher who eventually left Congregationalism for the Church of England. Afterwards he reflected on the preacher's dilemma: 'If he is a strong man, the possessor of popular gifts, he will be treated with plenty of consideration; but the consideration is not due to his office so much as to his personal qualities.' A more severe critic simply referred to 'this tendency of the Free Churches to man-worship'. Again, the system could produce a cosy relationship in which no one was challenged and everyone was entertained: one writer recalled that 'there was certainty in the pews and certainty in the pulpit, and the pews settled down snugly to hear the champion declaim his variations, so to speak, on a classically familiar theme'.[21]

Of course, sermon-tasting was one of the few traits shared by all church-going Victorians. If Anglicans flocked to hear Scott Holland at Westminster Abbey, Frederick Robertson at Trinity Chapel, Brighton, or Fr Ignatius during one of his missions, Roman Catholic ladies swooned under the eloquent passion of Fr Bernard Vaughan. Not a few Victorians followed Gladstone's example and shopped round; the Liberal Prime Minister much enjoyed Parker's Thursday sermons for men. Others, visiting Paris, would sit in Notre Dame to observe the pulpit techniques of French preachers although the listeners would have found it impossible to order a *bifteck* from a tolerant waiter. Where Nonconformist preachers differed was in their isolation: they stood alone without a liturgy on which to fall back or a priestly vocation which made good preaching a desirable but not essential option. They had, however, no doubt about the sacred nature of preaching. To A. M. Fairbairn, preaching was 'when the man possessed of God speaks of the God Who possesses him'. The biographer of J. A. Macfadyen recalled that 'whenever he preached he seemed overcharged with the sense of the reality and supreme importance of the Gospel'. Joseph Parker, before preaching in a village chapel, was overheard to say, 'Jesus be near me, very near me, near me all the time'. Hugh Price Hughes once referred to the 'unspeakable joy of beholding eleven penitents' who came forward because of his preaching. Some, like P. T. Forsyth or John Hunter, referred to the preaching as the 'Sacrament of the Word' and saw it as 'the distinctly Protestant Sacrament'.[22]

The emotional setting in which sermons could be preached was made possible by a sympathetic audience: indeed, reciprocity was essential. The great preachers were masters of their craft. E. E. Kellett wrote of Joseph Parker, 'Why should people to whom such a pleasure as this was open, desire to go to the theatre? Had they gone, they would only have heard the pupils: in the City Temple they heard the master.' J. C. Carlile wrote of Spurgeon's preaching thus:

> When the clock struck, the preacher came down from a little room behind the platform, followed by ten or a dozen men who looked like prosperous City merchants. It did not appeal to me, but when the preacher advanced to the platform and prayed, there was a transformation . . . It must have been the totality of the situation that made me feel that heaven was very near and the invisible clearly seen.

Spurgeon was, in short, 'like Paganini with one string'. When writing of R. F. Horton, A. G. Gardiner remembered that 'he leans forward with outstretched hands . . . He is torn with bitter agony. His voice is shaken by the tumult of his feelings . . . Outside some one touches you . . . with a light greeting. It is like the breaking of a spell.' Another admirer, a woman who went into the mission field, recalled that 'the silence of a great congregation, held by the power of an eloquence which we felt rather than understood, endued him with an "other-worldliness" which could not be explained'. The preaching of the Wesleyan Morley Punshon in the 1850s was described as follows: 'After the text was announced there was a kind of subdued rustling and expectancy . . . At intervals . . . there were breathing spaces when . . . the spell-bound hearers had a brief release and there was a movement . . . as of pent-up emotion set free.' The writer, Marianne Farningham, wrote of the preaching of her pastor at College Street Baptist Chapel in Northampton in equally rapturous terms: 'Not a sound was heard but the musical voice of the speaker, who held the great crowd in rapt and absolute attention. It was only when he paused . . . that the tension was relaxed.' Had such language been used of an Anglican or Roman Catholic Eucharist the user would have quickly been castigated by Victorian Nonconformists as a 'wafer worshipper'.[23]

Much was heard by the end of the Victorian era about changes in the content of sermons. Some complained that 'verbal inspiration [of the Scriptures] has become an untenable doctrine' and that 'doctrine has lost its hold of the pulpit'. Robertson Nicoll told A. S. Peake in 1898, 'You would not believe what hosts of letters I get, and do not print, about the kind of thing that is preached in many of our chapels just now, especially by the younger men'. The *Northamptonshire Nonconformist* listed three reasons for the 'decline' they saw in Nonconformity: the first was 'a cultured ministry which repels rather than attracts [for] it shoots over the heads of the people'; the second was a ministry which disregarded the central truths of the Gospel in favour of 'the latest theories of the . . . *Fortnightly* [*Review*] hashed up'; the third was a minister who 'dresses himself as much as a Church . . . parson as possible, as much as possible copies the ritual of the Establishment, and poses almost as a full-blown priest'.[24]

Complaints about the content of sermons were not new nor were they confined to Nonconformists. What was new was the diversity which people were finding by the end of the century: many of the greatest preachers remained 'orthodox' including Spurgeon and his many protégés or Wesleyans like Dinsdale T. Young and F. Luke Wiseman. Others, like Hugh Price Hughes or Joseph Parker, laced their sermons with political allusions based on the assumption that their listeners were Liberals, but their orthodoxy was not questioned. Still others like John Clifford, Horton, Silvester Horne or R. J. Campbell became exponents of a much more liberal or 'social' interpretation of the Gospel and in some cases, such as Clifford's, adopted a very 'open' view regarding miracles and traditional Christian doctrines. Clifford's unorthodoxy was never in doubt: 'The Church' he claimed, 'has made too much of theology.' Again he said, in an argument strangely reminiscent of Erastus, Richard Hooker and Matthew Arnold, that 'the State is more sacred than any Church . . . for the State stands for the whole people in their manifold collective life; and any Church is but a fragment of that life, though one of the most important fragments'.[25]

It was but a small step from this to the 'social gospel': one started with an application of the Christian Gospel to evils in society and errors in politics. This then led to an obsession with political and social questions with decreasing reference to the criterion by which they were being examined, namely the Christian gospel of salvation for all mankind. The attempt to see the Christian message in the secular world ended up in seeing the secular world in the Christian message and then in confusing the two. This writer remembers one Good Friday sermon in an Anglican parish church in which the preacher referred to the crucifixion not as the self-offering of God's only Son and an event unique in man's history but as an example of the 'little man' being maltreated by the all-powerful state. A metaphor based on a current political concern had ousted the doctrine of the atonement. Campbell's 'New Theology' movement which began in 1907 was an example of this same process at work. His claim that to see the atonement at work one should visit the House of Commons was made in those happy days before its proceedings were televised.

It is too much to say that 'ministers, uncertain about everything else, had at times found a refuge in social righteousness' and that 'Bunyan . . . might have said that social righteousness was his old village of Morality transformed, like Manchester, to a town, by the industrial revolution'.[26] While there were many ministers who advocated the 'social gospel' the majority remained orthodox in their belief and teaching. Again, men like John Clifford or Silvester Horne, active in Liberal politics, saw their preaching labelled as more 'social' than it actually was precisely because of their political work. On the other hand, others, like Joseph Parker, to whom Gladstonian Liberalism and Protestant Christianity were one faith, were not therefore accused of preaching the 'social gospel'. Clifford always insisted that there must be a real 'conversion' for each individual although he also thought that the belief in individualism had been pushed too far both in the Church and in society. With increasing concern for social problems as opposed to individual 'sins' came an increasing amount of 'social work' as opposed to individual acts of charity. The temptation was that the churches' social work, begun as a way to win the unchurched as well as to help them physically, would cease being the means and instead become the end. The justification for doing the work might be seen to lie in the material benefits it produced.

It was against this that the veteran Baptist minister, Alexander Maclaren, gave a warning when he asked 'whether the abundant works of the Churches at present are the outcome of life, or whether they are not, in some cases, galvanic movements that simulate vitality and mask death. Martha has it all her own way now.' 'We are' he said later, 'in danger of building so many mills and factories on the river's bank . . . that the stream will be all used up and its bed dry.' The change in emphasis was noted in 1893 by another Baptist minister, Thomas Morris: 'It is the fashion of the present day to exaggerate the importance and power of circumstances', to put 'society' above individuals, whereas Christianity, he argued, 'must begin at the centre, and not at the circumference.'[27] Insofar as the 'social gospel' aimed at a transformation of society in lieu of a conversion of sinners it was never the view of the vast majority of Nonconformist ministers. Insofar as younger ministers believed that a Christian state should improve housing, lay drains or provide pensions, they could be said to have advocated a form of social gospel. When viewed from a distance, however, were they that different from their fathers who had urged the state to legislate against intemperance or social impurity or, indeed, from mediaeval bishops who urged the state to build better bridges for pilgrims on their way to Canterbury or to put down heresy? It was not so much a new view as an old view applied to new problems. Again, we must remember that those sermons which got into print or were noticed and attacked in newspapers were not always typical: the typical is seldom noticed.

What had happened in the nineteenth century was a relaxation in the definition of orthodoxy: Nonconformists no longer saw their chapels in virtual juxtaposition to the world about them. This had been the view of the enclosed Calvinist chapel or Methodist station, hidden away from the high streets of life. Nonconformity had now become part of that high street and as such had a responsibility not just for the souls of the gathered faithful but for society as a whole. Guinness Rogers wrote that in the Victorian era 'our theological conception has changed and with it our spiritual ideal also'. Preachers now recognized '"God is Love" as the central truth of the Gospel' and saw that 'conversion' was far more varied than hitherto thought. This liberalizing trend was, of course, not confined to Nonconformity and marked the Church of England as well: witness the fierce debates over the doctrine of eternal punishment, the recitation of the Athanasian Creed and the verbal inspiration of the Old Testament.[28]

Because Nonconformists had done so well out of the changes brought about in the nineteenth century it is not surprising that increasing numbers assumed the inevitability of liberal progress to be as much part of the natural order as the law of gravity. Since so much had been done peacefully through economic change, population increases, emigration and Parliamentary legislation, it is not surprising that ministers, like others, naturally assumed that progress through the same channels would continue *ad infinitum*. Victorian culture, with its concentration on individual responsibility and the primacy of the family, had played the dominant role in shaping much of Nonconformity; it was inevitable that in its turn Non-conformity should absorb much of that culture into its way of thinking. The world, at least the British world, was better off in 1901 than it had been in 1801, so why should it not be even better in 2001? In 1937 the Congregationalist Albert Peel reflected on the late Victorian and Edwardian periods: 'Ministers who began their pastorates in the twenty years before the war look back in amazement at sermons they then preached, with their acceptance of the inevitability of progress.'

People were increasingly better informed about social ills as the century wore on and how these could undermine and inhibit individual responsibility and freedom. As we shall see in Chapter 6 the closing decades of the century and the early years of the new century were more concerned with the 'collective' approach than the individual, and younger ministers were only mirroring this change. Therefore, to a degree, the 'social gospel' was criticized not because it called for political action but because it called into question Victorian cultural and economic truisms. Some of those who attacked ministers' devotion to the 'social gospel' were attacking a penchant for education bills, county council elections and slum clearance, but they would not have been as upset by a renewed campaign for disestablishment, which, no less than educational reform, could not be achieved without political action. It was, therefore, to some degree the older generation attacking the younger, much as an eighteenth century minister might have attacked the political involvement by ministers in the 1830s and 1840s when they refused to pay Church Rates and supported the Rev. Edward Miall's British Anti-State Church Association.

In some ways the difficulty was not some ministers' demanding social solutions to social problems above individual solutions, but the underlying extent of the cultural absorption by Nonconformists discussed above. The question is one of degree and not of kind, for, were Christianity not to some extent shaped by those cultures in which it existed, it would not speak a language understood by the majority of those whom it addressed. It would then speak only to isolated minorities. Nonconformists had two identities – as Baptists or Methodists or Congregationalists and, secondly, as Nonconformists. The first was doctrinal and ecclesiastical; the second was peculiarly English and 'parliamentary' and, as such, political. There had always been an inclination among ministers to preach on their Nonconformity and not on their Christianity and to end up 'talking politics'. This was more so in the nineteenth century as Nonconformity grew stronger and more involved in the mainstream of national life, but it had always been the case.

Added to this was an acceptance of liberal Victorian culture to such a degree that it was assumed to be as eternal as the gospel itself. When these aspects of Nonconformity, its inherent political bias and its identification with Victorian values, led ministers into the political arena, it was not surprising that critics complained: 'The men whom the churches care to hear . . . are the men who speak most loudly upon the current political topics, and who . . . "play to the gallery" and, echoing the gallery's political watchwords, rouse the gallery to re-echo them in its turn.' It was the price Nonconformity had to pay for its absorption into the mainstream of liberal Victorian culture. There was, however, this to be said: there had been political involvement under Miall in the 1840s but this had been to achieve a narrow, sectarian goal – disestablishment. Political involvement by the end of the century, even if it was almost totally through the Liberal party, aimed to achieve national not sectarian goals. If that achievement would benefit Nonconformity, it would benefit others as well. Having said all this, there were still those who wondered if it was not all too easy to confuse the eternal with the transitory. A prophetic warning came from Canon Hensley Henson in his pamphlet *Cui Bono?*, published in the last years of the century. Nonconformists' 'strength and . . . weakness' he claimed, 'lie in the fact that they tend to reflect contemporary social and political movements'.[29]

However fascinating the 'social gospel' has proved to historians, it was not the most important aspect of the ministry to Nonconformity: this was the need to improve the quality of ministers' education in order to equip them for the position they had achieved in English life. When Robertson Nicoll came to England in the 1880s he went to Dawlish where he complained: 'Dissent here is nowhere . . . The ministers get about £80 a year and are quite uneducated. The Church . . . has it all its own way . . . No educated man could stand the Dissenters.' While Nicoll's judgement was reached in the heat of the moment the facts bear out his basic impression: a detailed survey of all the ministers of the four leading denominations in 1870 shows that roughly eight out of every ten Primitive Methodist ministers had no formal education beyond school and among Wesleyan ministers the numbers were little better, seven out of every ten. The situation was considerably better among Baptists where half the ministers had received some form of higher education. Better still was the situation for Congregationalists where seven out of every ten men had some form of higher education. By the first year of the new century – 1901 – the numbers without formal education of some kind were, roughly speaking, halved in all four denominations. Less and less did Nonconformists like to have it said of them as was said of the Primitive Methodist evangelist and erstwhile coal-miner, James Flanagan, 'He waited not for an abundance of knowledge but used what he possessed'.[30]

The cry by 1901 was for educated men 'of good social standing' to become ministers: 'Such men . . . are more needed now than before Board Schools provided hearers whose improved education demands preaching of a higher order than formerly.' The Primitive Methodists, whose work was mostly amongst working people, admitted with a sorrow they could not hide that 'the growing worldliness of men needs a faithful and independent ministry; the increased educational facilities and the advance of science challenge us to put the best talent we can produce into the pulpit'. The conference of 1891 was urged to 'create in your respective centres a healthier yearning for an educated ministry, which may also retain the grand, sterling qualities of our fathers'. Wesleyans had smarted most from criticisms that their ministers were neither educated nor cultured and admitted the need for a 'cultivated as well as a consecrated ministry', a ministry of young men of 'piety and culture' with 'a more thorough training . . . and a more complete equipment for the Ministry'.[31]

The principal means for educating Nonconformist ministers were the various denominational colleges. All the major denominations made great strides between 1870, when Board schools began supplementing the work done by older bodies to give elementary education to working people, and the end of the century, in creating a ministry with at least some higher education. In those years the number of Wesleyan ministers without any college training dropped by 51 per cent and the number of those attending a theological college rose by 46 per cent. Baptists saw the number of ministers without any college training drop by 32 per cent while those going to a college rose by twenty per cent. Those with a university degree rose by twelve per cent. For Congregationalists the percentage with a college training remained, surprisingly, the same. Primitive Methodists made the greatest strides of all: the number of their ministers without any college training fell by 60 per cent while the number with, rose by 59 per cent.

Naturally, much depended on the quality of the education these men received. The older colleges, which traced their history back to the eighteenth century's 'dissenting academies' had not kept the high standing they had then enjoyed. In the 1870s R. F. Horton's father, himself a Congregational minister, refused to let his son enter a Congregational college because, he wrote, 'there is not one of them fit for you to enter. The professors are of an inferior order, and very few of the students even approach mediocrity.' Charles Brown recalled Bristol Baptist College when he was there from 1879 to 1882: there was only one instructor while the course was 'not altogether satisfactory'.[32] The other change which took place was the growth of a minority who went on to take advantage of new opportunities to get a university degree.

The number of men in all four major denominations who had done a university degree more than doubled between 1870 and 1900, from 14 to 37 per cent. The traditional dependence on Scottish universities was replaced by the expanding university college system, London University and the Victoria University group of colleges.[33] It was a sizeable achievement.

The distance that had to be covered can be seen in the case of the Primitive Methodists: they had no theological college until 1881 and when the new college in Manchester faced collapse it was only saved by the generosity of Sir William Hartley. It was he who persuaded A. S. Peake to leave Merton College, Oxford, for Manchester in 1892. Peake introduced Greek, increased the course from one year to two and increased accommodation to sixty. Even so, expenditure per student, admittedly only a rough guide, fell from £81 per student in 1890 to £38 in 1901; it was not unusual for the college to spend more on the gardens than on buying books. Again, entrance to the probationary ministry, from which students were taken, was controlled by the districts, not the college. The problem was too many men applying for too few places; in 1895, eighty-seven men passed the required examination for the ministry although the college still had only sixty places. Even for those sixty, there were only vacancies in the circuits for twenty-seven.

For their part, Congregationalists suffered from a glut of colleges: there were eight in England, three in Wales and one in Scotland. There was virtually no denominational control. All was left 'to the working of chance or of economic forces . . . Clearly this is a thoroughly British policy, but it is also thoroughly pagan.'[34] If a man had a 'call' to a chapel he could become a minister without any denominational approval and with no educational qualifications required. Even so, by the beginning of the new century only six per cent of the ministers newly appointed to a church were without some form of higher education. Again, as with the Primitive Methodists, there were too many men chasing too few churches: 223 ministers in 1901 could not find a church. Expenditure in the various colleges varied tremendously: in Nottingham Institute (admittedly non-residential) it was £30 on each of its 60 students; Western College in Plymouth spent £136 but it had only fourteen students. As a general rule, expenditure only rose as enrolment fell. Baptists had six colleges in England and two in Wales although in 1904 the number was reduced to four in England through amalgamation. After 1893 expenditure fell although enrolment remained virtually at the 1890 level. Expenditure varied enormously: Regent's Park College in London spent £140 on each of its twenty-nine students in 1901, while Pastor's College, founded by Spurgeon in 1856, spent £64 on each of its sixty men.[35]

There were certain problems common to all nineteen denominational colleges: the first was the quality of men who entered the ministry and from whom students were recruited. Only the Wesleyans had a system whereby the national organization had any control and even they had problems. For the other three bodies the problem was the same: either the districts (for Primitive Methodists) or the individual chapels (for Congregationalists and Baptists) allowed men into the ministry who had no academic qualifications. Some colleges, such as Pastor's, existed specifically in order to train men who would not put off people by too much learning.[36] Again, some colleges were simply too small and had too little money: the Primitive Methodist college had only one tutor until Peake arrived. In 1901 the Congregationalists' Western and Hackney Colleges had only fourteen and twenty-one students respectively while the Baptists' Nottingham and Bristol colleges had only eleven and twenty-one. With so many colleges there simply were not enough funds to go round: a twelve year survey (1890–1901) of the Baptist colleges shows that of eighty-five annual budgets for which there is full evidence, fifty-five had over-spent. As a general rule the only way to spend more per student was to have fewer students. The colleges' incomes were either constant or declining.

The greatest problem, therefore, was not in getting men into the colleges but in raising the level of the education they received once they were there. Wesleyan colleges were established as theological training centres but Baptist and Congregational colleges, because of their origins as dissenting academies, still had a bias towards giving a general arts education and not just a theological training. As there was no national system of state secondary schools until 1902 there was a constant struggle between those who wanted to raise the level of theological education in the colleges and those who knew that many of the men coming into them had nothing but a primary school education. Charles Brown, for example, was born in Northamptonshire in 1855 and had to go to work as a boy when his father, an agricultural labourer earning 12s. a week, was taken ill. The boy earned 1s. 6d. a week scaring birds away from crops. At fourteen he began to work as a postman at 2d. a round, one round each morning. He left home in 1871 to work in Birmingham, was converted during a Moody-Sankey campaign, and in 1879 entered Bristol Baptist College.[37] It is not surprising that the course in Baptist and Congregational colleges ran to six years: there was a lot of ground to cover.

Salvation came from without: the development of some *de facto* secondary work in the higher 'standards' or years of Board schools, the improvements in the older grammar schools, the use of various 'institutes' dedicated to helping working men get more education, the creation of new, civic universities like Owens in Manchester, and the expansion of London University, gave men who wanted a basic education beyond primary school new opportunities, after which they could go on to a denominational college which was now more able to concentrate on theology. The theological colleges were eager to take up the new opportunities and transfer the teaching of arts subjects to the new colleges and universities. In 1881, for example, Lancashire Independent College abolished all preparatory classes as Owens College could do it so much better. When the Congregational Union officially urged this new course on the colleges in 1902 there was still a long way to go: A. M. Fairbairn warned Sir Alfred Dale, then Principal of University College, Liverpool, 'I think one has to be very careful as to giving the theological colleges power over the regulation of degrees. You must not let them level down the University, but rather use your position to level them up.'[38]

Wesleyans, along with Primitive Methodists, seemed less concerned with the need for an educated ministry than the Baptists and Congregationalists. They insisted their four colleges have a spirit which was 'practical rather than academical' although it was agreed that the 254 places provided in the colleges were not enough by the end of the century. A committee was appointed to report on the situation in 1901 because Conference wanted to know how to secure candidates 'of higher educational proficiency and others of special promise' and they wanted the committee's views on the 'desirability of raising the standard of the examinations for the ministry' as well as the possible need to give candidates 'a more thorough training . . . and a more complete equipment'.[39]

Two additional problems were shared by all denominations. The first concerned the large army of lay or local preachers: for every minister in the four leading denominations there were seven lay preachers. To onlookers these men were seen in many cases as 'Nonconformist ministers' and of many it could be said that 'his prayer was like himself, rough and earnest'.[40] All major denominations strove to raise standards for lay preachers; methods chosen included free circulating libraries and denominational courses and examinations. The second problem was the influx of men trying to enter the ministry by the end of the century; if we look at ministers actively engaged in church work in 1901 we see that three out of every ten Primitive Methodists, four out of every ten Wesleyans, five out of every ten Congregationalists and seven out of every ten Baptists had entered the ministry in the 1890s. (Except for the Baptists the influx did not lower the trend towards a more educated ministry: the total of all Baptist ministers without any formal higher education was only eighteen per cent by 1901. However among those men 'settled' in the 1890s it was over twice that, at 41 per cent.) Unlike the Church of England, Nonconformity suffered not from too few but from too many candidates. There was a real embarrassment of riches.

The problem of too many men wanting to become ministers and too many lay preachers who inevitably lowered the educational average pointed up a fundamental dilemma. Robertson Nicoll, with his journalistic exuberance, boasted in 1902 that 'the average Dissenting minister has . . . a better literary and theological culture than the average minister of the Church [of England]' who were 'the worst educated [ministry] in this country'. Against this was the tradition that Nonconformity was the religion of 'the people' and not of the 'privileged classes'. How far could a minister of the people be educated beyond their level? When Spurgeon opened Pastor's College in 1856 some of the first pupils were illiterate but he insisted that his aim was to equip 'a class of ministers who will not aim at lofty scholarship, but at the winning of souls – men of the people'. High standards of education were not needed for work among the 'neglected classes, to whom a more cultured ministry would have appealed less strongly'. Yet the same writer lamented that some of the first students 'in many cases alienated the more thoughtful minds from the denomination'. Primitive Methodists rejoiced that 'we are of the people, and know their needs' yet, as we have seen, they were also glad that 'our people are everywhere participating in the social and intellectual advance of the times'.[41] We saw earlier that critics in Northampton had protested against what they called a 'cultured ministry which . . . shoots over the heads of the people'. This was the voice of the 'grass roots' and not of the annual meetings in London. There was a genuine dilemma and conservatives like Spurgeon could, if they had wanted, cite a famous precedent: St Francis of Assisi never disguised his hostility towards learning yet, within a few years of his death, his new Order was dominating much of Europe's University life. Spurgeon might also have asked if an 'Oxbridge'-educated ministry had helped or hindered the Church of England's work among working people.

How far should Nonconformity work to avoid the type of praise given by the Bishop of Ripon in his 1892 article on Spurgeon: 'The Puritan type may mean heedlessness of culture and loss of sweetness and light, but it also means seriousness, earnestness and a courageous bearing.' Was this to be regarded as a compliment or a criticism? In the attempt to win society's approval by a cultured ministry that had both sweetness and light, would Nonconformity produce a ministry cut off from the faithful? Would one pay too high a price for approval? As one reporter said when talking about the Baptist minister and ex-butcher,

William Cuff of Shoreditch: 'When God calls into His vineyard men who are not scholars, we do not show our wisdom by disapproving of the choice.'[42] But, as R. J. Campbell pointed out, the respect paid a minister could often be based on his performance as a preacher and a leader. He did not have the 'prerogatives of his office' available to peasant priests in Russia, Spain or France or the traditional respect given to English clergymen as gentlemen if not always as priests. If his education were below that of his audience he could not fall back on the validity of the Sacraments he administered for support.

By the end of the century many were moaning that 'the pulpit can never again be what it was once – the chief organ of information to the people, the great agent in moulding public thought'. 'The journalist' the Baptist James Owen declared in 1890, 'the reviewer, the historian, the essayist have assumed the sceptre which the teacher in the pulpit long ago wielded.' This was a legitimate reaction to a real change: it was, arguably, the price exacted by the nineteenth century from Nonconformist ministers for the multitude of benefits they and Nonconformity had obtained from that century. Nonconformist ministers had become part of Victorian England as famous preachers, writers, controversialists, politicians and local leaders. They were better educated and better paid. They participated more fully in the intellectual and political life of their time – some argued that they participated too much – and reflected their society's values, again, perhaps, too much if the criticisms of the 'social gospel' were accepted. One Tory JP saw this reflected in the gradual substitution of the old toast of 'Church and State' by the newer one of 'Ministers of all Denominations', due he said, 'to the increasing importance of the Dissenting element'. Even so, he felt, it was 'a bitter morsel for old Tories to swallow'. The ministers of that 'element' held positions of authority and influence within their various denominations perhaps unequalled, whatever Owen might argue, in any Protestant country. Their identification with the Liberal, self-help, individualistic Victorian creed and their coupling of this with the Christian gospel gave them a bond with their congregations. It was ultimately because of this that Nonconformity, unlike the Church of England, was able to achieve something no church has equalled since: it attracted and kept *men* in church. Late Victorian Nonconformity was to a considerable extent a man's religion. An anonymous Anglican critic summed up the vitality and confidence of the ministry by the end of the century. Ministers were generally 'men of great ability' who read widely. As a group

> their enthusiasm is still that of a child who asks all kinds of fascinating questions about the new world in which he finds himself. A man like Mr Silvester Horne is regarded by his congregation with feelings of almost unmeasured adoration, due to the fact that he and they are really opening the book of life for the first time together and comparing impressions. Pastor and people are alike laymen.[43]

5

THE NONCONFORMISTS' SEARCH FOR DIGNITY

In 1895 the Congregational Chapel in Aylesbury agreed to repeat the Lord's Prayer during Sunday services; three years later the Church accepted a proposal from its younger members to have a vase of flowers in chapel during services and someone donated a vase. These were small events but when repeated up and down the country, they amounted to a vast change in Nonconformist attitudes towards worship.[1] There had gradually developed in chapel life during the second half of the century a desire for greater dignity, order and something akin to the 'beauty of holiness', if not that beauty itself. People wanted to get away from the stereotyped chapels of plain benches, unvarnished woodwork and oil-lamps, chapels filled with the drone of 'psalm-singing green-grocers' and their families. The desire for improved services was centred among Congregationalists and Baptists while what we might call a larger search for dignity pertained to all the major denominations; the Congregationalist, Dr George Barrett, told a 1900 meeting of the Free Church Council that 'Nonconformists have not yet enlisted the imagination as a handmaid to faith . . . We have yet to learn that form counts for something even in the holiest adoration of the heart.'[2]

There was also a growing belief that worship had a corporate dimension. Chapel services were, or should be, more than just opportunities to hear a sermon: when Major J. B. Pond, the American entrepreneur who arranged lecture tours for British writers visiting America, came to London in 1879, he visited Spurgeon's Metropolitan Tabernacle. He secured two admission tickets but when he arrived he found they were only good for the front doors where 'already hundreds were waiting'. Then he noticed an open gate and beyond it a side door which he approached; here he was told that his tickets were only good for the front door while the side doors were reserved for members. When asked why he could not enter, the guard replied, 'Oh, you can by dropping something in the box'. (As an American he would have been used to 'collections' being taken up during the service. In England the custom was still to rely on pew rents and on subscriptions being paid directly to the chapel. If donations were taken at a service, they were left at the door either on the way in or on the way out. By the end of the century the older ways were being overtaken by the American custom.) Pond then described what happened: 'I saw people were dropping pieces of silver into the box and passing in. I said to him, "How much am I expected to drop in?" He replied, "Anything you please. A half-crown is the usual amount."' Just to make sure of getting seats, Pond put in two half-crowns, not much under a week's wages for thousands of agricultural labourers. Once inside

a gentlemanly usher gave our party good seats. Already several hundred people had entered in this way, and before the doors were open the lower floor was about filled . . . When the main doors were thrown open, there was a general rush of men and women in all directions, carrying umbrellas and jumping over the pews to get to the very nearest available seats, and almost immediately every seat in the church was occupied and great crowds were standing against the wall in the back galleries. I think I never witnessed such a squabble of people rushing into a building. They created a dust that was almost suffocating.

Afterwards, however, Pond, himself a Baptist and used to Beecher's Plymouth Church, described the congregation as 'a very devout crowd of worshippers who entered into the spirit of the occasion and did worship the Lord and Mr Spurgeon with tremendous intensity'.[3]

It was against this sort of thing – the view that chapel attendance was nothing more than an opportunity to sit, to listen and, in part, to worship the preacher – that many Nonconformists reacted. In doing so they were part of their time. *The Christian World* noted in 1882, 'The great wave of Catholic sentiment which has been sweeping over the Established Church . . . has sensibly cast its spray over the Nonconformist bodies of the country'. Undoubtedly the Oxford Movement's influences had been felt outside the Church of England. The movement was arguably a result of cultural changes affecting not only Britain but America and Europe. The Rev. Arnold Thomas of Bristol told Congregationalists that 'it is good to make beautiful our buildings and services. No one need quarrel with the improvements that are taking place in these directions.'[4] Many Nonconformist leaders were outspoken in their criticisms of public behaviour at religious meetings and services: the Rev. Alfred Rowland told Nonconformists in 1898 that they were 'sadly deficient in reverence', while some services were marked by 'downright vulgarity' and an abundance of chattering and unpunctuality which often indicated a 'lack of inward reverence and true spirituality'. 'In many Free Churches I fear that awe is an unknown factor' and 'some who sneer at elaborately worked altar-cloths would do well to cultivate the spirit of those by whom they were presented.'[5]

The greatest occasions for offence came with the biennial meetings of the Baptist and Congregational Unions and the annual gatherings of the National Free Church Council. (Methodists, most notably Wesleyans, along with Presbyterians were recognized as being the best behaved.) These meetings were often passionate affairs: the deadening decorum which in the twentieth century has come to be identified with religious gatherings did not prevail in the nineteenth century. Victorians, who had yet to discover the stiff upper lip and the view that religion had always to be a serious matter, were passionate people who expressed their feelings freely and often loudly. Just as they loved colour, they loved oratory, even when they could not understand it: in 1901 delegates at the Free Church Council meeting in Cardiff stood up to welcome five former French priests. They were addressed by a M. Corneloup who told them that some 103 priests had 'escaped from the land of slavery . . . and had entered the . . . Canaan of the Gospel of Christ' due to his work. Afterwards one of these new Canaanites, M. Joseph Ver, spoke but unfortunately he knew no English. His French proved too voluble for the interpreter but the audience did not mind; cries arose of 'Let him go. Let him go', so the interpreter sat down and M. Ver carried on for five minutes more.[6]

It was normal for impassioned orators to be greeted by a sea of waving handkerchiefs and raised umbrellas. (Even during services it was not unusual for the audience to break into applause.) In that imperial *annus mirabilis* of 1897 Nonconformist representatives were invited for the first time in English history to take part in a royal celebration when thirty representatives were allowed places at St Paul's to witness the short act of worship in the midst of the Queen's Jubilee procession through London. At the Free Church Council's meeting an address of congratulation to Queen Victoria was adopted after which delegates sprang to their feet and burst into singing the National Anthem. The year before the Baptists had sent a telegram to Queen Victoria congratulating her on completing the longest reign in British history. When a reply arrived which simply said, 'The Private Secretary is commanded to express the thanks of The Queen for the kind message of congratulation which you have forwarded to Her Majesty', the assembly rose to its feet and cheered. As in so many things, the ways of the Victorians, while looked on with horror in late twentieth-century England, have survived in America; unashamed fervour in holding and expressing religious and patriotic beliefs which easily blend into one another is but one example.

The reaction was not against passionate expression of beliefs or against an audience's supporting a speaker: it was against excessive displays and rhetoric more appropriate to a political rally than to a religious meeting. R. F. Horton 'deplored the immoderate pleasure in witticisms and laughable anecdotes' that marred meetings of the Congregational Union. Hugh Price Hughes chastised the 1896 Free Church Council meetings for its vociferousness and insisted that all should 'submit to those restraints and regulations which the experience of the greatest representative assemblies of the world has proved to be necessary to an intelligent participation in the business as it proceeds'. The following year the new President, a Presbyterian, had to repeat the injunction, this time directed at the gallery, insisting that there be no applause, either 'by our hands, and still less by our feet'.[7] One should remember, however, that similar criticisms were levied at delegates to the Church Congresses of the period.

Some leaders spoke out against the new trend; in a paper on preaching delivered at a Free Church Council meeting the quixotic Joseph Parker defended congregational applause during a sermon because it encouraged the preacher and allowed the Holy Spirit to work through the listeners. (Ballet dancers of the same period used the same argument about applause during their performances.) Many opponents of the new desire for dignity were ministers trained by Spurgeon. A. G. Brown, who refused either to wear a white tie to show his ministerial status or to allow an organ in his chapel, was pastor of the East London Tabernacle. He insisted that 'we shall never win the people by keeping aloof from them . . . I would send dignity to the devil, where it came from.' Others, like John Clifford, regarded the new movement as a humorous irrelevance. When Hugh Price Hughes urged that he, as President of the Free Church Council, wear academic dress at Council sessions, a 'heated discussion' resulted. Clifford said he did not know which academic dress to wear as he had three London degrees, and 'I can't wear them all at once'. To the rejoiner that he wear the gown showing his 'highest proficiency' he replied, 'Ah, well, I should not need to put any other gown in my bag than I usually carry', by which he meant his night-gown, as 'that represents my greatest proficiency'. Hughes was not amused.[8]

There were, of course, other causes than ecclesiastical for the changing attitudes: public decorum, proper behaviour and increasingly complicated social rituals – as in mourning, dining, dressing and visiting – were part of Victorian middle and upper-class life and the churches could not stand outside these changes. In the Chairman's Address by the Rev. Arnold Thomas quoted above he went on to expand on a definition of the Nonconformist Conscience and in so doing showed how social attitudes and religious arguments had become fused. 'Our witness' he said, 'is to be for goodness', which he defined not only as being 'honest, temperate, chaste' and leading an 'upright, decent, useful life', but as the spirit or motivation behind all this. One must try to avoid, he said, what George Macdonald called the 'general disagreeableness of good people'. 'To put it plainly', Thomas concluded, one needed the grace to 'be a gentleman'. This is not the language of Spurgeon or of the stereotyped minister of hole-in-the-corner chapels. Ironically, in the midst of the education controversy of 1902, the Prime Minister, A. J. Balfour, who had known Thomas at Cambridge, singled him out amongst his opponents as 'a gentleman aiming at fairness'.[9]

Increasingly Nonconformity was becoming a religion of 'gentlemen' or at least of those who wished to become such, and gentlemen preferred dignity and decorum in religious worship. To a large degree this was centred, although not confined, to the newer, suburban churches, but it affected all aspects of Nonconformist church-life. (Once again Nonconformity was in step with the Church of England which likewise saw tremendous improvements in the quality of her religious services.) In Islington's famous Union Chapel, for example, the doors which opened into the auditorium had fixed to the wall beside them small boxes with a slit on the top; these were for worshippers' donations. Someone had been thoughtful enough to provide a felt lining to the bottom of the box so that there would be no noise from the falling coins. Union Chapel was also the home from 1852 to 1892 of Henry Allon. The Congregational historian, Albert Peel, wrote that 'it is probably true to say that no one did more to raise the standard of worship in Nonconformist churches' than he. This was especially the case with regard to the use of music: a memorial in Union Chapel referred to his 'successful endeavours to promote a nobler service of song in public worship'.[10]

Allon advocated the use of chanting but this was taken up by few chapels; the much greater growth lay in the use of hymns. In 1887, eleven years after Allon had advocated liturgical chanting, George Barrett edited the *Congregational Church Hymnal*. By the end of the century it had sold 1,250,000 copies and unlike Allon's own collection of hymns, it had been an official publication, part of the growth in musical taste and improved choirs. If music were important then choirs needed to be improved; in Gloucestershire a Nonconformist United Choirs Union was formed in 1892 and music festivals were held in Gloucester in 1892 and 1894. 'The Union was formed' records at Wotton-under-Edge show, 'with the intention of drawing these Congregational Church[es] into closer union with each other, and also of improving the service of praise in the house of the Lord.'[11]

Organs were also important for, just as Gothic was the 'English style' for churches, so the organ was the English instrument for church music. Congregationalists, for example, noted in their *Year Books* from 1898 to 1901 that they had installed 144 new organs; as early as 1873 William Shepherdson, a Member of the College of Organists, reminded Nonconformists that a hundred years before, organs 'were beyond the reach of small Churches, while as to Chapels . . . the placing of an organ . . . would have been regarded as an act of profanation.' Things had changed and 'the organ has now become a necessity. No Church or Chapel is complete without it.' Organs ranged from the 1,000 guinea pipe organ to 'The Sunday School Union's "New Baby Organ"' which sold for five guineas and promised a 'very sweet tone'.[12] Back at Wotton-under-Edge in Gloucestershire the Congregational Tabernacle's Mutual Improvement Society resolved in November 1893 'that the time has now come for an Organ to be obtained for the Tabernacle Services'. The following February the Church agreed and allocated £250; an organ was dedicated on 29 May 1895. The Church records noted proudly, 'That Memorial Organ on the very day of its dedication is *free* – it has no debt on it – it belongs to no human being – but like the sanctuary is dedicated to Almighty God & belongs only to Him.'[13]

Another leading advocate for a more 'religious' style of worship was also Congregational: John Hunter was pastor of four churches in Scotland and England. He is mainly remembered for his *Devotional Services for Public Worship*, first published in 1882. In it he insisted that 'worship requires serious effort, not only in the one who is to lead it, but in those who are to follow it and make it theirs'. He wanted people to kneel during prayer (as had once been done) and ministers to close their sermons with the *Gloria*

Patri. When he came to the King's Weigh House Chapel in Duke Street, London, off Grosvenor Square, he surpassed most of his contemporaries by introducing an elaborate ritual centred on a Holy Table. His methods had an appeal among the wealthy, professional classes who made up the congregation. In 1903 he addressed a conference in Liverpool where he made 'a Plea for a Worshipful Church'. 'It is time' he argued, that 'the Free Churches . . . had outgrown their fear of everything Roman or Anglican'. A congregation's attention should focus not on the pulpit, the choir gallery or the organ behind it, but on the Holy Table.[14]

Hunter, far more than Allon, was in a very small minority. Many ministers, especially those working in suburban areas and themselves graduates of universities, accepted the need for great decorum but decried liturgical worship; R. F. Horton attacked prescribed prayers, as used for example by Wesleyan Methodists, as belonging 'to a pre-Christian epoch'. The demand which grew up amongst Congregationalists and, to a lesser degree, Baptists was not for a radical shift in the nature of their worship but for the external embellishment of traditional worship: flowers, organs and stained glass, but not chants, Holy Tables and liturgical seasons. As Horton Davies, who has explored this subject deeply, wrote: 'More worshipful churches proved incentives to, if not a deeper, yet a better ordered and more dignified worship among congregations that had previously regarded worship as merely a preliminary to preaching.'[15]

The degree to which the trend had affected Nonconformist life can be seen by a return to the Metropolitan Tabernacle after Spurgeon's death. The pastorate had passed first to his brother; on his death it had reverted to one of the famous preacher's twin sons. It was some twenty years since Major Pond's visit and the visitor from Booth's enquiry team observed a communion service on a Sunday evening in 1901:

> Before us, in a sort of alcove brilliantly lighted . . . was a long table set out as one sees the Last Supper pourtrayed at Milan or elsewhere, with no one on the near side of the table . . . At the table before us Mr. Spurgeon occupied the central position;

the others were, I suppose, his deacons . . . Then Mr. Spurgeon rose, and all present rose with him, and, after breaking the bread, spoke the accustomed words: 'This is my body —.' Then from the back of the platform, where they had been seated, there stepped forward some twenty or perhaps thirty men, to whom were given silver plates containing little cubes of bread, and with these they moved down among the congregation . . . The pastor and deacons partook first . . . It was the same with the wine. Again all were seated, and again rose, the pastor taking the cup and speaking the chosen words, whilst those who served went with the cups among the congregation . . . Lastly, they brought round the collection plates . . . When this was all done, and partly, too, during it, prayer was offered and a hymn sung . . . Finally, Mr. Spurgeon spoke . . . and made his jokes. It was a marvellous scene – a strange incongruous medley of simplicity and ceremonial.[16]

Simplicity and ceremonial seem to express the changing pattern of Nonconformist worship but that worship was only part of a wider search for dignity, a dignity which was mainly realized in the new and improved buildings Nonconformity was erecting up and down the country.

To their own generation the new-found power and confidence of English Nonconformists were most visible in the buildings they erected in town centres, suburbs and villages throughout England. They influenced the appearance of England's expanding cities in the same way, and sometimes to the same degree as mediaeval parish churches and cathedrals had influenced the appearance of English villages and cities of their time. After Spurgeon's Metropolitan Tabernacle was erected in 1860 at the Elephant and Castle it quickly became one of the sights of London. It was Spurgeon who insisted on a classical design by which he meant a rectangular building with portico and six Corinthian columns. Just as Greek was to him a 'sacred language', so 'every Baptist place should be Grecian, never Gothic'. The Tabernacle cost £31,383, over a million pounds today. There were sixteen doors, excluding private entrances. The building, which was 174 feet long and 85 feet wide, had 5,000 seats on the floor and in two galleries. In addition there was standing room for 1,000.

The Building News said in 1860 that the new chapel, which was then the largest building in England for public worship, had solved Wren's query as to how 5,000 people in one building could all both see and hear a service. In the Tabernacle all but fifty had a perfect view. As Major Pond discovered, seat-holders were let in through side doors while *hoi polloi* had to come in through the front in the hope of getting what they could. 'There are dense, compact masses swarming everywhere around the chapel, like people round opera-house doors on a Jenny Lind night.' Inside, the building was remarkably plain with no pulpit but a platform or 'tribune'; the walls were painted a light green. One guide in 1861 ranked it with St Paul's and Buckingham Palace and began its report: 'We are not a race of giants, but we enter on gigantic works. We have, in our age, a predilection for great things . . . Mr Spurgeon and Mr Spurgeon's people were determined to have a great chapel.' It became 'unquestionably one of the sights of London'.[17] In 1898, six years after Spurgeon's death, the building suffered a disastrous fire and had to be rebuilt. Spurgeon's six Corinthian columns were kept but the number of seats was reduced to 2,700 due to the decline in the congregation after the great preacher's death.

Fourteen years later, on 19 May 1874, in the City of London, the City Temple, the new name for the old Poultry Lane Congregational Chapel, opened the doors to its new home on Holborn Viaduct. The Lord Mayor attended in state and a special service was intoned which included the Sanctus and a *Te Deum*. The building became known as London's Nonconformist Cathedral; unlike the Tabernacle, the Temple was elaborately furnished with stained glass windows and a tower of 145 feet in the 'Italian style'. The building was designed by the same Bradford firm which had built Sir Titus Salt's church at Saltaire. Like the Tabernacle, the Temple was built round the preacher, in this case Joseph Parker. The floor sloped slightly and the pews, which held 2,500, were slightly curved so that the preacher 'can be seen from every part of the building'. Behind the pulpit was room for an orchestra although in 1882 an organ was installed, something the more old-fashioned Puritan, Spurgeon, would never allow. As is always the case not everyone was pleased: one of Booth's team described it as a 'large and rather ugly building' although 'its interior looks well enough when crowded with people.' An even less sympathetic visitor, writing in *Truth*, described it as 'very like a City Hall in oleograph'. A twentieth century writer on church architecture called it a 'pretentious pseudo-classical building' whose principal feature was the famous '"Great White Pulpit"'. The total cost was estimated at nearly £70,000 (well over £2,000,000 today).[18]

Structures like those built for Spurgeon and Parker were only two of a myriad of building enterprises entered into by various Nonconformist denominations. London was now the home of striking Nonconformist churches like Christ Church, Westminster Bridge Road, the Wesleyan Hinde Street Chapel, Islington's Union Chapel or Mayfair's King's Weigh House, now the Ukrainian Catholic Cathedral of the Holy Family in Exile. Not all were built as auditoria in which an enrapt audience could listen to their chosen hero. As we have seen, attitudes were changing even when the builders were at work in the Elephant and Castle. Nonconformity was slowly and unevenly moving towards the idea of a worshipping community as well as a gathered audience eager to hear the Gospel preached. By 1902 one observer could note that the chapel had become

> a place for worship, instead of a theatre for listening. Money has been lavished upon towers, spires, gargoyles, tracery, carved capitals . . . and the general arrangements begin to approximate, in many instances, to those of a large parish church . . . the plastered wall, the unmanageable oil-lamps, the varnished reading-desk, and the big black stove have vanished forever.[19]

Occasionally an innovative structure was put up without spires and gargoyles: Congregationalists in the Hertford-shire villages of Braughing and Puckeridge spent £1,275 not just in refitting the chapels and manse but in building an unsectarian village centre where the minister acted as warden.

The greatest building work, however, took place in the suburbs and followed the prevailing fashions. With the building boom brought on by suburbanization, land for a chapel could now be bought in prominent locations: the days of buildings tucked into a court of back lane had passed. The 1897 President of the Baptist Union declared that Baptists were 'no longer treated as social pariahs, to be trampled under foot of men' as seen in their new 'sanctuaries in main thoroughfares' of which many were 'beautiful and costly'. They now carpeted the aisles and cushioned the pews while 'organ notes and well-trained voices' led the congregations. In the event it had not been so much religious 'discrimination' as the limits imposed by lack of money and of land in over-built ancient towns and villages. Today, when councils like that in Tewkesbury restore old Meeting Houses – in Tewkesbury's case a Baptist chapel down a narrow lane opposite the great Abbey Church – Baptist visitors are as surprised as everyone else at the austerity of the past. All this vanished in the suburbs.[20] By the end of the century expenditure on building new churches, improving existing ones, paying off debts, erecting towers and spires and on constructing missions, settlements, central halls and school rooms had reached incredible amounts.

This building campaign soared in the 1890s: Wesleyans, Baptists and Primitive Methodists (there are no accurate statistics for Congregationalists) spent at least £8,316,920 on building, equivalent to some £275,000,000 in 1990. Because Congregationalists were such a wealthy denomination the true figure would be considerably larger. The importance of this expenditure is realized when we contrast it with the £701,469 these three same denominations spent on ministerial training and the £692,054 spent on home missions. In the case of the Primitive Methodists, the poorest of the four leading denominations, the Connexion faced a debt of £1,003,207 by 1901. Ironically, while they erected 660 churches, they closed thirty-three for every twenty-one new ones they built. In most cases the money went on replacing or improving old buildings, not in building chapels where there had been none before. Both Baptists and Wesleyan Methodists actually had fewer churches in 1901 than they had had in 1870.

As we have seen Nonconformists benefited greatly from rising standards of living and the movement to the suburbs. The Primitive Methodists boasted that their

Connexion was 'year by year . . . erecting new chapels, some of them magnificent and even sumptuous in their appointments'. As the denomination most solidly based in the countryside, they also realized they had little choice in the thousands of new streets with their red and yellow brick terraces that were covering England's acres. 'Families are more inclined to settle permanently as worshippers in good, commodious, and well-situated buildings than in small, ill-arranged, and badly situated chapels.' In other words the money spent was one way of stopping 'leakage' to other denominations; the new chapels also tended to enhance loyalty and to lessen disaffection over trifling matters.[21] While Nonconformists were not 'ashamed of the many-windowed chapel, the vulgar conventicle', a Chairman of the Congregational Union told his audience during the 1897 May meetings, they had shown that they could 'also appreciate the noblest architecture, and pay for it, too!' Indeed, they could.[22]

A demand for the 'noblest' architecture inevitably meant that Nonconformity was caught up in the debates over the value of Gothic architecture which went on for most of the Victorian period. The two sides may be called the Goths and the Greeks, and while the Goths won the war, the Greeks took quite a few battle honours. When the Birmingham architect Joseph Crouch looked back on the nineteenth century, he reflected that 'the spirit of Evangelical religion in England has changed in a singular manner during the past fifty or sixty years. This change has been chiefly in the direction of the broadening of its outlook on life.' The victory of Gothic architecture showed that Nonconformity had kept pace with the spirit of the times; to have done otherwise would have turned them back into hole-and-corner chapels appealing, like the Quakers with their simple meeting-houses, to 'men and women of a certain temper'.[23] It is ironic that the man who did so much to revive Gothic design, Thomas Rickman, was himself a Quaker. His 1817 book, *An Attempt to Discriminate the Styles of English Architecture*, asserted that Gothic was essentially an English architecture. The idea that the appropriate design for those new churches being built for England's expanding towns should be

'Gothic' first gained public favour as a result of the 1818 Church Building Act. Many of the new parish churches built with the funds provided by Parliament were in 'Commissioners' Gothic'. The first recorded Nonconformist Gothic chapel came in 1839 when Sir Charles Barry, who started work on the new Houses of Parliament the following year, designed a new church for Upper Brook Street Unitarian Chapel in Manchester, although the interior design still had the pulpit as the central feature against the east wall and facing the congregation.

By the 1840s Gothic was growing in favour among Nonconformists generally. Denominational year books were featuring 'Gothic' chapels: these were usually brick buildings of traditional rectangular shape but with pinacles, mullioned windows, buttresses and arches. Internally the design was the same. In 1847 the *Congregational Union Year Book* included a thirteen-page section, 'Remarks on Ecclesiastical Architecture as Applied to Nonconformist Chapels'. The author rejoiced that 'the improvement in public taste . . . during the last twenty-five years has at length reached the meeting-houses of Nonconformity'. Gothic was not only the English style but the 'Christian' style. Lancashire Independent College, one of the denomination's theological colleges, was especially commended for its 'Gothic' design which included cloisters, a tower and 'orial [sic] windows'. Brick must be eschewed for stone whenever possible.[24]

Three years later the Methodist minister, F. J. Jobson, who had trained as an architect, published a practical guide with the blessing of the Wesleyan Connexional authorities. His aim was to overcome a fear of 'extravagance' in chapel design; God did not dislike adornment, but *unnecessary* adornment'. Gothic architecture, he insisted, 'is ENGLISH CHURCH ARCHITECTURE' and, by implication, if Nonconformists wanted their denominations to be considered as part of the Christian Church in England then their buildings must be Gothic. However, the design was only to affect the outside; inside things must remain the same. There were to be no aisles, crosses or altars; the pulpit must be against the end wall facing the congregation. Also, like the writer in the Congregational *Year Book* he insisted that Gothic architecture was 'the most *economic* style of Chapel Building'. The book was said to have had a sizeable effect.[25]

In 1853 the English Congregational Chapel-building Society was founded to help local chapels and two years later the Rev. J. C. Gallaway published for the Society a tract on *Practical Hints on the Erection of Places of Public Worship*. Congregationalists must convince their fellow Englishmen that they were 'fully up to the spirit of the age'. 'We are aiming not at the elaboration of a few but at the erection of many temples or houses of our Lord' and therefore 'cheapness in the construction of each is indispensable to success' and Gothic chapels need not be expensive. Their great value was that Gothic structures 'are seldom mistaken for Mechanics' Institutes, Post Offices or Banks'. Congregationalists should welcome the erection of towers and spires not, he insisted, 'for the sake of display still less as affecting mere imitation of a wealthier body [*i.e.* the Church of England] but for purely practical purposes.' These included 'conspicuousness' to attract the public and space for lobbies, clock chambers, staircases, belfries and better ventilation. Galleries should be avoided, to get away from the idea of a theatre with an audience watching an actor but the pulpit must still remain the central feature. A lecturer at the Architectural Exhibition of 1861 noted that 'we cannot afford to ignore the element of association which now more than ever connects our idea of churches with good Gothic architecture. We want our churches to be church-like.' 'Dissenting Gothic' had arrived: external Gothic features cheaply built, combined with traditional arrangements inside, or what Sir John Betjeman later called 'terra cotta Gothic, riddled with dedication stones'.[26]

Throughout the Victorian era there were constant criticisms of the devotion to Gothic architecture and especially 'Carpenter's Gothic'. R. W. Dale accepted in 1862 that the sneers against Dissenters' Gothic had some validity but, he added, 'we can only say that we are inexperienced hands at this work. We are improving already, and hope to do better still by and by.' Amateurishness and lack of money were the prevailing weaknesses. The writer, Christopher Stell, has pointed out that of some 600 'architects' whose buildings were described in the

Congregational Union's *Year Books* in the nineteenth century, 'very few' are credited with having built more than one or two. 'R.D.W.' told his fellow architects in 1859 that 'Since the revival of gothic architecture, and the general advance in public taste, a great advance has been made in chapel-building' regardless of the style chosen. Money, however, remained the chief problem. If the architect chose Gothic and was asked, as increasingly he was asked, to provide stained glass windows, columns for aisles, 'showy' decoration and in some cases even chancels, holy tables and clerestories, he faced an impossible task. Always he had to exercise 'great economy'.[27]

While the demand for 'great economy' meant that Dissenting Gothic became a byword for machine-produced, dull buildings, this was not always the case. Observers agreed that Nonconformist buildings improved with the century, especially during the last twenty-five years. To a large degree this was due to the examples of famous churches such as Christ Church, Westminster Bridge Road, to which we have referred before. The new building, opened in 1876, cost £62,000 (approximately £2,000,000) but this included not just the church but the organ, the famous Lincoln Tower, the land and the various subsidiary buildings. The architect did not try to reproduce a mediaeval church with aisles and chancel but chose an octagon shape with one side designated as an 'east end' with a window under which stood a Holy Table. The pulpit was to the side. When Booth's assistant visited the church he praised it as a 'great and successful attempt to adapt the aspiring and inspiriting beauty of Gothic architecture to the congregational ideal'. 'The worshippers' he continued, 'are still regarded mainly as an audience but the house is manifestly a house of God': Newman Hall intended it to be both a non-denominational centre and a 'Cathedral of Nonconformity'. At Ashton-under-Lyne the congregation of Albion Church spent £50,000 (£1,600,000) on the 'Nonconformist Cathedral of Lancashire'. The 'early perpendicular' building was 175 feet long with windows designed by Morris and Burne-Jones and a hammer-beam roof. The spire was 200 feet high. Most of the cost was met by the wealthy Congregationalist, Abel Buckley, who had been the MP for Prestwich Division in the Home Rule

Parliament of 1885. (W. H. Lever would soon follow Buckley's example with his 'Christ Church' in Port Sunlight.)[28]

Where there was a wealthy patron the chances of a first-rate building were obviously greater. In Liverpool Miss Ruth Evans donated £25,000 (£825,000) to build a Congregational chapel at Rainhill to seat 650, as a memorial to her brother, Joseph, a colliery proprietor at Haydock. The new building had an organ and the obligatory tower, this time 120 feet high. In addition there was a gymnasium, swimming baths, club house, reading and 'cocoa' rooms. In Bolton, W. H. and J. D. Lever gave the money to build Blackburn Road Congregational Chapel to replace a temporary prefabricated 'iron church'. The new building had both an organ and stained glass windows and was meant as a memorial to the brothers' parents. In Port Sunlight W. H. Lever paid for Christ Church Congregational Chapel. In West Ham, Mr James Duncan, 'a large employer of labour in that locality' gave £4,000 (£132,000) to build Union Congregational Church, Victoria Docks, and provided funds for its upkeep. In Halifax, as we have seen, the Crossley family provided most of the funds for Square Congregational Chapel. In Bristol the Wills family got the young William Butterfield, a relation through marriage, to design Highbury Chapel. This was the only Nonconformist chapel Butterfield ever designed and in 1976 it became a parish church.[29]

The greatest single expenditure on a Nonconformist chapel came not from the Congregationalists but from the Baptists and not in England but in Scotland. In 1894 the Coats Memorial Baptist Church in Paisley replaced the old Storie Street Chapel when the congregation moved into the northern suburbs after the decline of the area round Storie Street. It was paid for by the Coats family and cost a phenomenal £100,000 or £3,300,000 in 1990 terms. It was built as a monument to Thomas Coats, the man who had established the family's cotton thread empire. The style was Gothic and followed 'the best traditions of mediaeval church architecture, but to meet more advantageously the requirements of Protestant worship the nave is kept broader and shorter'. Stone, not brick, was used. While there was a chancel and a holy table the chancel was not long and the table was not put against the east wall; the pulpit was to the side, an unusual feature in Baptist Gothic buildings. There was the obligatory tower which rose 220 feet above street level. 'The edifice', the *Baptist Union Hand Book* declared, 'may fairly claim to be one of the finest ecclesiastical buildings reared in this generation.'[30]

Towers and spires had become something of an obsession with Nonconformists during the last forty years of the century. A glance at the architectural section of any of the annual handbooks published by the leading denominations or a survey of the denominational press shows how important they had become. This was largely but not exclusively an obsession of Congregationalists, much as it had been of mediaeval bishops. Frequently the tower had to be left unfinished or left on the drawing-board, awaiting more funds. At Lavender Hill in London in 1900 the Congregational church added a tower and spire to a church built in 1883. In 1897 Congregationalists in East Dereham raised £500 by public subscription to complete their tower, complete with chimes and clock, to celebrate Queen Victoria's Diamond Jubilee. In Leeds, Newton Park Union Church not only had a seventy-foot tower but a clock which Leeds Corporation agreed to illuminate at night. Whether or not this constituted a form of 'corporation establishment' was not recorded. Other denominations had their share of towers and spires; indeed, one of the more prominent of Oxford's dreaming spires is that of the Wesley Memorial Chapel on New Inn Hall Street. Its spire was said by a contemporary guide to Oxford to form 'a conspicuous addition to the architectural adornments of the city'.[31]

Gothic architecture was never, however, totally accepted. In many cases small congregations, especially in villages, simply could not afford even 'Dissenters' Gothic'. They continued to build plain, cheap red brick chapels. In 1896, for example, the year in which Radnor Park Congregational Chapel in Folkestone spent £7,000 and Albion Church in Ashton-under-Lyne spent £50,000 on new buildings, Congregationalists at Rothbury in Northumberland built a new chapel for £1,400 but they were fortunate in having the land given them by Lord Armstrong, the arms magnate. Again, among Baptists, a survey of 248 new buildings erected in the last decade of the century shows that of the total, 60 per cent cost under £2,000 and 42 per cent cost under £1,000. Primitive Methodists, the most rural of the four leading denominations, built a total of 660 chapels between 1890 and 1901 and the average cost was £1,151. 14s. 6d. and many would have been under the average.

Again, those who preferred the Greeks to the Goths were never vanquished. As we have seen, two of the most famous chapels built in the Victorian era, Metropolitan Tabernacle and the City Temple, were not Gothic. While the heyday for Greek columns was between the 1830s and the 1850s, the classical style carried on although not to the same degree. They tended to be built round ministers who disliked the slowly developing penchant for what were called 'liturgical' forms of worship associated with Gothic chapels. Such men included Dale of Carr's Lane, the first Greek revival chapel in England, Spurgeon and Parker. The classical style, which included Spurgeon's Greek temple facade, was used by all denominations and stretched from Belvoir Street Baptist Chapel in Leicester, built in 1845, to the Wesleyan Hinde Street Chapel in London, built in the 1880s with a two-storeyed portico-front copied after St Paul's Cathedral.

Spurgeon's was the greatest single influence in ensuring that the Greeks were never totally defeated. One of his many acts was to open the Pastor's College, originally in the basement of the 'Monster Tabernacle'. From here he sent out young men committed to his style of preaching. They took with them the word 'Tabernacle' which came to mean in architectural terms a building in rectangular shape, with a Greek temple frontage outside and inside, little decoration and preaching in the conservative, earthy, evangelistic and Calvinistic tradition. Such buildings tended to be comparatively inexpensive. Woolwich Tabernacle, erected between 1895 and 1896, sat 1,690 but cost only £13,936 for both the land and the building. The secret was that the man made the Tabernacle. When 'A Travelling Correspondent' in the 1870s asked why Shoreditch needed a Tabernacle, he answered 'because a man has lately settled there who, as a preacher of the Gospel, can attract a full house'. The preacher in this case was the Rev. William Cuff, a Spurgeon man. After 1860 Tabernacles reached Battersea Park, South Lee, Dulwich, Peckham, Highgate, Barking, Enfield, Poplar, Shepherd's Bush, Uxbridge Road, Walthamstow, Croydon and Tunbridge Wells.[32]

One final reason why Gothic's victory was never complete lay in the new Settlements and Central Halls which Nonconformity erected in town centres. Any form of 'ecclesiastical' architecture was seen as a hindrance to the 'unchurched millions'. The Leysian Mission on City Road was opened in 1904 by the Prince and Princess of Wales (later King George V and Queen Mary). The cost was £110,000 (over £3,600,000). The Wesleyan mission had been started in 1886 by the old boys of The Leys School as a settlement for the poor of Finsbury and it had the usual assortment of activities such as clubs, bands, and concerts. It was designed not to resemble a church of any sort but, if anything, a town hall.[33] Likewise there was little 'church like' about Whitefield's Tabernacle on the Tottenham Court Road to which C. S. Horne came in 1903 while the Wesleyan mission at Ancoats, Manchester, had an eclectic design consisting of Tudor half-timbers plus towers.

Gothic design always had its critics. Some at the grass roots feared that it was a rejection of traditional Puritan virtues. In 1863 J. A. Tabor wrote a pamphlet attacking the new Gothic building put up for Lion Walk Congregational Chapel in Colchester. He denounced the 'vainglorious erections . . . of . . . gorgeous edifices with . . . lofty and defiant spires' because they proved that Nonconformity had become 'tainted with the spirit of the world'. Protestant Christianity was not an *'Exhibition*, but an internal, vital principle'. The new buildings were 'so many monuments, not of piety, but of pride – not of spirituality, but of rank carnality'. More often critics attacked the craze for Gothic architecture not because it was wrong in itself but because the mediaeval arrangement, as opposed to mere decoration, was not suitable to a religion based on preaching, not on eucharistic sacrifice. In 1862 the architectural historian, James Fergusson, denounced Victorian Gothic, by which he meant a servile copying, as a 'forgery'. It was not a 'true' style because it had not developed within an era to meet a genuine need; it was merely copying the dead and it 'degrades architecture from its high position of a quasi-natural production to that of a mere imitative art', a criticism often levied by professional architects against the wishes of the man in the street. The simple fact was that large numbers of Victorians, if not the vast majority, liked Gothic.[34]

In 1870 the architect James Cubitt denounced the Gothic design for chapels as being as 'undesirable as it is inappropriate' for Protestant worship. His attack was not so much on 'Gothic' decorations but on the cruciform pattern with columns, aisles and a chancel. He felt 'their day is nearly over' and recommended alternative styles. 'If we are ever to have a real modern church, it must be by adopting a fresh church arrangement.' In 1876, the same year in which Christ Church Westminster Bridge Road was built, Cubitt had an opportunity to put his theories into practice. He was chosen to design a new building for the Congregationalists' Union Chapel in Islington. While the congregation was only prepared to spend £25,000 (£825,000) they also only wanted 1,650 seats which took some of the pressure off Cubitt. In his design he is credited for seeing that 'auditorium planning need not be inconsistent with good architecture'. Like Christ Church, Union Chapel was an octagon which focused on the pulpit without being centred on it. Unfortunately for Cubitt he had to have a gallery but he made it far more acceptable by supporting it with pointed arches. He also designed a fascinating roof of wood and glass. The organ was behind the pulpit but was hidden by an attractive grill. The building was set in its own garden, since vanished, and was built of red brick. Ten years later came another blow for Cubitt when a large tower was added; while it was 'ecclesiastical', it was not Gothic. Nicholas Pevsner later referred to it as having a 'blustering High Victorian effect'. If the building did not look like a church, Cubitt could have replied that Englishmen needed to ask themselves what a church *should* look like.[35]

Twenty-two years later Cubitt returned to the attack

when he published his *Popular Handbook of Nonconformist Church Building*. He accepted that people had a right to prefer buildings 'such as custom and habit associate with the name of "church"'. The need was to reconcile the 'ecclesiastical' and the 'congregational' elements, and while he insisted that 'Nonconformist churches must, beyond all question, be built to see and hear in' he had nothing good to say about the vast preaching halls, such as the Metropolitan Tabernacle, with a bit of tracery and the proportions of a barn. He also criticized the competition among Nonconformists 'of having the "highest spire in the neighbourhood"'. Cubitt's greatest savagery was reserved for the '"Meeting-House Gallery"' which he described as 'about the crudest attempt ever made at providing seats for a certain number of people over the heads of the rest', a 'failure practically, and a horror artistically', 'uncouth' and a 'gigantic misfit'. He was delighted that 'Dissenters' Gothic' seemed to be a thing of the past. The things 'one most misses in the Nonconformist church-building of to-day are character, self-reliance, individuality'. While there were still some mongrel structures – 'half meeting house, half music hall' – things were improving. Let Nonconformity 'only have courage to develop on its own lines, to be itself, and not a pale imitation of Anglican architecture, and the possibilities before it are very great.' By the 1890s architectural styles generally were changing and Gothic had largely run its course; Cubitt's arguments were in step with the times.[36]

The reaction against Gothic continued despite its decline. In 1902 J. Compton Rickett, Liberal MP for Scarborough and a wealthy coal merchant, denounced Gothic architecture in his book, *The Free Churchman of To-Day*. Except in a few cases it was pronounced a failure because of the need to use cheaper materials. He wondered if it was ever right to spend 'large sums of money . . . in attempting to compete with' the Church of England. Could Nonconformists 'with advantage surrender the outline of the meeting-house' which often 'more fitly accords with the genius of the Free Churches than many an ambitious structure which ministers to the cultured taste of a suburban congregation'? In 1911 P. T. Forsyth insisted that a Protestant church 'must be primarily an auditorium'.

Even though Gothic was 'the purest, most adequate, and most congenial expression of the Christian spirit in architecture', Nonconformity needed its own expression.[37]

The difficulty with all these criticisms is that they never specified exactly what was the 'correct' style for Nonconformist chapels. In the event, Gothic was succeeded in the 1890s by a variety of new styles. The first we must call Eclectic Gothic: this used red brick and stone facings and, as Cubitt suggested, a variety of designs for towers, some of them quite ingenious. It eschewed the Gothic spire and mediaeval internal arrangements. Chapels on this pattern were barely distinguishable from parish churches of the same period and they both fitted perfectly into the leafy suburbs for which they were intended. In many instances they closely resemble Protestant churches built in America except that there stone was used as frequently as brick. The architect most commonly associated with this work was George Baines who designed quite a few churches for Baptists. Other new styles were created by adapting traditional designs other than Gothic as Cubitt had suggested; as we have mentioned before, Hinde Street had a facade based on St Paul's Cathedral while Westminster Congregational Chapel, near Buckingham Palace, had a 'Lombardic' design. In the village of Thornton Hough in Cheshire, W. H. Lever gave a Congregational chapel in 1907. He had it named St George's Church and also had it built in the centre of the village in impeccable Norman style with nave, transepts, chancel, altar, choir stalls, altar rails and tower. There was even a lych gate.[38]

Yet another new style was created when Nonconformist buildings adapted the designs of the public buildings which arose in the final years of the nineteenth century. This may be called the 'monumental or Renaissance', a style which made an enormous impact on 'townscapes' throughout Europe, especially in the years before and after the Great War. It is now mainly associated with government offices in most major capitals and in Britain with the Methodist Central Hall in London and the Civic Centre in Cardiff, both designed by Rickards and Lanchester. In Brighton the monumental style was to find favour with Nonconformists planning a new church, not a denominational headquarters like Central Hall. In 1898

Union Chapel was created by joining Union Street and Queen Square Congregational churches. R. J. Campbell, pastor of Union Street, became the minister of the new church, inadequately housed in the Gothic buildings in Queen Square. The old Gothic was felt to be as inadequate in the 1890s as the old meeting-house had been in the 1860s so plans were made for a new building worthy of their pastor whose fame was rapidly increasing. Land was bought, an architect hired and the cost agreed: £70,000 (£2,310,000). It would be yet another 'great Nonconformist cathedral'. The architect's plans were exhibited at the Royal Academy in 1899. The building would be built of stone and there would be niches in the outside walls to be filled with statues of dissenting saints like Cromwell. Inside there would be seating for 2,000. To the German architectural historian, Hermann Muthesius, the building's 'expense, splendour and technological worth will have no equal amongst English nonconformist buildings'. However, after Joseph Parker died in 1902 the City Temple invited Campbell to take his place. He therefore left Brighton for the greater glory of London; fortunately for his less famous successors, 'the scheme never materialised'.[39]

One example of the monumental style which did get built was the Wesleyans' new London home, the Central Hall in Westminster. For years it had been a dream of Methodist leaders like Hughes, Sir Robert Perks MP and Sir Henry Lunn to have a 'monumental Connexional building' worthy of Wesleyanism. They were lucky when the freehold of the old Aquarium Theatre, opposite Westminster Abbey, came up for sale. It was a perfect site because the building, for which a quarter of a million pounds (£8,250,000) had been set aside from the Twentieth Century Fund, was meant to be 'a challenge to the Church of England'. The historian, Robert Currie, has justly described it as the 'architectural monument to Methodist ambitions at the beginning of the twentieth century'. Nothing better illustrates the change in English religious life produced by the nineteenth century than the proximity of the Wesleyans' new Central Hall to the Anglicans' new Church House (put up between 1891 and 1902) and the Roman Catholics' Westminster Cathedral further down Victoria Street.[40] The building's hall is still frequently a venue for those exercising their Nonconformist Consciences on current political controversies.

Whatever the criticisms that were and are levied against Nonconformist chapel building in the nineteenth century, no one can deny that it was a tremendous undertaking. Nonconformity did not will migration into the towns nor the migration out again to the suburbs but it did meet the challenges presented by these mammoth social changes. The worse criticism, of course, is not that Carpenter's Gothic was cheap nor that most of the styles chosen were imitative but that it did no good. Newman Hall, whose Christ Church, Westminster Bridge Road, was to many the epitome of Gothic extravagance, is said to have told F. B. Meyer's biographer, 'Had I my time over again with my present knowledge, I would build a Workmen's Hall at Westminster and use the surplus money to build three or four churches in the suburbs of London'. This was a criticism not of Gothic design nor of church building but of extravagant expenditure.[41] An even greater criticism is that the vast sums spent should have been spent elsewhere, especially in missionary efforts among the growing number of Englishmen who never went to church or chapel. The expenditure was a commentary on the disunity within Methodism and the lack of supervision within the Baptist and Congregational Unions.

Critics then and now say that Nonconformity did not create a new architecture after they had given up the old seventeenth and eighteenth-century meeting house. Nonconformists could not win: if they followed normal Victorian uses and imitated the past, whether it was Greek, Gothic, Lombard, Norman or St Paul's Cathedral, they were and are criticized for not having a new style. If, on the other hand, they had remained loyal to the meeting-house style they would have still been criticized for not having a style which met the needs of their time. If they stood apart from their era, assuming human nature can ever do this, their fear was that they would have faded away as irrelevant oddities; if on the other hand they became fully part of their century their fear was that they would not be giving an alternate witness, another voice.

Their imitation was not wrong and, if they were actually a vital and in some cases dominant part of English Christianity, was their 'imitation' of Gothic buildings any more wrong than that of their Anglican competitors? What was wrong was cheap imitation. Likewise, they did use innovative architects, men like George Baines, W. W. Pocock, James Cubitt and Alfred Waterhouse. If their buildings were garish then so, too, were most Victorian creations. As Bishop Edward King, at the opposite end of the English religious spectrum from Nonconformists, noted, 'We live in an age of decoration . . . It is in all matters, not merely ecclesiastical ones, that the spirit of adornment has caught hold of us, and unless there is positive wrong in any of these things, we have no call to repress them.' It was Cubitt who noted that 'artistic knowledge and cultured tastes are not now confined to what are sometimes called the upper classes' and the German historian, Muthesius, saw that 'within Nonconformity, each individual layman's romanticism has begun to show itself – as seen in the architectural achievements of the Congregationalists'.[42] Those who eschewed colour and decoration, like Spurgeon, and built what were really mammoth meeting-houses with a Greek front, were criticized for lack of taste and for concentrating too much on the preacher. Those who, like Newman Hall, let Gothic design take over, were criticized for being imitative and for demeaning the sermon.

It took professional journals like *Building News* and foreign observers like Muthesius to recognize Nonconformity's achievements. In his book, *Die neurere kirlichliche Baukunst*, Muthesius devoted one-third of his space to Nonconformist buildings and noted the proposed Union Chapel in Brighton, Melbourne Hall in Leicester, Newman Hall's Christ Church, Union Chapel, Islington, Victoria Hall, Ancoats, Manchester and Whitefield's Tabernacle. He was impressed by the variety, originality and eclecticism of Nonconformist architecture: 'The grateful lesson, which, as the preceding [discussion] obviously shows, English Nonconformist architecture has given architects, serves as a means of liberation which, from the architectural point of view, deserves a thorough consideration.' In some cases even those more conservative chapels which stood aside from the changing fashions made notable contributions to their own town's architecture. In Bedford, Bunyan Meeting House still possesses bronze doors of a very high quality and showing scenes from Bunyan's works. They were given by the Duke of Bedford, who also gave a statue of Bunyan to Bedford Corporation. (Another member of the Russell family, Lord Charles, used his influence as the Queen's Serjeant-at-Arms to get William Hale White's father the position of Door-Keeper to the House of Commons.) The fact remains, however, that there was a certain defensive quality in many Nonconformist discussions on their new buildings; the Editor of the *Baptist Times* insisted in 1902 that 'to-day, under changed conditions, we are false to no principle and to no tradition in making our Sanctuaries beautiful as well as useful'.[43]

In 1914 Ronald Jones argued that 'Everyone will now agree that a building should sincerely interpret the object for which it was erected, and should be the natural outcome of the conditions . . . of its own period and place'.[44] The trouble was that the old meeting-house had become a symbol of religious and cultural isolation. Nonconformity no longer felt itself to be a gathered community of dissenters but part and parcel of the English Christian Church and for better or worse the architectural tradition of that Church and nation was Gothic. To revert to an old style would be to try to set back the clock and deny the progress which had been made and made under divine providence. If Nonconformists were imitators they were no more so than Anglicans or Roman Catholics. The tension was never resolved. Even within the bounds of their overwhelming devotion to Gothic they showed by the end of the century an openness to new styles which other denominations were not as quick to learn. If their new buildings did not look like churches they had a right to say that people should re-examine what they thought a church *ought* to look like. The debates which raged round their building programmes were themselves healthy signs, showing that they were in the mainstream of Victorian life which is where they wanted to be. The one fact which does stand out is this: in the creation of the Victorian town, just as in the life of the ancient universities, in the spread of learning and in the writing and publishing of Victorian literature, Nonconformists were a vital element in English life wielding an importance far beyond their numbers.

6

THE MOVE TO UNITY

It is hardly surprising, given the enhanced status, power and influence which the nineteenth century had brought, that Nonconformists had come to identify the Christian religion with the values and secular goals of their times, the most important of which was an acceptance of the inevitability of progress through change. The older dissenting bodies – the Baptists and Congregationalists – had largely thrown off their heritage as 'gathered communities' founded on an old High Calvinism for a more flexible biblical Protestant creed in a world of expanding knowledge and opportunities. They had retained a firm conviction, despite the talk about the 'social gospel', of the need for personal salvation through individual conversion, a belief which accorded with the century's emphasis on individualism. Methodists, likewise, were being gathered up into what the veteran Congregational leader, J. Guinness Rogers, called 'the general intellectual movement of the generation', even if at a slower pace. The century had been one of tremendous change and older views, like the emphasis on individualism, were being modified and in some cases challenged by the closing decades of the century. Then, as always, various 'catchphrases' were strung together like shells on a necklace to form a complete view that was repeated over and again and formed men's attitudes. The two most important catchphrases, certainly by the 1890s, were the 'law of evolution' and what may be called the spirit of organization. As Sir Percy Bunting, Methodist editor of the *Contemporary Review*, wrote: 'The influence of the evolutionary idea in all subjects of human thought is permanent, and has deeply affected theology.'[1] The 'law' of natural evolution or development, especially when popularized by Herbert Spencer and applied to society, was said to parallel traditional Christian reliance on Divine Providence and meant that the expansion of Nonconformity at home and the extraordinary growth of British power and influence abroad could be seen as part of the same phenomenon.

Many leaders, including the imperialist Hugh Price Hughes, the Fabian Socialist John Clifford and the Gladstonian Liberal Joseph Parker, also urged the need for organization and cooperation. To them the traditional emphasis on voluntarism and private initiative, which had laid the foundation for Nonconformist power, needed re-examination or what a later generation would call 'rationalization'. Nonconformity's dependence on *laissez faire* and, in the case of Methodism, on competition among five separate bodies, had not always worked for the best and there had been a lot of wasted effort. The 1901 President of the National Free Church Council was only pointing to the obvious when he told his audience that there was throughout the country and Empire 'an irresistible movement towards co-operation, combination, collectivism, solidarity, centralisation . . . The whole bent of thought, and what we call the spirit of the age, point straight in that direction.' He added that 'the survival of the fittest is sometimes the apotheosis of the unfit'. Here again Nonconformists were only adapting current political and social ideas to religious ends. In politics Charles Dilke had referred to 'Greater Britain' and Joseph Chamberlain to Imperial Unity, while the quixotic Lord Rosebery, with his usual flair for vacuous terms, demanded 'Efficiency' in government, education and industry. As an anonymous pamphleteer wrote, 'The growth of an Imperial sentiment in politics . . . is not more remarkable than the corresponding sentiment in favour of the unity of all baptised Christians'.[2]

As we have seen, attitudes had been changing regarding the corporate nature of chapel life and of the individual Christian's duty concerning social ills. People were coming to accept that Nonconformist chapels should look like 'churches' and that Nonconformist services should be more 'dignified' and 'ecclesiastical'; it was not surprising that people should come to view the nature of the Church itself in a different vein from their forefathers. This increasing emphasis on 'dignity' was not only a reference to behaviour within the chapel but to the nature of the Church as a body. As one of Nonconformity's most severe but incisive critics observed, 'powerful influences have intervened to elevate the corporate as opposed to the individualist aspect of dissent'.[3]

These changing attitudes can be seen as part of the general reaction against the older voluntarism. Signs of change had been evident within various protest movements, like the Teetotallers, from the 1850s when they realized that without state action they could not achieve their goals. A widespread reaction, however, can be dated from the 1880s. Knowledge of the effects of urbanization, industrialization and poverty proliferated throughout society, partly due to the efforts of Nonconformists like Rowntree, Cadbury, Mearns and General Booth; fears developed about the industrial competition from America and Germany; demands grew within the Liberal party for more state action with regard to education, public health and housing. Increasingly people looked to the state to provide services, to regulate more of the affairs between men and to effect overall improvement in the quality of the nation's life. The Empire likewise needed organization if it were to survive. All this was perhaps an inevitable reaction by a new generation to the old creed of individualism and *laissez faire* which G. W. E. Russell, a Liberal MP and High Churchman, denounced in a *Manchester Guardian* article at the turn of the century as 'this intellectual but unmoral theory'. To him, 'the cause of collectivism seems to be the cause of Social Progress. It is the new and better Revolution.' When Joseph Parker urged a radical reorganization of the Congregational Union to create a 'Congregational Church' he asked pointedly, 'What right has Congregationalism to stand outside the law of evolution?' Increasingly the answer was: none at all.[4]

For centuries one of the most telling criticisms of Nonconformity had been its penchant towards disintegration, what Edmund Burke called 'the dissidence of dissent'. In his *Letter to Sir Hercules Langrishe* of 1792 Burke carried the argument to its logical conclusion:

If mere dissent from the church of Rome be a merit, he that dissents the most perfectly is the most meritorious . . . He that dissents throughout with that church, will dissent with the church of England . . . A man is certainly the most perfect Protestant, who protests against the whole Christian religion.

The problem extended both to Old Dissent – what had become in the nineteenth century Independents or Congregationalists and Baptists – and to the Methodists who were wracked by schisms until 1849. Silvester Horne, in his popular survey of nineteenth-century Nonconformity, admitted, 'The easiest accusation to sustain against Nonconformity has been hitherto its tendency to disintegration and division'. Other leaders, like the Rev. Alexander Mackennal, pointed out that the original Separatists of the sixteenth century had not venerated that 'extravagant individualism against which we are now witnessing a somewhat excessive revolt'. Extreme religious individualism, he insisted, was an outgrowth of the Methodist Revival, amongst other sources, presumably because of its emphasis on individual experiences of 'salvation'. The essence of Congregationalism, he insisted, was not isolated individual salvation but a 'pure and disciplined' Church, an argument which retained a traditional Calvinist flavour. A Congregational Union pamphlet issued in 1901 cited Article XXIV in the Savoy Declaration of 1658 which had warned against too many 'distinct societies' and Article XXVI, which urged co-operation. The tract also admitted that 'there are churches that ought never to have come into existence, churches of dispute and personal pique or eccentricity'.[5]

The Old Dissent had traditionally held that 'the Church' meant the gathered, local body of true believers. Organization to control local initiative, let alone to define belief and practice and to fight the eighteenth-century tendency towards Unitarianism, had not been easy to achieve. The power the respective Unions exercised over Baptists and Congregationalists was very small, compared to that of the various Methodist Connexions. Another tract in the same Congregational Union series argued that to join a local church was, in effect, to join 'Christ's universal church', which was 'Christ's own society', not a 'private society organised by pious men.' As often happens, this younger generation of 'Tractarians' who were leading the crusade on the side of 'collectivism' joined forces with the older generation like J. A. Macfadyen who had remained Calvinist in their views and 'deplored the modern nondenominational spirit, the temper of indifference to questions of church order', the spirit which saw local churches as 'mere voluntary associations for religious purposes, with power to determine their own polity and prescribe their own sphere of action'.[6]

In many chapels a more traditional, eighteenth-century practice as to church discipline was followed well into the twentieth century. These were located mainly in rural areas and in smaller market towns where conservative practices inherited from the past stood a better chance of survival. These were chapels which did not have the 'coming-and-going' of suburban churches where people sought out the latest new preacher or moved on once their income increased. At Holmer Green Baptist Church in Buckinghamshire, for example, in February, 1890, 'the deacons were requested to visit Mr and Mrs R— — — in consequence of their long absence from Communion'. In April 'The visitors reported the result of their interviews with Mr & Mrs R— — — . . . and no action was taken'. The problem, however, did not go away and in January, 1897 'A revision of the Church Roll was then made and the following name was erased for absence from Communion[:] Miss R— — —.' Two other people were to be visited regarding their absences. In Amersham, the church meeting of the Lower Meeting House (Baptist) heard in 1892 that 'several of our young members have been absent from the means of grace [communion] for many months and it was resolved that they be visited by two members of the Church'. Five years later the Meeting considered another problem and in its wisdom inverted the common law assumption that an accusation was not a conviction: 'The Case of Mr. H. R— — — — was brought before the Church, who had misconducted himself and at the recommendation of the Pastor and Officers was suspended until his guilt was proved.' The Minutes do not tell us in what Mr R— — —'s 'misconduct' consisted and he is heard of no more.[7]

Like the Baptists in Holmer Green, the Amersham

Baptists' main problem concerned attendance; following traditional Christian practice they held that the indispensable sign of membership, of being 'in communion', was partaking in the Communion Service, whether this was held quarterly or, in their case, monthly. In 1898 the Church Meeting resolved to draw up the membership list on the basis that 'those who wished to be regular communicants be voted upon at the Church Meeting'. The following year the question of non-attendance arose. It was resolved that any member absent for twelve months should be visited by a deputation to 'ascertain the cause'. Afterwards the church would decide each case 'on its merits'. Members also appointed six 'pew-stewards' who were 'to look after the pew demands [rental fees] and the non-attendance of Divine Service and the monthly ordinance [i.e. Communion].' In 1900 the two senior deacons were appointed to look into three cases of 'non attendance to the table' and reported back that there were twenty-one cases out of a membership of 109. It was obviously a real problem. Of the three cases investigated by the deacons, one was put on probation and two, 'after confession and promises for better attendance . . . were left upon the Church books'. To some all this will appear to be petty, intrusive and narrow-minded along the lines of 'What right had they to . . .'; to others it will appear an example of the chapel's commitment to their beliefs. The Baptists of Amersham were only doing what the universal Church had done for centuries in insisting on partaking in the Communion as a sign of being 'in communion' with the church. As the *Prayer Book* enjoined in the Notes appended to the Communion Service, 'every Parishioner shall communicate at the least three times in the year, of which Easter to be one'. It shows that the older, 'high' view of the Church had survived and that not all Nonconformist chapels could be lambasted as mere preaching barns in which the faithful could hear the minister dilate on the role religion could play in politics.

It was the Congregationalists who suffered most from what R. F. Horton called an 'exaggerated and perverted notion of independency', partially because of their history and partially because there was a greater diversity of beliefs than in the other denominations being discussed.

The 1898 Chairman of the Union told his listeners that 'religious atomism is the bane of Congregationalism'. 'Among us the sin of schism is too often committed and too quickly condoned.' Local churches had a 'spiritual responsibility to the Church of God'. The most important challenge to the *laissez faire* mentality within Congregationalism came from Joseph Parker in 1901 when as Chairman he placed a cat among the pigeons with his usual dexterity. He had himself witnessed the 'dissidence of dissent' as a child: his father, a stonemason in Hexham, left the local Congregational chapel when the new minister turned out to be an Arminian, and migrated, somewhat illogically for a Calvinist, to the local Wesleyan chapel. When the offending Arminian left he returned to the fold. Not surprisingly he had not been happy as a Wesleyan.[8]

Parker called for a 'United Congregational Church' and despite vociferous interruptions from the floor he asked, 'Is it really a glorious thing to be absolutely independent of each other?' He wanted more control in order to level up, to get rid of 'jerry building being described as Congregationalism'. He wanted all the theological colleges to be combined into three, at Oxford, Cambridge and Durham; he wanted the numerous funds, societies, urban work and foreign missions combined for greater effect. He spoke not because he felt that the denomination was threatened or was losing ground but because the status quo did not give Congregationalism the dignity its growing wealth and membership had earned for it. Parker was applying Herbert Spencer's law of social evolution and the current devotion to organization to the denomination. It was an act of confidence, based on strength, not of fear based on weakness. Greater unity would strengthen the weakest link in the chain, the village minister: 'When sneerers and wonderers ask [him], "Hath any man brought him ought to eat?" it will soon be made clear that good men eat at the table of Divine plenteousness.' A new constitution was adopted in September 1904 but Congregationalists fought shy of using the word 'church', with the implication that local chapels were *de facto* parishes within a new national body, and retained their old title of 'Union': churches remained the local bodies of gathered believers. It proved only a partial victory for Parker who had died in 1902 and it was not until 1919 that the first Moderators or *de facto* bishops were inducted to ensure higher, more uniform standards and greater control from London.

To many people, talk of greater denominational unity was nothing more than the application to religion of current political nostrums like collectivism or, worse, 'socialism'. Among the more doctrinally united Baptists some conservatives were rather defensive by the end of the century and accepted the need for a middle course between 'exaggerated and ill-directed individualism' on the one hand and 'exaggerated and ill-directed socialism' on the other. Others, however, retained their traditional belief: T. M. Morris declared in his 1893 Presidential Address to the Baptist Union that the 'fashion of the present day' was to 'exaggerate the importance and power of circumstances' whereas Christianity was based on the individual. The Church, he insisted, was 'nothing more than the aggregation of these individuals.' Two years later the Union President, J. G. Greenhough, called up the old world to attack the new: he expounded traditional Calvinism with its high doctrine of church order although he accepted that it had 'little favour' in 1895. Then he attacked the new belief in collectivism as a political, not an ecclesiastical cry: socialism would produce a 'kingdom of Lilliputians, not men'. 'If there be no free play for the individual forces there will be a speedy decay of manhood.' In the following year the President argued that man's nature had been used by God and that state-imposed collective responsibility was unnecessary: Christian altruism had worked through an 'inevitable though almost undetected stimulation of Egoism'.[9]

The argument against individualism in religion and politics was led by men like J. C. Carlile and John Clifford. (Clifford's London church had emphasized the corporate nature of Christianity by having a service of 'infant dedication' while retaining baptism by total immersion for those who had experienced 'conversion' at a later date. They were by no means alone in this practice.) In 1899 Clifford, as President of the Baptist Union, had argued that 'that separate entity called the individual is not a concrete existence . . . You cannot insulate a man . . . The highest life of the unit is only attainable through the fullest life of all.' Salvation may begin with the individual, he argued, but is only fulfilled in a life of shared brotherhood. Four years later Carlile argued that 'the Church is an organism and an organisation. As a living body in which dwells the Divine Spirit, it is fashioned and shaped by the Divine Power. It is a Divine creation.' The Church is not merely 'a company of faithful men in which the pure word of God is preached' but is in truth, 'Christ in the world'.[10] We may question how far these arguments were heeded, given the radical reputation of their proponents. Where a 'corporate' sense of the Church survived it usually did so, as at Holmer's Green, through the survival of the older, Calvinist tradition which was alien to men like Clifford.

To Methodists the talk of collectivism remained largely a political debate because, despite their numerous schisms, all five Methodist connexions had strong central authorities much envied by some Baptists and Congregationalists. Methodists might reject the right of Rome or Canterbury to speak with authority on matters of faith, but they had no doubt about Conference's role as *ecclesia docens*. The Wesleyans, especially, maintained a very 'high' view of their Connexion and of Methodist order: 'Its remedies have been tested everywhere' Conference declared in 1896, 'and the first failure has yet to be recorded.' In short, the connexional system seemed infallible. There were those like Hugh Price Hughes who joined in the reaction against individualism because they felt it had narrowed the churches' work among working people:

> The manhood of England has been largely alienated from the organised Churches because we have been so absorbed by the interests of the individual soul as to neglect the woes of society, and so preoccupied with the delights of heaven as to overlook some of the most urgent duties of earth.[11]

Methodists' main concern was not so much the debate over collectivism v. individualism as over reunion of the various Methodist divisions. There was, of course, talk of union all round; it was in the early 1890s, as we have noted, that the historic divisions between General and Particular Baptists were finally consolidated into the

Baptist Union. In the year in which Joseph Parker made his controversial speech the Baptists and Congregationalists held some of their 'May Meetings' jointly but talk of the two denominations uniting found little support. With Methodists, however, the talk of reunion bore fruit not only at home but abroad where English divisions had been taken by emigrants. In Canada a united Methodist Church was created in the 1880s and in Australia in 1902. In America the divisions over slavery in the 1840s and 1850s continued with separate Northern and Southern churches. In England there had been talk of reunion since the 1830s and some reunions had taken place. Most talk occurred among the four non-Wesleyan groups although in 1886 Hughes and his *Methodist Times* began urging a total reunion which would create one church. As we have seen, in 1907 the Methodist New Connexion, the Bible Christians and the United Methodist Free Churches united to form the United Methodist Church. To their 'uniting conference' came the Lord Mayors of London, Bristol, Cardiff and Leeds and with them twelve other mayors, all sixteen of whom were members of the new body. Also among the visitors was a representative of the National Free Church Council, the most important example of Nonconformist 'imperialist efficiency' to emerge in the nineteenth century.

The movement for a national Nonconformist forum, and with it for a union in some form of English Nonconformist churches, was a product of the 1890s. If the 'Free Church Movement' was bound up, at least in its leaders' minds with the cause of union, it was also bound up with politics, at least in the minds of its supporters. A union of Baptists or of Methodists could be based on shared theological foundations; a union of Nonconformists could only be based on the one thing they shared, their non-conforming status as English Protestant Christians outside the established church of the land. The movement could never be separated from political questions whatever its leaders wanted, for the question of non-conforming raised the question of establishment, itself a political question dating to the anti-church rate campaigns of the 1830s and the creation of the British Anti-State Church Society by

Edward Miall in 1844. In 1853 this became the Liberation Society and nearly fifty years later, Joseph Parker said in the midst of his speech on reorganizing the Congregational Union, 'Every Council of Free Churches is an auxiliary of that Society [Liberation Society], whether nominally so or not'.[12] The question of establishment raised *mutatis mutandis* other causes dear to radical hearts. It was as much the way of the world for a Congregationalist keen on disestablishment to be keen on electoral reform, state education and 'reform' of the House of Lords as it was for an Anglo-Catholic priest who was a member of the Confraternity of the Blessed Sacrament also to belong to the Guild of All Souls.

There had been for many years various organizations to co-ordinate Nonconformist work in both political and religious fields and the oldest bodies dated back to the previous century. The General Body of Protestant Dissenting Ministers of the Three Denominations had been formed in 1727 and included ministers from Baptist, Congregational and Presbyterian chapels in London. Although they were not avowedly political, they did make political pronouncements and had a 'privilege of approaching the Throne' which, by the end of the nineteenth century, had lapsed through disuse. During the height of the controversy over the 1902 Education Bill, its membership numbered 396 but attendance at annual and special meetings ranged from 'small' to 'fair'. A second body was the Protestant Dissenting Deputies which had been founded in 1732 and was, by the end of the nineteenth century, healthier than its older friend although *The Christian World* noted in 1901 that it 'seems to have fallen on evil days'. At that year's annual general meeting there were 'about 35' present of whom one-third were reporters. The annual report was long and 'somewhat pessimistic' and the meeting was 'by no means characterised by enthusiasm.' During the 1902 controversy the annual meeting could only muster forty attenders despite the attraction as guest speaker of W. S. Caine, Liberal Member for Camborne.[13]

The nineteenth century had seen a variety of *ad hoc* political bodies. The Protestant Society for the Protection of Religious Liberty flourished between 1811 and 1857 and was especially active in the heady days of 1827–1829, when the Corporation and Test Acts were repealed. The Society had eventually been eclipsed by the more active and famous Liberation Society. However, by the end of the century it was in no better health than the older, eighteenth-century bodies: the 1902 Parliamentary Breakfast saw only thirteen MPs present. Despite the desire of some supporters to 'take advantage of the condition of the Public mind, brought about by the . . . Education Bill' the Society was unable to make any real headway.[14] In 1893 Nonconformist MPs formed a Committee for Religious Equality under the chairmanship of Sir Osborne Morgan to challenge the Church Defence Committee formed the same year. Five years later there was another attempt with a Nonconformist Parliamentary Council, led by R. W. Perks, Lloyd George and J. Hirst Hollowell but the venture was not warmly received by the Nonconformist establishment. All of these bodies had either been confined to MPs or had been expressions of 'Political Dissent' and had overlapped in membership, support and aims; all had been shunned by most Methodists.

There were, of course, bodies devoted specifically to religious aims. A 'Society for Promoting Ecclesiastical Knowledge' was formed in 1829 (a balance to the older, Anglican Society for the Promotion of Christian Knowledge); in 1846 the Evangelical Alliance was begun although it was not, at least in the beginning, mainly Nonconformist.[15] The need, however, was for a permanent body to deal with matters affecting Nonconformity, to encourage unity amongst the various denominations or at least to cut down on needless competition, to present a united Nonconformist 'witness' when required and to give a 'Nonconformist' answer to political questions whenever possible, that is, when this could be done without alienating the Methodists, especially the Wesleyans. The Church of England set an example in its semi-official Church Congresses which date from 1861. Seventeen years later the Congregational Union's Executive called for a Nonconformist equivalent but nothing came of it. The differences in history, theology and practices, combined with historic jealousies and denominational structures which prospered as membership grew were enormous stumbling blocks.

The only solution appeared to be to go round existing denominational organizations and to create a new body which would emphasize non-political aims and gather a following based on individuals, not denominations. Not surprisingly the impetus for what became the National Council of Evangelical Free Churches (normally called the National Free Church Council) came from a Congregationalist, J. Guinness Rogers. An article by him advocating a national Nonconformist congress appeared in Hughes' *Methodist Times* on 20 February 1890 and was written at Hughes' request. Rogers' call was supported by the Baptists John Clifford and F. B. Meyer and the Methodist New Connexion leader W. J. Townsend in the 27 February issue. Local 'Nonconformist Councils' based on individual, not denominational, membership had already been formed in Worcester in 1881, in Stratford-on-Avon in 1884, in Leamington and in Warwick in 1890. Another would follow in Walsall in 1892; it was obviously largely a Midlands phenomenon.

In 1891 the *Review of the Churches* began publication and it included representative editors from not only Nonconformity but from the Roman Catholic Church and the Church of England. There were also monthly round-table meetings, the first of which included a paper on reunion by Gladstone. In that same year a circular was sent to every Nonconformist minister in England and Wales by the Rev. J. B. Paton and a committee which included Hughes, Clifford, R. F. Horton, J. Scott Lidgett, Richard Westrope and A. T. Guttery. Its aim was to encourage the establishment of 'Unions of Evangelical Churches' on the town or district level and based on individual membership. The aim was cooperation to secure 'social redemptive work' which must by nature be 'thoroughly and systematically undertaken'. At the same time the first inter-denominational ministerial conference met at Grindelwald, in Switzerland.[16]

In November of the following year, 1892, the first 'Free Church Congress' met in Manchester and was composed of personal delegates. There was no Congress in 1893 although there was an important meeting in Birmingham where the new movement was gaining strength due partially to the support of the Cadbury family. In 1894 a second Congress was held in Leeds and delegates began constructing a national organization composed of county federations and councils in towns with a population over 50,000. The movement was not without criticism from those whose support might have been taken for granted; Robertson Nicoll pronounced the 1894 Congress a 'failure' because 'it does not represent Nonconformity and it is wholly lacking in enthusiasm and initiative.' He added that it also omitted the question of disestablishment.[17] It had refused to discuss an issue which to many was becoming a red herring in an attempt to win Presbyterian and, more importantly, Wesleyan support. The organization was already suspect because of the support of veteran radicals like Clifford and Rogers, and Liberals like Hughes.

The Council's Liberal bias, however, was never really in doubt: when the 1895 meeting met in Birmingham the Conservative Mayor welcomed delegates. The official resolution said in reply that the gracefulness of his welcome was only increased because he 'did not belong to any of the Free Churches . . . and did not belong to any section of those political parties to which they might be supposed to belong'. There was seldom a meeting in which some speaker did not refer to the need for disestablishment and resolutions were passed in support of Welsh disestablishment, temperance and international arbitration, and against Tory bills on education. One speaker warned the Liberal party leadership that Nonconformists were not 'mere hewers of wood and drawers of water . . . As Free Churchmen we will not be the helots of either Mr John Morley or Mr Chamberlain.' No one thought the speaker should have added that they would not hew wood for Lord Salisbury; the divisions within the Council which would become so painfully evident over the Boer War were between Gladstonian Liberals and Liberal Imperialists, with the odd Liberal Unionist added for decoration, not between Liberals and Conservatives.[18]

New councils began appearing throughout England and Wales. They described themselves as a 'movement' for the simple reason that 'movements' tend to be better things (implying progress and struggle for right against entrenched powers) than 'establishments' or 'institutions'. Later decades have seen other organizations use the term so that we speak in the twentieth century about the trade union 'movement' or the 'peace movement'; we seldom think to describe the Conservative Party, the Confederation of British Industry or the North Atlantic Treaty Organization as 'movements'. In 1895 the Congress had delegates from two county federations and sixty-eight towns. The 50,000 limit had been dropped. In 1896 the fourth Congress resolved itself into the first National Council with a permanent staff and offices, at first in Birmingham and then in the Congregationalists' London headquarters, Memorial Hall. By 1896 leadership had passed to London and to three men – Hugh Price Hughes, C. A. Berry and Alexander Mackennal and there was a new emphasis. Coordinating social work amongst Nonconformist churches, stopping overlapping, as in Paton's 1891 circular, and providing a national forum for debate and possible agreement remained goals, but the real inspiration was the desire to build an extra-denominational basis for a grand scheme which would unite English Nonconformity into one body. As one President put it, 'this Federation forms the great Free Church of Great Britain'.[19] (In fact the Council was confined to England and Wales and did not exist in Scotland.)

By using the term 'evangelical' the leaders were purposefully excluding Unitarians who could easily be sacrificed in order to get Methodists. It was also something of a reassurance to conservative waverers frightened of political radicalism; the Council was committed to evangelization of the Christian gospel. By adopting the Scottish term, Free Church, instead of Nonconformist, the movement was showing that it was making a new start with an eye to the twentieth, not to the nineteenth or even eighteenth century. It was also a positive term with none of the negative connotations of Nonconformist or Dissenter. In theory delegates met not as Nonconformists but as evangelical Christians who were free of state control because outside the Established Church. The movement was also the best example of the 'spirit of the times' working within Nonconformity; if evolutionary progress led to Lord Rosebery's 'Efficiency', a decline in unnecessary competition and a new emphasis on cooperation and order as opposed to unregulated competition, then the twentieth century demanded a better organized Nonconformity to assume the place hitherto occupied by the Church of England. Robertson Nicoll, who now supported the movement, told the 1896 Council that 'our business is to claim our heritage boldly, hopefully, with ceaseless energy and unflinching resolution'. Two years later John Clifford told delegates that 'unification is and has been the note of our time'.[20]

Enthusiastic supporters claimed that the movement gave to 'the Free Churches a unity they have never had before' although this same observer recognized that it was 'the Establishment that lies at the foundation of our contention'. The new Council hoped to provide evidence of unity by having unified positions on public questions and unified activities on the assumption that where there is smoke there must also be fire. Annual Councils continued and there were special conferences on the Education Bill of 1896, the Armenian massacres, the 'Ritualist Crisis' in the Church of England and the 300th anniversary of Cromwell's birth. There were special services to commemorate the Queen's death in 1901 as well as 'United Communion Services' which took place at each National Council. Money was not lacking: George Cadbury promised £600 a year for five years beginning in 1895 and his brother, Richard, agreed to do the same. After the latter's death in 1899, his brother raised his contribution to £900 per annum. Cadbury's financial support continued to his death as did his two stipulations: the movement should avoid politics if possible (it was not possible) and it should try to create Free Church parishes to end 'overlapping' between denominations (it did so but to little effect). Between 1897 and 1900, George Cadbury alone gave £3,065 as well as an original gift of £2,000. W. P. Hartley also made donations so that the movement could be said to have been financially based on Quaker chocolate and Methodist jam. It received no funds from any denomination although the Congregational Union provided office space in London.[21]

One of the movement's greatest assets, perhaps its

greatest, was its Organizing Secretary from 1895 to his death in 1910. Thomas Law was a shrewd Yorkshireman from Sowerby. He was born in 1854 and in 1877 became a circuit minister in the United Methodist Free Church. He was released from his duties by Conference the year after he became Secretary. Law was 'obsessed by one large and absorbing idea', the creation of a single, united, powerful 'Free Church of England', and he 'personally formed almost every Council in England' which by his death meant over 1,000. In 1910 the Executive decided that Law, who seems to have been suffering from nervous exhaustion, should be dismissed and sent Sir J. C. Compton Rickett to break the news to him. The wretched man made his way to Brighton where after one bungled attempt he walked off the pier and killed himself by drowning. The obituary in *The Times* said that while he was known as the 'chief engineer of a great ecclesiastical machine', to his friends he was a 'most kindly man'. Without him, Arthur Porritt later recalled, 'the momentum of the movement swiftly spent itself' and although many had criticized him greatly for his involvement in Liberal party manoeuvrings (which will be discussed in Chapter 9), all recognized his gift of organization, something which 'amounted to genius'. It seems reasonable to say that without Law there would have been no NFCC, at least not in the powerful form it reached in the early years of the twentieth century.[22]

In 1899 the movement's leaders achieved a striking *coup* when they published, without reference to the annual Council, a 'Free Church Catechism'. The Catechism was Hughes' brain-child and was published on 5 January as a penny pamphlet. By March 1900, 190,000 copies had been sold in England and there were special Welsh and American editions. In Liverpool the local School Board, which controlled the state primary schools in the city, voted by a majority of one to use the Catechism for its 'non-denominational religious instruction'. The Free Church Executive was embarrassed by the action and refused permission even though specifically 'Nonconformist' principles had been expunged by the Board. Prebendary Wace of Canterbury praised the pamphlet during the 1899 Church Congress and Charles Gore, from the opposite wing of the Church, called it 'an extraordinarily important document' because it defined what the nineteenth century's latest religion, 'undenominational Christianity' actually was. However Gore pointed out that it was silent on the 'characteristic doctrines of Calvinism and many of those [doctrines] most associated with popular Protestantism'.

The Catechism was considerably in advance of the thinking of average Nonconformists in England and Wales and reflected more the thinking of the self-appointed leaders than the followers; this was especially the case in the section on the church in which it emphatically taught the existence of a visible Christian Church and not an invisible 'union' of believers, a very 'high' doctrine. It was an exercise to prove the existence of a Nonconformist unity which only came into existence by the exercise. Supporters, however, were keen on its value and C. Silvester Horne wrote that its creation showed that no one could now argue that Nonconformist 'unity cannot be permanently reared because of an inadequate basis of agreement in matters of faith'. The movement's historian has described it as 'a landmark in Free Church history' although he admitted 'it did not take hold on the life of the Free Churches in the way that might have been expected'.[23]

The National Council annually met in a variety of cities in March, so as not to clash with the customary 'May Meetings' of the various denominations. These annual Councils normally lasted for three days and were composed of official sermons, addresses and conferences on various topics. Perennial favourites included 'overlapping' in towns and villages and, tied to this, the creation of 'Free Church parishes', urban work among the unchurched millions, the role of women in Nonconformist church life (there was very little), the need for house-to-house surveys, the present state of the Church of England (normally the increasing power of the Ritualists and their threat to England's 'Protestant heritage') and political questions such as land redistribution in the villages or, especially, education. Divisive questions like the Boer War were carefully avoided if at all possible. There was an Annual Report read by the Secretary and a United Communion Service, something which upset some of the more 'strict' Welsh Baptists.

On a local level Free Church Councils grew not only in number but in the work they undertook. Whereas in 1890 there were said to have been two councils, by 1901 there were 720. In addition there were regional and county federations: by 1901 these had risen to thirty-six, with each centred on a major town to enable the stronger, urban Councils to help the weaker, rural ones. The Council's work can be divided into four areas: religious, social, 'nonconformist' and political. The religious work centred on evangelism: George Cadbury supported 'Free Church parishes' in order better to coordinate as well as to encourage evangelistic effort. 'In this way' he declared in 1895, 'they would do a thousand times more good than by denouncing Roman Catholics, Unitarians or anyone else.' There were united missionary services and neighbourhood 'visitations' after which the names of those visited were passed on to a minister of their denomination. In Birmingham the survey covered 160,000 houses over a forty-eight square mile area although the 75,000 reports turned in were officially recognized as 'unreliable' due to ignorance or incomplete forms. Still, the reality of the unchurched millions was brought home.[24]

By 1900 it was reported that 500,000 households in England and Wales had been visited. Councils began Saturday night entertainments to lure people away from pubs. There were open-air services during the summer on the beaches at Yarmouth and Bournemouth and there were inter-denominational Communion Services as an exercise in ecumenism. There were exchanges of pulpits, especially between village and town, lay preachers' unions were organized and, by 1898, there were two full-time national missioners, the more famous of whom was 'Gipsy' Smith. A 'Simultaneous Mission' throughout England and Wales was planned for the first month of the new century; the Queen's death on 21 January did not alter plans and some said the mission was helped by the heightened emotions produced by her death.[25]

The social activities of the Councils were numerous and varied according to the locality. Watch Committees were organized to keep an eye on prostitution and the granting of licences to publicans. In some areas nursing corps were organized to visit the poor and, sometimes, a Free Church

Help Society to assist in cases arising from previous visits. In Gillingham there was a 'Free Church Employment Bureau' and in Newport a home for 'friendless girls'. Some Councils established a Legal Advice Bureau for alleged cases of discrimination against Nonconformists. The Hambledon Council sponsored a fortnight's holiday for forty-six London school-children while another, in the north of England, got the local School Board to institute a regular course of lessons in temperance. There were choir contests, religious retreats, boys' clubs and cycling clubs. The London headquarters created a 'circulating library' paid for by the Cadbury brothers, which numbered 7,000 volumes by 1900. Ministers could borrow up to fifty books at a time. That same year the National Council began a Free Church Temperance Crusade to obtain one million new pledges.

The third division was the propagation of Nonconformist principles. Various councils organized lectures and magic-lantern shows; pamphlets and tracts were distributed by the thousands and there were courses of study complete with examinations in Nonconformist history and teaching with prizes for the winners. Local magazines were started and in time there was a national monthly, *The Free Church Chronicle* as well as a monthly magazine for the family, *The Freechurchman*. In addition to the official annual Reports there was a *Hand Book* and in 1900 they were combined to form the *Free Church Year Book*. The NFCC published an eleven-volume historical series entitled 'Eras of Nonconformity' edited by C. Silvester Horne, a *Free Churchman's Legal Handbook* to aid ministers and chapel officials, hymnals, leaflets (100 for 1s.) and booklets.

Political involvement at the national level was, as we shall see in Chapter 9, fraught with dangers. On the local level, where a much greater chance of agreement could be assumed and where Hughes could not veto their action, political work was easier. J. Scott Lidgett, head of the Wesleyans' Bermondsey Settlement, warned delegates in 1901 about their political work:

The Free Church Council, special emergencies apart, will therefore best serve the administration of its city or town, neither by meddlesome interference with it, nor by attempting to be represented as such in its political caucuses, or even on its administrative boards; but by training men who, representing its views and coming under its influence, have at once the strength of character and the breadth of conception, which will cause them to secure its great ends . . . in the ordinary arena of public life.[26]

The advice was not followed. Local councils did avoid using national party labels but there was no real need to use them anyway. Political work was made easier by the number of elected bodies; in addition to borough and county councils there were, after 1894, rural and urban district councils and the various *ad hoc* boards, the most important of which were the Boards of Guardians and the School Boards. These last were elected by all ratepayers including women, who could also be elected; in addition, electors had a cumulative vote with as many votes as there were members of the local board. This last provision was included in the enabling legislation to allow for representation of minority religious groups, but it made the triennial elections a running denominational sore and made the Boards particularly sensitive to pressure from minority interests. By the 1890s it was the established practice for Nonconformist ministers, along with local clergymen, to stand for election to the Boards. They were, therefore, a superb battle ground for the new movement.

Thomas Law reported in 1896 that in one Lancashire town the local Council nominated nine men for election to eleven vacancies on the Board of Guardians and all nine were elected. In another Lancashire town the Council nominated four candidates for the School Board of whom three were elected. In Nottingham a six-year period of 'clerical' dominance of the School Board was ended in a recent election when the Council put forward eight 'unsectarian' candidates and all were elected. Similar victories in elections for other School Boards, rural and urban district councils as well as town councils were reported in Lincolnshire and Norfolk. As Law said, 'we are realizing our power, and are beginning to use it.'[27] In 1898 he reported that in Bridlington the local Council opposed candidates for the Urban District Council election who favoured Sunday concerts on the Parade and were able to get one 'anti-musician' at the top of the poll. In 1899 the Secretary could report that at a special election in the village of Barnton, near Northwich, to decide on whether the new school should be Church of England or 'unsectarian' the Council put up 'Progressive' candidates who won the election. The following year Law told his audience that Council candidates won School Board elections in Stratford-on-Avon and Sutton Coldfield while in Cardiff they worked to return an 'unsectarian' majority.

Aside from elections, Councils were able to use pressure to win victories for Nonconformity. In Leeds the Council secured a Nonconformist chaplain in the Infirmary; in Sheffield the Council worked with local clergymen to provide an inspection team for religious instruction in Board schools. The Rochester and Chatham Council accepted a similar invitation from their local School Board: hitherto the Board's inspector had been an Anglican priest so that Anglican 'exclusiveness' was yielding in this microcosm to the new England. In Leicester the Council got a Nonconformist chaplain for the workhouse and it was also able to ensure that the new public cemetery would be 'unsectarian', that is, without an Anglican Chapel. In Chichester the local Council was able to force the Bishop to dedicate, and not to consecrate, the new chapel at the local asylum; even the mad could not escape the Council's power. In Kirkby-in-Ashfield the Council successfully petitioned against the establishment of a Sunday postal collection. In Dewsbury the Council got the magistrates to cooperate in reporting pubs which gave sweets to children under thirteen in order to entice them inside while the Wigan Council got the Home Secretary to investigate the local police force. In Sheffield the Council got the local School Board to stop supplying boys in Standard VII (the oldest class in the schools) with dummy rifles; the Board also agreed to stop teaching them how to use them. The *British Weekly* reported that by 1899, 460 out of 646 Poor Law Unions had Nonconformist chaplains. Of the 186 without chaplains there were voluntary Nonconformist services in 128 leaving only 58 Unions without a Nonconformist 'presence'.[28]

By the turn of the century the Free Church Movement presented an imposing facade but it was only a facade. Guinness Rogers admitted that 'the Federation may not be so potent a factor as its promoters suppose, and one of its nearest perils may be the temptation to take itself too seriously'. Many leaders did just that: Hugh Price Hughes could declare in writing that the National council 'represents the view of a majority of the Christian people of England'. It did of course no such thing.[29]

There were many weaknesses which could not be cured. Wesleyan support, as the *Spectator* observed in 1897, 'was not so extensive as outsiders might gather from some inside declarations'. While prominent Wesleyans like Hughes, J. Scott Lidgett, R. W. Perks, Charles Kelly and Henry Lunn were active and, in Hughes' case, vital to the movement, the majority held aloof and Conference refused to take any notice of the Council. Many conservative leaders were openly hostile to it. While most Primitive Methodists were more favourable, their Conference likewise took no notice. The one exception in both cases was the Simultaneous Mission of 1901 but as this was avowedly non-political their normal wariness was made even more obvious. Surveys of local records that have survived show clearly that the rank and file of local Councils were overwhelming Baptist and Congregational. Law was only giving credit where due when he said that these two groups 'have from the first been the main-props of the new National Free Church movement'. Likewise, both Unions repeatedly gave their support.[30]

National growth was uneven; in the north of England it quickly took root although in the northwest and in Wales it grew more slowly; it was always weak in Liverpool. It grew slowly in the West Country but rapidly in the South of England, the Midlands and in London. To a very large extent the movement was urban; as Arthur Porritt later recalled, the councils 'were never as strong in the provincial areas as Law represented'.[31] Its leadership established itself in London although its real strength was centred in the towns and cities of the Midlands. Statistics gave a misleading impression. It is true that by the time of Law's dismissal the number of Councils had grown to 1,005. But Councils varied enormously in size and strength: the Chew Magna FCC could not compare with that of Leicester, Coventry or Birmingham. Much of the Councils' work was simply duplication of what was already being done by denominations or denominational societies. The movement was, despite all its rhetoric about the need for 'organization' and Roseberian efficiency, one of the last examples of Nonconformist voluntarism because ultimately it was only a collection of men, and sometimes women, who wanted to promote their identity as 'Free Churchmen'. The National headquarters could advise local Councils but it could not order or control them.

The Councils could never rid themselves of their reputation as just another manifestation of Political Dissent for the simple reason that the charge was essentially true. If one looks at the speeches, reads the pamphlets and studies the discussions of Councils one sees that an aggressive political tone was never far from the surface and this was before their wholesale involvement in the debates over the 1902 Education Act. During this, the Wesleyan Sir George Chubb, referred to the 'pernicious influence of that self-constituted and irresponsible body, the Free Church Council'. Again, while the cry for disestablishment was not a major factor in the political make-up of Hughes or Perks, it was so for the bulk of the movement's leaders, men like C. A. Berry, Alexander Mackennal, John Clifford, J. B. Paton, A. T. Guttery, W. J. Townsend, C. Silvester Horne, R. F. Horton, J. H. Hollowell, J. Carvell Williams, J. E. Ellis, Henry Broadhurst, J. Compton Rickett, Albert Spicer and W. P. Hartley. Berry might insist that the movement owed its existence to 'the present-day inspiration of the Holy Ghost. To no other, to no less divine a source can I trace the movement', but as we have seen, other speakers, like Joseph Parker, were more perceptive while the 1897 National Council president admitted that 'perhaps it can scarcely be denied that in some of our earliest Nonconformist Councils . . . at first the inspiration was to a large extent political'.[32]

To others the Councils were a natural response to the growing power of the High Church party in the Church of England. In 1899 Silvester Horne in his *Popular History of the Free Churches* claimed that Councils 'came together under the shadow of a great common peril . . . whenever sacerdotal intolerance had to be resisted the machinery should be in existence . . . The Councils took root.' Hughes admitted that one reason for the slow growth of the movement in Wales was that the Church of Wales was in a minority 'and there did not exist the sense of peril which, he feared, must be admitted, had done so much in driving them together in England'.[33]

Most Nonconformists were genuinely distressed at the changing character of the Established Church; whatever they might say to the contrary, they lived in the shadow of 'the establishment' and continued to feel a certain proprietary if illogical interest in the Church. They seldom could avoid looking over their shoulders at her and when forced to explain this, they normally fell back on one of three arguments. The first was that they were legally members of the National Church by virtue of being Crown Subjects; this was nonsense of course as the tolerance introduced after the 'Glorious Revolution' recognized Dissenters' right to exist, even if it were a restricted right. What restrictions had been imposed were largely removed in the nineteenth century. The second explanation was that as English Christians and as Protestants they had to fight the inroads of Popery wherever it occurred. Roman Catholics could be tolerated but not pseudo-Romanists in the guise of Anglo-Catholics. The third was that Non-conformists still continued to 'pay for' the Church: a Primitive Methodist home missioner complained in 1896 in a mixture of theological disagreement and social envy of the '"little priestling"' who is 'clothed with national authority and paid by national money'.[34] Once again this was not the case. Endowments dated from the earliest days of England's Christian history and compulsory Church Rates were no longer being levied throughout the Kingdom. In 1896 it had been well over half a century since Parliament had made specific grants to build parish churches and if Church schools got grants they did so as voluntary, not as Church schools: Roman Catholic, Methodist and 'British' schools were equally entitled to the grants.

As Anglican church discipline was tightened and as the Oxford Movement spread its influence throughout the clergy the happy-go-lucky attitude of older Broad and Low

Churchmen was put on the defensive. The humorists needed to find new caricatures for the clergy; the older, fox-hunting parson was replaced by fanatic young curates. Nonconformists were left bewildered. A. M. Fairbairn complained that the clergy had become 'more professional than social' and the Baptist C. F. Aked attacked 'the funny little assistant priest, who has taken the place of the old-fashioned curate', the man who says

> with the ineffable modesty that, because he stood in the direct line of the Apostolic Succession, he had a better right to preach the Gospel and to administer the Sacraments, and was more a minister of Christ than Dr Dale or Mr Spurgeon or Henry Ward Beecher . . . what could they do but laugh?

Hughes, for his part, never tired of pointing out his opponents' errors. His daughter wrote, in a biography even more adulatory than most Victorian daughters' biographies of their fathers, 'He loved conversing with all manner of persons, but I do think he preferred a parson to any other. There was so much that he could tell him.'[35] Of course, none of us particularly likes an opponent to change his tack, let alone his apparent nature, and Nonconformists who had listened to Dean Stanley and remembered the latitudinarianism of Thomas Arnold found it difficult to tolerate Lord Halifax and Bishop King. The success of the Anglo-Catholics and the revival of the Church of England produced by both Evangelicals and High Churchmen did not fit into the plan prepared for the new century: it is no coincidence that both Anglo-Catholicism and the new Free Church Councils were mainly confined to England's towns and cities. It was Protestantism, not Anglicanism, that should be the vibrant, all-conquering force. The Church of England was meant to wither and die on the vine, not to survive.

Many Nonconformists, including here especially the Wesleyans, felt that the defence of Protestantism was now their concern. (For many years the *Wesleyan Methodist Year Book* included a section on the 'Statistics of Popery', something not found in the annual publications of the other main denominations.) The official National Council resolution 'deeply deploring' the Anglo Catholics' language and their audacity in referring to the Reformation as a 'flagrant wrong', resolved that such behaviour was inconsistent with 'the letter and . . . spirit of their contract with the State'. If the Church of England, which many preferred to call simply 'the Establishment' or, copying the Scots, 'the Episcopalian Church' violated its 'contract' and failed to provide a Protestant religion for England, then the Nonconformists, cooperating through the Council, would willingly take up the contract and deliver the appropriate religion. In 1901 the question of the Sovereign's Accession Declaration and Coronation Oath became public when Edward VII, with his High Church views, let it be known that he thoroughly detested the clauses denouncing the Mass. Primitive Methodists, Baptists and Congregationalists took no public position although many of their leaders like Clifford and Parker agreed with Edward VII's attitude in 1901–2 and favoured omitting the passages. Wesleyans, however, declared their 'strenuous opposition to any change . . . which would, in the slightest degree, weaken the guarantees of the Protestant Succession'.[36] That same year they took up that old chestnut, the inspection of laundries attached to Roman Catholic (and now Anglican) nunneries; they were annoyed that these had been excluded from the Factory Bill then before Parliament.

One of the many boasts made by the Free Church Council's driving force, Hughes, was that the Free Church Council was the real representative in England not only of undiluted Protestantism but of the *de facto* Church of the English-speaking world. With a somewhat carefree use of statistics he claimed at one National Council meeting in 1897 that the delegates represented 70,000,000 Nonconformists, on the assumption that they represented all non-Anglican and non-Roman Catholic Christians in the English-speaking world. They did of course no such thing for membership was on a voluntary basis and they only represented the local Councils who had sent them. The year before Hughes had told his audience that

the future belongs neither to small States, nor to small Churches, but to great Federal unions of self-governing communities . . . I believe that our future and the future of the British empire, and therefore to a great extent the future of the human race, depends [sic], under God, upon the extent to which the churches we represent are able to distinguish between denominational loyalty and bigotry . . . between denominational activity and schism.[37]

It was increasingly to those churches outside England, to Hughes' seventy million, especially those in America, that English Nonconformists looked for reinforcements. The world produced by the English diaspora had increasingly played an important role in Nonconformist life; in the first year of the new century the anonymous critic in the *Church Quarterly Review* acknowledged the 'spectacle of vast religious organisations throughout the whole Anglo-Saxon world'.[38] It is to the importance of this often under-estimated 'Anglo-Saxon world' and the influence it had on English Nonconformity that we shall now turn.

7

NONCONFORMISTS
AND THE ANGLO-SAXON WORLD

In 1906 a ship left England bound for Australasia. Once at
sea the Church of England chaplain read the Prayer Book's
'stately intercessions' on the first class deck. Down below,
in the third class, James Flanagan, a Primitive Methodist
minister who began his working life at seven and taught
himself to read at twenty-one, preached and 'frequently
pleaded with the God of earth and sea' for a safe journey.
Once in New Zealand, Flanagan, the Home Missionary
Advocate and Connexional Evangelist, found himself in a
very different world from England. He was presented to
the Governor, Lord Plunkett, who presented him with a
portrait of himself. When he visited Parliament he was
shown to a seat beside the Speaker in the House of
Representatives. The Liberal Prime Minister, Sir Joseph
Ward, came up to shake his hand. As he toured the Colony
he was introduced to mayors, civic leaders and clergymen,
men 'with an outlook, who had escaped the ruts of
tradition'. He travelled on to Australia where he was the
guest in Adelaide of the Lord Chief Justice and his wife
who were fellow Methodists.[1] No story better illustrates
the importance of the English-speaking world that Britain
had brought into being, than James Flanagan's reception.

Nonconformists were as alive as other Englishmen to
the wealth, influence and achievements of the Empire and
the 'English republic' across the Atlantic. Love of the
Empire and a belief in its mission cut across all
denominations, ages and social classes. It was not the
prerogative of Conservatives or 'Imperialists'. It was the
radical MP, Sir Charles Dilke, who had created the phrase,
'Greater Britain', and it was the radical Baptist minister,
John Clifford, who later wrote of his Empire tour under
the title, 'God's Greater Britain'. When the Wesleyan,

Hugh Price Hughes, returned from a tour of Egypt he burst out: 'Everywhere, justice and the Pax Britannica. The very donkey boys were full of it. They said to me, "Wonderful! wonderful! a donkey boy and a cadi [civil judge] equal before the law! Wonderful, wonderful!"'[2] As the century wore on more and more people became convinced of the need to 'organize' the dispersion of the English race round the globe. Nonconformists were slower to attempt some degree of unity than the Church of England, which began the Lambeth Conferences in 1867. It was not until 1881 that the world's Methodists held their first Oecumenical Conference in London's City Road Chapel: the suggestion had come from America. Ten years later the Congregationalists followed suit with their first International Council: the suggestion here had come from Australia. In 1904 the first Pan-Presbyterian Council was held and in 1905 the Baptist World Alliance was formed at Exeter Hall.

If Nonconformists were slow to start, once they had they were eager to point out that while in England the Church outnumbered them (as far as baptized members were concerned), in the Empire and America it was a different story as regards active members. The 1902 *Free Church Year Book*, for example, had tables showing that while Anglican 'communicants' came to 3,367,052, equivalent statistics for Methodists, Baptists, Presbyterians and Congregationalists numbered 18,231,588. The future was also theirs: Nonconformist Sunday School students came to 14,091,034. The message was clear: throughout 'the great English Republic, which we call . . . America, and . . . the yet vaster territories of the British Colonial Empire' it was Nonconformity, not Anglicanism, which bore the brunt of English Christian witness.[3]

Because of geography, population and economic ties, America was the most important element in Nonconformity's new awareness of its international strength. It was in the development of the 'special relationship' between Britain and America that Nonconformists once again influenced subsequent English history, however little that contribution has been valued by historians. New ways of thought, concentrated but largely ineffectual attempts to persuade the British that they are 'European', a fear of talking about the English 'race' and its diaspora round the world and the virtual disappearance of the word 'Protestant' as an adjective to describe anyone other than Ulster fanatics, has meant that a once powerful cultural and historic bond is little understood in the late twentieth century. A shared Protestant Christianity, combined with the legend of the persecuted Puritans seeking refuge in the new world to worship freely (and *pari passu* to prevent those disagreeing with them from worshipping at all) and based on the Authorized Version of the Bible, Shakespeare, Bunyan and Foxe's *Book of Martyrs*, transcended political separation.

The very fact that terms like 'dissenter' and 'nonconformist' made no sense in America shows the attraction that she held for English Nonconformists: America to them was what England might become. As Tocqueville wrote, 'the American is the Englishman left to himself'. America had no established church and provided the free market place for religion with no state monopolies which Nonconformists wanted in England. Joseph Parker returned home from a visit, to refer to the 'spirit of equality and brotherhood [which] everywhere prevailed' and Silvester Horne praised the 'freer ecclesiastical atmosphere of America'.[4] The bond between the mother country and her former colonies grew stronger as the century wore to its close. America was hailed as the 'great English Republic' and orators hoped that England would become a country in which 'all denominations will be as free from State patronage or persecution as they are in the great land over which waves "the star-spangled banner"'.[5] To A. M. Fairbairn, one had to visit America 'to discover how far we have travelled out of the darkness towards the light', while to R. F. Horton, it was a land with 'truth open to all who have eyes to see it and those who have not eyes held in wholesome restraint from meddling with those who have'. To John Watson, who travelled under his pen-name, Ian Maclaren, and was undoubtedly pleased with the £19,200 (over £600,000 in today's currency) earned from public readings of his novel, *Beside the Bonnie Brier Bush*, 'the American influence was in general reforming and deoderizing'.[6]

When poor Col. Griffin was laughed at for suggesting

that Baptists establish a University in England, the laughter did not come from the descendants of Matthew Arnold who saw them as psalm-singing greengrocers, but from his fellow Baptists. In America Baptists built universities like Chicago, Brown, Colgate and Baylor as well as imposing churches on New York's Fifth Avenue to compete with the Presbyterians, Episcopalians and Roman Catholics. When John Clifford, who began his working life in a mill, wrote home after preaching in New York, he told his family that, 'Mr J. D. Rockefeller came and spoke to me, thanked me, and said he would like to take hold of my skirts when I ascended and go up with me. Attended a luncheon . . . one of the most magnificent and costly I ever attended.' 'The Americans', he concluded after giving the Commencement Address at Chicago, 'are an inexhaustible marvel.'[7] Ironically, Rockefeller was exactly that type of capitalist he would have despised back in England.

Few Englishmen would have disagreed with Archbishop Benson when he was describing the visitors to London for the 1887 Jubilee. He referred to 'the Americans in general, as well as the foreigners'. The bond was as strong as it was between those who had emigrated to Australia, New Zealand, Canada or Southern Africa: it was a shared race, religion, history, language and culture. It took a foreign observer like Alexis de Tocqueville earlier in the century to describe 'the people of the United States as that portion of the English people which is commissioned to explore the wilds of the New World'. Where there were differences they were between London and America, not England and America and were no greater than between London and the provinces where the industrial revolution was changing the world. In Birmingham people 'never have a minute to themselves. They work as if they must get rich by the evening and die the next day. They are generally very intelligent people but intelligent', Tocqueville added, 'in the American way.' Here was the bond: it was the provinces, not London society, which were peopling America and it was in the mushrooming towns of industrial England that Nonconformity was strongest. Matthew Arnold put it more succinctly:

America is just ourselves, with the Barbarians [upper classes] quite left out, and the Populace nearly. This leaves the Philistines [middle-classes] for the great bulk of the nation; – a livelier sort of Philistine than ours, and with the pressure and false ideal of our Barbarians taken away, but left all the more to himself and to have his full swing.[8]

This bond held despite the massive immigration into America after the 1840s of peoples who had nothing in common with England, let alone with the Puritan and Protestant traditions. Oliver Wendell Holmes, the product of a Boston culture based on Puritanism, reflected on these changes after an 1886 visit to England. He accepted that those of English descent were decreasing as a percentage of the population but their cultural loyalty was as strong as ever, as was their influence in shaping American thought, especially through literature. As the twentieth century has shown, this bond was strong enough to withstand even greater demographic changes than Holmes ever could have feared. In his book, *One Hundred Days in Europe*, he wrote: 'Our recently naturalized fellow-citizens, of a different blood and different religion, must not suppose that we are going to forget our inborn love for the mother to whom we owe our being.' Holmes was addressing those who traced their roots back to the Puritans: 'We must not forget that our fathers were exiles from their dearly loved native land, driven by causes which no longer exist. "Freedom to worship God" is found in England as fully as in America, in our day.' While recognizing the changes that were taking place Holmes described a characteristic which has survived intact:

It is true that the wonderful advance of our people . . . has transformed the wilderness into a home where men and women can live comfortably, elegantly, happily, if they are of contented disposition . . . [Yet] give him [the American] all these advantages, and he will still be longing to cross the water, to get back to that old home of his fathers, so delightful in itself . . . The less wealthy, less cultivated, less fastidious class of Americans are not so much haunted by these longings . . .[9]

Holmes had felt that 'Protestant England and Protestant America are coming nearer and nearer to each other every year. The interchange of the two peoples is more and more frequent, and . . . is likely to continue increasing'. This 'interchange' took many forms. Economically, of course, it had never ceased and had been to both countries' benefit. However, as we have noted before, by the end of the nineteenth century Englishmen began to worry about American competition, especially in cheaper means of manufacture. It was a Nonconformist shipowner, Sir Christopher Furness, who warned that England must realize that 'we are neither omnipotent nor omniscient, that as our fathers have struggled to obtain supremacy, so we their sons must struggle to maintain it'. Equally, of course, the massive emigration of Englishmen, many of whom were Nonconformist, continued up to the outbreak of war in 1914. After that year it never neared the peak of 470,000, which occurred in 1913.[10]

If the traffic in emigrants was almost totally from the British Isles to America, the exchange in religious influences has often been seen as going the other way, from America to Britain. In the eighteenth century, for example, Jonathan Edwards' defence of High Calvinism was read and appreciated in England; ministerial exchanges between the two countries never ceased and religious developments and controversies in one country normally occurred in the other. As early as 1805 Lorenzo Dow visited England and was the first of those many American evangelists committed to 'saving Britain'. By the 1830s the number had increased and these visits coincided with fundamental changes in English Nonconformity, especially within the older Calvinism of the eighteenth century among Congregationalists and Baptists. The most important of these evangelists, in addition to Dow, were James Caughey and Charles Finney, whose last revival tour ended in 1860. It was only thirteen years later that the most famous evangelist, Dwight L. Moody, launched his first revival campaign which reached its peak in 1875. He returned to England in 1881–3 and in 1891–2. As important as the preaching of Moody were the songs of Ira Sankey with their simple words, clear message and catchy tunes. Nothing like them had ever before been heard in England. It has been estimated that Moody and

Sankey were heard by upwards of one-and-a-half million Londoners in 1875.[11]

The American influences on English Nonconformity were far more than just catchy songs, the taking of collections during services, 'American organs' and individual communion cups. There was the underlying, common culture, a Protestant bond strengthened by those churches which built up their own special relationship: in 1874, for example, it was the American Ambassador who laid the foundation-stone for the 'Lincoln Tower' at Newman Hall's new Christ Church, Westminster Bridge Road. The tower, designed by Sir Gilbert Scott, cost £7,000, which was met half by Americans and half by Englishmen. To Hall, the 220 foot tower was 'second to none . . . erected in London during the last one hundred years'. The tower had a suitable motif of stars and stripes and somewhat ironically commemorated a man no more remarkable for his Christianity than for his constitutionalism. In 1891 the Methodists held their second Oecumenical Conference in Washington. The meetings showed

> the great part which Methodism is called to play in the Providential order of the world, through its influence among those nations which seem appointed to lead the development of mankind. Methodism is knitting those spiritual bands which will help to draw the scattered fragments of the English race into that great Confederation which every wise statesman desires.

In 1899 the second International Congregational Conference met in Boston and the Governor of Massachusetts, the Mayor of Boston, the Bishop of Massachusetts and the President of Harvard participated. The meetings, English Congregationalists were told, helped to cement Anglo-American relations, 'one of the most potent factors in preserving the peace of the world'.[12]

In 1896 it was, once again, the American Ambassador who laid another foundation stone. This time it was for a new church in Gainsborough to honour the Lincolnshire-born John Robinson, pastor to the 'Pilgrim Fathers' although he did not actually sail in the *Mayflower*. In 1883 the pilgrim fathers' theme led the Rev. Henry Allon, minister of Islington's Union Chapel, to ask for a piece of the 'Pilgrim Rock' (the rock onto which the pilgrims were believed to have stepped) for his chapel. The trustees of the Pilgrim Society obliged and sent a piece of the relic which was placed in a special niche above a door to the right of the pulpit.

In talking about American influences on English Non-conformity we must not give an unbalanced picture. Certainly by the last third of the nineteenth century the influences were becoming more noted although they had always been there. While England sent no revivalist as famous as Moody she did send a number of famous ministers and the works of her most famous preachers were avidly bought and consumed in America. Men like Spurgeon, John Stoughton, R. F. Horton, J. H. Rigg or F. B. Meyer could be as famous in America as in England. Even lesser known men were received with open arms and, in some cases, cheque books: when the Rev. J. A. Macfadyen went to America to 'supply' the pulpit of Brooklyn's Central Congregational Church he was offered a church in Chicago at the princely stipend of £2,000 – over £60,000 today – but he turned down the offer. During the latter part of the century visits by famous Nonconformist ministers as great public figures, and not as denominational delegates or visiting preachers, became part of American cultural and religious life.

In 1867 Newman Hall visited America, or at least the northern states, where he was assured a warm welcome because of his support of the North during the recent war. Senator Sumner, the chairman of the Senate's foreign affairs committee, wanted him to address the Senate but decided this would be a bad precedent. Instead Sumner went with various other senators, representatives and the President, Johnson, to hear Hall speak in the largest Presbyterian Church in Washington. Hall later had the honour of being presented to Johnson. When Congress assembled the Speaker of the House of Representatives asked Hall to give the opening prayer and on a Sunday he preached before both Houses in the Capitol building. Once in New York he was invited to Wall Street where he addressed the assembled and hushed stockbrokers who had suspended business with the understanding that the talk would not exceed three minutes. Afterwards the brokers and traders erupted into 'God Save The Queen', a thank-you from northern capitalists for his support of the North during the war. It was during this trip that the idea of a 'Lincoln Tower' arose. Hall's devotion to America became a byword and in the 1880s he was called 'an American preacher' although one listener added, 'though allusions to things American are frequent in the sermons . . . he is heartily English in thought and speech'.[13]

In 1877 a new strand was created in the bond between Nonconformist England and Protestant America. R. W. Dale was invited by the theology faculty of Yale University to give the Lyman Beecher Lectures on Preaching. Beecher, the paterfamilias of the well known family, had been one of the major liberalizing influences in American Puritanism (despite his rabid anti-Catholic feelings) and had helped to transform the old High Calvinism into the broader stream of liberal protestantism. He was also a key factor in transplanting New England religion to the newer Northern states, especially Ohio. Dale was the first English-man asked to give the lectures and it was a visible sign of a shared heritage. He toured widely but was dismayed at the corruption of public life which had arisen after the Northern victory and the Republican domination of Washington, led by men like Sumner: 'The rogues do public work in order to make money, and the honest men neglect public work in order to save money. Judged by the laws of public morality, there is not much to choose between them.' Before returning to England he was asked to persuade Gladstone to come over for the 1878 Yale 'commencement' but he would plead in vain. On his return he also acted as an unpaid adviser to Yale about other possible English choices. One of the men he approached was Spurgeon who gave him this characteristic response: 'I sit on my own gate, and whistle my own tunes, and am quite content.'[14] Despite Spurgeon's refusal, the University went on to invite several famous ministers to give the annual lectures. These included R. F. Horton in 1893, followed by John Watson in 1896, P. T. Forsyth in 1907 and C. Silvester Horne in 1914.

Famous ministers like Horne, Clifford, Watson, Horton, Charles Berry of Wolverhampton's Queen Street Congregational Church and Forsyth often visited America to conduct long preaching and lecturing tours. Sometimes they had the help of the same Major Pond who had visited Spurgeon's Metropolitan Tabernacle. The redoubtable Joseph Parker made four visits although it was not until 1887 that he made a lecture tour which was not a success due to ill health and financial disagreements. Although Pond praised him as a 'middle-class Englishman . . . the personification of all their sterling traits and sturdy characteristics', there were problems over whether or not he should have taken a fee for giving a eulogy on his friend, Henry Ward Beecher, at Beecher's Brooklyn church. The most successful tour was that of John Watson – 'Ian Maclaren' – in 1896, two months after the publication of his best-seller, *Beside the Bonnie Brier Bush*. In under ten weeks Watson, 'dressed in a plain business garb – rather more like a Scotch merchant than a minister', had ninety-six engagements, mainly readings but including some lectures. Pond, who 'cleared' $35,795.91 was, not surprisingly, enthusiastic and offered Watson an additional $24,000 if he would extend his tour by twelve weeks but the exhausted man refused. The Major later claimed that his takings on Watson's tour exceeded that from H. J. Stanley's after his famous meeting with Dr Livingstone. He also said, to the delight of those Nonconformists who read his memoirs, that Watson's tour was far more successful than Matthew Arnold's. (Part of Arnold's failure had been due to his poor delivery as few could actually hear his mumbled address.) In Washington, Watson and his wife took lunch with President and Mrs Cleveland who later came to that night's lecture. In 1899 Watson came on a second tour and this time went to the far west. Like almost all other ministers he avoided visiting the defeated South as such a trip would not have fitted the received view of America which both hosts and visitors wished to retain. (Sometimes a fleeting visit to Kentucky was included.)[15]

There were also, throughout the century, various international bodies (which in the nineteenth century, as now, frequently meant bodies dominated by or confined to Britain and America) concerned with promoting various radical reforms or building up new ventures like Sunday Schools. Through these bodies there was a continuous exchange of Englishmen and Americans in which English Nonconformist ministers took the lead. These were particularly important in the decades before denominations established their own international organizations. Anti-slavery, temperance, teetotalism and Sunday Schools each had international conferences normally either in America or in England. As the century wore on and transatlantic travel improved, the exchanges increased.

In addition, traditional anti-popery was as alive in America as in England and politically as important, especially after the arrival of Catholic immigrants in the 1840s. The Evangelical Alliance was founded in 1846 largely under the inspiration of a Polish Jew, Ridley Herschell, who had been converted in London and became a notable Nonconformist preacher in the capital. He probably served as the model for Trollope's Joseph Emilius in *The Eustace Diamonds* and *Phineas Redux*. The Alliance, which increasingly became a *de facto* Nonconformist organization, existed not just to fight popery but Puseyism and also to coordinate Evangelical work. From its first meeting it was also identified with the anti-slavery movement and this meant that it did not establish itself in America, where many religious leaders were wary of too close an identification with such a divisive issue. When Joseph Parker paid his first visit to America in 1873 it was for an Alliance conference: on that occasion the delegates were presented to General Grant, the President.

A more important transatlantic forum for cooperation and exchange of knowledge was the Teetotal Movement in which Nonconformists predominated. The Temperance movement, requiring an oath to moderate drinking or to abstain from certain drinks, seems to have begun in America: the first Temperance society was established in Puritan Connecticut in 1789. By the 1820s the movement had spread to England. The British and Foreign Temperance Society was formed in 1830 and was dominated by the Church of England. Teetotalism, however, was a radical, working-class, provincial and largely Nonconformist movement which began in Lancashire in 1832. It insisted on a total abstention from not only spirits but beer, the staple drink of the working man. It was part of the larger movement of self-improvement by working people and not surprisingly, given Nonconformist domination, it used religious language and insisted on 'conversion' and renunciation. It soon established its own organization and meeting houses which were hardly distinguishable from chapels. Not surprisingly Teetotalism at first ran into opposition from some Nonconformists who saw it as a rival pseudo-religion. With the passage of time attitudes changed and support grew, mainly from Baptists, non-Wesleyan Methodists and smaller Congregational chapels. Although by the end of the century all four leading denominations had temperance committees and urged parliamentary action to curb 'the trade', Teetotal organizations were confined to the Baptists and Congregationalists. The degree to which these denominations had come to terms with Teetotalism and a sign of the strength it had acquired are seen in some figures for 1890. The Baptist Total Abstinence Association recorded a membership for England and Wales of 1,315 ministers and 205 ministerial students or nine out of every ten Baptist ministers and candidates.

The teetotal movement had another important effect: once it took root in America it strengthened the Anglo-American bond. In one area American Teetotalism then affected the English movement which in turn set an example for Nonconformity as a whole. In both countries the movement away from the pure gospel of self-help to a demand for state action can be dated from the late 1840s. On 2 June 1851, the state of Maine enacted its famous act 'for the Suppression of Drinking Houses and Tippling Shops' – the 'Maine Act'. It was an attempt at prohibition that was never wholly successful but it did set an example. Two years later in Britain the United Kingdom Alliance began its work to secure state action. Teetotallers did not stop insisting on the primary importance of individual commitment but the change in attitude did begin to filter through Nonconformity as a whole and it would have long-lasting effects on attitudes towards the state.

The second area where Teetotalism strengthened the

Anglo-American bond lay in visits between leaders from both countries and this was especially the case with the Rev. Lyman Beecher who visited England in 1846 and stayed with the publisher, John Cassell, in his St John's Wood house. Beecher was not only keen on Teetotalism but on the abolition of slavery. The two causes were closely linked from the 1840s and it is not surprising that when Cassell visited New York in 1853 as a delegate to a World Temperance Convention he would also use Beecher connections to see the anti-slavery 'Underground Railroad' at work in Ohio. From early days English Teetotallers had felt it their duty to correct their American brethren when they fell short, a trait which has become an intricate part of general English attitudes towards America. (In this way they were of course only following the examples set down in the 1820s and '30s by British visitors to America such as Captain Basil Hall or Mrs Frances Trollope.) In 1850 the *Teetotal Times* recorded an 'atrocious outrage'. The Sons of Temperance, a secret American Temperance body, had excluded Negroes. In the same year the paper gave considerable coverage to the tour of the Rev. Kah-ge-ga-gah-bowh, an Ojibway chief, who was a Teetotal crusader. What is important, however, is that the chief was also promoting the idea of an all-Indian state and felt that persuading English Radical opinion would help his cause in America. The fact that Englishmen were upset at what the Sons of Temperance did and that American crusaders felt they could advance their cause by rousing English opinion show the degree to which a common culture had survived the political separation of the previous century. The 'special relationship' was well under way.

The Beechers, however, became something of an institution in their own right. The paterfamilias, Lyman, was exceeded in fame and influence by his son, Henry Ward Beecher, minister of Brooklyn's Plymouth Congregational Church from 1847 until his death in 1887. Beecher was the prototype of the 'political parson' and put some of his words into action, or rather, equipped others to do so. During the fighting in Kansas Territory in the 1850s between Southern settlers who brought their slaves with them, and Northern settlers who wanted no Negroes in

Kansas, abolitionist terrorists like John Brown began murdering the families of Southern farmers. Beecher, safe in Brooklyn, began sending not only his prayers for the abolitionists but arms in boxes labelled Bibles. This gave rise to the phrase Beecher's Bibles, a harkening back to the nickname – Breeches Bible – for the translation of the Bible issued in 1560. Yet, in Brooklyn, Beecher acted somewhat differently as Dickens found when he paid his last visit to America in 1868. The author went to Beecher's chapel to give a public reading. When he arrived at the chapel, which sat about 3,000, he was shocked to learn that 'a certain upper gallery holding 150 was "the Coloured Gallery". On the first night not a soul could be induced to enter it.' This had been kept secret from Dickens by the chapel trustees.[16]

Beecher's reputation as a preacher, let alone as a Man of God, was not universally accepted. When Lord Rosebery toured America in 1873 he went to Plymouth Church and was 'greatly disappointed'. Beecher, he found, could not equal Spurgeon in oratorical powers and, of course, Spurgeon was never a political parson. The preacher's arrogance and pomposity made Rosebery erupt: 'He is a buffoon without the merits of a buffoon.' One of Beecher's favourite oratorical gimmicks, which he used to great effect in England, was to lean down from the dais to tell a humorous story but only audible to the front row. They laughed. The row behind leaned forward to ask what was so funny and were told the story. The third row followed suit and before long enough people were laughing and questioning that Beecher raised his hand and told the story so that all could hear.[17]

In 1874 Beecher's career received a setback of sorts when a newspaper editor with whom he had worked sued him for alienating his wife's affections. The jury hearing the suit was unable to reach a decision and although the six-month trial was reported in England it did not destroy his reputation. This had been built during the American War when he toured England to rally support among Radical and Nonconformist circles for Lincoln's armies. He had also become a close friend of Joseph Parker who had visited America in 1873 and 1884. The two had much in common: conceit, fame, unorthodox pulpit manners and a trenchant belief in liberal progress. In 1886 he came on his last lecture tour, managed by Pond, and at the invitation of Parker. His first lecture was given at the City Temple. The following year Parker paid his first visit to America to give his own series of lectures on non-religious topics such as 'Mr Gladstone' or 'Clocks and Watches'. He delivered fifty lectures in the course of three months but, as we have noted, was not a great success.[18]

One final example of the influences which the Beecher family exerted on English life is, of course, the anti-slavery novel of Henry Ward Beecher's sister, Harriet Beecher Stowe. Seldom in history has a work of fiction had such influence in forming public attitudes and the full fruit of this influence would only be recognized in 1861: it was Lincoln himself who would refer to the little lady who started the war. Dislike of American slavery had never vanished and was a favourite topic for novelists like Mrs Trollope to tackle in the 1830s. It was part of that 'love-hate' aspect of the special relationship between the two countries. Englishmen could always apply a degree of moral superiority, when necessary, to the upstarts across the Atlantic, by condemning Negro slavery. Their American allies among the northern intelligentsia were led by the Beecher family and in this the Nonconformist contribution to Anglo-American relations was vital.

Mrs Stowe was the wife of an ill-paid professor in an Ohio teacher training college and she shared the family's abolitionist feelings. She also collected tales from those runaway slaves who escaped via the Underground Railroad. She wrote her novel to attack slavery and to supplement her husband, Calvin's, income. Although she was a somewhat morbid woman she also had a vivid imagination and was able to combine an exciting story with a good dose of sentimentality, much as Ian Maclaren would do later. The novel first appeared in serialization in 1851 and was then published as a book. By the end of September that year it had sold 100,000 copies. It first appeared in England in April 1852 and was not a success despite good reviews in trade journals. She knew that success would come if she could convince readers that it was not a novel designed as mere entertainment but a moral tale designed to expose an evil and enhance the moral status of the reader. She had therefore sent advance copies to Prince Albert, the Earl of Shaftesbury and Charles Kingsley to whom she referred to 'that awful book I have been forced to write'. In another letter to a Scottish admirer, she said 'I can only say that this bubble of my mind has risen on the mighty stream of a Divine purpose'.[19]

In September the log-jam thwarting the 'mighty stream' gave way: throughout that month London publishers of the book were furnishing to one distribution house alone some 10,000 copies a day. Before 1852 was out Mrs Stowe's 'awful book' had sold an amazing 1,000,000 copies, over three times the total sold in America. A Welsh translation was soon published by John Cassell and eventually the book was translated into all the major European languages. There had never been such a literary success in England. Unfortunately, as there was no international copyright agreement, Mrs Stowe received nothing although one publisher, James Bosworth, did promise to pay her threepence on every copy sold at 3s. 6d., less than she could have expected from a modern royalty. A favourite comparison among the book's enthusiasts was to see in Uncle Tom a 'Christ figure'. 'Reader', John Cassell wrote in his own introduction to his English edition, 'we must caution you in reading this book to take care of your heart.' In 1853 Mrs Stowe came to Britain to be lauded while Calvin came to lecture on Teetotalism. Not everyone, however, liked Mrs Stowe: Thackeray began, but does not appear to have finished, a spoof, now in the New York Public Library, which begins: 'An army of 500 thousand ladies with tasteful banners on which poor Gumbo is displayed kneeling in his chains . . .'. The ladies carried with them 'their Koran, their Book of Mormon, the book of their law'.[20]

The book was a triumph not just for the 'Nonconformist' Mrs Stowe but for English Nonconformity. It was the Nonconformist Beecher connection and the special relationship between American and British reformers which Nonconformists were doing so much to cement that paved the way for Uncle Tom. The book's success, like that later of Moody and Sankey, showed that it was Nonconformity, not the Church of England, which had conquered one of the most important mountain peaks of public morality and sentiment produced in the Victorian era. It was a conquest which would be theirs for more than half a century. This was symbolized in 1908 when the World Sunday School Association held its sixth conference in Washington, under the presidency of F. B. Meyer, the Baptist who succeeded Newman Hall as minister of Christ Church, Westminster Bridge Road. The House of Representatives adjourned to enable Congressmen either to watch or to march in the procession of delegates past the east front of the Capitol.

The special relationship was not without its trials, one of which occurred some thirteen years before the Sunday School march-past in Washington. Late in 1895 a diplomatic storm blew up between Britain and America over Venezuela. At issue was a boundary question between Venezuela and British Guiana which had been under discussion for some time. President Grover Cleveland sought to make political capital by 'twisting the lion's tail' and gave an ultimatum to the British Government: an American commission appointed by Cleveland would investigate the dispute and decide the matter. Britain would have to accept the decision or America would enforce it by arms. It was one of the worst examples of the American penchant for using foreign affairs to win elections. In London the government's policy was clear, as Lord Salisbury told the Queen in a cypher telegram: 'Until United States [make] some communication to us no further step on our part is necessary. My impression is that if we remain quiet this feeling will shortly disappear.'[21] If the government were calm most people in Britain took the American threats seriously: the thought of war was inconceivable and Nonconformity united in support of a negotiated settlement.

Again the Beecher connection was used. The Rev. Charles A. Berry was one of the many Nonconformist ministers to visit America: in 1887, on his second visit, he had preached at Beecher's Plymouth Church, a visit organized before the American's death. Indeed, Berry was offered the Brooklyn pastorate after Beecher's death but declined it. At the height of the crisis his church sent a

cablegram to Brooklyn: 'Queen Street Church, Wolverhampton, sends greetings and prays for perfect peace
between England and America. Berry.' In reply came
another cablegram signed by Beecher's successor: 'The
great congregation of Plymouth Church by unanimous
rising vote returns greetings. We join in prayers for peace
with kin beyond sea. Abbot.' (Two years later Berry paid
his fifth visit to America where he spoke 101 times and
travelled over 3,000 miles. When in Washington both
Houses, in an extraordinary mark of respect, asked him to
give the opening prayer as they assembled for the fifty-
fifth Congress.) The Congregational Union's executive
cabled to Washington on 7 January 1896 also urging a
peaceful settlement.

The day before, W. T. Stead, now editor of the *Review
of Reviews* and, before that, of the *Pall Mall Gazette*,
wrote to Arthur Balfour, First Lord of the Treasury in
Lord Salisbury's government. Stead, a Congregationalist,
and the son and brother of Congregational ministers, had
gained fame for his 'new journalism', in which newspapers
'made' news as well as reported it. He now urged the
establishment of a permanent tribunal for settling Anglo-
American disputes. Later that same month he forwarded
a copy of a declaration in favour of arbitration signed by
Nonconformist ministers so that the Foreign Secretary
could approve the wording before it was sent. In addition
the National Free Church Council supported a peace
mission by W. R. Cremer, Radical MP for Haggerston
from 1885 to 1895 and a Wesleyan. Cremer had started life
as a joiner and had then become a trade unionist. In 1870
he established what became the Workmen's Peace
Association of which he was secretary. He had travelled
widely in America on behalf of peaceful arbitration of
international disputes and in 1893 had persuaded the
Commons to resolve in favour of an Anglo-American Treaty
of Arbitration. He would be re-elected for Haggerston in
1900 and in 1903 would be awarded the Nobel Peace
Prize. When he died in 1908 his Memorial Service was
held at Horne's church on the Tottenham Court Road.[22]

Although the crisis passed without armed conflict,
Nonconformists added a call for a permanent 'court' to
settle disputes between nations to their long-standing

demand for international arbitration to avoid war. However, in 1898, when America went to war with Catholic Spain over Cuba, international arbitration was forgotten and English Nonconformists were united in their support for Protestant America. As we shall see, this was a unity they found impossible when their own country went to war with the Boers in the following year. In 1898 the Baptists expressed their 'sympathy with the people of the United States in their honourable resolve to put an end to the intolerable oppression by Spain in the Island of Cuba.' The President of the Baptist Union called on the United States' ambassador but unfortunately he was out. He had better luck when sending a cablegram to the American President who replied, 'The President deeply appreciates the friendly sentiment expressed by you on behalf of the influential body which you represent.' The following year the Baptists rejoiced in the American victory and recorded the 'confident hope that henceforth America and Britain will alike and together, in every part of the world, be the friends of the oppressed and down-trodden, the champions of civil and religious freedom, and the promoters of righteousness and peace.' Congregationalists at the 1899 May meetings gave a rapturous ovation to the American deputation to show their support for America's 'high-minded purpose'. Not to be outdone the Wesleyan Methodists rejoiced in 1898 'in the growing sense of kinship that marks our relations with the United States', expressed their 'warmest sympathy' with America's efforts to 'disburden suffering peoples of the pitiless and truculent misgovernments under which they have groaned' and rejoiced that 'In fusing together the two great divisions of the Anglo-Saxon race, the Churches have played the chief part although', they added as a reprove to their more 'political' friends, the Baptists and Congregationalists, 'like their Lord, they do not cry nor uplift their voice in the highways of International politics'.[23] The whole question of political cooperation between Methodists and what they traditionally called 'the Nonconformist churches' was one which vexed leaders like Hugh Price Hughes. In 1890 a chance arose for united action but even here divisions remained.

8

NONCONFORMISTS AND
THEIR PECULIAR CONSCIENCE

On 15 November 1890 Captain William O'Shea, one-time MP for Galway City, sued his wife for divorce and cited Charles Stewart Parnell, the 'uncrowned King of Ireland', as co-respondent in his wife's adultery. In so doing Captain O'Shea unwittingly offered English Nonconformity a chance to influence politics unequalled since the early 1870s. The response to the divorce had a profound effect on Nonconformity. To a considerable degree it defined their involvement in politics for almost twenty-five years and, even after that, it left a legacy which has influenced English political and religious life to our own day. It gave rise to a phrase – the Nonconformist Conscience – which plagued or honoured Nonconformists, depending on their point of view. The controversy surrounding the divorce gives us a unique opportunity to look at one of the most fascinating aspects of English Nonconformist life.

For four years Ireland – 'the Irish problem' – had dominated British politics and made the name of the Irish Nationalists' leader, Parnell, famous. For at least eight years the affair had been known in political circles as well as the fact that Captain O'Shea had accepted his wife's infidelity in order to further his own political career. The real question now was: what would the Liberal Party do? Its leadership had known that a storm was brewing for months and had hoped that Captain O'Shea would stop 'casting mud at Parnell' if he made no defence against the charge. O'Shea had said before the trial that he must be guided by his counsel. Unfortunately for the Liberals this was Sir Edward Clarke, Tory MP for Plymouth and the most famous advocate of the day. Liberal leaders feared he would 'be likely to do his best to get as many nasty things out as possible'. 'I fear' John Morley added in a

note to Gladstone, 'there is [sic] plenty of them.'[1] Whatever
happened, it was obviously Parnell and the Liberal policy
of Home Rule, not Kitty O'Shea's adultery, which would
be on trial. Could Gladstone, a paragon of virtue to those
Nonconformists who had stayed with him after 1886, lead
a Liberal party pledged to Irish Home Rule now that it
was certain that, if Home Rule were gained, the first
Prime Minister in a Dublin government would be a man
publicly branded as an adulterer? Could Nonconformists
seriously be expected to continue following Mr Gladstone
wherever he went?

On 17 November the scandal broke and on the following
day *The Times*, still smarting from the public exposure of
its attempt to discredit Parnell the year before, took a high
moral tone: 'Even the least prudish', it said, 'draw the line
for public men above the level of a scandalous exposure
like this.' Gladstone's position was clear as he told John
Morley: the Liberals must 'be passive, must wait & watch',
although personally he admitted, 'I again & again say to
myself the words I have already quoted, say them I mean
in the interior & silent forum "H'ill na dee" ["He'll never
do"]'. He added significantly, 'It is yet to be seen what our
Nonconformist friends . . . will say.'[2] On the same day
Morley sent Gladstone a cutting from that evening's edition
of *The Star* which contained a letter from John Clifford: 'If
the members of the Irish Parliamentary party do not wish
to alienate the sympathy of the Radicals' and 'indefinitely
postpone' Home Rule, 'they must insist on Mr Parnell's
immediate retirement. *He must go.*' The principle at stake
was clear: 'Men legally convicted of immorality will not be
permitted to lead in the legislature of the Kingdom.' It was
a painful decision but 'the only right course'. However
Clifford wrote not as a Nonconformist but as a Radical
and keen supporter of Home Rule.[3] Nonconformists were
to be summoned into battle, and Gladstone's peace
disturbed, Morley told him, by W. T. Stead, who was
'going to raise his *fiercest whoop*' against Parnell's
remaining in the post of leader. He was going to 'appeal in
his most vehement style to Catholic Ireland and Nonconformist England' through *The Review of Reviews*.
Stead's appeal, however, would be to Christian, not
Nonconformist, morality in those areas where it would

have most impact on Irish and Liberal party leaders.[4]

Behind the scenes Roman Catholic leaders were also acting but without the publicity which leading Nonconformist ministers, who were also known supporters of the Liberal party, invariably attracted. On 21 November Cardinal Manning, Archbishop of Westminster, wrote to his old friend, Gladstone, to tell him that he had already written twice to the Archbishop of Dublin and had let the Irish bishops 'know my mind'. His view was that Parnell, a Protestant, 'cannot be upheld as leader. No political expediency can out-weigh the moral sense. I trust that the Irish people will on reflection see this. The politicians will not . . .' He urged Gladstone to speak out: 'If you say "do not fetter my freedom of action, & take away my strength by putting the cause of Ireland in opposition to the public feeling & instinct of England, & my chief supporters" – Mr Parnell would retire. . . .'[5]

The first specifically Nonconformist attack came on Wednesday the 19th in a letter to the *Pall Mall Gazette* from John Clifford and Joseph Parker. They wrote that if the divorce suit showed the Irish leader had committed adultery, then 'Parnell must go'. The following day another shot was fired across Parnell's bows in *The Methodist Times*, the organ of its editor and founder, Hugh Price Hughes, one of the few leading Wesleyan ministers to support Home Rule. 'Of course, Mr Parnell must go. We apologise to our readers for discussing so obvious a point.' He added as a reminder to Liberal leaders that there would be no Home Rule without the 'hearty co-operation of the religious Nonconformists of England' and that if there was any hesitation in getting rid of Parnell, 'the Liberal Party in England will be shattered'.

On Tuesday, 25 November, the Commons reassembled to discuss the Irish Land Purchase Bill. Throughout the week *The Times* continued its attack on both Parnell and Gladstone. One of the suggestions put forward was that Parnell withdraw for a while as Irish leader. On 28 November the paper published a letter from 'A Wesleyan Minister' which argued that while this might satisfy the national conscience it would never satisfy Nonconformity. The writer, who was Hughes, demanded that Parnell retire altogether from public life for 'nothing less will satisfy the Nonconformist conscience'. The paper referred in its lead article to the 'vociferous demands of what a correspondent to-day calls the "Nonconformist conscience"'. A phrase had been born which has proved far more lasting than Captain O'Shea's marriage or Parnell's leadership of the Nationalist Party.

The following week *The Times*, while agreeing the Nonconformist assertion that 'morality cannot be divorced from politics, and that character is indispensable to public men' issued a caveat to Nonconformist spokesmen that 'all morality is not summed up in the negative virtue of abstinence from a breach of the seventh commandment'. The correspondence columns of the paper had given birth to a new phrase in the English language. Was the term only a slang expression or did it reflect a reality and if it did, what was this 'conscience' of English Nonconformity to which Hughes referred? Some leaders, like the veteran Congregational minister, J. Guinness Rogers, attacked the new term as 'slang' and denied that Nonconformists had a 'keener sense of what is due to right than other Christians'. He stated the obvious: it was those 'special circumstances', by which he meant increasing Nonconformist power within the Liberal party after the split of 1886, which had given them 'a prominence'. After the 1886 general election seventy per cent of the parliamentary Liberal Party were Radicals and the majority of these men were Nonconformists. It was nothing more than this.[6]

Other Nonconformists, especially Congregationalists and Baptists, disagreed and were sure that as Nonconformists they had acquired through their history of 'suffering' a special awareness of and sensitivity to wrongdoing in high places and corruption within an 'establishment' both religious and political which was based on compromise and exclusion. Politics were never far removed; W. T. Stead defined Congregationalists as 'the heirs of Cromwell and Milton and the Pilgrim Fathers, and the representatives of the extreme Democracy which knows neither male nor female, and which makes the votes of the whole Church the supreme and only authority in the Church'. 'Nonconformists', insisted the Congregational minister, Dr Alexander Mackennal, 'represent the continued effort of believers to get back to the primal source of Christianity.' 'Political Dissenters' he continued, were 'the only seceders who can permanently influence for good the national life or even permanently maintain a high standard of social godliness.' His fellow Liberal and Congregationalist, R. F. Horton, went even further: 'Dissenters *as such* are more religious than they who conform just because their convictions are strong enough to compel thought and to nerve them for suffering in a cause which is despised.' A Baptist writer in 1890 recalled her father's resistance to Church rates and his injunction: 'If you will be consistent Nonconformists, you must expect to suffer in purse and position, and be wronged in every relation of life.' One of the most important ingredients in the Nonconformist heritage was the resistance to church rates when non-payment was based not on a desire to break the law but because of the dictate of individual conscience, the higher law within. The words 'conscience' and 'conscientious' were frequently used and writers liked to quote the saying attributed to Lord Palmerston, 'In the long run English politics will follow the consciences of the Dissenters'.[7]

Of course a lot of this was, by the 1890s, sentimental poppycock, an historical legend harping on battles which had already been won. There was also a division between Methodists on the one hand and the Older Dissent on the other. As we shall see, Methodists tended to interpret the term as an insistence on Public Morality and 'Social Purity' while Congregationalists and Baptists saw it in a more political light. In addition there was a background of personal and denominational motives which influenced the history of the new term. The degree to which it influenced people's behaviour would be seen in the extreme political action which Nonconformity adopted in the opening years of the new century. What was a slang phrase to some was, to others, a true and timely definition of their calling.

Suffering was the key and where all divisions of English Nonconformity had suffered more or less equally over the years had been at the hands of English writers. Tradition-ally hostile views of Nonconformists were part and parcel of Victorian literature. There was a persistent tradition in nineteenth-century writing, especially in novels, of portraying Nonconformity as narrow, vulgar, provincial and, often, hypocritical. The hostility did not begin with the Victorians: Sydney Smith, who, though a clergyman, was far from being a Tory, analysed Methodism in the *Edinburgh Review* in 1808 and his analysis is remarkably similar to those of Mrs Trollope, when writing about American fundamentalists in 1832, and Matthew Arnold in 1869. To Sydney Smith, Methodism was a 'conspiracy against common sense, and rational orthodox Christianity'. 'Accordingly,' he wrote, 'there is not a madhouse in England, where a considerable part of the patients have not been driven to insanity by the extravagance of these people.' The history of Methodism, as of all the Nonconformist denominations, illustrated a common pattern beginning with Wesley and Whitfield:

> They were men of considerable talents; they observed the common decorums of life, they did not run naked into the streets, or pretend to the prophetical character; – and therefore they were not committed to Newgate. They preached with great energy to weak people; who first stared – then listened – then believed – then felt the inward feeling of grace, and became as foolish as their teachers could possibly wish them to be: – in short, folly ran its ancient course, – and human nature evinced itself to be what it always has been under similar circumstances.[8]

Perhaps the single most important novelist to attack Nonconformity was Charles Dickens who, in Anthony Trollope's words, 'gibbeted cant in the person of Dissenters'. In 1840–41 he portrayed Little Bethel in *The Old Curiosity Shop* and for millions this became the model of a dissenting chapel:

> It was not badly named in one respect, being in truth a particularly little Bethel – Bethel of the smallest dimensions – with a small number of small pews, and a small pulpit, in which a small gentleman (by trade a Shoemaker, and by calling a Divine) was delivering in a by no means small voice, a by no means small sermon, judging of its dimensions by the condition of his audience, which, if their gross amount were but small, comprised a still smaller number of hearers, as the majority were slumbering.[9]

Thackeray, in *Vanity Fair*, written in 1847–8, had his 'strong-minded Lady Southdown', a keen Evangelical who patronized 'the Reverend Luke Waters, the mild Wesleyan; or the Reverend Giles Jowls, the illuminated Cobbler, who dubbed himself Reverend as Napoleon crowned himself Emperor'.[10] In the 1860s the popular novelist and the Queen's favourite, Mrs Oliphant, brought out *Salem Chapel*, and described a chapel made up of 'greengrocers, dealers in cheese and bacon, milkmen, with some dressmakers of inferior pretensions, and teachers of day-schools of similar humble character, [who] formed the *élite* of the congregation'.[11] Trollope, in those novels set in England, paid little attention to Nonconformity and told his first biographer that he never really knew anything about them. Unlike Dickens, however, he always tried to be fair. In *The Vicar of Bullhampton*, a new Primitive Methodist chapel is built in the village. Civilized men 'acknowledged that it was ugly, misplaced, uncomfortable, detestable to the eye, and ear, and general feeling, – except in so far as it might suit the wants of people who were not sufficiently educated to enjoy the higher tone, and more elaborate language of the Church of England services'. The Methodist minister, Mr Puddleham 'is an earnest man, who, in spite of the intensity of his ignorance, is efficacious among the poor . . . and . . . considers it to be his duty to put down . . . the Church Establishment'.[12]

It was George Eliot who first showed that a writer could construct entire novels round Nonconformity, the 'little hidden world' of places like Lantern Yard Chapel described in *Silas Marner*. Silas's church was, admittedly, a 'narrow religious sect' and an example of the 'obscure religious life which has gone on in the alleys of our towns'. This was seen when the congregation drew lots to see if Silas were really guilty of theft. Even so, the chapel was still a place 'where the poorest layman has the chance of distinguishing himself by gifts of speech, and has, at the very least, the weight of a silent voter in the government of his community', a form of do-it-yourself religion. In *Felix Holt*, the congregation of the Baptist Malt-house Yard Chapel had changed from the quiet backwater of an eighteenth-century market town due to the Industrial Revolution; it 'began to be filled with eager men and women, to whom the exceptional possession of religious truth was the condition which reconciled them to a meagre existence, and made them feel in secure alliance with the unseen but supreme rule of a world in which their own visible part was small'.[13]

The pattern was of narrow-minded, uneducated, provincial people, somehow out of step with English life but, to some, providing religious needs which the Established Church did not, or could not, meet. Occasionally, as with George Eliot, chapel democracy earned Nonconformity a degree of praise. It is not surprising therefore that Mrs Craik chose a Nonconformist background for her novel, *John Halifax, Gentleman*, published in 1857. Her aim was to show that a poor orphan could be as much a 'gentleman' as someone born to a secure social position. Even this was a back-handed compliment as it implied that John Halifax could really be a gentleman despite his dissent as well as despite his being an orphan. It presumed among her readership an unwillingness to accept that Nonconformists, any more than orphans, could readily be accepted as gentlemen.

Mrs Humphry Ward's 1888 publication, *Robert Elsmere*, was perhaps the most famous 'religious' novel of the nineteenth century, though the reasons for this baffled intelligent readers then and continue to do so today; G. W. E. Russell rightly described the book as an 'ideal representative of skin-deep culture'. *Punch* featured a cartoon showing the confused young priest and hero of the novel, Robert Elsmere, on his knees before his sceptical friend saying, 'Pray, pray, don't mention the name of another German writer, or I shall have to resign my living.' Mrs Ward set out to show how the clergyman is beset by doubts based on 'German philosophy' or higher criticism, doubts instilled in his mind by a sceptical squire. He rejects traditional Christianity for a new, 'rational' religion which is combined with work among the lower orders. Mrs Ward's purpose was to attack orthodox Christianity, and Nonconformists once again were given a back-handed compliment. The clergyman criticizes a Nonconformist minister whom Mrs Ward describes as a 'strong coarse-grained fellow of sensuous excitable temperament, famous for his noisy "conversion meetings", and for a gymnastic dexterity in the quoting and combining of texts.' The sceptic turns on him: 'I am all for your Ranter. He is your logical Protestant.' Elsewhere the 'evangelistic exploits' of Wesleyan Methodists who go about saving souls in odd places is held up to ridicule in words similar to Sydney Smith's criticisms eighty years earlier. To Mrs Ward the real battle was between orthodox Christianity and a new religion based on man, not between church and chapel, and Nonconformity suffered for believing too much, not too little.[14]

By the end of the century the pattern established for Nonconformists – narrow, ignorant and provincial – remained. When Arnold Bennett published *A Great Man* in 1904 he had much fun with his hero, Henry Knight, also a Wesleyan Methodist from the Potteries. When Knight was introduced to a reporter who gave him his card, 'He wondered what "P.A." meant. Not till later in the evening did he learn that it stood for Press Association, and had no connection with Pleasant Sunday Afternoons.' Even when writers like George Gissing were only making references to the sounds of an English Sunday including church bells, which he disliked, he especially singled out 'the most aggressively pharisaic conventicle, with its one dire clapper'.[15] As with many stereotypes this had grown out of date. While village red-brick chapels did remain, the bulk of Nonconformists were middle-class and urban. When in 1897 the Anglo-Catholic Fr James Adderley brought out his novel, *James Mercer*, marginally better than Joseph Parker's attempts, he referred to Nonconformity's 'hardness and sourness', 'self-righteousness' and 'withering contempt' but he had to qualify it. These traits were found in 'small dissenting chapels'.[16]

This need by writers to define chapel life only in terms of small, unrepresentative backwater communities outside the mainstream of Nonconformity shows both the assimilation that had taken place and the strength of old views. Just as it was essential for Nonconformists to keep the old traditions alive to retain their sense of identity, so was it essential for writers to do the same; a wealthy Congregational or Baptist suburban church in North London would never have sufficed as the setting for a 'chapel community'. A prosperous industrialist who entered Parliament, a suburban shopkeeper whose daughters taught in the local Board school and whose sons won a place at a grammar school and went on to qualify as solicitors or accountants would never do.

However much writers from Sydney Smith to Mrs Ward lumped all Nonconformists together in one stereotype, such was not the case as we have seen. Many if not most Wesleyan Methodists disliked too close an association, and the divisions over Irish Home Rule had done nothing to bring Nonconformists, including Wesleyans, closer together. Not surprisingly, therefore, when Hugh Price Hughes wrote to *The Times* in 1890, he acted from a mixture of motives, some of which were political. While many Nonconformist laymen and some leading ministers, the most famous of whom were Spurgeon, Joseph Parker, Newman Hall, Henry Allon and R. W. Dale, had joined Chamberlain, John Bright and the Duke of Devonshire in disavowing Gladstone's leadership in 1886 rather than support Home Rule, the majority appear to have remained loyal to Gladstone. Of the four leading denominations, Wesleyan Methodists had the greatest number of those who were either Liberal Unionists or Conservatives. Indeed, the Nonconformist Unionist Association, established in 1888, was inspired and guided by the Wesleyan businessman Sir Henry Chubb.[17] As a 'Home Ruler' within Wesleyanism Hughes had a degree of political sensitivity sharper than those within Old Dissent. To him the Irish nation owed Nonconformity a certain amount of deference and when he devoted his regular Sunday afternoon talk on 23 November to 'The Public Moral Aspects of the Parnell Case' he referred several times to the undefined 'sacrifices' which Nonconformists had made for Ireland. 'But' he added, 'there is one thing we will never sacrifice, and that is our religion. We stand immovably on this rock . . . and we are certain that any politician who is the acknowledged enemy of God and Social Purity can under no circumstances be the true friend and rightful leader of men.'[18]

There was a second political aspect, this time to do with denominational politics. As we have seen, Hughes was one of the leading 'triumphalists' among prominent Nonconformists and advocates of unity. He made his point clear in a lead article in his paper on 11 December entitled 'What United Nonconformity Can Do'. It began, 'The extraordinary and almost unprecedented political crisis through which this country has been passing is a positively startling illustration of the power of British Nonconformity when it is united'. The Liberal Party had to be saved from the 'journalists and wire-pullers', who sneered at Nonconformist influence. Hughes contrasted Nonconformity's lead with the 'absolute silence' of the Church of England and the Roman Catholic Church: 'This great battle of public morality – one of the most serious that has ever affected the course of English history – has been fought and won by the Nonconformists and the Nonconformists alone.' Unity was essential in order to gain three goals: temperance, social purity and peace. Their aim was to 'demand righteousness in the laws and policies of this empire', especially as the Established Church, 'silenced with the gold of the State', would do nothing.

Part of Hughes's problem lay in convincing his fellow Wesleyans that they really belonged both within the Liberal Party and within the ranks of a united Nonconformity. He wanted to stem the tide of defections to the Conservatives and Liberal Unionists. This meant identifying themselves not only with those Methodist bodies which had seceded from Wesleyanism and which drew on lower social classes, but with the 'older dissent' – Congregationalists and Baptists – from whom they had always stood aloof and in whose history they had no share. Wesleyans had traditionally eschewed the terms 'dissenter' and 'nonconformist'. This is why Hughes used the term 'religious Nonconformists', by which he included Methodists, as opposed to 'political Nonconformists' by which he, and others, meant Baptists and Congregationalists. Politically many Wesleyans were still wary of too close an involvement with the 'older dissent'. They remembered its Radical reputation gained through association with movements like teetotalism, opposition to Church Rates and the 'taxes on knowledge', electoral reform and worst of all, disestablishment. Inevitably involvement in these movements brought Nonconformists into cooperation with non-religious Radicals. This had especially been the case in the campaign for disestablishment. Wesleyans boasted in 1892 that a century before 'our Methodist fathers had little direct political power, yet, in the judgment of impartial historians, they saved the land from revolution', while the year before, Conference declared:

> We are thankful for the direct and the indirect influence of our Church. It has told profoundly on English society. Though it has never passed as a social reformer, yet it has gone down to the lowest strata of the community . . . it has rescued men from sin; it has created a sense of self-respect; it has trained intelligence and conscience; it has led to the formation of habits of industry and sobriety . . . As a consequence it has changed the social rank of myriads of Englishmen.

Wesleyan Methodists' own social rank had been changing: as Sir Henry Chubb told Lord Salisbury in 1885, Wesleyans 'belong to a much higher social class than used to be the case'.[19] With their social improvement their old evangelical fervour which Sydney Smith had so disliked had subsided into a sound middle-class respectability combined with a strong anti-popery which made sympathy for Ireland particularly difficult. By controlling – publicly – Liberal Party decisions Hughes hoped to convince Wesleyan Methodists that there was a safe place for them within the vast folds of Liberalism.

Hughes's view was that Wesleyans should be as independent in politics as they had become in doctrine. He reasoned that only as Nonconformists influencing the Liberal Party could they play the role in national and imperial politics which their dignity demanded. To him, therefore, the term 'Nonconformist Conscience' meant something quite distinct from what it meant to men like Horton, Clifford or Mackennal. To Hughes it was a question not just of public morality but of 'social purity', the term he frequently used. In 1886 during the sordid divorce case which ruined the career of the Liberal MP Sir Charles Dilke, Hughes had used many of the same phrases he used in 1890. Indeed, the Parnell campaign was essentially a repetition of the earlier one. In 1886 Hughes demanded that Dilke clear his name or resign else 'the Liberal Party will stink in the nostrils of good men'. Nonconformity demanded 'moral men in the . . . Commons' and, he warned, without Nonconformity the party would be 'smashed into fragments'. Unfortunately for Hughes, the day after his warning was printed Chamberlain resigned over Home Rule and the country faced a major political upheaval.[20]

There was a test case in 1891 when the crusading atheist, Charles Bradlaugh, MP for Northampton, was gathered to his fathers. The first name suggested to the local Liberal Association was Dilke's but within six hours, the *Northamptonshire Nonconformist* declared, this was seen to be impossible. The Nonconformist Conscience had been, it agreed, 'pilloried in a portion of the public press as an object for reviling, and we are told that it is as invertebrate as the conscience of a man bent only on the aggrandizement of self'. In Northampton it was 'not seared' but 'manifested itself in its power and if in any quarter Sir Charles Dilke's name had been seriously considered, it was at once relegated to the limbo of impossibilities'. 'We know' the paper declared 'that a man cannot be an acceptable politician if he be a social monster; we know that a man cannot be fit to make laws for his fellows if he does not do his best to keep the Decalogue . . . Nonconformists cannot release their conscience to honour a man who legitimately is covered with dishonour . . .' Dislike of Dilke was unrelenting: when W. T. Stead was asked by the editor of the *Albermarle Review* to write an article he refused: 'If I were one of your Staff, even as an occasional contributor, I should have to be associated with Sir Charles Dilke as another occasional contributor. Leaving his adulteries altogether out of the question, he has lied, and is still lying to an extent which, if it became general, would make human society impossible.'[21]

Another factor was a change in attitude among Nonconformists towards the role of government. As we have seen, by the closing decades of the Victorian era the early nineteenth-century devotion to the 'voluntary' principle was on the wane. All this had obviously been attractive to Nonconformist churches which were, by definition, 'voluntary' religious bodies, that is, not established by law. But as reform movements failed to realize their goals, as the extent of social problems grew with urbanization and as knowledge of these problems exploded, reformers turned to government to aid them and then itself to effect desired changes. It became illogical to hold that moral reform could come through the state if those who devised these reforms were themselves 'immoral'. As the 1891 Wesleyan Methodist Conference resolved, 'the responsible representatives of the nation ought to be men of unstained character'. The following year the Conference asked for legislation to exclude from 'our Houses of Legislature' any man 'judicially convicted of flagrant immorality'. The task now was to gain control of government, not avoid it.[22]

To insist that the Christian moral code could apply to public as well as private relations was not new; what was new was the view that immoral behaviour was sufficient ground for leaving public life for ever. Those groups who defined morality for the democracy and issued expulsion notices on offenders, bodies such as the Methodist Conference and men such as Hughes, would therefore be assured a secure place in the new order. This was only proper, they said, because the Church of England did nothing. A purified Establishment was part of the wider campaign for Social Purity, something dear to Hughes's heart. He had long been a supporter of Josephine Butler in her work with prostitutes and in her campaigns against the white slave trade and the Contagious Diseases Act. A 'pure' society was one which attacked and abolished the 'trades in vice': drink, gambling, war, pointless industrial strife, and 'impurity' by which was meant prostitution and pornography. In this the denomination followed him and in the 1890s resolved in favour of 'social purity' regarding temperance, gambling, Indian and Chinese prostitution (as affecting the British army), opium, Sunday observance, marriage laws in Malta, public preaching, slavery in Africa, the problem of pleasure (something which traditionally bothered Puritans) and, somewhat ironically given Hughes's example, overblown language by journalists.

For his part Hughes combined his devotion to Social Purity with his political radicalism. In 1894 he insisted that Nonconformists must 'expel from Parliament, local as well as national, men of impure lives' not merely because laws based on righteousness could not be made by the unrighteous but because 'of the supremacy of man as man – that man, created and redeemed by God, was greater than rank or wealth. Democracy was the recognition that character was above cash, and brains above birth. So they insisted that they would have men of pure character, high intelligence [and] true humanity to make and administer our laws.' Lloyd George, whose extra-marital affairs were unknown to Nonconformist leaders, expanded this point in 1899 when speaking at the Cromwell Tercentenary Commemoration. Cromwell was 'a great fighting Dissenter' who 'was perhaps the first statesman to recognise that as soon as the Government became a democracy the Churches became directly responsible for any misgovernment. His great idea was to make Christ's law the law of the land.' In the heat of his oratory Lloyd George's grasp of Cromwell's political thought was rather feeble and his view of the churches' role as a veto on Parliament was something of a constitutional innovation. He did not specify how this theocracy would work nor did he define what constituted 'misgovernment'. Given Nonconformist effectiveness at blocking educational legislation in the 1890s one suspects he meant the churches should act through concerted pressure as well as through support of the Liberal Party. One thing was clear to men like Lloyd George, Hugh Price Hughes or Guinness Rogers: in the new, democratic century it would be the Nonconformists who would count, not the Church of England. In Rogers' words, Nonconformists were 'the backbone of the army of progress' and 'if Nonconformists are not the party of the people, there is no strength in them'.[23]

Among Congregationalists and Baptists the term, 'Nonconformist Conscience', had a decidedly political ring to it. When Guinness Rogers said that '"The Nonconformist conscience" is simply a slang phrase' and that Nonconformists did not claim a 'keener sense of what is due to right than other Christians' he was attacking the use to which the term had been put, especially by those who wanted to discredit policies Nonconformity supported, not the reality behind the term. Writing seventeen months after Parnell's fall and with a general election only months away, he warned the Liberal leadership that Nonconformity had 'saved' the party in November of 1890 and reminded Irishmen that Nonconformity had preserved the cause of Home Rule. Most telling was his warning to professional politicians and those 'wire-pullers and newspaper editors' who disliked Nonconformist power, that 'they will, nevertheless, have to reckon' with it because 'Nonconformity remains and is likely to remain a powerful factor in English political life'. Rogers, a friend of the 'Mustard King' Jeremiah Colman, had spent several pleasant weekend parties at his Norfolk country home in the company of Gladstone. He knew as well as everyone else did that, despite appearances, Gladstone would not live forever and that with his retirement a new era awaited the party. He also knew how little Nonconformity could depend on the loyalty of Nonconformist MPs like Herbert Asquith, Augustine Birrell or Arnold Morley, surrounded as they were by the lures of the Establishment and the restraints of parliamentary life. Of Morley, Birrell would write that the millionaire's son had 'grown up a man of pleasure without a shred of real Nonconformity about him'; of Birrell, A. M. Fairbairn had written in 1889, 'he is not ashamed of his Nonconformist descent – at least to me – yet thinking and speaking of Nonconformity as something outside him with which he was largely over and done'. (The same could have been said about Asquith.) Fairbairn wished it were 'possible to get over this attitude'. As the years ahead would show, it was not.[24]

Nonconformist leaders were as aware as everyone else that as the British electorate grew (it had more than doubled between 1869 and 1886) the importance of working men grew within it. Men like Hughes were keen to impress on all voters, especially the newer ones, that political debate was not about 'class' issues, economic questions or mere self-interest, but about great issues and philosophies, about the 'spirit and the character of the Legislature' and about morality. Their task was to preserve a Gladstonian mentality for the world after Gladstone's death. We must always remember the awe with which 'Mr Gladstone' was held by Nonconformists. Joseph Parker, though he disagreed over Ireland, wrote to congratulate his hero on his birthday in 1895. Parker was not a humble man yet his letter was as follows:

> Dr & Mrs Parker shrank from telegraphing to Mr Gladstone
> on his birthday lest they shd. be intrusive even in appearance,
> but now that persons of their own social rank have telegraphed
> they cordially & reverently join in every expression of deepest
> regard for Mr & Mrs Gladstone.

Some attacked Nonconformists for not always sticking to
that high moral tone which they shared with Gladstone,
for example with regard to the actions of the Land League
in Ireland. Here Rogers argued that boycotting and
adultery were not the same and that the churches had
denounced violence. In 1890 Nonconformist leaders
'obeyed their moral instincts, and these instincts have
proved right' even if some 'action may have been unwise,
or hasty, or Pharisaic'. However critical the Liberal veteran
was of Hughes's and Stead's actions, he was still pleased
to see that the Wesleyan Methodists were coming nearer
to the Old Dissent. Fundamentally, he argued, Nonconformity was 'something more than a mere objection to a
particular Church. It is an assertion of the right of the
individual conscience, a protest against invidious class
privilege and distinction, an emphatic testimony on behalf
of liberty and progress.'[25]

To Baptists and Congregationalists, political principles
and activity were and always had been intertwined with
religious beliefs. To believe as they did meant that they
could not be part of the national Church, that they, like
their ancestors, were legally non-conforming Christians.
The 1900 Chairman of the Congregational Union was the
veteran campaigner for disestablishment, J. Carvell
Williams, Liberal MP for Mansfield, who had founded the
movement's paper, *The Liberator*, some forty-seven years
before. 'There has always been a Nonconformist Conscience'
he told delegates, 'or there would have been no Nonconformity; but it has been in recent times . . . that the views
of the Nonconformists have influenced the course of public
events . . . in favour of justice, of morality, and of freedom.'
England owed her liberties to the Nonconformists for
without them, he had written fifteen years before, 'we
should have been a people without rights, without
freedom, without hope, trampled under foot alike by
tyranny and priestcraft'.[26] Baptists were equally proud of
the power of the Nonconformist Conscience and quoted

with evident pride Gladstone's statement that he looked to the Nonconformists for a 'consistent application of the principles of the Kingdom of God to the business of public life'. 'That is,' the Rev. Samuel Vincent said in the year Gladstone died, 'Christ in Nonconformity affects all our national life! Now, that is no mean part to play in politics and religion in the foremost empire of the world.' In saving Britain from 'priest and demagogue' Nonconformists will 'help the whole world'.[27]

It is worthwhile noting that there was no official comment on the Parnell scandal by Baptists, Congregationalists or Primitive Methodists precisely because it was seen as a case of public morality, not the Nonconformist Conscience. The *Primitive Methodist World* even went so far as to criticize Hughes's language in 1890. Although their conferences did pass resolutions against gambling, intemperance and the Prince of Wales' involvement in the Baccarat gambling scandal, Primitive Methodists insisted that their mission was 'to preach the Gospel in opposition to Romanist, Ritualist and Rationalist'. As the most working-class of the four leading denominations, they simply had a different perspective. In 1893 conference declared that

> God has used our church as He has used no other religious community, in caring for the poor . . . Our history speaks to us, and in unmistakable language commands us to devote our attention mainly to the toiling masses of our countrymen . . . and to stand shoulder to shoulder with them in all their efforts to improve their condition.[28]

During the 1890s another factor influenced the changing nature of the Nonconformist Conscience in addition to the Parnell Case and the efforts of Hugh Price Hughes. One of the most important elements in 'political nonconformity' during the Victorian era had been the cry for disestablishment. By the nineties, however, this had begun to wane. The 'Liberation Society' had followed a cautious policy for many years and had eschewed a moral campaign, preferring political pressure. To a degree they had been successful: in 1868 only 95 out of 382 Liberal MPs had supported disestablishment; in 1895, after the party's defeat in a general election, the number stood at 162 out of

175. The following year, however, only 86 of these 162 actually voted for a disestablishment resolution in the Commons.[29] The difficulty with the demand for 'disestablishment' was that while Nonconformity's last remaining constitutional goal remain unachieved, nineteenth-century legislation had largely removed their grievances and given them *de facto* disestablishment. Nonconformity's political strength along with Victorian urbanization had acted as the catalysts in dismantling the seventeenth century's Restoration Settlement through the repeal of the Test and Corporation Acts, the abolition of compulsory Church Rates, the opening of the ancient grammar schools and universities to Dissenters, the extension of the franchise and the abolition of the corn laws. The Burial Act of 1880, promoted by Williams, allowed Nonconformist ministers to conduct burials in parish churchyards. (A 1900 act gave Nonconformist ministers equal standing in corporation cemeteries with ordained clergymen.) The 1898 Marriage Act removed a long-standing grievance of Nonconformist ministers: until then they needed the presence of a Registrar at a marriage. After 1898 they, like parish priests, acted as registrar if their chapel had been duly authorized.

Also, of course, Nonconformity was shored up by statute law along with the Church of England and disestablishment might endanger the whole structure. Might the Nonconformist baby go out with the Anglican bath-water? It was to Parliament that people looked for those laws that made and kept Britain a 'Christian' country and it was ultimately Parliament which could give Nonconformity the recognition it craved. Parliament was blamed for continuing the Church of England's 'establishment' but not for keeping the Sabbath holy or for enforcing the Christian Church's rules on consanguinity in marriage, for restricting gambling and the licensing of public houses, for putting down prostitution and increasing the age of consent in India to twelve or maintaining laws against blasphemy in Britain; all these were enforced by Parliament. In addition Nonconformist chapels had legal existence because of the laws relating to charitable trusts. Individual chapels, along with the five Methodist connexions, had also benefited from special legislation making it easier to hold property and the Congregational Union was incorporated under an act of Parliament. Parliament had made Nonconformist chapels exempt from the operation of the Charitable Trusts Acts. It was Parliament which in 1844 enacted legislation to sort out those disputes between ministers and trustees over disputed changes in doctrine.

It was to the Chancery Court that the Congregational Union went in 1898 to demand, unsuccessfully, that the trustees of Lord Wharton's Charity, founded in 1692 to provide money for Bibles to the poor, should have a majority of Nonconformists. In 1890 the Wesleyan Conference thanked Sir Henry Fowler, himself a Wesleyan and Liberal MP, for introducing a bill to improve the appointment of trustees to Wesleyan trust properties. The following year Conference told members that it could not legally change the name of the Connexion to 'Wesleyan Methodist Church', which it wished to do, without an Act of Parliament. Conference went ahead to give official approval – much as the Church of England would do in 1928 after Parliament had rejected the revised *Prayer Book* – by printing the new title above the ponderous legal description to read, as in 1892, *Wesleyan Methodist Church. Minutes of Several Conversations at the One Hundred and Forty-Ninth Yearly Conference of the People Called Methodists, in the Connexion established by the late Rev. John Wesley, A.M.* For years there had been talk of Methodist reunion and various schemes had been considered. When, finally, the three smallest denominations, the United Methodist Free Churches, the Methodist New Connexion and the Bible Christians united into the United Methodist Church in 1907, it could only do so through an Act of Parliament, 7 Edward VII, Cap. lxxv.

If Nonconformists had to go to Parliament for reform, so did the Church of England and she had no guarantee that her wishes would be met. In 1896, for example, Archbishop Benson of Canterbury asked the Attorney General to introduce a patronage bill because 'the traffic in Livings is an unbearable evil & scandal'. It was getting worse: although livings were decreasing in value, clergymen were still buying them as a long term investment. Three years later the 'crisis' over the Bishops' inability to curb Anglo-Catholics was aired in Parliament when Low

Churchmen demanded legislation. Likewise, it was Parliament which gave Nonconformists as well as Anglicans privileges under the law. Ministers, like clergymen, were exempt from jury duty and from being forced to serve in the militia. Chapels, like parish churches, were exempt from rates, income tax, Poor Law rates and, normally, land tax. Chapels registered with the Registrar-General were protected by law against 'riotous, violent or indecent behaviour during the celebration of Divine Service' and their ministers were protected against any molestation or disturbance. The penalty was a fine not to exceed £5 or imprisonment for up to two months. Nonconformist ministers were now able to become paid chaplains to workhouses and gaols. Finally, denominational colleges which trained ministers were specifically exempted from the Endowed Schools Act of 1869 which allowed for the withdrawal of students from the school's religious observances or instruction. The colleges shared this exemption with those bastions of privilege, the public schools. Chapel and Church alike existed within a legal framework created by Parliament and to some degree they were equally established in law.[30]

A new cry was heard in the nineties – 'religious equality' – which had been foreshadowed by the cry for political equality or universal suffrage. The new demand was often put in economic terms. Orators and writers demanded the equality of the market place for all, with no Anglican monopoly; in a free competition the best would undoubtedly win. Disestablishment would come about *pari passu*. Although the new terminology did nothing to reverse the decline in the disestablishment lobby, it did indicate new ways of thinking which in effect made the old battle-cry irrelevant. A. M. Fairbairn argued that 'The Church that makes the best citizens is the best Church for the State, the true national Church'. A Wesleyan body put it quite clearly: 'Whatever Church can succeed in winning for Christ the non-worshipping multitudes who are unfortunately at present a distinct majority of the English people . . . will inevitably become in the hour of its victory *the* Church of England.' The term was not without its critics. High Churchmen attacked the 'new catchword' and pointed out that in law Nonconformist chapels already had equality. What Nonconformists really wanted was 'official and social equality of all persons who call themselves "Christian ministers"'. It was, in fact, a 'mere class cry' by ministers. The anonymous writer in *Church Quarterly Review* quoted an article by Guinness Rogers in *The Congregational Review* of January 1890, which admitted that human nature will always prefer a 'prince of the church' to a nonconformist minister. The real need, therefore, was to 'disestablish human nature'.[31]

Despite the criticism, the new term quickly grew in popularity because it was positive in tone and assumption and it went well with the new term, 'Free Churches'. This was said to express the situation as it was: Nonconformists were 'free' because they were not 'tied' to the State. Any sense of inferiority was now on Anglican shoulders, not Nonconformists'. It was not a label based on what people did *not* do but on the inherent virtue of their position. If only Nonconformists were 'free' the Anglican majority were left to consider their own alternative condition. The new term also reminded Nonconformists of the Italian politician Cavour's oft-quoted dictum devised when attacking the position of the Catholic Church in Italy: 'a free church in a free state'. It was also a term which was more attractive to those Methodists who disliked the term Nonconformist.

Some Nonconformists ignored the semantic changes and the legal and social realities and continued to revel in a fantasy world of nostalgia. Joseph Parker told a session of the 1896 Free Church Council that the heavy burden of being a Nonconformist was always present, 'now coming in one form and now another, now accepting one load and now another, now a pain severe, now a sneer unworthy'. Even so, he continued, Nonconformity 'will conquer all the Lord Mayors and it shall yet bring spring and summer over the face of the whole earth', a somewhat odd assertion from him, considering the broad-minded help which the City of London had given his own congregation when they erected the City Temple in Holborn. Parker did admit in his badly written novel, *Paterson's Parish*, that 'The cost is now mainly social' but, he insisted, 'the best chances of life must always be on the side of an established church'. Nonconformists, insisted the Rev. Thomas Green in his

1890 Chairman's Address to the Congregational Union, 'are not in the same position as adherents of the Establishment [Church of England]. They are in the comfortable association of the majority, and of the wealthy . . . They never need trouble to think about their principles . . . But a Dissenter is the object of continued proselytism.'[32]

Some leaders recognized that the Nonconformist, 'brooding over his wrongs . . . often more justly angered by patronage than by indifference or scorn, is driven to exercise, in criticism and protest, powers he would gladly devote to other and more spiritual service'. But grievances provided their own comforts, identity and sense of 'community' as Anthony Trollope had seen:

> There is nothing perhaps so generally consoling to a man as a well-established grievance; a feeling of having been injured, on which his mind can brood from hour to hour, allowing him to plead his own cause in his own court, within his own heart, – and always to plead it successfully.

When the Nonconformist attack on the 1902 Education Act erupted, the *Coventry Herald* reminded its readers that one motive behind the campaign might well be the 'familiar resentments that belong to human nature' and from which they 'have no immunity'.[33]

Others took a different tack. In 1893 the MP for Monmouth District, Albert Spicer, was Chairman of the Congregational Union. Spicer, a partner in the well known stationers, James Spicer & Sons, had gone to public school and studied at Heidelberg. As a man who was Chairman of the London Chamber of Commerce, a keen Imperialist and possessor of a house on the right side of the Park, he was not perhaps the best speaker to dwell on the sufferings of Nonconformists. He told his hearers, instead, that 'we are recognised and looked to do our share in providing for the religious needs of the people.' Likewise, a Congregational Union pamphlet declared that 'Nonconformist Churchmen are not going to apologise to any brainless masher for their belonging to the Free Churches. They believe that their work is needed more than ever.' Baptists could also rejoice in their new found strength: 'We are no longer treated as social pariahs, to be trampled under foot of men. Not many leases to-day contain an obnoxious clause forbidding the "erection of a Dissenting Chapel, a slaughter-house, or other nuisance".'[34]

A triumphant note with little if any reference to a history of social discrimination was far more in accord with Methodist thinking. In 1895 the Wesleyan conference claimed that 'the influence of Methodism as a spiritual force . . . is greater than ever'; two years later Conference added that 'in members, adherents and influence Methodism was never stronger, or in possibilities of development more full of promise'. Even the Primitive Methodists declared in 1893 that

> God has used our church as He has used no other religious community, in caring for the poor . . . Our history speaks to us, and in unmistakable language commands us to devote our attention mainly to the toiling masses of our countrymen . . . and to stand shoulder to shoulder with them in all their efforts to improve their condition.

In 1897 Conference boasted that England 'would scarcely have been what it is to-day but for the influence of that religion of which Primitive Methodism is the type and expression'.[35]

The difficulty faced by Nonconformists was summed up by Guinness Rogers when he argued that 'the Congregationalist of to-day is no more known by a special narrowness in social life than is a member of the Society of Friends by the special garments which once were distinctive of his people'. Here was the rub. If the Congregationalist, or for that matter, the Baptist or Methodist, were indistinguishable from his neighbour in dress, home, work, or the size of his mortgage repayments; if the 'discrimination' from which he suffered was nothing more than the snobbery indigenous to English soil, where was the foundation for a 'Nonconformist Conscience' nurtured in suffering? The distance between rhetoric and reality was becoming perilously wide. Would the English capacity for absorption kill the exclusiveness which had given Nonconformity its special 'witness'?[36]

Some Nonconformists sought to square material well-being and increasing absorption into the expanding mainstream of English suburban life with the legend of 'suffering for conscience' sake' by transferring the latter to those small village chapels left deserted, weak and vulnerable by Nonconformist migration into the towns and cities of England. Orators and novelists waxed eloquent over the sufferings of rural Nonconformists. They were aided by the increasing ferocity of debate between Nonconformity and Anglo-Catholics, which rose to a peak in the 1890s. In 1889 a Primitive Methodist publication published a story called 'A Vicar's Freak' centred on the incumbent of Hoo St Walburgh [sic Werburgh]. This priest allegedly refused the Sacrament to a woman because she had attended a Wesleyan chapel. Unfortunately for the priest his patron was said to be none other than James Plaisted Wilde, first Baron Penzance. Penzance, far from being a character from Gilbert and Sullivan, was a Law Lord who had been brought out of retirement and rose-growing in Surrey to be the first judge of the infamous court set up by the Public Worship Regulation Act to enforce discipline on Anglo-Catholic clergy.

The magazine said that Penzance had tried to 'suspend' the priest but whether his effort was as a judge or a patron was not stated; nor did the paper say on what grounds he, as patron, felt he could do so. The clergyman refused to comply and the publication commented: 'Some of these clergy . . . get their heads filled with strange notions of their importance, and think they can have State pay and yet flout the representatives of the State as they please. Mr Benson [the incumbent] will find that Lord Penzance is rather too many [sic] for him.'[37] The difficulty with the story is that the patron of Hoo St Werburgh was not Lord Penzance but the Dean and Chapter of Rochester. In addition, the Vicar, P. G. Benson, retained possession of his living for many years still to come. Finally, Benson had been ordained in the Church of Ireland in 1861 and as an Irish clergyman it is highly unlikely that he would have been 'high' enough to refuse the Sacrament to someone for attending a Methodist service. Stories of suffering became part and parcel of most denominational meetings. One minister, again a Primitive Methodist, decried the 'vicious landlordism in close and active alliance with a bigoted clericalism'. He went on to tell his listeners at the 1896 Free Church Council a story about a parish priest who, when visiting a dying woman who later became a 'poor dying girl', tried to 'proselytise' her. The speaker, who was her minister, heard of the incident and challenged the priest to 'try his hand on her minister as a more manly and worthy course'. The cowed priest naturally retreated from the field.[38]

There were those who decried the exaggerated stories and pointed out that 'great is the responsibility of men who thus poison the springs of rural life . . . [and] read into the hearts of their opponents the suspicion and hatred which possess their own'. Sometimes Nonconformist MPs raised questions in the Commons about alleged 'voluntary school rates' which Tory landlords and clergy were said to force poor Dissenters to pay. The Baptist MP, George White, did this in 1901 regarding the parish of Terrington St. Clement in Norfolk. This may well have been one of those cases where everyone, squire and cottager, Churchman and Nonconformist, agreed to have an unofficial rate levied alongside the official Poor Rate. This allowed everyone to get round the need for a School Board with its higher rate. Answering for the Government, Mr Walter Long, President of the Local Government Board, agreed it was a practice 'open to much objection' and said he had ordered it stopped. Although the state school would have had 'nondenominational' religious instruction, it would also have cost more; at the grass roots, rhetoric had given way to reality. Baptist orators however, reflected the confidence and optimism of their denomination and one Union President declared that 'Rural Nonconformity breathes more freely. Its heart beats faster. There is health in its face . . . This fine factor in English life . . . and manhood is not going to die.' Like others he was convinced that the problem could be traced to the Anglo-Catholics who had replaced the old-fashioned, easy-going vicar who never 'interfered': 'If we can only be indulged with a little more priestly arrogance, and a lot more petty persecution, we shall have more and stronger men for our town, as well as village, churches.'[39]

Nonconformist novelists made use of this obsession with Anglo-Catholics. The Baptist novelist, H. E. Stone, as we noted earlier, created a Fr Shiftweight, a 'black-haired, thin shaven . . . lisping vicar' as a suitable villain. The

Methodist novelist, Silas K. Hocking, earned a considerable reputation amongst readers who enjoyed his type of fiction by describing the sufferings of rural Nonconformists; his novels are now mainly collected for their colourful bindings. The following is a representative dialogue from his novel, *Reedyford: or, Creed and Character*, between a haughty rector named Mr Stubbs and an appropriately humble sexton named John:

> 'You've no right to think on those subjects,' said Mr Stubbs, sternly, 'you should accept without question the teaching of the Church.' 'What Church?' said John. 'There is but one Church, man' said the rector, 'the Established Church of England, all those other sects are schismatics.' 'Oh,' was the laconic reply. 'Yes, sir! And I shall request for the future that you accept the teaching of the Prayer Book without question.' 'I'd prefer the Testament, if you'd no objection.' 'But I have an objection; you ignorant people don't understand the New Testament when you read it.' 'Oh, don't us,' said John, rather nettled at being called ignorant.[40]

Historians and observers at the time recognized that the 'problem of the countryside' was due to a variety of causes. Migration into the towns and cities of England continued after England had emerged as the world's first urban society and rural decline quickened. Between 1851 and 1901 the number of agricultural labourers fell by some forty per cent. In the 1890s alone it declined by eighteen per cent. Low wages were a contributing factor. As late as 1913 the highest average weekly wage for farm workers was 22s. 6d. in County Durham while the lowest was in Oxfordshire at 14s. 11d. Bad sanitation, over-crowding, often in delapidated houses, the absence of secure employment, increasing mechanization, changing patterns of farming requiring fewer men, and a system of education for their children which the government admitted was 'not sufficiently practical' also were factors. Farmers, for their part, were hampered by the long agricultural slump, the lack of any fixity of tenure if they were tenant farmers, high rates which were not reduced for farmers until 1896, the lack of sufficient capital for improvements, low profits, expensive transit to market and greater competition from cheaper foreign imports.[41]

Observers pointed out that villagers themselves tended

to discriminate little between Church and Chapel. Writers commented on the general atmosphere of 'sheer indifference tinged less often with bitterness than with a kindly toleration'. One Yorkshirewoman, whose husband brought home 9s. a week as an agricultural labourer in the North Riding, told one investigator: 'I doan't gan to chapel, no mair dis he . . . and we bean't no worse'n them as dea.' The sociologist's conclusion was that religion was an 'expensive, even a prohibitive, luxury which is apt to have a deteriorating effect.' Not everyone accepted the description of 'sheer indifference' while reporting that the only evidence of 'vital religious life' lay in the chapels; but even here their appeal was not so much to agricultural workers as to 'sturdy small-holders who are perchance lay preachers or in the most secluded villages where the minister has slipped into the shoes of squire and parson'. In 1909 a study of Corsley, in Wiltshire, concluded that 'the bond of union between members of each Nonconformist community appears to be close' with the better-off helping the poor. Help normally came from the Communion Fund; at Holmer Green in Buckinghamshire, the deacons of the Baptist Chapel were authorized in 1899 'to use the Communion Fund for the relief of necessitous persons whether members of the Church or not in such cases as they may deem advisable'.[42]

For years reformers had argued that the extension of democracy to rural communities would not only overthrow the Tory squire but the parson as well. In 1894 the Parish Councils Bill was adopted; it was popularly called Fowler's Bill because it was sponsored by Henry Fowler, President of the Local Government Board, the son of a Wesleyan minister. To the Liberal government the Bill's enemies were quite clearly 'the Lords, the Squires and the Parsons'. Great things were expected from the legislation on the assumption normally made by politicians that problems can always be solved by acts of Parliament. One Methodist writer greeted it as 'this glorious charter'. Clergymen, Eliza Champness continued, 'will not now be the only people whose word is law in the villages'. If the Nonconformist hope was that the clergyman would be replaced by the minister it was not to be. A study of the first elections in December 1894 showed that few clerics of any description were elected. Traditionally Nonconformist East Anglia, for example, in 392 elections had only thirty-seven Nonconformist ministers returned. In Norfolk, of 1,011 councillors returned, only seven were Nonconformist ministers.[43]

As we have noted above, the changes wrought in the Church of England by the High Church movement, especially among the younger clergy, infuriated Nonconformists who, like the rest of mankind, preferred the opposition to remain the same. The changed character of the clergy added an edge to the Nonconformist Conscience, especially with regard to the village. Methodists felt the changes most because they had been the nearest to the Church which now, increasingly, spurned them as Nonconformists. In the official denominational history of Methodism published in 1909 the writers insisted, despite all the evidence, that the decline in rural Nonconformity was due to two factors: the first was 'an intolerant clergy [which] have usurped a degree of authority which was fatal to freedom of religious worship'; the second was 'social barriers' whereby 'convinced Nonconformists have been excluded not only from the amenities which they could spare, but even from the legitimate exercise of influence in civil life'.[44]

The one significant study of village chapels, which was examined in Chapter 2, confirmed rural apathy but did not bear out the wholesale charges about 'discrimination'. In 1894 the Primitive Methodists, seventy per cent of whose 'stations' remained in rural areas, discovered that just under 83 per cent did not bother to reply to the questionnaire. The report came up with only ninety-nine cases of 'discrimination' against the chapel and forty cases against individuals while the total rural membership in Great Britain in 1901 stood at 100,647.[45] Once again rhetoric and reality had parted company. People, faced with a choice, normally prefer rhetoric and Victorian Nonconformists were no different. The Nonconformist Conscience, one orator declared, did not need any 'phrase-making journalist . . . to give it a name' because it was still alive in suffering village communities. This conscience was built on 'principle and not pedigree, true hearts and not coronets, character and not wealth.' Nonconformity was an affirmation of 'simplicity and spiritual worship as against a delusive sensuous excitement'. Where better could this be found than in the village chapel where 'the smallest gathering in the meanest place becomes incomparably superior to the most magnificent sanctuary that the genius and taste of wealth of man can fashion'.[46]

In 1890 the 'Nonconformist Conscience', which drew on its legacy of suffering and renewed itself with tales of romanticized village chapel life, had played an important, perhaps decisive, role in the affairs of two political parties because of its power within Liberal ranks. The Parnell affair had stimulated Nonconformist leaders like Hughes, Clifford or Guinness Rogers who wanted Nonconformity to continue to play a vital role in national politics. Between 1890 and 1905 Britain had a Tory government for twelve years and the Nonconformist Conscience found opposition easier than support. In domestic policies it was mainly heard on education and matters of public morality but in foreign relations it also spoke out. In the Venezuelan crisis it had urged a peaceful settlement, the avoidance of a 'fratricidal' war with America and the value of international arbitration. In the years between 1895 and 1897 it also spoke out with regard to the waves of massacres carried out against Christians in Turkish Armenia. Here it spoke not to urge peace but to force international action by Christian Europe to help fellow Christians. It was the voice of right against government manoeuvrings and international diplomacy and it failed.

The protests over Lord Salisbury's refusal to intervene were not, of course, confined to Nonconformists but theirs was the most important religious campaign. The height of the protests came on 29 April 1896 when a special Memorial Service for Armenian Martyrs was held at Hughes's St James's Hall. Most of the audience came in mourning and some of the biggest names in Nonconformity were on the platform: Hugh Price Hughes, John Clifford, Monro Gibson, F. B. Meyer, Oswald Dykes, J. B. Paton, Percy Bunting and Henry Lunn. Also on the platform was the Liberal aristocrat, Lady Henry Somerset, a veteran temperance campaigner. Clifford had already allowed his church in Paddington to be used by exiled Armenians for their religious services. The Radical MP for Holmfirth, H. J. Wilson, described as 'the Nonconformist Conscience incarnate' was at the meeting and wrote to his wife:

> Lady Henry Somerset got an 'ovation' when she finished – the biggest of any. The 2nd best was Dr. Clifford, when he began. A long list of noblemen & bishops, etc. was read out as sympathising. Gladstone was cheered loudest, & Genl. Booth next. These incidents prove what a power the 'Nonconformist conscience' is, – it formed the bulk of the meeting.[47]

In the event there were moves behind the scenes, as there had been in 1890: Canon Scott Holland asked Bishop Davidson to urge the Queen to approach the Russian and German Emperors about a joint demand by the great Christian powers that the Sultan stop the massacres. Although Victoria disliked the thought of war even more than the massacres themselves, she made the approach, but to no avail. The Nonconformist protests on behalf of persecuted Christians will always stand to their credit as much as Christendom's refusal to act stands to its discredit.

The greatest test for the Nonconformist Conscience came in 1899 with the Boer War. The Armenian protests had arisen from a genuine and credible outrage at the sufferings endured by fellow Christians and were based on the reasonable proposition that a great power's foreign policy should be based at least in part on religious factors. Here Radical, Liberal, Liberal Unionist and Conservative Nonconformists could unite. Likewise the demand for a peaceful settlement with America united all Nonconformists as it did all Englishmen. Increasingly, however, such unity would be rare. R. F. Horton admitted in 1897 the difficulty facing Nonconformists and foresaw that it would only get worse because 'large numbers . . . are Conservatives now, and still more are Liberal Unionists; while in that political cleavage of the future, between old Liberalism and the Labour Party, both sides are equally represented'. It was in 1899 that the Nonconformist Conscience came to grief. Was the Boer War wrong in inception? Should new territories be added to the Empire in order to protect English settlers in the Boer Republics? Were the means by which it was being fought 'barbarous'? Was the government being duped by a Machiavellian Colonial Secretary, Chamberlain, himself a Nonconformist? Was it a war, as some Radicals claimed, merely to extend British capitalism and not to protect the integrity of the Empire?[48]

A good number of leading ministers opposed the war including John Clifford, J. C. Carlile, Alexander Fairbairn, Silas K. Hocking, F. B. Meyer, C. Silvester Horne, J. H. Hollowell, Alexander Mackennal, Alexander Maclaren, C. F. Aked and A. T. Guttery. In addition Horton and J. Guinness Rogers were mildly opposed; Rogers argued in December 1899 that the war was 'offensive to the moral sense' but reminded fellow-opponents that the Boers were not without guilt. The task was to 'muddle out of it'. Opponents were mainly Baptists and Congregationalists with some Primitive Methodists, Quakers and members of the United Methodist Free Church (one of the minor Methodist denominations). Wesleyans were noticeably absent. Roughly speaking the Nonconformist Conscience had split along the lines of Old Dissent *versus* Methodist. Hocking recalled that the Stop the War Committee, of which Clifford was President, had behind it Quakers, Unitarians, a 'considerable number of Baptist ministers', a 'few Congregationalists' but that 'The Methodists, as a whole, ignored us'.[49]

On 14 December 1901 the *Daily News*, now owned by George Cadbury and a leading opponent of the Boer war, printed the names of 5,270 ministers who had signed the 'Peace Manifesto'. The paper hailed it as a sign of the alliance between English and European Protestants against the war. Soon, however, a debate erupted about the importance of the Manifesto. The Rev. W. E. Blomfield, pastor of Queen's Road Baptist Church in Coventry argued that as there were 14,609 Nonconformist ministers in the United Kingdom, the overwhelming majority had not signed. One-half of all Baptist ministers, two-thirds of all Congregational, over two-thirds of all Presbyterians and four-fifths of all Wesleyan ministers had not signed: 'So much for the solidarity of the Free Church ministers.' Of course, one can do a lot with statistics; there were, at the end of 1901, 10,097 ministers in England and Wales, where, after all, the vast bulk of Nonconformists lived.

When one places the 5,270 names against this total, their strength grows to over half (52 per cent). Some ministers suffered because of the stand they had taken. The windows of John Clifford's church were smashed. Hocking found that preaching engagements were cancelled and that some bookshops refused to carry his novels. His home would have been destroyed by a mob on Mafeking night had not the mob attacked the wrong house.[50]

One should add that in many cases the anti-war position taken by a minister did not necessarily reflect the thinking of his congregation. Indeed, it does not seem unreasonable to assume that the strength of anti-war feeling was stronger within the Baptist and Congregational ministry than within the laity. Also, there were several influential ministers who actively supported the war. The President of the Wesleyan Methodist Connexion for 1899–1900, F. W. Macdonald, was one. Macdonald, one of whose grandsons was Rudyard Kipling, urged Wesleyans to contribute to the Lord Mayor's Transvaal War Fund for wounded soldiers and by May 1900 they had given £10,483. When the minister of City Road Chapel, the Wesleyans' London shrine, invited Joseph Chamberlain to attend a fund-raising luncheon, the invitation had to be withdrawn when a storm of opposition arose. Later Macdonald asked Chamberlain to a private dinner party which included Hughes and J. H. Rigg, Principal of the denomination's Westminster Teacher Training College, a past President of the Connexion and for many years editor of *London Quarterly Review*. For his part Hughes used *The Methodist Times* to support the war with his accustomed vigour. Another famous minister in favour of the war was the Presbyterian, John Watson. In addition, Joseph Parker, whom those in the Radical tradition would have hoped to include in the anti-war ranks, supported the Government. Finally, both leading Nonconformist newspapers, *The Christian World* and the *British Weekly*, supported the war.[51]

While the anti-war movement had little success with most leading denominations, they had some success with the Baptists. John Clifford was Baptist Union President in 1899 but moderated his official address. He urged Baptists to 'take the higher path again' even if the anti-Boer reports of the 'yellowest paper of the yellow press' were true. The official resolution which was unanimously adopted was moderate and urged a peaceful settlement. It did, however, recognize the difficulties facing the government and the legitimate grievances of British settlers in Boer territories. The Union further dampened the anti-war spirit in 1900, with a general election looming. It urged Baptists to remember that there were other issues than the war, issues like licensing reform, housing of the poor, education, land law reform and 'religious equality'. It went on to 'condemn' war in general without specifically mentioning South Africa. It reaffirmed its belief in international arbitration and welcomed the creation of the new International Court at the Hague. The growing anti-war feeling found expression, however, in the following appeal to Baptists to 'seek to awaken the public mind to the alarming growth of militarism; to the revival of racial animosity; to the moral not less than the physical evils of war; and to cultivate in every possible way the spirit of international brotherhood'. Its last word on the war came in 1901, in a 'Patriotic Declaration' of loyalty to the new King, when it referred to the 'horrors of war' and prayed 'for a speedy settlement of an honourable and lasting peace'.[52]

Congregationalists were simply too divided to speak with one voice although in 1896 their Union had denounced, in a resolution on International Arbitration but with reference to the Jameson Raid, the 'vainglorious and militant temper' of that event. In 1900 the denomination's spring meeting refused to act, despite appeals from 414 Dutch ministers and the Congregational Union of Natal because of 'the wide differences of opinion that exist in the churches'. In the autumn, the Chairman, the Radical MP J. Carvell Williams, sadly admitted that 'We have been so sharply, so miserably divided . . . that this union has thought it better to keep silence than to speak'. He went on to denounce the growth of militarism and the jingoistic fever. In 1901 the Union did agree sufficiently to urge on the government 'a magnanimous and conciliatory policy' in order to achieve a 'secure and lasting peace'.[53]

The two major branches of Methodism were frightened of divisions along political lines and the Primitive

Methodist Connexion refused to comment on the war. Wesleyans were warned of the dangers involved when churches got involved in political battles: 'Public action' the 1900 Conference's Annual Address warned, 'tends to become political and political differences are a standing menace to our religious unity. Only by an exercise of constant forbearance . . . [and] by a firm control of personal temper . . . shall we escape . . . dissension.' In 1900, while Congregationalists stayed silent and Baptists gave tacit approval to the anti-war movement, the Wesleyan Conference warned the Government against 'arrogance and abuse of power' and against forgetting the rights of the 'native races'. It went on to 'rejoice at the ardent patriotism that this crisis has elicited, at the readiness of devotion shown by all classes' in the Empire. It saw in the fervour of patriotism 'an example to the people of Christ'. The number of Wesleyan Methodists in the Armed Services (Army, Royal Navy and Militia) almost doubled between 1890 and 1901, from 18,898 to 36,639 – an increase of ninety-four per cent. Given that English Nonconformists had only made up some four per cent of the Army in figures released in 1880, Methodists undoubtedly made up the vast majority. (Wesleyans were the only major denomination to give the number of their men in the Services.)[54]

Opponents of the war naturally looked to the National Free Church Council for support but were again to be disappointed. They later complained that 'the "irresistible force" then was not the Nonconformist (or any other) conscience, but a music-hall excrescence of braggart Jingoism, which drove the Council of . . . the Free Churches ignominiously to its tent'. Its attitude was nothing less than 'the Great Apostasy.' In 1900 the annual meeting saw a head-on clash. That year's president was the Wesleyan C. H. Kelly, and the executive had stated that the war was not to be discussed. Clifford, however, drew up a private resolution calling for peace which he circulated on the floor. Kelly asked Clifford to withdraw his resolution after which he came onto the platform. There he pulled the resolution out of his pocket. It was concerned, he said, not with the war but only with peace terms: it would be a 'somewhat pathetic spectacle' if the Council, which claimed to speak for all of Nonconformity, took no stand. The resolution was rejected and Kelly later announced that the petitioners had changed their designation from 'representatives' of the churches to 'members of various Nonconformist churches' to avoid splitting the movement.[55]

Finally, in 1901, the Council agreed without debate to adopt *nem. con.* a resolution moved by the 1900 President, Alexander Mackennal, a strong pro-Boer. It decried war in general, recognized the differences of opinion concerning the war's origins and urged all Nonconformist denominations to pray for peace and a just settlement. The Council had to beware not only of offending strong supporters, like Hugh Price Hughes, but of alienating the Wesleyan Methodists without whose support the Council could never succeed. Likewise delegates could not offend men like George Cadbury; although he denounced the war, he also feared too close an involvement by the Council in politics. More importantly, Cadbury and his brother Richard had long been among the movement's greatest financial supporters. Some local Free Church Councils, like that in Sheffield, were able to influence the course of events locally. The Sheffield Council successfully memorialized the town's School Board against its decision to supply all boys in Standard VII (the highest form in state primary schools) with dummy rifles and to enforce compulsory drill. While such successes were possible on the local level, none was on the national. The success in 1890 had come about because Nonconformity and the Liberal Party were, at the end of the day, united and because Nonconformity could speak with one voice. In 1899–1901 both Party and chapel were hopelessly divided and the Nonconformist Conscience lost its voice.[56]

Ever since it first saw the light of day, the Nonconformist Conscience had its critics. Those within Nonconformity, like Guinness Rogers, modified their criticism as the heat of debate caused them to see the moral advantage the term gave Nonconformity. The 1892 article in the *Church Quarterly Review*, which was specifically addressed to the new cry, 'religious equality', attacked the 'selfish clamour of "the Nonconformist Conscience"' and behind it the Nonconformist minister, the 'spoilt boy of the State, the petted child of the municipalities' because he is 'the chaplain to a powerful minority, which possesses votes enough to turn the scale at a parliamentary election'. J. R. Diggle, Tory Chairman of the London School Board from 1885 to 1894, had much experience in dealing with Nonconformist opponents and was genuinely hated by them. He admitted that 'the early Nonconformists undoubtedly had grievances' but added that 'the existence of those grievances appears to have resulted in a state of mind which is totally oblivious of the grievances of others. Thus there has been a quasi-monopoly of grievance in the Nonconformist mind.' This had allowed the selective radical consciences of men like Edward Baines in the earlier decades of the century who could weep over the alleged condition of Negro slaves in America while forgetting the child labourers in their own country. Perhaps the most trenchant contemporary criticism came from the historian and Liberal Unionist MP for the University of Dublin, W. E. H. Lecky. He argued in his book, *Democracy and Liberty*, that the bulk of Nonconformist leaders had been silent over Irish nationalist leaders' 'complicity' in terrorist acts and that their silence was only broken in 1890 by an 'explosion of moral indignation' because 'it was intolerable that a truly religious party should be in alliance with a politician guilty of such an act'. 'Can those who witnessed this grotesque exhibition wonder' he asked, 'at the charge of Pharisaism and hypocrisy which foreign observers so abundantly bring against English public opinion? Can they be surprised that "the Nonconformist conscience" is rapidly becoming a byword in England, much like the "moral sentiments" of Joseph Surface?'[57]

While most Churchmen strongly attacked the term, some, like Fr James Adderley, envied the Nonconformists their conscience and, charitably forgetting the divisions over the Boer War, praised them for having a 'really united opinion'. 'Never let us be so unChristian as to laugh at the Nonconformist Conscience. Would to God there were a Church one!' The Tory *Blackwoods Magazine* wrote that 'the Nonconformist Conscience is as flexible as india-rubber. You can pull it any way you like, and you will find it always stretches away from truth or honesty.' It was 'as valiant as Ancient Pistol himself'. In 1903, admittedly in the heat of the debate over the 1902 Education Bill an anonymous book attacked what it called the 'Nonconform-istconscience' as having 'no openness, no honesty, [and] no receptivity for frankness'. 'Like the Zulu' the writer continued, the Nonconformist 'waxes fat for want of war.' Nonconformity produces 'hordes of smugs, prigs and toshers'. Its most famous ministers are seized by a 'vulgar thirst for publicity, fame, notoriety'. The rank and file of its ministry come off little better; the Nonconformist minister

> is merely human. He goes with the crowd, the worldly crowd, and where success and prosperity are, there he will be also. His entire training and upbringing qualify him for this. He is destined from the earliest period of his studies to be a great man in a little world, and from the moment he is set to go straight for the rostrum or the pulpit he has it impressed on him that he is not as his fellow-creatures are, but a superior animal.

In eight out of nine cases the minister was 'designed by nature to be a working man, a clerk or an elementary teacher'. A somewhat less outraged critic felt that 'while the Church of England has largely learned the lesson of charity and toleration, many modern Dissenters linger in the persecuting stage of evolution'. This writer especially singled out the Free Church Council and its leaders, Hughes, Clifford and Horton who constituted a 'ministerial oligarchy leading a political caucus', a 'Nonconformist House of Lords'. Over the years the Nonconformist Conscience came to mean for many a selective application of rigid rules. E. E. Kellett, the Methodist writer, recalled in the 1930s that 'Nonconformists were accused of having conscientious scruples about the vices of others, while hugging their own. Like the old Puritans, they "compounded for sins they were inclined to by damning those they had no mind to".'[58]

To others the phrase became an object of fun, a symbol of applied but selective morality. When examining the accounts of a Church school in his diocese Bishop Stubbs came across the term 'occasional monitor'. 'What is that? Oh, I see,' he said, 'I suppose it is the *Nonconformist conscience.'* Although Max Beerbohm quipped in the third volume of the *Yellow Book* that 'The Nonconformist Conscience makes cowards of us all', the most famous literary use came in Oscar Wilde's 1892 play, 'Lady Windermere's Fan' in Act III when Cecil Graham says to Lady Windermere:

> Oh! gossip is charming! History is merely gossip. But scandal is gossip made tedious by morality. Now, I never moralise. A man who moralises is usually a hypocrite, and a woman who moralises is invariably plain. There is nothing in the whole world so unbecoming to a woman as a Nonconformist conscience. And most women know it, I'm glad to say.

Perhaps the 1899 Chairman of the Congregational Union remembered the play, or perhaps he was referring to the long literary tradition regarding Nonconformity, when he said:

> It is easy to raise a laugh at the Nonconformist Conscience. To some minds anything pertaining to Nonconformity appears to be chiefly matter for amusement. But let the stupid world make merry as it will, I rejoice in the Nonconformist Conscience, and am deeply thankful for it.[59]

As we have seen, the Parnell Divorce Case, the subsequent popularity of the phrase, and certain political successes in the 1890s led observers to see in English Nonconformity a much greater political unity than existed. The Boer War showed this. Guinness Rogers was correct when he said that the Nonconformist Conscience, as it operated in 1890, was only the accepted Christian conscience applied to men in public life. Nonconformity had power within the Liberal Party and this power allowed it to stand outside the give-and-take of parliamentary life and to act as a 'monitor' – to use Bishop Stubbs' phrase – as well as a prophet. As such it could draw the Party back to fundamentals, much as trade union leaders and annual conferences would do to the Labour Party in the years after the Second World War.

Behind the apparent unanimity lay a basic disagreement as to the role Nonconformity should play in political life. To Congregationalists and, to a lesser degree, to Baptists, being credited with a peculiar 'conscience' was a recognition of an historical truth: it showed that to be a Nonconformist meant to be involved in political struggle through the party of reform. It was, as the Congregational writer W. B. Selbie pointed out, a voice 'which the forces of privilege and reaction have every reason to fear'. To Methodists it meant something quite different, the application of the Christian moral code to men in public life to the extent that a violation meant the end of a man's career. In effect, in either interpretation, it gave all the churches, but in practice the Nonconformists, a perpetual veto in national politics. To the anonymous writer in the *Church Quarterly Review*, it betrayed a collapse in the old belief in voluntarism and a new 'Erastian faith in Parliaments'.[60] Put in different terms, it showed the extent and nature of Nonconformity's power and the degree to which it had been absorbed into the mainstream of English life. The greatest test to which Nonconformity's peculiar conscience would be put came in 1902 when the Government introduced an Education Bill which, at the time, was seen as undermining all the cherished hopes and dreams for the new century, the century that was meant to be theirs and theirs alone.

9

PASSIVE RESISTANCE
AND NONCONFORMIST POWER,
1902—1914

In Coronation year – 1902 – the confidence with which Nonconformists viewed the new century was strengthened by the highest authority in the Empire. The new King personally commanded that Nonconformist representatives be invited to the Coronation for the first time in history. It was a fitting recognition of their strength and influence throughout society as well as politics. In the Commons, well over half those Liberal MPs who queued to take the new Oath of Allegiance were Nonconformists – 106 out of 186.[1] In the summer of that same year the Boer War ended and with it, those arguments that had so divided the Party as well as Nonconformists. It also seemed that the vexed question of Irish Home Rule had receded. The one annoyance to many Nonconformists was that the Conservative Government, now in its seventh year, was still committed to doing something about education despite numerous setbacks.

When Arthur Balfour, First Lord of the Treasury, introduced the Government's massive Education Bill in 1902, he took both Liberals and Nonconformists by surprise. Education was, of course, of vital importance to that class from which Nonconformity drew its greatest support; it was the key to social advancement and self respect. The School Board system of 1870 was regarded with an almost religious devotion by Nonconformity and this helps to explain many Nonconformists' almost hysterical opposition to the bill. Nonconformist fury did much to bring about the great Liberal victory in 1906 and included a 'No Rate' movement – 'Passive Resistance' – which bordered on illegality and involved thousands of otherwise respectable people being brought into open court. Almost 200 Nonconformists, including ministers, even went to gaol. Passive Resisters saw their campaign as drawing on the old traditions of the Nonconformist Conscience – of suffering for conscience' sake. During the agitation leading Nonconformist bodies committed themselves to political involvement on a scale unknown in their history and three of the four leading denominations urged their members to disobey the law. As a result of all this Nonconformity had an influence over politics which it had never enjoyed before and which it has never enjoyed since. These years, from 1902 to 1906 give us an insight into English Nonconformity enjoying the full rigour of that strength and confidence which had been building up during the closing decades of the last century.

The Government's Education Bill proposed a complete overhaul of state education even more radical than the 1896 bill which they had had to withdraw. In that year, as the Clerk of the House of Commons later recalled, they suffered 'probably the severest humiliation that a strong government has ever experienced'. They had been forced to give up a major bill partly because of Nonconformist threats, yet their goal remained the same: a state system of secondary schools and, in elementary education, a secure future for denominational schools. The church school, Balfour declared, was not 'a relic of an ancient system permitted as a matter of compromise to remain . . . out of harmony with the needs . . . of a progressive community' but the 'normal . . . machinery for education'.[2]

Nonconformists genuinely, if naively, felt hurt at the introduction of Balfour's bill which undermined all their assumptions not only about the future but about their own importance. One point in the *British Weekly*'s attack was that the Government had 'utterly ignored' Nonconformity and one Primitive Methodist minister asked Chamberlain, 'Why did not the Government consult the leading men in the Free Churches as well as the Anglicans and Roman Catholic Bps. and priests? Do we not pay taxes, rates then why this disrespect?' The lack of reference was because other than Wesleyans, Nonconformists had made no direct contribution to meeting the nation's educational needs other than through their support of 'British' Schools and of their own public schools and teacher training colleges which were mainly Methodist or Congregational.[3] Throughout the century, starting with Brougham's 1820 bill to set up a national system of rate-supported elementary schools, Nonconformists had opposed any legislation which retained the Church's role in education. Again in 1870 their power had caused Gladstone to modify his original bill to their advantage.

By 1902 the needs were so great that only a radical restructuring would save the day. The bill not only created a new system of secondary schools but abolished the Boards so beloved by Nonconformists. In their stead it made county and borough councils the local educational authority – the LEAs – for all schools, elementary and secondary. While it retained the restriction that in all schools 'provided' by the state, religious instruction must be 'non-denominational', it incorporated all those denominational schools which were prepared to allow one-third of their committees of management to be nominated by the LEA. In return for this they would receive rate aid. This meant that rate-payers would be paying *inter alia* for Anglican, Methodist and Roman Catholic instruction whatever their own religious beliefs. To many if not most Nonconformists this was a direct challenge to their view of the future which was based on expanding educational opportunities as part of a state system within which the Established Church would play a steadily decreasing part. Voluntary schools would not now disappear: the legislation 'makes permanent what was decaying and sure to die', Nicoll declared.[3] Even worse, it meant: 'Rome was on the rates.'

The Nonconformist commitment to the School Board system requires a closer look. Their devotion was based on several factors: since 1870 these Boards had done much to educate those people from whose ranks many if not most Nonconformist denominations drew their members. They had given Nonconformists, especially ministers, opportunities to take on political work in their towns. They had provided the type of 'non-denominational' religious instruction which appealed to Nonconformists.

They were seen as a force for 'democratic education' which would come to perfection in the new century. In their work in city centres, the Boards had indeed effected great improvements in the lives of their pupils and were a means by which Nonconformists who sat on the Boards or taught in the schools could reach the 'unchurched millions'. They knew that the battle for religious supremacy in the twentieth century would be won or lost in the cities and here Board schools, the natural allies of Nonconformity, predominated. To Wesleyan Methodists they were also a means not just of undermining the Church's claims but of combating the growing influence of the High Church movement. Finally, in the 1890s education had been the one issue on which Nonconformists, divided over Home Rule and then the Boer War, could unite.[4]

Before we can understand this commitment and the influence it was to have on Nonconformist history we need to know something about Board schools. This topic has been dealt with extensively elsewhere and here we need only give a basic outline.[5] In 1870 Gladstone's first government passed an Education Act popularly called after its sponsor, W. E. Forster. The bill was a compromise to fill the gaps which still existed despite the extraordinary efforts of voluntary groups during the century. These gaps were mainly in the expanding towns and cities of England. Elementary schools for 'the people' had been provided by the Church of England, the 'non-denominational' British and Foreign School Society, the Wesleyans and the Roman Catholics. Boards were to be created if a local referendum showed a need and they were to get their funds from a local rate. They could, if they wished, give rate-aid to voluntary schools in their area. Radical Nonconformist groups like the Birmingham-based National Education League, wanted no religious instruction at all in the new schools and attacked any rate aid to church schools. The original bill also allowed Anglican religious instruction to be given in the new Board schools, for the rather obvious reason that the majority of pupils would naturally have been Anglican. Strenuous opposition, led by the Central Nonconformist Commitee under R. W. Dale of Birmingham, forced the Cabinet to change its mind on both points. England would now have two rival systems of primary schools.

The new Boards could have religious instruction or not, as they saw fit although by the early 1890s there were only some ninety Boards with no religious instruction and seventy-one of these were in Nonconformist Wales. Those Boards with religious instruction had to ensure that such teaching was 'non-denominational'. Teachers could say that there were three persons in the Trinity but not that the Church of England teaches that there are three persons. Likewise each Board could decide on the nature and content of its religious instruction; in Birmingham Nonconformist power was strong enough to ensure that 'R.I.' only included the reading of the Bible without comment. Interpretation depended on the children's theological skills. The changes forced on the legislation were examples of the power of a committed minority over a less committed majority: the Nonconformist tail had wagged the Liberal dog.

In effect the state had established a new and alternative form of religion, 'non-denominationalism', and this became the chief reason for growing Nonconformist support of the new schools. Although in 1901 Wesleyan Methodists had 458 day schools with 160,675 pupils, they still agreed with the view adopted by Baptists and Congregationalists. They wanted 'the establishment of School Boards everywhere . . . of sufficient area' but they added one proviso: the Boards must provide a 'Christian unsectarian school within reasonable distance of every family' especially in villages. Baptists and Congregationalists still believed that 'the responsibility for the religious education of the young rests upon the Church of Christ and not upon the State', but had come to accept that religious instruction should be given in state schools. Not everyone agreed what the nature of that instruction should be, but few continued Joseph Parker's adherence to the old view that state schools should have no religious teaching of any sort.[6]

By the end of the century the tables had largely been turned. Nonconformists had resigned their old belief in 'voluntarism' because they knew that religious instruction independent of the Church of England could only help them towards their inevitable victory. For her part, the Church of England had resigned her old dependence on the secular arm, which had been withering since the 1820s, and now stood for the voluntary principle to maintain choice through the existence of church schools. Behind this was the view, shared with Roman Catholics, that it was the moral responsibility of parents, not government, to educate their children in schools of their choice. As Cardinal Vaughan told one correspondent, the parents' right to choose was 'the basis in natural law upon which the whole denominational system is erected and justified before the State'.[7]

Nonconformists' identification with the School Boards also reinforced their view that they alone were the churches of 'the people' and that the new type of religious instruction was what average people wanted. They would have been delighted with a secret government memorandum of 1896 in which it was argued that 'the simple teaching of evangelical Christianity appears to be acceptable to large numbers of Churchmen and to the great majority of Nonconformists'. One retired Chief Inspector of Schools, Sir Joshua Fitch, wrote about the situation in London: 'No practical difficulties have arisen in the interpretation or in the actual working out of the very simple and intelligible programme of the School Board.' One should add that Fitch was a Wesleyan Methodist.[8] The difficulty was, of course, the lack of any guarantee that the teaching would remain distinctly that of 'evangelical Christianity'; this is what had led to the furious London Board election in 1894.

Board schools were essentially the schools of working people supported by the rates of the middle classes. They were also the schools of the towns and cities: seven out of every ten children in Board schools lived in urban areas. What this meant was that Board schools were moving, like thousands of Nonconformists, into the suburbs while inner city areas were left to voluntary schools, largely Church of England and severely limited for funds. In the suburbs, Board schools would have had increased revenue and better provision and here they would have taught the children of the upper working classes who made up such a large proportion of Nonconformists, those whom Lloyd

George described in the Commons as 'the best citizens in the land, the most intelligent artisans, and the best of the middle classes'. The number of Boards had grown enormously, allowing their supporters to see them as the natural basis for a complete national system of education which would include secondary schools as well; by the turn of the century roughly two-thirds of the population were under their authority. Their schools were newer and better built, they provided a wider range of lessons, they spent more on education and their teachers earned higher salaries. In 1870 the cost for each child in average attendance had been £1. 5s. 5d.; by 1900 it had risen to £2. 17s. 7½d. in Board schools but only £2. 6s. 4½d. in voluntary schools. Finally they were 'democratic' schools, controlled by Boards directly elected by rate-payers including women.[9]

However, their strength was more apparent than real. The Boards did not really form the basis for a national system. The majority of school places, as opposed to pupils, remained in voluntary schools. The majority of Boards were confined to urban areas. The majority of schools were still voluntary and the majority of pupils were still educated in voluntary, not Board, schools. What Board schools there were in rural areas suffered from exactly the same problems as voluntary Church schools: apathy and lack of income. Indeed, in some villages it was only organized Nonconformist demands and not genuine educational needs which forced the erection of a Board school. As a result both village schools suffered from small enrolments and little revenue. Behind these unnecessary Boards lay the stories of persecution suffered by little Nonconformist children being forced by haughty Anglo-Catholic vicars to recite the Rosary or attend the parish church. This was more rhetoric than reality and as such was a favourite theme of MPs like Lloyd George. On one occasion in the Commons, Lloyd George waxed eloquent about the sufferings of one young Nonconformist but Balfour had the unusual pleasure of silencing him by demanding the name of the parish and the priest involved. Neither piece of information was forthcoming. When the Primitive Methodist Conference surveyed 'village Methodism' they asked the 838 circuits under Boards, 'Is the

School Board system more favourable to our work than the Sectarian system?' While 376 said they thought the Board system better, 462 actually preferred the 'sectarian' system which really meant Church of England schools. Despite the reality, Conference still preferred to join Baptists and Congregationalists in demanding a universal Board system with non-denominational religious instruction. Of course, all parents had the legal right to withdraw their children from religious instruction in Church Schools, but few used it: an 1891 survey in the Diocese of Southwell, for example, showed that of 84,053 children, only 205 were withdrawn from all or part of the class and of these, twenty-six were Roman Catholics or Jews.[10]

The Boards were not as popular as Nonconformists maintained: of the 2,563 Boards created, 1,369 or 54 per cent had only come about through an Order of the Education Department after the local area had refused to act. Likewise, Board elections, which occurred every three years, attracted notoriously low polls. In their support of the School Boards Nonconformists were not in step with changing attitudes. There were, in the words of one civil servant, 'signs that the *ad hoc* election . . . is now regarded by a considerable body of public opinion as no longer the most satisfactory arrangement'. While Sir Henry Campbell-Bannerman, Liberal leader after 1899, moaned about 'our County Council philosophers & the Haldane-Webb set' younger men felt that those *ad hoc* authorities established as part of the nineteenth century's piecemeal reforms should yield to a more ordered system based on county and borough councils. It was another example of the philosophy of 'Efficiency'. The Royal Commission on Secondary Education, chaired by the Nonconformist James Bryce, reported in 1895 that 'The electorate is already overburdened with elections and is growing restive under their combined annoyance and expense.'[11]

The one feature of the Boards which most discredited them in popular estimation was the battle over religious issues and personalities which accompanied so many elections. These were renowned for the bitterness of religious fighting, the most famous of which came in London in 1894. The ferocity was helped by electors' having as many votes as there were members of the local

Board or, in London, as there were delegates from the local division. This 'discredited freak of perverted ingenuity' as the Boards' own publication called it, was created to ensure representation of minorities. In the event it only encouraged religious warfare: like most theoretically devised schemes it had achieved unexpected results. (In part it explains why Nonconformist ministers often stood for and were returned to their local Board. They had a good chance of being elected, given the support of a devoted following and the smaller number of votes required.)

On the other side of the debate, many Churchmen had changed their views and were demanding that the Church of England live up to her historic responsibility for teaching the nation's children. This group, normally High Churchmen, saw in the Boards' 'non-denominationalism' 'a new denominationalism more intolerant than all it condemns', a 'false ideal' which 'would mean ultimately the decay and death of all specific religious conviction'. Likewise, some veterans of 1870 came to feel that they had created something of a Frankenstein monster. In 1894 Gladstone denounced 'any undenominational system of religion, framed by or under the authority of the State' as a 'moral monster'. In that same year John Clifford admitted that if forced he would defend a Unitarian's giving religious instruction to Christian children rather than have an agreed syllabus which was orthodox in its teaching but which 'discriminated' against the Unitarian or atheist teacher. Many found it frightening that the subject and nature of religious instruction were entrusted not just to *ad hoc* boards but to the beliefs of individual teachers.[12]

Despite the School Boards' weaknesses, they enjoyed by 1901 almost total support from Nonconformists. Indeed, that same year Robertson Nicoll urged Nonconformists to threaten a 'No Rate' campaign to fight a small bill to establish a system of secondary schools under county and borough councils. As there was to be no religious instruction in the new schools there was no question of religious scruples being offended by having to pay for religious instruction of a denomination not one's own. The action, which would involve refusing to pay a portion of any new rate designed for the new schools, was merely to strengthen the Liberal opposition. In the event the bill was withdrawn. In his call Nicoll was drawing on the old tradition of 'persecution for conscience's sake' and harkening back to the Church rate controversy of the 1830s. In some places, like Halifax, home of the Crossleys, this had carried on into the 1870s. Older Nonconformists could remember that a 'No Rate' campaign had been revived in that same decade by some in protest at a clause in the Forster Act which allowed the new Boards to pay school fees for parents too poor to pay the fees at those voluntary schools which they wanted their children to attend. In this case the protesters were resisting Board rates on the older argument that 'it is not within the competence of the Legislature to provide religious teaching for the people'. As the bulk of the fees paid were in Manchester and Salford one suspects many of those receiving the aid were Irish Roman Catholics. The offending clause was withdrawn in 1876.[13]

Calls for non-payment of rates or 'passive resistance' – after the Church of England's opposition to James II – were also heard in the 1890s from Churchmen like Bishop Jayne of Chester who wanted larger government grants for voluntary schools. One clergyman refused part of his School Board rate because he objected to 'non-denominational' religious instruction and in the debates over the 1896 and 1897 Education Bills, calls for non-payment had been heard by extremists on both sides. A similar ploy had been used by the 'anti-vaccination' campaign, starting in 1873 although this was undermined by a relief act passed in 1898. Even so, in 1902, 1,535 'anti-vaccinationists' were fined.[14] The tradition, therefore, was still very much alive.

From the moment the 1902 bill was introduced Nonconformist leaders rushed into the attack with a ferocity that surprised the Government. To Balfour it was an 'extraordinary campaign of lies . . . and . . . total indifference to the interests of education'. It would be led by three of the biggest names in Nonconformity – Hugh Price Hughes, Joseph Parker and John Clifford. The movement therefore was seen by conservatives as another campaign by Political Dissent. Clifford, famous as a 'pro-Boer', quickly emerged as the most important of the three through a series of articles in the *Daily News* in which he denounced the bill as 'blind and bigoted', 'mean . . . despicable . . . unauthorised . . . unconstitutional . . . tricky . . . [and] unscrupulous'. 'The State', he wrote, 'is in danger; yes, that is the fact.' 'It is a battle for life' and a 'fight for the birthright of British citizens.' Sometimes his exuberance outran propriety as when he told the Women's Liberal Metropolitan Union that the bill 'emasculated education'. Arthur Balfour, who succeeded his uncle, Lord Salisbury, as Prime Minister in the summer of 1902, took Clifford's letters, despite their 'unrelenting scream', seriously enough to answer them in scathing detail in his own pamphlet which was published on 4 December. He contrasted the willingness to pay taxes which went in part to Church schools with the threatened refusal to pay part of the rates which went in part for the same object, and turned a favourite anti-popery cry against Nonconformists: 'Is there not a certain over-subtlety of distinction in this ruling which, if I may say so without offence either to Dr. Clifford or the Jesuits, is almost Jesuitical?'[15]

Clifford's great fame rested on his oratory. The Baptist historian, E. A. Payne, once told this author that he had heard Clifford as an old man and that 'he must have been almost invincible a decade or so earlier' – that is, during the education controversy. Clifford was an extraordinary man of great personal kindness and Christian charity, unless engaged in a public debate when his rhetoric knew no bounds and he went at his enemies with a Quixotic disregard for consequences. Helen Wilson, daughter of the Liberal MP, H. J. Wilson, once listened to the famous Baptist minister during a discussion about miracles, which to Clifford were unimportant. The phrase within square brackets was crossed out in the manuscript.

> He struck me as a decidedly lovable kind of man, quite capable of loving his enemies, but quite incapable of [comprehending any point of view except the one at which he stands at the moment.] understanding even his friends . . . He knew he was right, and why should he bother about the consciences of people who did not agree with him?[16]

Calls for passive resistance appeared even before the first reading of the 1902 bill. In a little-known woman's magazine, *The Light of Home*, the Liberal MP for Norwich, George White, a keen Baptist and supporter of the Free Church Councils, urged non-payment of any school rate designed to help denominational schools or to pay for denominational religious instruction: 'This and nothing else will save the situation.' The Editor of the monthly magazine was J. Edward Sears who would emerge as a vital force in the movement. However, the real call for passive resistance came from Nicoll ten days after the bill's introduction: 'Free Churchmen will, we . . . think, be compelled to resist' and he urged the Free Church Council to 'give a clear lead'. The next week he told readers that the bill 'deals the deadliest blow to the very existence and future of Nonconformity . . . and will practically hand over the children . . . to the clergy . . . of England and Rome'. Nicoll freely admitted that 'I like a good hot controversy if I am sure of my side'.[17] Nicoll knew he could count on activists in the network of local Free Church Councils. As one local paper would note, 'the Free Church Council leaders are everywhere the most conspicuous and, in some places, the only "Passive Resisters"'. The Council's Secretary, Thomas Law, boasted on 3 April that 'we have now a formidable machinery by . . . which we can organize resistance to any measure which threatens the rights of Nonconformists'. The question for Nicoll was whether or not he could get the Council itself to take up organizing the campaign. Two days after Law's boast, Hugh Price Hughes and Joseph Parker came out for 'conscientious resistance'.[18]

Nicoll knew full well that the real task facing 'political dissent' was the need to apply pressure on the Parliamentary Liberal Party. Nonconformity appeared to dominate the Party: as we have noted, over half of all Liberal MPs were Nonconformist. To outsiders like Viscount Wolmer, who entered the Commons as a Liberal Unionist MP in 1885, the Liberal Party was 'greatly influenced, & sometimes dominated, by a body of Radical nonconformists, whose hatred of the Church of England knew no bounds. The leading ministers, of whom Dr Clifford was a type, were supported in the House of Commons by a band of men . . . who would have destroyed all church schools if they could.' Yet the domination was only apparent and Lord Wolmer was judging the strength of the band by the sound of the drums. Many MPs were only nominally Nonconformist, especially when we remember how much money one needed to become an MP and how wealth tended to loosen one's Nonconformity. In addition, some younger MPs, especially the 'New Liberals', wanted the Party to become one of social reform through state action and to break away from the old dependence on Nonconformity. Their magazine, *New Liberal Review* declared, 'We shall rejoice no more gladly in the coming Nonconformist victory than we rejoice in their present eclipse'. On 16 April Campbell-Bannerman and Herbert Gladstone received a deputation from the National Free Church Council which officially stated their opposition to the bill. Thirteen days later the veteran Liberal MP, Sir William Harcourt, told 'C-B' that he had met Bryce, Fowler and Asquith – all three Nonconformist to varying degrees – and agreed 'without *eclat* that the point of attack should be directed at the Rating question without popular control', i.e. giving voluntary schools rate aid without having a majority of the school governors appointed by the LEA. In other words, the party's opposition would not be based on the religious objection felt by Nonconformists at having to pay for Anglican or Roman Catholic religious instruction.[19]

Campbell-Bannerman replied that 'the mere rating objection' was not enough: Nonconformists 'have a question of principle beyond the mere question of uncontrolled rating' and if the party did not recognize the religious dimension 'we shall come to infernal grief'. 'So long as our solid Non.Cons. are satisfied I am content: but surely that is a *sine qua non.*' 'C-B' thoroughly disliked the bill and wrote, 'I hope our people will stand no compromise, but take a bold line against the whole scheme. I am sure we shall come to grief if we do not take a strong line . . .' Yet even he did not much care for 'fanatical noncons' nor for Wesleyan Methodists – 'those fellows have a great gift of suspiciousness'. (He once said of Hughes' paper *apropos* its support for the Boer War: 'I presume it is a religious newspaper. It cannot be a newspaper of the Christian religion.') He was supported by Bryce, 'our education pundit', whose attitude was that 'we want no compromises, for none could satisfy our friends in the country, now in a real good fighting mood'.[20]

Nonconformist opposition was a mixed blessing to Liberals: a national campaign of passive resistance might be a valuable weapon in stirring up support and reuniting the party but it might also become a rod for their own backs, especially if charges of conspiracy were taken seriously. For the fourteen Nonconformists who as Liberal Unionists were now supporters of the Conservative Government, the future was much more worrying. Joseph Chamberlain, Liberal Unionist leader in the Commons, had little sympathy for Nonconformist objections. He complained about his own denomination, the Unitarians, that they 'were rapidly becoming the mere creatures of the political orthodox Dissenters, who, as my father always said, are infinitely more illiberal than the Church at its worst times'. His own efforts to alter the bill, which he did not much like, in order to meet some Nonconformist objections were unsuccessful.[21]

Among other Liberal leaders there was a mixed attitude toward the question and an obvious reluctance at too close an identification with Nonconformity: in October 1901 Asquith had warned that legislation touching both primary and secondary schools would cause 'infinite confusion & division among us'. While he joined Campbell-Bannerman in publicly opposing the new LEAs his friends doubted his sincerity as he had moved away from his Nonconformist upbringing. As always, the former Prime Minister, Lord Rosebery, had just enough influence over the Liberal Imperialists or 'right wing' of the party to cause trouble and at first no one was sure what his attitude would be; what was certain was his 'delight in acting the critic and making utterances as a half-leader'. A civil servant at the Treasury noted that many MPs were 'dubbing R[osebery] a "rotter"' because of his 'shilly-shallying'. Luckily for the Liberals he came out against the bill and in support of Nonconformist opposition although he found Clifford's 'polemical methods' to be 'quite hateful'. To his supporter, 'Imperial' Perks, Rosebery had recognized the central fact, namely that Nonconformists 'are really the motive force of provincial Liberalism'.[22]

Although Harcourt had worked with Chamberlain in the Birmingham Education League thirty years before, he now had little time for 'dissenter Radicalism'. Even so, he came nearest to Rosebery in supporting Passive Resistance in a letter Clifford published in the *Manchester Guardian* on 10 June 1903: here Harcourt referred to the Tories' 'permanent, unchangeable, tyrannical majority in the House of Lords'. For his part the Liberal Imperialist, R. B. Haldane, made no bones about his support for the central principles of the bill and wrote in private: 'The attitude of the NonCons. over the Education Question is very bad. They will not look at the larger aspect of the matter . . . [and will not see] the impossibility of the Liberals being able to deal with it.' While Sir Edward Grey opposed the bill and repeated the party's arguments, he disliked too close an association with Nonconformists and told one friend that one of the things that makes public life so distasteful was that 'everything has to be overstated & put almost brutally if it is to have any effect'. Perks' boast that 'at last we have a united Party . . . there is no schism; we have not had to form any league; there is absolute unity' was something of an exaggeration. The parliamentary Liberal Party would need careful watching if Nonconformists were to become allies in securing a Liberal majority in the next election.[23]

In May Nicoll called for a national organization to coordinate a no-rate war but failed in his demand that the National Council become the coordinating body: its Organizing Committee met on 12 May in response to a letter from him but 'did not see their way to take up his suggestion'. They also rejected a proposal that they should urge Nonconformist leaders to boycott the approaching Coronation. On 12 June Balfour received the National Council's deputation: its leader, A. M. Fairbairn, ended his speech with an open threat of resistance: 'We should not be worthy of our citizenship, or of the interview . . . granted us, if we did not frankly say that to the legislation which creates an ecclesiastical monopoly in the schools of the people we will not submit.'[24] In the event, while Fairbairn supported resistance he would avoid the campaign, arguing that conscientious opposition could not be organized.

One key question was what would the Methodists do. All four smaller divisions came out against the bill but only the Primitive Methodists endorsed Passive Resistance. They called upon their ministers 'to resist this retrograde and disastrous movement with all possible power and at every possible stage and in every possible way and to the utmost extremity'. The Wesleyans were divided and Conference was torn by acrimonious debates. Hughes introduced the official resolution which called for the retention of School Boards and for a public majority on the governing committee of any voluntary school receiving rate aid. R. W. Perks, who really wanted Wesleyans to transfer all their schools *en bloc* to the Boards, seconded Hughes' resolution: unity must be maintained. A conservative counter-resolution welcomed the bill and agreed an LEA majority on voluntary schools' governing committees only if the school's denominational character was not lost. This was rejected by a vote of 471 to 66 and the Hughes' resolution was accepted by 454 to 68. Hughes wrote later that 'many Methodists are still merely Nonconformists. They are not Dissenters, and cannot be expected to share the deep convictions and feelings of their Dissenting brethren.'[25] Passive Resistance would have little support from the Wesleyans.

On 31 July Nicoll issued his call to arms in a lead article headed by a quote from *Pilgrim's Progress* – 'Set Down My Name Sir'. He declared that there could be 'no resistance except the refusal to pay rates . . . Those who will do nothing but speak have turned their backs, and the Christian has no armour on his back.' If Nicoll was frustrated with the Free Church Council he had better luck with backbenchers. By July Lloyd George was writing to him and agreeing that 'the time has arrived when we should take counsel together as to our next step'. He had already asked Clifford to the House for a chat and now wanted 'a more complete understanding between those who conduct the campaign in the Country and the Members who fight the Bill in the Commons.' His hope was that a 'great agitation well organized and skilfully directed might break them down in the Autumn Session. The House of Commons is not yet convinced that the Nonconformists in any part of the country except Wales mean business.' Augustine Birrell's sardonic reference to the 'impotent rage of Nonconformity' would not have amused Lloyd George who shared the general Nonconformist fear that the Liberal front bench wanted to avoïd a religious battle for fear of offending Irish Nationalist MPs whom they might need to call on some day to form a coalition government.[26]

During that summer of 1902 people were more concerned about the end of the Boer War, the King's sudden illness and the delayed Coronation than about education. After the summer recess Campbell-Bannerman asked Bryce to sound out Nonconformist opinion both inside the House and in the country. Within a fortnight twelve back-benchers wrote directly to Campbell-Bannerman: 'We, the undersigned, have been fighting the Education Bill day by day in the House . . . There is only one thing which arouses comment outside, and gives us constant discouragement – i.e., the very small numbers of the party in most of the Divisions . . . Generally very little more than half the party have been present.'[27] Lloyd George's hopes for a reinvigorated Liberal opposition came to nothing. Things were better outside Westminster: a 'giant demonstration' took place in Leeds on 20 September at which somewhere between 110,000 and 150,000 Nonconformists attended. Balfour's educational adviser, Robert Morant, said there were 80,000 not 150,000 and that they 'were largely sight-seers'. It was here that passive resistance marches were first played. The most famous was 'Men of England' with music by W. H. Bell and words from Shelley's 'Masque of Anarchy'. Another, by the Nonconformist educationalist, J. Hirst Hollowell, 'England, Rouse Thy Legions', and a third, 'Arouse, Arouse, Ye Englishmen!', urged Nonconformists to see that 'the banner of the free e'er waves o'er England's schools, and that a papal hierarchy ne'er over Britain rules!'.[28]

At the Congregational Union's autumn meetings Silvester

Horne proposed an amendment to the official resolution denouncing the bill. It stated that the Union was 'prepared to advise its members to refuse to pay the rates' should the bill become law. The amendment was carried with only about six voting against it and Horne wrote in his diary, 'the superior persons discredit this enthusiasm, but I question whether they know the intensity of feeling'. In October the Baptists followed suit and vowed, with only twenty-three votes against, 'to offer passive resistance . . . and to render' the bill 'unworkable'. That same month answers to an NFCC survey about passive resistance came in and showed that 489 councils had answered its questionnaire and of these, 412 agreed to enrol names of potential resisters; twenty-nine opposed the idea and forty-eight were non-committal. The National Council therefore agreed to receive names even though 'conscientious objection has been ridiculed by persons of eminence in the State and by writers in the Press'.[29] In Wales county councils were voting to refuse to enforce the bill if enacted.

Many religious leaders were becoming seriously worried about a renewal of the old Chapel v. Church warfare in the new century and there were secret talks between Bishop Randall Davidson of Winchester, Hugh Price Hughes and J. B. Paton but these came to nothing, partially because of 'the tone and terms of Dr. Clifford's letters with their amazing statements'. By November the campaign had reached a critical state as Lloyd George told Nicoll:

> Something must be done. It is now too late to reverse the policy of 'no rate'. The leaders of the Free Churches have committed themselves too deeply for reconsideration & they must go through with their threats otherwise they will make Nonconformity contemptible in the eyes of the nation.
>
> However, I have no doubt as to their organising first. The Bill is as obnoxious to-day as it ever was.

The bill was not always so 'obnoxious' to Lloyd George. He had written to his wife on the day it was introduced: 'Balfour is developing a most revolutionary Education Bill . . . Up to the present I rather like the Bill. It is quite as much as one would expect from a Tory Government – in fact, more than anyone could anticipate.'[30] Yet for Lloyd

261

George rank and file opposition had proved too strong a force not to be turned to good purpose for the party and for his own position within it.

On 1 December the Free Church Council's General Committee met. The Council was divided; some newspapers, like *The Christian World*, attacked the whole idea; certain famous figures like A. M. Fairbairn and J. Guinness Rogers would have nothing to do with any such campaign; George Cadbury was hostile to overt political work and the Council could not survive without his money. Finally, as Clifford later wrote, 'high legal authorities said we might be indicted for conspiracy and our Councils broken up'. After a 'full and frank exchange', the normal euphemism for a flaming row, the Committee agreed that it was 'not expedient' to organize a No Rate campaign. When it seemed inevitable that the Council would not act, a National Passive Resistance Committee had been formed in the last week of November. Clifford was appointed President and well-known members included Robertson Nicoll, George White MP, C. Silvester Horne, F. B. Meyer, R. J. Campbell, J. H. Shakespeare, editor of the *Baptist Times* and secretary of the Baptist Union, Thomas Spurgeon, pastor of his father's Metropolitan Tabernacle, the minister of Wesley's Chapel on the City Road and Thomas Law. The committee eventually had forty-six members of whom thirty-six were ministers. Over half the members were either Baptists or Congregationalists. By the end of 1902 both Hughes and Parker had died and Clifford was left in '"sudden solitude" as a Free Church leader with magnetic qualities'. He became, for better or worse, the driving force behind the movement and stamped his personality on it.[31]

On the day after the bill's third reading the King's private secretary wrote to Balfour congratulating him on 'the skill, temper and patience which, if he may be allowed to say so, you have shown in steering such a difficult and very controversial Bill through the House'. Thirteen days later, on 18 December, the bill received the Royal Assent. Yet the Government, which had won such an outstanding victory in 1900 was now extremely unpopular, both with the electorate and with many back-benchers who saw the hand of the High Church party behind the bill. (Balfour's cousin, Lord Hugh Cecil, was a famous High Churchman and the basis for most of these rumours.) Some felt that the 'country wd. turn out the present govern . . . at this moment . . . principally due to the Educ.on. Bill' and others sensed a 'general impression about that the Ministry are tottering'. Outside Westminster the Government faced an extraordinary situation: the official leadership of three of England's leading Nonconformist bodies had called on their members to resist an act of Parliament through a coordinated campaign of civil disobedience. Chamberlain had warned Balfour months before that

> the Bill has brought all the fighting Nonconformists into the field . . . Their representations and appeals to the old war cries have impressed large numbers of the lower middle & upper working classes who have hitherto supported the Unionist Party without joining . . . I think there is no doubt that very large numbers of Nonconformists will . . . be induced to refuse the payment of rates.[32]

This in turn would allow Nonconformity to force the Liberals into repealing the act should they regain office. The Nonconformists' bluff had been called and they now had until April, when the Act began coming into force outside London, to turn their threats into reality.

The movement's organizers used the time between December and June, when the first wave of rate demands was expected, to make good their threats of a national No Rate campaign. In April George White took over as President of the Baptist Union. The jam manufacturer, William Hartley, announced he would become a 'Resister' as did the tea magnate, F. J. Horniman MP. He joined the growing ranks of MPs who were pledged to the campaign. Already Robert Perks, H. J. Wilson and White had committed themselves and in time at least nine MPs 'resisted'. From its London offices the National Committee issued reports and a sample letter announcing a Resister's refusal to pay. It distributed leaflets explaining the intricacies of the criminal and educational laws and even published a do-it-yourself guide, *For Conscience' Sake. The Manual of the Passive Resistance Movement*. From November 1902 there was a national news magazine, *The*

Crusader, which started as a monthly but changed to weekly publication in October 1903. It was edited by the same man who had edited *The Light of Home*, J. Edward Sears. He was a London architect, the son of a Baptist minister, and active in local politics: from 1898 to 1901 he was a member of the Hendon School Board and from 1901 to 1907 he sat on the London County Council. Most important of all, he was a keen member of the Metropolitan Association of Free Churches. (His good work was rewarded when he was selected as Liberal candidate for Cheltenham, which he won in 1906.) Sears also sold a Passive Resister button for twopence (or 7s. 6d. for a hundred) which showed a crusader mounting a flight of stairs. In one hand he carried a lance and in the other he held a shield displaying the Cross of St George. This was the magazine's emblem. The motto round the edge was 'We Demand Alteration of Education Act'.

In May there was an enormous procession to Hyde Park, partly to protest against the Government's 1903 bill which extended the Education Act to London and partly to advertise Passive Resistance. Here a knight dressed in chain mail rode carrying his lance and shield, presumably paid for by the *Crusader*. Yet another song was composed – this time to the tune of 'Men of Harlech' – and began 'Hark! the clerics are advancing: In the schools you'll see them prancing, Hungry at the children glancing . . .'. On 6 April Mr Lewis Wing of Weston-super-Mare withheld part of his rate payment but the first case to get national attention occurred on 28 May when a young Derbyshire farmer, Thomas Smith, appeared before the Belper magistrates' bench. Rather unfortunately for the movement, Smith, a Primitive Methodist local preacher, admitted, 'I am a bit used to this sort of thing, for I am one of the anti-vaccination people', an admission gleefully picked up by critics of the movement like the *Daily Telegraph* which commented on 5 June, 'From this we may infer that Mr. Smith's conscience is at once delicate and comprehensive'.

By June there were 206 Passive Resistance Leagues and the number eventually grew to 648. These leagues organized meetings, distributed literature, sent off statistics to the National Committee and, when rates were due, arranged for the repurchase of goods distrained and sold. The Norwich League, for example, met four times in 1903–4, five times in 1905 and twice in 1906. The leagues also had to decide the notional amount resisters should deduct from their rate payment which they felt would go to denominational religious instruction. The Coventry and District League, for example, told its members on 18 January 1904: 'At a Meeting of the League, held at Cow Lane, on Tuesday, January 10th last, it was resolved that the Members tender payment of the Current Rate . . . less 2d. in the pound thereof.'[33] (Amounts normally varied between threepence and sixpence in the pound although the smallest amount was one-half a farthing.) They also drafted a Manifesto defending their actions and drew up a roll of members and supporters.

It was at meetings where the roll was signed that the religious nature of the campaign was most evident. The average Resister had no doubt that he was 'witnessing for Christ'. One Devon meeting at which the Roll was signed was described as follows:

> The chairman signed first 'Knowing he would have to suffer', then 'a solemn stillness – a stir, a footfall' and the signing proceeded with ministers, businessmen, old and young coming forward. 'Yes, the deed is done! What visions rise before their view! There would be persecution but did not Christ say "If any man will come after Me, let him deny himself, and take up his cross, and follow Me."?'

Sometimes emotion undermined the lessons learned in Sunday School as when one Kent Resister said that 'with all reverence . . . it needed that Christ should die a second time, for here was one set of men . . . robbing another set'. Suffering, however, was felt to be essential, not just for Christians but for Nonconformists. Clifford wrote to the Shoreham Citizens' League: 'We are despised, condemned, and hated to-day, as our fathers were; but we are serving God and our country by this conviction of the supremacy of right.'[34]

The movement was noted for its revivalist overtones, a recurring No Popery theme and its ever-present political bias. Hymns were sung in court and prayer-meetings often preceded and followed distraint auctions and court-room appearances. One Resister described how his wife sang 'Peace, Perfect Peace' when their furniture was being taken away for 'she felt, as never before, the reality of the peace which passeth understanding'. One Resister at Cullompton, Devon, told magistrates: 'I object to pay the rate because I believe the money is required to train up children to kiss the Pope's toe. As regards the Pope's blessings, personally, I would rather have a basin of milk-broth.' The National Committee in London always insisted that Resisters were acting 'from a conscientious and religious standpoint' but everyone knew the campaign was a bye-product of the Free Church Movement and was led by the most famous 'political dissenter', John Clifford. Matters were not helped in 1903 when Clifford accepted the Presidency of the reorganized Liberation Society and Lloyd George accepted the Vice-Presidency. The Society's executive had said in the summer of 1902 that it 'has now an opportunity greater than at any previous period and one which on no account should be missed'. When R. J. Campbell, a Liberal Imperialist follower of Lord Rosebery, told a rally that the movement must not become 'an institution to further the interests of one political party – the Liberal party', he was greeted with cries of 'Withdraw!'.[35]

Many Leagues were called 'Citizens' Leagues' and not 'Passive Resistance Leagues' because some Resisters acted from political motives alone. When H. J. Wilson became a Resister he insisted he did so 'to make the further protest involved in the indignity of a summons, magisterial proceedings, and distraint'. He resisted because the Act was 'a reactionary and unjust law' and not from any 'high religious ground'.[36] Sears always used his newspaper to further Liberal interests and assumed that a victory for Resisters was the same thing as a victory for the Liberals, which it was. As *The Coventry Herald and Free Press* pointed out on 8 May 1903, 'The organisation of conscience becomes in part at least an organisation of political forces'. It would be simplistic to argue that clever manipulators in London – Nicoll, Lloyd George, Thomas Law, and Sears – manipulated the simple faith of provincial Nonconformists for political ends because Resisters were perfectly aware that in politics religious beliefs mattered, whether

Nonconformist, Anglican or Roman Catholic. This was especially the case concerning education. In all honesty they argued that their aim was not so much political as parliamentary while their motives were religious because based in conscience. The degree to which a man's conscience was not just a product of his religion but of many factors of which religion was only one, the degree to which one could be solicited to take up conscientious objections and the extent to which such objectors could be organized was something Resisters left to philosophers.[37]

For those people who made up the rank and file of Nonconformists few things counted as much as respectability. Passive Resistance brought them into magistrates' courts and forced them to see their household goods hauled out into the street for auction – in its way a form of middle-class martyrdom. Most domestic rates came half-yearly and when a Resister returned his payment minus his deduction a summons arrived which commanded him 'in His Majesty's Name, to be and to appear . . . to show cause why you have not paid and refuse to pay the same, otherwise you shall be proceeded against by Default as if you had appeared, and be dealt with according to law'. When appearing before the magistrates, Resisters could then pay the amount due plus the cost of the summons but if they refused a warrant was issued allowing the bailiffs to seize any goods, except tools necessary to the individual's livelihood, which belonged to the protester wherever they were kept. Enough goods had to be seized to pay the amount due plus any costs. The normal procedure was then to sell the goods through a public auction. If there were no goods or if the bailiffs could not gain entrance, the authorities could ask the court to commit the Resister to gaol: if the amount owing did not exceed ten shillings the maximum sentence was seven days.[38]

The variations on this theme were numerous. In some places, such as Reading, local authorities refused to issue summonses, wishing to deny Resisters the opportunity to gain 'cheap martyrdom'. In Yorkshire, two district councils refused to levy a rate and were themselves summonsed. Some sympathetic Benches adjourned all resistance cases in the hope that the government would amend the law. Occasionally magistrates would leave the Bench rather than act against friends or those they admired. Some local councillors resigned or announced they would not stand for re-election, rather than be party to issuing the rate. On several occasions a Resister would have the amount withheld plus his costs paid anonymously. Sometimes this was done for 'the peace of the parish' and sometimes to embarrass Resisters, as at Bradford where there was a 'Passive Resisters' Anti-Martyrdom League' and at Brighton where the 'Active Resisters' did the same. Normally courts scheduled all resistance cases to be heard at the same time partially to reduce costs and partially to save the court's time by reducing the number of speeches. Resisters normally, at least in the beginning, marched to the Court. Once there the inevitable temptation was to make a speech to justify the situation. Normally magistrates let them do so but at Glastonbury one magistrate simply referred to them as 'you stupid people'. When the Cambridge bench refused to let Resisters make a statement they simply walked out of court and when a Salisbury protester referred to the 'priest-ridden Government' another magistrate burst out laughing. At Leicester some 280 Resisters appeared in November 1904 and sang 'O God, Our Help in Ages Past' without any attempt to prevent them and at Norwich, one Resister, fearing an unsympathetic bench, wore a red jersey with a sash inscribed, 'We Will Fight the Government!'.[39] Occasionally magistrates were themselves Resisters and at Leeds the mayor signed an order for distraint on his own goods.

These court appearances could be unnerving for respectable people. One Sheffield Resister wrote:

> A long list of 'felonies', 'drunks', disposed of, the discipline of the Court relaxed. The genial smile and patient condescending manner of the magistrate were contagious . . . Still, to breathe the atmosphere and stand where just before the criminally accused had stood, was offensive to delicate nerves.

Here was an inherent dilemma: Resisters wanted to be seen as martyrs but took umbrage if they were not treated differently from 'real' criminals. Sometimes there was humour and occasionally even violence. At Bournemouth in September 1905, George Stay of Pokesdown read a poem reminiscent of William McGonagall to the Court and was greeted with applause:

> A law that justice passes by,
> And injustice seeks to justify,
> In vain demands respect or fear,
> And that is why I'm standing here.

Occasionally Resisters were ejected from the court-room when the Bench refused leave to make a speech or once, when a Resister's friend called one constable a 'coward'. In London, the windows of one of the chapels attached to Clifford's London church were broken.[40]

Once a distraint order had been issued, the next step was for the goods to be seized and the auction held. Local authorities did not have to enforce the warrant and if they refused, the Resister's name could be struck off the electoral roll. All told some 154 Resisters lost their vote and *The Crusader* noted that 'perhaps the fact that resisters are willing to sacrifice their political existence . . . will convince their cynical critics that they are sincere'. When the authorities did enforce the order it could be a dramatic event. One such distraint was watched by a Resister's young daughter who later described it to this writer:

> The heavy front door was opened to them by my Mother . . . (This door was opened only on special occasions, such as when the Duchess of Somerset came in for a rest and tea as she passed the farm to the race-course. Ordinarily, everyone used the side entrance.)
>
> My Mother received her unwelcome visitors with dignity . . . they seized the first pieces of furniture they saw . . . but she explained that they belonged to friends who had gone to Canada and had left them in her charge. The men then went forward to take the hall stand and another chair. Finally the door closed on them, leaving my Mother upset but resolute, and leaving me bewildered and not a little alarmed to see parts of my home being carried away.

Sometimes seizures were excessive and sometimes no one could be found to do the work, especially in villages. Items seized varied enormously and included a mousetrap, a 107 pound head of Cheddar cheese and a pony belonging to the local Primitive Methodist minister. At the auction it was bought by friends (the normal procedure), decked with ribbons, photographed for the front page of *The Crusader* and placed at the head of a procession which set off to 'Onward! Christian Soldiers'. The normal item to be seized was any silver object as it was easiest to carry and most sure of fetching sufficient funds. Electro-plated tea pots were the most vulnerable and in some houses these became known as the 'Passive Resistance Teapot'. At Creaton, near Northampton, Resisters met after the sale at the Congregational Sunday School room to pass a resolution of thanks to the auctioneer who was also a Resister. After this the chairman read one of the innumerable telegrams fired off by John Clifford: 'The first duty of the hour is resistance to the education policy of the Bishops. it [sic] revives the Roman Catholic tyranny. Clifford.' As the years wore on these sales began to get a somewhat farcical reputation as Resisters either bought their own goods back (which they were encouraged not to do) or arranged to have friends buy them. Sears warned in April 1904, 'in a number of cases, the word "farce" has already been used.'[42]

In some cases Resisters were committed to gaol and by November 1906, when records stop, 189 Nonconformists had been imprisoned for having no goods to be distrained: of this total, 118 were imprisoned once, forty-six twice, fourteen three times, four, six times and two were gaoled seven times. In March of that same year a survey of 172 prisoners showed that Primitive Methodists provided fifty-four, Baptists forty-two, Congregationalists thirty-seven, and Wesleyans sixteen; the balance came from smaller denominations. A third survey in July 1905 showed that of 188 prisoners, eighty-three were ministers and 104 were laymen. There was one woman. One Resister who was sent down for five days for refusing to pay 6s. 6d. plus costs was the Rev. Richard Dalby who had been an assistant of R. F. Horton at Hampstead and was, after 1903, the minister of the Congregational Church at New Eltham in Kent. He left an account of his time in gaol of which the following is his summary:

Perhaps a word should be added to make clear that with all the courtesy of the officials and the comparatively mild treatment a debtor undergoes, it was real imprisonment. There was the lack of the ordinary comforts and appliances of life, the sense of subjection to routine control, and the close confinement in the small apartment (without out look) except for chapel and exercise. Nor could one forget the sense of injustice and that the chief agents causing it were fellow Christians . . . but it will make many of us watch more carefully than ever from disregarding the consciences of others. The anxiety and pain caused to friends is not to [be] lightly thought of.

There was compensation that the day of true religious freedom and educational efficiency was being helped on, – and there were other compensations too!

As the months wore on and the Government neither fell nor amended the Act, demands grew for more imprisonments to show that the Resisters 'meant business'. No one doubted that 'gaol birds' were the heroes of the movement: one West Country Methodist minister wrote to his local Free Church Council from Exeter Prison: 'I quite believe God has as much called me to do this as He has my two daughters to serve Him (as missionaries) in China.' The reading of the letter produced 'profound sympathy'. In 1905 Clifford transferred his goods to his wife so that he would be imprisoned. He reasoned that to allow one's goods to be sold meant that the money raised still went to denominational teaching. He was therefore indirectly still paying. Paddington Borough Council's Finance Committee simply refused to accept the transfer as valid and therefore got out of seeing the movement's leader put into gaol. Normally, magistrates tried to avoid imprisoning Resisters and in many cases reduced sentences to confinement in court. When the Rev. A. G. Prichard was imprisoned for one day for 1s. 1d., he asked, 'Where am I to go now, your worship?', to which the chairman replied in exasperation, 'Oh, Sit down!'. One by-product of all this was that a special conference of Resister 'Gaol Birds' resolved to see the Home Secretary about 'sanitation, discipline and labour tests . . . and the whole system of spiritual administration' in gaols.[43]

271

On 13 January 1904 *The Times* declared that Passive Resistance was 'now a flagging and expiring' movement but the paper was expressing a hope, not stating a fact. Undoubtedly the campaign had not fulfilled the dreams of its earliest adherents and some resisters, like the Primitive Methodist minister, G. R. Bell, discovered that suffering for conscience' sake was 'too easy' because of the politeness of officials and the routines into which the movement quickly fell. His solution was for a massive increase in imprisonments.[44] It is not easy to say exactly how many Nonconformists became Resisters because of the difficulty of relating summonses to individuals summonsed more than once and also because some areas had quarterly rates while the majority had semi-annual. A reasonable estimate is that between 7,500 and 10,000 people resisted and this matches estimates at the time. Even the outside estimate of 10,000 would mean that less than one-half of one per cent of all Nonconformists listed in the 1904 *Free Church Year Book* (some 2,020,834) had joined.

The movement grew during the first eighteen months, that is from June 1903 to the end of 1904 and then remained static until June 1905 when, with a general election in the offing, adherents began to fade away. The real loss came in 1906 after January's landslide Liberal victory. This would, of course, support the view that Resisters' motives were essentially political for the political make-up of the Government should make no difference to the alleged injustices which the Act produced. Geographically the movement was spread across England. Its strength, however, lay in the Midlands, the Home Counties, the West Country and London, although resistance could not begin there until 1904 because the 1903 London Education Act did not take effect until 1 May 1904. While it spread into villages, it was essentially a movement based on provincial towns and cities as was Nonconformity itself. It was the movement of a committed and highly motivated minority. If the metaphor is not too inappropriate it may be called the froth of a heady brew which was English Nonconformity: this is borne out in the fact that the movement was strongest where urban Nonconformity was strongest, in those towns and cities with populations between 10,000 and 100,000. It was overwhelmingly a layman's movement although its leaders were normally ministers and it was composed predominantly of Baptists, Primitive Methodists and Congregationalists. Nor surprisingly, given the nature of home ownership, it was mainly a man's movement made up of younger men from the upper-working and lower-middle classes. Of the three denominations it seems fair to say that the Baptists, for whom at the turn of the century the outlook was 'full of hope' and who were arguably the most active Nonconformist group, were the most active, closely followed by Primitive Methodists.[45]

From the beginning, however, Passive Resistance was compromised. Some leaders, like Guinness Rogers and Fairbairn, had refused to join; the Quakers, famous for their consciences, stood aside as did all but a handful of English Presbyterians. The Free Church Council had been forced to sever itself officially from Resistance and while many local councils were in effect Passive Resistance committees almost half – forty-eight per cent – had either not cooperated with the original proposal in 1902 or had ignored the questionnaire. The movement was weak in London and virtually non-existent in Liverpool. To innocent bystanders it was never taken seriously as a movement of conscience. When the results of the 1901 Census were published they showed that there were 97,383 insane persons in the United Kingdom: *Punch* commented, 'It is appalling to think that this number was reached even before the Passive Resistance movement was started'. *The Schoolmaster*, the journal of the National Union of Teachers, was more serious and its editor, T. J. Macnamara, MP wrote that 'both Parliament and the country are so sick and tired of this interminable struggle' that compromise ought to be easy. The leader of London's Progressive Party, whom Resisters saw as a natural ally, refused to discuss their case: T. McKinnon Wood, himself a Nonconformist, said, 'We shall have enough to do . . . without making our Education Committee a battle-ground for ecclesiastical controversy'. While the TUC felt in 1902 that 'the principle of taxation without representation might justifiably be met by the refusal to pay the taxes [rates] imposed', by 1904 its Parliamentary Committee was urging members to 'see to it that "education" is not . . . swamped by controversy over the "religious difficulty"'. Keir Hardie, writing in his *Labour Leader*, referred to the 'squabbles of rival Christian sects' and the 'putrefying remains of Liberalism' upon which Nonconformist arguments were based.[46]

On the whole the movement received some support from Liberal papers and, not surprisingly, none from the Tory press. The *Daily News*, edited by A. G. Gardiner, was a firm supporter and saw Resistance as a 'weapon which accords peculiarly with good citizenship'. *The Star* and the *Morning Leader* also gave support. The *Westminster Gazette*, edited by J. A. Spender, voiced the mainstream Liberal view: it gave considerable coverage and saw Resistance as a warning that Nonconformists were 'not reconciled' to the Act. All other national papers opposed the movement in varying degrees: as the *Daily Chronicle* said, 'so long as we elect our governors by counting heads, we must abide by the results . . . Even the burglar helps to pay for the policeman.' *The Standard* referred to 'those misguided persons who are endeavouring with more noise than effect to defeat the Education Act', while the *Pall Mall Gazette*, as far back as 1902, referred to the 'theatricals of the Nonconformist conscience'. The *St. James's Gazette* found Resisters 'preposterous' while *The Times* referred to the 'great body of undemonstrative but sincere Nonconformist opinion which views with utter distaste the policy of their vociferous leaders'. A survey of thirty-one provincial newspapers shows that the majority were either hostile or indifferent: the deciding factor was their political bias.[47]

Another weakness arose when some Nonconformists, and even some Resisters, agreed to take part in the administration of the Act which was, for Resisters, illogical to say the least. Should a Resister accept his local authority's nomination as one of the Council's two 'representative managers' on a Church School's management committee? In Dorset, the pastor of the Congregational Church at Wareham was taken to task by his congregation after he had agreed to sit on the local Church school's management committee. He explained that this did not diminish his 'resistance'. He had agreed, he said, in order 'to represent the Nonconformists of this Town' and this satisfied his critics. The worst cut of all, however, came from the Wesleyan Methodists who decided to cooperate with the government. They agreed to take rate aid and changed the make-up of their schools' governing bodies so that one-third were parents' representatives, one-third were nominated by the LEA and only one-third came from the Connexion. The Wesleyans' action did meet the objection which Chamberlain had made and which Nonconformists repeated, that the Act 'does not give effective Public control over money publically contributed'. They were able to placate the radical wing, led by Perks, by agreeing that they would build no Wesleyan schools where a 'Christian unsectarian school . . . under the . . . Cowper-Temple' clause existed. However, to thwart any would-be minister's desire to resist they appealed against a court decision that their ministers could be registered as occupiers but lost. Eventually a county court decided that the Circuit Stewards and not ministers were the legal occupiers of any manse.[48]

Passive Resistance was, therefore, largely a campaign by the traditional forces of Radical Dissent, this time joined by Primitive Methodists. While it would prove an effective weapon against the Tories, it was not a truly conscientious movement unless we assume that men's consciences can be organized by a triumvirate of Nicoll, Clifford and Sears. Their appeal succeeded because it tapped traditional Nonconformist dislike of the Church of England, inherited anti-Popery and those deep traditions of suffering for conscience' sake which, as seen in the discussions over the 'Nonconformist Conscience', had become vital to those people who took not only their faith, with its belief in personally 'witnessing', but their Nonconformist heritage, with its tradition of suffering, seriously. While not discrediting those who felt they were acting from honourable motives, we must admit that they were to a degree manipulated by Nicoll and Sears if not by John Clifford. One is reminded of Balfour's dictum in his answer to Clifford: 'Some there may be who think that, if a thing be said often enough, it must be true; if it be said loud enough, it must be important.' Likewise, any self-induced 'martyrdom' always has something of the farcical about it. The tears shed at the loss of a much-loved electroplated teapot only truly inspired sympathy when bystanders did not recall that the owner who refused to pay part of his rates happily paid all of his taxes from which came grants to voluntary schools. Writing almost a century before, Sydney Smith commented:

> When a human being believes that his internal feelings are the monitions of God, and that these monitions must govern his conduct; and when a great stress is purposely laid upon these inward feelings in all the discourses from the pulpit; it is, of course, impossible to say to what a pitch of extravagance mankind may not be carried, under the influence of such dangerous doctrines.[49]

However marred Passive Resistance was as a conscientious movement, was it effective politically? When writing to Edward VII in May 1905 Balfour referred to 'the religious controversy which is causing friction' and this is not an unreasonable summary of the Government's attitude. The Prime Minister admitted 'to finding it exceedingly difficult entirely to understand' Nonconformist grievances although he was reluctant to 'embitter feelings in Protestant Christianity already so weakened by division'. The Government's official attitude was explained in a letter from Balfour to *The Times* on 26 June 1903. Here he denounced the movement as 'a policy . . . quite unworthy of the citizens of a free country'. The real motive was not 'constitutional but sectarian'. With this he had no quarrel so long as Resisters' 'practice is consistent' and 'they show themselves ready to give to others what they claim as of right for themselves'. Their 'moral imperative' could not form any 'coherent principle underlying the present agitation'. 'These gentlemen', he argued, were 'fighting not for principle but for privilege' and the movement was a 'conspiracy against the cause of ordered freedom' and unworthy of Nonconformists. In 1904 he told one correspondent that Resistance was an 'evil precedent for the future of free institutions'.[50] As we shall see, it did form a precedent.

Despite their public pronouncements, the Government made several attempts at meeting Nonconformist objections even though Balfour privately felt, when he wrote his letter to *The Times*, that 'the Education Bill fever will be allayed in twelve months'. In the autumn of 1903, in March 1904 and in November 1904 there were attempts at settlements but they came to nothing. This last attempt arose when R. J. Campbell, now at the City Temple, called on the Prime Minister with a suggested compromise. It is no wonder that the Liberal Imperialist, Campbell, was 'politically dubious' to *The Crusader*. Perhaps Sears had heard that in 1899 he had offered himself as a Liberal candidate but had withdrawn. He told Herbert Gladstone that he feared 'his own people might turn against him on selfish grounds'. In his memoirs Campbell wrote that it was Gladstone who asked him to stand. He eventually joined the ILP. Unfortunately Balfour told him that he doubted if 'any compromise could be successfully attempted *before* the General Election; that it would be scornfully rejected by the other side; that it would dishearten our own people'. A permanent solution could only come after 'the other side, by painful experience, had found how difficult it was to deal with it from their own point of view; they would then be in a very different frame of mind'.[51]

A far greater problem facing the Government was the 'Welsh Revolt' where Nonconformist leaders with Lloyd George at their head decided to use the machinery of local government, and not individual action, to fight the Government. Nicoll was furious at this because his campaign would now be restricted to England. Fourteen of the sixteen Welsh LEAs simply refused to enforce the act. There was a fear that English councils like Northampton or the West Riding, where Nonconformity was strong, might follow their example and in November 1903 the Cabinet decided on a 'short measure putting them straight'. The bill giving Government power to circumvent local revolts became law but was never enforced. In September 1904 Welsh affairs reached a crisis. Balfour was told that 'Lloyd George has roused a mob which he cannot now quell . . . [he] frankly admits that the real objective is disestablishment in Wales'. Although they had nearly fallen out over the Welsh action, Lloyd George still asked Nicoll for his 'powerful aid' and the NFCC for a pledge of their support. The General Committee resolved that the Council 'will earnestly support the general policy which they [the Welsh LEAs] have announced' and if conflict became inevitable the Council would give its 'utmost moral and financial aid'. They still hoped, in somewhat inverted logic, that the Government would 'recede from their unconstitutional policy'. Newspaper reports spoke of £100,000 being raised for the Welsh revolt, money necessary to allow the LEAs to set up their own system of non-denominational schools as they had in effect closed down the state system in order to avoid giving money to Church schools.[52]

In May 1905 Lloyd George reported to the NFCC's Education Committee that while there was as yet no need for English money, 'a little later it would be necessary to appeal to the Nonconformists in England'. By September 1905 Balfour was told that the Free Church Council 'are now definitely taking up the Welsh affair. *They* do this because they recognise Lloyd George as a useful protagonist, and the Welsh business as a likely fighting ground for *their* purpose. And Lloyd George, who has always tried to avoid being rushed by Dr Clifford and Co. is now unable to keep them at arm's length . . . particularly because he needs their money bags.' When Lloyd George was tempted to a compromise which allowed a 'right of entry' into council schools outside school hours to give denominational religious instruction a telegram arrived from Thomas Law: 'You must be with us . . . if not you will ruin your reputation and mine.' This brought him into line although it remains a moot point as to who – the Welsh MP or the London Free Church leaders – used whom when. Between December 1902 and December 1905 when the Government fell, there were several occasions when compromise seemed possible and every time some party in the tangled affairs of educational politics – Passive Resisters, the Free Church Council, Lloyd George, the Government or the Church of England drew back. Undoubtedly the Resistance movement both encouraged the desire for peace by keeping the controversy alive in England and made it impossible to achieve. One ramification of the controversy was that the bill to establish a new bishopric for Birmingham had to be delayed. Balfour felt it was better to 'lie low' until things had cooled.[53] It was a most extraordinary situation:

an organization nominally religious was secretly manoeuvring with an MP and councillors from fourteen Welsh LEAs to flaunt an Act of Parliament and was pledged to raise large sums of money to finance an illegal system of schools and all under the banner of 'conscience'.

Of course, the single most important factor in political life between 1902 and 1905 was not education but Chamberlain's projected tariff reform or Imperial preference. This vitally affected the Resisters' impact on the Liberal Party. As far back as 1902 the Government were worried about Chamberlain's ideas on 'corn duty' and the Chief Whip reported that 'it is the one thing he is afraid of at an election, and that if he were the agent of the Liberal Party he would undertake to "sweep the country" on that issue'.[54] This is exactly what the Liberal leadership hoped to do and those MPs who had been uneasy at too close an identification with Nonconformity and Passive Resistance, saw in Chamberlain's new campaign a way out of their dilemma. Again, unlike education, defending free trade involved no legislation should Liberals win the upcoming election and would not endanger any coalition with the Irish Nationalists. For Passive Resisters it sounded remarkably like a death knell.

There were Liberals, however, who warned against taking Nonconformists for granted. 'It would not do, when we are going into battle', Bryce felt, 'to blunt the edge of the Puritan sword.' The immediate problem lay in those Unionist MPs who were prepared to leave the government benches and work with Liberals in defence of Free Trade if some arrangement could be made. The Liberal Chief Whip reported on Christmas Eve, 1903: 'It will be necessary I think to meet two or three of the leading Noncons. about the Free Fooders. Probably they could be got to see that the general position would be strengthened by the return of Free Fooders when it was pretty clear that our men would not have much chance.' On Boxing Day 'C.B.', like Bryce, still loyal to the Nonconformists, warned that 'we cannot compromise any of our other controversies'. Nonconformist leaders, he wrote, 'are naturally & justifiably suspicious of concessions'. Throughout all this period the Liberal Chief Whip was coordinating election strategy with Thomas Law. They met at least six times between 1903 and 1905 to coordinate the selection of Liberal candidates for Parliament. Law had become 'the Noncon. Chief Whip' and by September 1903 the Council were already 'promoting various candidates to wh. they will contribute . . . Much satisfied with his [Law's] argument'. With regard to the Free Fooders, Gladstone got Law to agree that 'each case wd. be considered on its merits . . . Wishes to discuss remaining vacant constituencies to arrange candidates'.

There were, of course, other groups making demands and other voices expressing anxiety: the Liberals promised Nonconformist leaders that a bill to meet their demands on education would be the first priority but could they openly commit the party to a policy attacking Church of England schools? Not surprisingly, in the same month in which Bryce wrote to Clifford asking him to be accommodating he was secretly negotiating with the Archbishop of Canterbury: not every Liberal voter was a Nonconformist. Likewise, no one knew what size majority the Liberals would have if they won an election. To make sure of a majority they might well need the support of Irish Nationalists and to get this they needed more than a renewal of a pledge to Home Rule. They agreed that in any new education bill, Roman Catholic schools should receive 'some sort of separate and distinct treatment'. When making the pledge Bryce had qualified it by saying that the party had only 'some slight hopes that a fair arrangement may . . . be made' and that Nonconformist leaders must not think 'we were deserting them'. It was still a pledge.[55]

If Liberal 'wire-pullers' needed reminding of Nonconformity's strength they got it in 1904 in the seven by-elections won that year by Liberals: of the seven successful candidates, five were Nonconformists. They also got it through frequent public warnings. In July 1904 Clifford was quoted as saying, 'The Liberal Party cares nothing for Passive Resistance'. In February 1905 Perks publicly warned his party's leaders that they 'were mightily mistaken if they thought the Nonconformists did not mean business. He would marshal all the forces of Nonconformity against any Liberal Party or administration which did not put in the forefront of its programme the repeal or amendment of the . . . [Education] Acts.' Another example of what Nonconformist muscle could do came when the Secretary of the Home Counties Liberal Federation complained, 'I can't get any place in the Home Counties to take an R.C.'. He cited the case of Hilaire Belloc. He had been forced to abandon his candidature at Dover because the 'extreme section simply won't have him, & they have come up here for another candidate.'[56]

Despite Nonconformity's undoubted power there were several in the party who feared their influence: George Cadbury, whose money helped to keep the party alive, did not want Liberals to appear as the hand-maid to Nonconformity. This would forfeit their claim that they and not the Independent Labour Party were the only party that could promote 'the interests of the millions of underpaid & suffering men, women & children in this country' who cared little for religious controversy. When the political world was daily expecting the fall of the Balfour government the Liberals' Chief Whip warned against taking office before an election could sort out which pressure group had most strength: 'Labour men, Irishmen, cranks of all sorts and last but not least the *Noncons*. wd. hammer at you and all our candidates to extract their pounds of flesh.'[57]

In the 1906 general election Nonconformist work and candidates would prove extremely important. As early as March 1905 the Free Church Council had publicly announced that they would enter the forthcoming campaign on behalf of the Liberals. Within days of the Liberals taking office in December 1905 the Council's General Committee adopted a national syllabus for religious instruction to show that Nonconformists had positive answers to their well-orchestrated complaints. They also issued an unprecedented 'Election Manifesto'. When the election came in January, leading Nonconformist ministers toured the country in support of Liberal candidates which included C. Silvester Horne, while pamphlets and leaflets poured out of the Free Church offices in London. In Manchester the Primitive Methodist College (where A. S. Peake had become a Resister) postponed examinations to allow students to work for a Liberal victory and in Taunton, A. D. Crossman, 'Tailor, Outfitter, Hatter and Hosier' of 10, North Street, left a prayer meeting that had begun at 7 a.m. at Albermarle Chapel 'to ask God's blessing on the Election' to write to the Liberal candidate, Arthur Ponsonby. He added that they would 'continue to pray throughout the day'.[58] God, it appeared, in at least one constituency, stood out against the Liberal landslide and favoured the Tory candidate, Sir Edward Boyle.

On the national level Providence was more Liberal: of 670 MPs returned, 401 were Liberals. The Tories and Liberal Unionists had lost 215 seats in what proved to be a Liberal landslide. Of the Liberal MPs elected, between 187 and 210 were Nonconformists and of these, between 157 and 180 were Liberal. (It remains difficult to establish definite totals for both Nonconformists and Nonconformist Liberals.) Twenty-four of the new MPs were Passive Resisters. The National Free Church Council's General Committee hailed the results as 'an answer from God to the united prayers of the Christian Churches of the land' but as the popular vote only gave the Liberals 306,400 more votes than the Tories it seems more a product of the British electoral system. It has become standard historical practice to comment on the number of Nonconformist MPs as the largest number ever to be elected which is true. Within the Liberal Party, however, the percentage of Nonconformists actually fell from the 1900 peak, even if we take the higher figure of 180 as accurate. In the 1900 election the percentage had been over half whereas in 1906 it fell to just under 42 per cent.[59]

Nonconformist strength in Wales, the work of Thomas Law, the efforts of the Free Church Councils and underlying all else, especially when we remember the limited nature of the franchise, Nonconformist concentration in the towns and cities, had done the trick. Although Nonconformists constituted only some fifteen per cent of the English population they made up roughly one-third of Parliament. Politicians at the time agreed that controversy over the 1902 Act, kept alive by the Passive Resisters, had ensured the support of English Nonconformity. The controversy had also ensured that education would not be forgotten in the wake of the Tariff Reform crisis:

within weeks of the election the new Liberal Government had agreed that their first major piece of legislation would be a bill to meet Nonconformist demands.[60] The Promised Land seemed in sight and the gamble of Passive Resistance had paid off and handsomely at that. The temporary set-back of the 1902 Act would be put right and the inevitable victory of Nonconformist forces in the new century was once again ensured. Nonconformity was healthier, stronger and more united than ever before, largely due to the controversy over education. The degree of political involvement undertaken by the Free Church Council was, after all, known but to a very few leaders. To the man in the pew it seemed as if the election and, behind it, the identification of Nonconformity with the forces of Liberalism and Progress had been truly 'an answer from God'.

When Campbell-Bannerman formed his new Liberal Government he included nine Nonconformists in the Government: Asquith, Birrell, Bryce, Lloyd George, Burns, Sidney Buxton, Sir Henry Fowler, Haldane and John Morley. In February the Cabinet agreed to give education top priority: the debt to Nonconformity would be honoured. Yet, there were warning voices. The High Church MP, Lord Hugh Cecil, wrote, 'I sometimes fear that Noncons. are inclined to overrate their powers & to be irreconciliable in proportion'. Soon Lloyd George, now President of the Board of Trade, began to advise caution: speaking at the NFCC's banquet to honour Nonconformist MPs, he said, 'Let . . . the nation . . . see that Nonconformity had the moderation, the wisdom, and the restraint essential to any party which sought to govern.'[61]

Augustine Birrell, President of the Board of Education, was given the task of devising another comprehensive bill which would hopefully meet Nonconformist demands while keeping the basic structure of 1902: the old demand that School Boards be brought back had been left to wither away. He had a difficult time and backbenchers grew restive at the leadership's moderation. Winston Churchill, now on the Liberal benches as one of the Free Fooders who had so worried Nonconformists, wrote, 'I do not suppose we are likely to attain the millenium; but a few Big Acts by way of instalment ought certainly to be put on the Statute Book.' 'Big Acts' are always difficult both to plan and to get through Parliament and education acts are as difficult as any. MPs were easily bored by the subject and many if not most had their children in private schools anyway. Birrell found he got 'very poor support from the Cabinet' but fortunately he never lost his sardonic wit. Perhaps he was musing on his own future reputation among Nonconformists when he wrote of Lord Loreburn's being made Lord Chancellor instead of the Nonconformist, Haldane. For his part it mattered little because 'to speak profanely, one lawyer's arse is very like another'.[62]

The Cabinet was divided, Irish MPs, acting on behalf of the English Roman Catholic hierarchy, were proving difficult, and finally the Church of England, led by Bishop Knox of Manchester, was rousing herself to fight with a spirit hitherto thought the prerogative of Nonconformists. The bill basically gave Nonconformists what they wanted: it effectively confiscated denominational schools which would have been forced to have nondenominational religious instruction on three days a week with their own instruction confined to two days. The majority of school managers would be from outside the denomination. If four-fifths of the parents in any school petitioned, then denominational RI would be given on all five days instead of three but this was confined to areas with a minimum population of 5,000, i.e. excluding small villages. It was a sop to urban Roman Catholics, not village churchmen.[63] Tories, inspired by Balfour, put up a fierce resistance against a measure which to their eyes undermined a national system of education to meet the demands of the most vociferous part of a minority. Typical of the many pleas Balfour received was a telegram from the Rector of Bugbrooke: 'Oh Sir, in this the hour of their bitter grief and shame don't let the country clergy your most devoted followers cry in vain to you to help them save their schools from base surrender.'[64]

In the event Nonconformist euphoria was to prove short-lived. The Bill was heavily amended by the Lords and even though many Liberal MPs moaned that it was 'fatal to let Lords think they cd. do as they liked' because this might endanger larger programmes of social reform, the Government did not force the issue.[65] Even the King's work for a compromise came to nought and the bill was abandoned. Birrell was rewarded for his efforts by being sent as Chief Secretary to the relative peace and quiet of Ireland which Bryce left for the even safer haven of the Ambassador's residence in Washington. Nonconformist strength had helped to put the Liberal Party into government but in so doing had shown the Church of England that what was sauce for the dissenting goose would do just as well for the conforming gander. If the Lords erred in throwing out a measure on which the Liberals had campaigned, the Liberals erred in trying to restructure a national system of education to fit the demands of a minority of the country. Nonconformists were learning the hard way that the power to influence was not the same as the power to control.

The Government had not surrendered to the Lords as much as fallen back, the better to fight another day and in so doing had kept the loyalty of the Nonconformists even if they were frustrated in seeing their educational goal achieved. The Prime Minister's private secretary noted the strength of the 'general indignation against the H. of Lords' and was relieved that there had been 'no alienation of the extreme Noncons. which further [?] compromise would have inevitably brought about'. True to their word, the government did attempt a 'Passive Resisters' Relief Bill' in 1907 to the fury of the Board of Education. In the following year a second comprehensive bill was brought forward to settle the debt to Nonconformity by guaranteeing an 'unsectarian' primary school in every district and an abolition of rate aid for church schools. However it too came to nothing when faced with total opposition from the Church of England. The Government, now under Asquith, who had never shared Campbell-Bannerman's loyalty to Nonconformists, had had enough: Bryce admitted that while education 'was worth a great deal as an issue in Jan. 1906', the 'cards have been so played that it is worth little now – perhaps indeed it would tell against, not for'. Not surprisingly Clifford wrote to the Prime Minister to warn that Nonconformists were 'losing heart' and his warning reminded the Government that they must tread very carefully. While ministers for their part simply wanted to get the 'wretched business out of the way' no one would act 'if Clifford was against him': this was said two days after Clifford's letter arrived in Downing Street.[66] If Nonconformity could not get the bill it wanted it would at least be able to ensure it would not get any bill it did not want.

In 1909 Nonconformist political hopes received another blow, far greater than Chamberlain's proposal for Tariff Reform. Lloyd George's radical budget and the attack on the Lords which followed meant that education could no longer be a priority for the Government. During the heyday of the Resistance movement before the decline set in in 1905, Sears and others had warned that Nonconformity might well have to join in destroying the House of Lords before they could get the educational system they wanted and now they were being proved right. Lloyd George wrote to his old comrade in arms, Nicoll, again asking for his aid: without Nonconformists' 'active and zealous co-operation in every constituency, we cannot hope to win; at least the victory would be such a doubtful one as to leave us weak, embarrassed and impotent'. 'It is Nonconformity alone' he went on, 'that can bring the middle class to our aid.'[67] It was the same argument the politicians had used in 1904 over Tariff Reform but this time it held water. Only after Britain had a new Constitution with the power of the Commons increased even further, would the power of Liberal Governments to pay off their supporters be guaranteed. A new educational system to meet Nonconformist criteria could only come after the defeat of the Lords.

In the event things turned out largely as Lloyd George had foreseen: the Constitution was redrawn and the Lords' powers were curtailed but by the end of 1911 British politics had entered a new era. The Liberals had lost their overall majority and were now weak and embarrassed if not impotent. Asquith's Government could only carry on with the support of Irish Nationalist and Labour MPs. Any new reform of education would have to be on a quite different basis from that of 1906 to 1908. Nonconformity had also changed: it was in 1910 that the long-standing dispute over the Free Church Council's political work came to a head when Thomas Law was ousted with such fatal results for him personally. Thereafter the Council was wary of the corridors of power. Government could meet some Nonconformist demands without legislation. One standard grievance had been the 'single school district' – areas, normally villages, where the only school was a Church one. In 1907 a grant of £100,000 was made available to build council schools in such areas when requested – like the old village Board schools built when no one but a Nonconformist lobby wanted them – but not even half of the money was allocated.[68] A later bill to 'bus' Nonconformist children from villages with only a Church of England school to nearby council schools was vetoed by Nonconformist leaders.

In 1911 the fourth education minister since 1905 was appointed. This was the Quaker, J. A. Pease, a Cambridge double blue and the inheritor of his father's banking and industrial fortunes. He still made the expected public references to the 'grievances of the Nonconformists' but added, when addressing Liberals in Grantham, that 'One of the things which struck him more than anything else . . . had been how the denominational controversy had impeded the progress of education almost in every branch'. A voice from the hall cried out, 'The best of luck to you, sir'. Older leaders, like John Clifford, could lament to the handful of Passive Resisters who carried on their protest that 'We have been beaten. Our numbers have decreased . . . The illusory expectation of speedy deliverance led some to surrender. The magistrates are gracious. "Sales" fail to attract attention'. Just the opposite was the case: Nonconformity was winning. The *Free Church Chronicle* pointed out 'there was much more in the administration of the Education Act . . . than many people are aware of' and, if properly used, would 'bring about the end desired' – the disappearance of Church of England schools for working people. Pease pointed out that for every seven children in Church schools in 1902 there were six in 1911 and of every three children in Board schools in 1901 there were four in Council schools in 1911. Between 1902 and 1911, 4,742 voluntary schools had been closed or transferred to the LEA. Ironically, all Nonconformity had to do was to stand back and let the hated Balfour Act do its work of eliminating Church schools for them.[69]

While the Government would still not touch education without prior Nonconformist approval, after 1910 they added a proviso. They would only introduce legislation if such were seen as 'an integral part of an advance in the direction of educational reform' since they did not want to be seen to be paying off a debt to Nonconformity.[70] Almost every year after 1910 saw plans for bills to amend the 1902 Act and all were first cleared with Nonconformist leaders. None got beyond the planning stage. Finally, in 1914 the Government decided on a comprehensive bill for the autumn session but the bill would only be introduced if 'the controversies of the past, which played so important a part from 1900 to 1911, were to be, by general agreement, dropped'. The real problems were continuity of education – only one in every ten children went on to secondary school – improving the quality of teachers and the physical condition of children, organizing scholarships, coping with schools that were too small – normally Church schools in villages – and the need for nurseries. It was a very different world from 1902.[71]

Even Nonconformity cared less for education. In March 1914 Nicoll told Lloyd George that the 'really notable feature' at the Free Church Council was not education but 'your land scheme'. This is what 'excites enthusiasm'. As 1914 wore on Pease got on with his plans: in June and July he conferred with Lloyd George, Clifford and other Nonconformist leaders regarding three alternate proposals. Then, on 3 August he had dinner with the Prime Minister. After the ladies had withdrawn to enjoy Margot's acidic wit, Asquith carried on with his drinking but showed emotion 'which was most unnatural to him . . . nothing theatrical about it, it was real & genuine – & with quiver of his lips, tears in his eyes & a break in his voice he took me quietly by the hand as I left the room, & in the doorway said "Jack, God moves in a mysterious way his own . . ." & failed to finish the quotation'. The following day Asquith's ramshackle Government found themselves and the Empire at war. In September the Norwich and District Citizens' League met and resolved, despite

Clifford's plea for the few remaining Resisters to carry on, that 'during the war we suspend our agitation and hold ourselves free to resume our protest anytime after the War is over'. A week later forty-six members met and signed a letter urging all subjects to close ranks in the face of the 'extraordinary international crisis'.[72] They never met again.

AFTERWORD

With its traditional connection to improvement and learning the word 'culture' is an appropriate one to apply to the Nonconformists. The world they created was, within living memory, a power within the land. To late twentieth-century Englishmen and to their descendants, it will appear as remote as the abbeys and priories of Pre-Reformation England. English Nonconformity by the end of the last century had all the attributes of power: it was vibrant, self-confident and arrogant. Within its ranks it contained a diversity which was a sign of health but one that was balanced by a body of shared beliefs, assumptions and traditions. Increasingly Nonconformists were discovering bonds which could unite them. They shared a common, confident vision about their future. Nonconformity had its own institutions, colleges, libraries, schools and charities; it had its own calendar of services, Class Meetings, Sunday Schools, outings, May meetings and chapel teas, however much despised by Matthew Arnold; it had its own movements which touched and improved the lives of millions – Bands of Hope, Pleasant Sunday Afternoons, Mutual Improvement Classes, Sunday Schools. It had its own heroes and giants – Charles Haddon Spurgeon, Hugh Price Hughes, Joseph Parker, John Clifford, R. W. Dale, its own buildings which often dominated their environment and in which they could take genuine pride; it had its own newspapers, publishing houses and international organizations.

Were that all, there would be less reason for historians to be concerned with it. English Nonconformity was much more than a cultural phenomenon, especially when the term is used in its newer, sociological, sense: it was part of a much wider, Victorian culture, most of whose attributes it increasingly came to share. As we have seen, there were few aspects of English life that were not touched in some manner by Nonconformists: industry, commerce, literature, journalism, publishing, town planning, travel, education, research, the universities, art, science, social work and even the stage. Most people know, through the phrase, 'The Nonconformist Conscience', that it affected politics both at the local level and by filling the ranks of the Liberal Party with local party workers and MPs. Between 1905 and 1914 it established a virtual veto over legislation on education and was constantly consulted by leading ministers; in 1908 England had her first Nonconformist-born Prime Minister. It was a power both in the Empire and in that special relationship between England and America. Yet by 1919 it seemed to many then, and to more later, dated and something of a relic. Since then it has declined as a power in the land and its numbers have shrunk as a proportion of the population. How could a force which had been so influential in English life for so long and which, by the end of the nineteenth century, was so powerful decline so quickly in the decades after 1919?

Several explanations have been offered and there is a vast amount of work that needs to be done before historians can attempt a satisfactory answer. Here we can only discuss certain explanations and offer tentative answers. Some have seen the cause of Nonconformity's decline in the effects of the Great War. Nonconformity threw itself into the war effort and Nicoll wrote in his paper within two days of the declaration of war a call to arms under the title, 'United We Stand'. All divisions – education, land reform, disestablishment in Wales, home rule in Ireland – must be laid aside. The older views of Radical Dissent had to be expunged even if they lingered in the popular imagination. In November 1915 one Essex farmer commented on the enthusiasm to enlist and recalled that when as a young man he had 'joined the Yeomanry, his chapel relatives looked upon him as a reprobate, who had done something desperately wicked. The other day at Chelmsford he saw one of these people, "a Pharisee and the son of a Pharisee", in VTC [Voluntary Training Corps] uniform, marching about as if slaughter was his honourable trade.'[1]

When war was declared, John Clifford was the most

famous of the Victorian political parsons and 'pro-Boer' left in England yet he thoroughly supported the war even though he would defend Conscientious Objectors. Within three months over fifty men from his London church, men whose characters and outlooks he had largely formed, had volunteered. By 1915 the Primitive Methodists noted that some 30,000 of their men were in the Colours: these formed over fifteen per cent of their total membership and probably not much under one-third of the male members. Indeed, it was the 'establishment' figure, Lord Lansdowne, not the inheritors of the Nonconformist Conscience, who led those advocating a negotiated settlement to end the war. Historians may be right in regarding the war years as doing more than anything else to increase the absorption of Nonconformity into the mainstream of national life. This was symbolized when George V and Queen Mary attended the Royal Albert Hall on 16 November 1918 for the Nonconformists' Thanksgiving Service to mark the end of the war. Three years later the King invested John Clifford, with the Companionship of Honour. Indeed, under Lloyd George honours rained on leading Nonconformists: unlike so many of these honours, those given to Nonconformists had been earned, not bought.

It is, of course, easy enough to find many comments claiming that the Great War marked an unparalleled change in English life. Nicoll's biographer wrote in 1925:

> Through the spring and early summer of 1914, people in London were concerned mostly with strikes and militant suffragettes and Irish rebels. We went about our business and our pleasure in placid fashion – as men did before the Flood. Then suddenly the sky darkened and thundered, the earth rocked under our feet, the day of judgment had begun.

We recall the comment cited earlier that, after the war, ministers were amazed at the pre-war confidence with which they accepted the inevitability of progress. Sir William Nicoll – he had been rewarded with a knighthood in 1909 for his services to the Liberal government – wrote in October 1914: 'The War has altered everything. One feels sure of nothing now. All the old foundations are shaken, and we do not know what we can keep.'[2] People who survive any great historic experience are not always the best judges of its lasting effects. They are often inclined to confuse its immediate effects – in this case the terrific loss of life, the growth of state control, the electoral changes, the inflation and the changes in social behaviour produced by the war effort – with fundamental changes to the nation's life. With the passage of time we can see that much if not most of English society carried on after 1919 as it had before 1914. There was little of the upheaval that threatened Scotland, or that occurred in Ireland, let alone in the shattered Romanov, Hohenzollern and Hapsburg empires.

Often those who say the war 'changed everything' cannot say exactly how this affected average people as opposed to authors, historians, journalists or the writers of memoirs. People also tend to forget that many of the changes attributed to the War were actually only hastened by it, that they most likely would have come in due course without a war. Likewise, the years preceding 1914, when judged strictly by British standards and not European, were in many ways more violent than those between 1914 and 1919. For their part, however, the Wesleyan Methodist Conference of 1920 had no doubts. The Conference Address referred to the 'swirl of rising dissatisfactions and disputings' and the

> ominous drift of untoward and foreboding things – the passion for pleasure, senseless extravagance, distaste for work, defiance of authority, ready resort to violence, lamentable laxity in sexual morals, flaunting disregard of the binding obligations of marriage and family life.

It is true that the War, like most wars, helped to relax moral standards and to bring on changes in social behaviour by quickening the pace of life, but Conference had also declared that 'we cannot with sufficient earnestness recommend plain living, simple habits, and self denial. Do not make the lot of your children too easy': this admonition was written twenty-eight years before, in 1892.[3]

Where historians are justified in asking about the effect of the War is in the loss of men and the effect this had on England's churches. The 772,785 men killed formed twelve out of every hundred men mobilized but the casualties were unevenly distributed. The likelihood of being killed was 'substantially higher' among officers than among the ranks and therefore higher among the classes which produced officers: men from public schools and the ancient universities. The Church which suffered the greatest loss was the Church of England not just because of her influence in the public schools and universities but because the bulk of men in the ranks, as well as the 'officer class', were Anglican: we must remember that Nonconformists formed only about fifteen per cent of the population. Finally, historians have known for some time that in statistical terms war deaths did not equal, let alone surpass, the number of men who probably would have left the country over the same period as emigrants to the colonies or America.[4]

One way of looking at the effect on Nonconformity, although admittedly only a rough index, is to compare membership totals for 1914 with those for 1919. In comparing annual membership figures we find that the membership of the four leading denominations did fall but only by 26,843 or 2.23 per cent. It would have been greater if the Congregational total had not actually increased by almost 6,000.[5] The decline, where it occurred, could have been due just as much to the influenza epidemic which swept Britain in 1918–1919 as to the war. We cannot argue too much from these figures because there had been individual years when membership decreased in periods when overall, it was increasing. Likewise, membership figures did not discriminate according to sex so that an increase of women could have offset to some degree the loss of men.[6] The fact still remains that between 1901 and 1931 there was an increase in the membership of all four major denominations, in some cases by over seven per cent despite war losses.[7]

The deaths of men from England's Nonconformist churches in the War, however harmful they were to the potential leadership of the churches, do not appear to have created a vacuum which in turn precipitated a crisis in chapel life which in its turn led to a 'decline' in political power and social influence. Are we justified, then, in looking at wider causes, causes which are often loosely referred to as cultural changes? The trouble with this approach is that it is so difficult to be precise and to produce concrete arguments. Bishop Hensley Henson and numerous conservative ministers had warned for many years of the problems involved in too close an identification of the Christian gospel with the beliefs and goals of the era in which it is preached. If there had been a wholesale change in English attitudes, behaviour and assumptions after 1919, if that year had truly marked the death of Victorian attitudes, then one could argue that the foundation for Nonconformist strength went out with those attitudes, like the baby with the bath water in which it had played too long. It is possible to cite numerous statements that this was the case, that Victorian culture was thrown overboard after the war: the future Tory Prime Minister, Stanley Baldwin, whose mother had been brought up a Wesleyan Methodist, told a group of Methodists in 1926 that 'We do not all realise in what a changed world we are living', but he went on to add this caveat, 'Superficially it is a frivolous world, full of "jazzing" and pre-occupation with pleasure, but under the surface it is intensely serious.'[8]

We have noted before the comment that many ministers in the 1930s looked back with amazement at their assumption before 1914 that human improvement and national progress were inevitable and that all that was needed was a more efficient organization of resources. Undoubtedly the 'thinking classes' – those who read and write memoirs, authors, journalists, ministers and so on – had undergone a tremendous upset because of the war. To what degree they reflected 'average' people's thoughts is not easy to know. Likewise, many came out of the War not to reject all the old assumptions but to build on them. John Clifford was no less 'radical' in 1919 than in 1914 and was more determined to fight militarism and to press for international arbitration and cooperation, now through the League of Nations. The War had, after all, achieved its aim of putting down Prussian militarism and defending the rights of small nations. Belgium was intact and the Kaiser was in exile in Holland. To Liberals there were two extra bonuses: the despised Romanovs were dead and in central Europe nationalism had been triumphant in the creation of the Successor States of Czecho-Slovakia, Poland, Yugoslavia and Hungary.

We should remember, however, that Nonconformity had survived other cultural changes of tremendous, though not of equal, significance or changes concentrated in such a relatively short period as the Great War. These included: migration from villages into towns, the growth of suburbs, the decline of the Calvinist tradition in favour of a more liberal Protestant view, the problems produced by Darwin, the difficulties over 'higher criticism', the decline of many town centres, the altered nature of the Church of England due to the High Church movement, the growing rejection of voluntarism in preference for state action, the development of the Imperial vision, the political divisions caused by 1886 and the unmistakable decline in religious attendances which progressed with the century. Nonconformity had survived them all, had grown, had adapted and had prospered. As we have already noted, it continued to grow in the first thirty years of this century and if its percentage of the population shrank, it had been shrinking since at least 1871. These thirty years formed a period, especially in the 1920s, when social change was, arguably, quickening its pace and politics were even more unsettled than in the late 1880s.

To a large degree the argument about a Nonconformist 'decline' based on a wholesale rejection of Victorian culture is really an argument about 'political culture' – Nonconformity's increasing identification with the Liberal Party and with the acceptance that progress was inevitable. Politically Europe had undergone a sea-change and as the twenties wore on people realized that more harm had been done than good. The Allies' 'victory' over Germany began to seem irrelevant: the growth of communism not only in Russia but, for a while, in Hungary and Germany, the collapse of the Hohenzollern dynasty, the demise of ancient institutions like the Hapsburg Monarchy, replaced by the weak and ultimately doomed states created by the politicians at the Versailles Peace Conference, and the horrific inflation which swept across so much of Europe caused widespread disillusion. In Britain the twenties saw the break-up of the Liberal Party into warring camps, the rise of Labour, the changes in the Conservative Party over Protection and the gold standard, talk by leaders like the fourth Marquess of Salisbury of a new Christian centrist party, widespread labour unrest and strikes, the General Strike of 1926 and the economic collapse which unseated the second Labour Government. The Tory Party itself was changing, not just in regard to Protection or the gold standard but in regard to its leadership. The party of the Gentlemen of England and of King and Country had as its leader from 1911 to 1925 the 'damned Scotch dissenting ironmonger', Bonar Law, and the successor to the High Church Baldwin in the 1930s was the Birmingham Unitarian, Neville Chamberlain.

Gladstone as an old man had pondered the future of politics. 'He takes a gloomy view of the position', Arnold Morley told Sir William Harcourt, 'so far as the Party & Political life generally are concerned. The next fifty years will not at their termination bear comparison with the half century that has passed! It is perhaps natural for him to think so, but I fear it is true.'[9] However, before we place too much emphasis on an old man's reflections we should recall that Victorian political life had never been static, as Gladstone's own career had shown. The politics of the 1850s, dominated by Palmerston, were not the same as the politics of the 1880s, dominated by Gladstone or the politics of the 1890s dominated by Balfour and Chamberlain. Political life was constantly changing: the Irish Nationalist Party seemed ruined in 1890–1891 but by 1910 they were a tail to wag Asquith's dog. The Tory Government of Arthur Balfour seemed doomed because of the split over Imperial Preference and the 1906 election debacle. Even though it recovered its popular vote by 1910 it spent a total of seventeen years in the wilderness and did not form a government until 1922. Since then it has been the dominant party in British politics.

The Liberal Party had split over Home Rule and spent the years between 1886 and 1892 and, again, from 1895 to 1905 on the Opposition benches. It was badly divided over the Boer War and increasingly over the role of government in what was becoming the Welfare State. Yet in 1906 it had won a massive victory only to stagnate in 1910, after which it could only carry on with the help of Labour and the Irish. Nonconformity had weathered those divisions and those long periods out of office and, as we saw, used them to good advantage by increasing its influence within the party long before the 1906 election. Indeed, Nonconformity's political power had been growing and making itself felt decades before the Liberal Party came into being. Again, some in the years immediately before the 1906 election felt that Nonconformity had established too close a link with the Liberal Party and its machinery. But this was true not of Nonconformist denominations so much as the Free Church Council and its Secretary, Thomas Law.

We must ask if the Nonconformists were any more closely identified with the Liberals than the Church of England was with the Tories. Political alignments along religious divisions were an accepted part of Victorian political life. If politics cut across religion, religion cut across politics whether one were a High Churchman like Lord Hugh Cecil, urging more government help for Church schools, an Evangelical like Lady Wimborne, paying money to the Liberal Party in return for the nomination of Low Church bishops, or Nonconformist ministers like Silvester Horne or Hugh Price Hughes, urging support for the Liberals in order to get legislation on education or reform of the marriage laws. The Tory Party as naturally turned to the Church for support in the nineteenth century and as naturally was given it as Liberals turned to the chapels for support. When Archbishop Benson warned Balfour that younger clergymen were turning against the party, Balfour could only remark that:

I am glad to think that the loyalty of the Conservative party to the Church is of a different character. And even when the Archbishop's prophecy has come to pass – and the Conservatives are permanently excluded from office by the efforts of Churchmen, he will find that the Church may still count upon the affection and support of those who alone in the past have lifted a finger to preserve or to reform her.

There was simply a shared community of interests. As the radical Congregational minister, J. Hirst Hollowell, pointed out in less elegant terms in 1904: 'No one, of course, ever noticed a smell of politics about a vicarage.'[10] Where Anglicans differed from Nonconformists is that they were beginning to see a genuine, and growing, multiplicity of political allegiances: the old Church-and-King philosophy held true but there were many Churchmen who were Liberals, Liberal Unionists and, in the case of some younger priests, Labour, regardless of their 'label' within the Church. Within those Nonconformist denominations we have been surveying, the division tended to come largely between Wesleyan Methodists on the one hand and Congregationalists, Baptists and Primitive Methodists on the other. Only among Wesleyans did observers think a man might be something other than a Liberal.

Those Nonconformists who did assume that to be a Nonconformist was to be a Liberal never sold their souls to the Liberal Party. Nonconformists frequently warned that they must not be taken for granted and constantly remembered that there were denominational goals which were not party goals: English disestablishment was the most obvious. (Not only Gladstone, but Harcourt and Rosebery were each in his own way devout Anglicans while the party never adopted disestablishment for England.) There were always voices warning against too strong an identification of Nonconformity with the Liberal Party, if not with Liberalism, and Nonconformity was never totally behind the Liberals, either before 1886 or afterwards. Again we return to the statistics of growth between 1901 and 1931: when the Liberal Party was losing supporters and disintegrating, Nonconformity was increasing its numbers and working to achieve greater unity. Baptists and Congregationalists – the two bodies with the loosest organizations – worked to achieve greater structural unity while a new Free Church body was created to establish closer ties to the denominations, something the old Council had never achieved. The differences between Nonconformists and Churchmen were to a considerable degree that Nonconformists were more open about their ties to the Liberals than Churchmen were about their ties to the Tories: Hughes's campaign to get Parnell disowned by Gladstone was a good example of this. If John Clifford took to the platform in 1902, Robertson Nicoll went to his desk to write to Lloyd George while Thomas Law took himself to Westminster to see Herbert Gladstone. It was with men like Law and Nicoll that Nonconformists learned that effective work can be done in private as well as on the platform.

In 1915 Lloyd George wrote to Nicoll about the postponement of the Welsh Disestablishment Act and commented in passing, 'One never knows what a general election will bring forth, but at the post-bellum election the country will be impatient of the obtrusion of stale issues.'[11] Nonconformists like Nicoll fully understood this: after the collapse of the Liberals' second effort to get a new comprehensive education bill in 1908 Nonconformists dropped many of the demands made before the general election. Of course Nicoll could have pointed out that 'stale' issues could prove surprisingly fresh: it was the Liberal Government which rediscovered the value of temperance legislation as an aid to the war effort. Likewise, after the war Radical Dissent's old cry for a reduction in armaments and the need for international arbitration became suddenly very relevant with the creation of the League of Nations.

In the short term the split in the Liberal Party affected Nonconformist power: sixty-five Nonconformists stood under Asquith's banner as opposed to fifty-nine under Lloyd George's Coalition banner. Should the split in the Liberal Party prove its undoing, there was no reason why Nonconformity should not make itself felt within the Labour Party. R. F. Horton had pointed out in 1897 that 'large numbers' of Nonconformists are conservatives now, and still more are Liberal Unionists' and he predicted that 'in that political cleavage of the future, between old Liberalism and the labour party, both sides are equally represented'. Indeed, there were forty-seven Nonconformist candidates in the Labour Party in 1918 and of the fourteen ministers who stood, eight were Labour. In certain areas the 'Nonconformist' view and the 'Labour' view differed: on education the new party wanted nothing to do with the older, chapel v. church battles. Yet on many other issues Nonconformists, at least the non-Wesleyans, could readily support a Labour candidate. If Nonconformity were never again to have the power it had enjoyed over the Liberal Party between 1902 and 1908, it had to remember that these years were extraordinary and could not be repeated. The pattern in the nineteenth century was of influence through shared goals and local work and there was no reason why this could not be repeated in the twentieth century with Labour. When Stanley Baldwin addressed those Methodists in 1926 he pointed out something he had noticed in the House of Commons:

> I find there, especially among the Labour Party, many men who fifty years ago would inevitably have gone into the Christian Ministry. They have been drawn into political life from a deep desire to help the people . . . I certainly agree with many observers that since the war the manifest forces of Satan have been more conspicuously at large . . . On this account I feel it to be so important that a church like yours should send its quota of young men into politics to-day.[12]

Without the gift of hindsight there is no reason why a Nonconformist in the 1920s should not have assumed that whereas his Victorian fathers had supported Liberals, he and his friends should support Labour with the same possibility of influence if not control. If individual Nonconformists devotedly adhered to the Liberals and felt their political power decreasing with the party's that was their choice: it was not inevitable.

It may well be that the War, cultural changes and political upheavals, while important, are not the cause of Nonconformity's ultimate decline. That cause may be the same factor that brought about Nonconformist growth in the first place: urbanization. The 1931 Census pointed out a change that had occurred in English life between 1901 and 1931: urban growth before 1901, as we have already seen, depended on the movement of people into towns and cities from the surrounding countryside. After 1901, the Census had discovered, growth was no longer due to migration but solely to 'the spreading or the decentralisation of the towns themselves'. Along with this, the pace of increase, both in the population as a whole and in towns in particular, had fallen: what increases there had been 'represent little more than the natural development of the urban areas themselves'.[13]

This statement did not mean that only from 1901 did cities provide their own growth, but that from 1901 this source was the only source of that growth. Throughout the nineteenth century towns and cities, as they grew because of emigration, began to replenish themselves. As the years wore on, growth due to emigration lessened while growth due to the cities' own birth rate quickened. By 1901 internal growth was the only growth. May it be that the very force which gave Nonconformity its foundation in Victorian England also ordained its ultimate decline? We noticed in Chapter 2 that Nonconformity during the last thirty years of the century, and we suspect in the decades before then, did best in those towns with a population between 10,000 and 100,000, followed by those with populations between 100,000 and 250,000. In the nine cities with populations over 250,000 it was even less strong. It would not appear that Nonconformity could not exist in the largest cities, as if there were something in the climate of a city with a population in excess of a certain figure, that was hostile to Nonconformity. Indeed Nonconformity prospered in the suburbs of the largest cities and showed remarkable resilience in devising Institutional Churches, Settlements and Tabernacles to cope with new demands and new social groups both in declining town centres and in expanding suburbs. It appears that Nonconformity could not thrive in those towns where growth due to internal regeneration as opposed to migration had become first the main means of growth and, then, the only means. The larger the city the more likely it was producing its own growth: London was almost doing this by the early 1890s. Nonconformity waxed strong because of rural migration into the cities. When this migration began to wane, so did Nonconformist power.

Much research needs to be done into this field and here we can only sketch a tentative explanation. To do this a survey has been made of 435 towns which, by 1901, had a population of over 10,000. We can say that as a general rule, while the four major denominations grew in membership, their percentage of their towns' growing population steadily declined, due, it would appear, to the towns' own increasing ability to grow without recourse to rural emigrants. Nonconformists could bring their religion with them into the towns and out again into the suburbs and they could perhaps hand it on to the first or even second generation to be born there, but they could not, in the end, square chapel going with urban life and the faster the pace of growth produced by the towns themselves, the slower the ability to keep up with it.

This was not always the case, but generally so. In London and Liverpool, between 1871 and 1901 the Nonconformist proportion of the population actually increased but only just, from 2.38 to 2.41 per cent for London and from 1.84 to 2.29 per cent for Liverpool. In the seven other largest cities the Nonconformist proportion declined in all but Bristol where it rose from 5.04 to 5.44 per cent. If we look at the next group of towns, those twenty-four whose population was between 100,000 and 250,000 by 1901, we find that there is adequate information for twenty-two. Of these, all but seven saw the Nonconformist strength decline. In the next group, those forty-two towns which by 1901 had populations between 50,000 and 100,000 and where Nonconformist growth was strongest, we still find that of the forty where we can make some comparison, the Nonconformist percentage of the town's population fell from the 1871 level in all but ten. In the final group, those 360 towns with populations between 10,000 and 50,000 by 1901, a study was done of all the towns with a population of 30,000 to 50,000 and of forty-five of the sixty-eight towns with populations between 20,000 to 30,000. Here we find that of the seventy-one towns, there is adequate information for thirty-eight and of these, Nonconformist strength fell between 1871 and 1901 in all but ten. The pattern then is that the smaller the town the greater the chance that the stage had not been reached when urban growth came from within: as a result Nonconformity not only held its own or increased in absolute numbers but was able to increase as a percentage of the population. In no case did the increase keep pace with the growth in population. Of course these are only the roughest of guides and this is only at best a factor, however important it may be. Equally, in many cases there were local factors which go a long way to explain the changes.[14]

Victorian Nonconformity therefore seems to have benefited from a unique coming together of a variety of historical events, the most important of which was rural migration: Nonconformists, and those people to whom Nonconformity would have an appeal, moved into the expanding towns of England. Once there they tended to prosper, as did those chapels which they attended. In due course they moved into the suburbs. Wages rose, the purchasing power of the pound increased and prices generally fell. Those who benefited most in the Victorian economic miracle were the lower-middle and upper-working classes, again those people who filled Nonconformist pews. They benefited from expanding educational opportunities in a century devoted to increasing literacy, self-education and personal achievement. Nonconformity was able to produce a ministry which itself came from the same classes and backgrounds of those to whom the minister preached. The minister reflected these great Victorian goals and was in a sense a 'self-made man' preaching to 'self-made men'. He was able to establish a strong bond between pulpit and pew, something which the Established Church was not able to do and which increasingly no Church seems capable of doing. With good reason, therefore, some worried that the minister might grow away from his followers if he became too sophisticated and learned. The price for too much education might be the creation of an intellectual priesthood whose mysteries were alien to average people. It was a culture which had a great appeal to men and in which men predominated and as such must be somewhat unique in English history.

Nonconformity was overwhelmingly an urban culture despite its fondness for the village life its adherents had left behind. If it lost the ability to keep up its growth when rural migration lessened and then stopped, it found it could not thrive in an urban environment. The reason for this was not that there was anything essentially hostile to religion in town life or in the life of those towns over a certain size, because the inability was general; it lay in the fact that Nonconformists suffered from their own prosperity and with it, from their absorption into the mainstream of urban life. Here the majority of Englishmen did not regularly go to church or chapel. Here Nonconformity, with its own insistence on the 'internalization' of the Christian religion suffered badly: people who believed that religion was essentially, and then completely, a way of life based on a regard for others and a private belief in God, had no need to go to church and even less, to chapels where the emphasis was on preaching.

Nonconformists were frightened of what they called 'leakage to the Establishment'. It is impossible to say how many Nonconformists 'went over' to the Church of England but one suspects large numbers did so, far larger than those Anglicans who became Roman Catholics although they have been given most of the attention both by propagandists and historians. Yet the far more important 'leakage' was to no church at all. The more Nonconformist chapels became part and parcel of suburban life, the greater the risk of this loss through what Professor David Martin, writing about the 1980s, has called the 'open door towards the wider community'.[15] As the Victorian era wore on, more and more alternatives to Sunday chapel-going were created: these may have accelerated after 1919 with the growth of cinema and wireless but, other than the radio, they were not created then. The Victorians had their day-trips, cycling expeditions, band concerts in the parks (unless stopped by the local Free Church Council), art galleries, amusement palaces and, increasingly, respectable Sunday papers. The same problem has faced the Roman Catholic Church in England as the descendants of Irish immigrants move up the social scale, out of the terraced streets and into the suburbs. Indeed, in the late twentieth century it may be said that the Roman Catholics have largely ousted the Nonconformists in the chief supporting role to the national church. As Archbishop Robert Runcie put it, 'the Roman Catholic Church is now making for a centre stage role in the ecumenical play'.[16] In due course they, like the Nonconformists, will be absorbed into the suburban culture of which T. S. Eliot wrote in *Choruses from 'The Rock'*:

And no man knows or cares who is his neighbour
Unless his neighbour makes too much disturbance,
But all dash to and fro in motor cars,
Familiar with the roads and settled nowhere.

305

The decline of Nonconformist culture may well have been brought on by forces which at one time had given it strength and confidence. It has nevertheless left a legacy which has permeated English society even among those who are unaware of its source. Its chief contribution to the English character lies in that 'conscience' which, once peculiar, is now more or less universal.[17] At times it can be sanctimonious but at other times it can point with a clarity envied by many other nations to standards of public as well as private behaviour and decency that mark a civilized society enjoying, if not replenishing, the fruits of a Christian past. It insists that public men should adhere to traditional standards of behaviour, that there is not one moral law for the powerful and one for the rest, that each individual is in some sense morally responsible for the problems of the world. If the world of the chapel and the Sunday School, the teas and the Pleasant Sunday Afternoons, is gone, to be only a chapter in the long history of English religion and to survive only in folk memory and history books, then the legacy of the Nonconformist Conscience may be Nonconformity's most enduring memorial.

MANUSCRIPT COLLECTIONS CONSULTED

Acland MS Papers of Sir Arthur H. D. Acland, Bt, Bodleian Library, Oxford.

Allon MS Papers of the Rev. Henry Allon as editor of the *British Quarterly Review*, Dr Williams's Library, London.

Asquith MS Papers of H. H. Asquith, Bodleian Library, Oxford.

Aylesbury Church MS Church Minutes, Aylesbury Congregational Church 1877–1910, Buckinghamshire Record Office.

Balfour MS Papers of Arthur Balfour, British Library.

Baptist Union MS Minutes of the Baptist Union General Committee, 1902–1908, Baptist Church House, London (abbreviated in the notes to BU MS).

Board of Education MS Files relating to educational legislation and administration, ED 24/13A to ED 24/32, ED 11/63 and ED 13113E, Public Record Office.

Bristol Free Church MS Minutes of the Bristol and District Federation of Evangelical Free Churches, October 1898 to May 1971, by courtesy of Mr C. Stirzaker, then Secretary of the Somerset Free Church Federal Council (Bristol FC MS).

Broad Street Chapel MS Minutes of Church Meetings, Broad Street Baptist Chapel, Nottingham, 1820–1902, University of Nottingham.

Brougham MS Correspondence between Henry Brougham and John Cassell, University College, London.

Bryce MS Papers of James Bryce, Bodleian Library, Oxford.

Cabinet MS Drafts of bills, committee reports, correspondence etc. circulated in Cabinet, Public Record Office.

Campbell-Bannerman MS Papers of Sir Henry Campbell-Bannerman, British Library (C-B MS).

Chamberlain MS Papers of Joseph Chamberlain, University of Birmingham.

Clark MS Diary of the First World War kept by the Rev. Andrew Clark, Bodleian Library, Oxford.

Creaton Congregational Church MS Minutes of Church Meetings, Creaton Congregational Church, Northamptonshire, 1903–5, Northamptonshire Record Office (Creaton MS).

Davidson MS Papers of Randall Davidson, Archbishop of Canterbury, Lambeth Palace Library.

Devonshire MS Papers of Spencer Compton, 8th Duke of Devonshire, Chatsworth.

Dilke MS Papers of Sir Charles Dilke, Bt, British Library.

Durham Primitive Methodist MS Minutes of the Quarterly Meetings, Durham Primitive Methodist Circuit, 1902, County Durham Record Office.

Franklin MS Collection of newspaper cuttings, bills of sale, distress warrants and other items relating to the Passive Resistance movement, Queen's Road Baptist Church, Coventry, by courtesy of the Minister and Deacons.

Free Church Council MS Minutes of the General (1902–6), Education (1905–13) and Organizing (1902–3) Committees of the National Council of Evangelical Free Churches, Dr Williams's Library, London (FC Archives).

Gainford MS Papers of J. A. Pease, 1st Baron Gainford, Nuffield College, Oxford.

Gladstone MS Papers of W. E. Gladstone, British Library.

Haldane MS Papers of R. B. Haldane, National Library of Scotland.

Hamilton MS Papers of Sir Edward Hamilton, Permanent Secretary to the Treasury (1902–7), British Library.

Harcourt MS Papers of Sir William Harcourt, Bodleian Library, Oxford.

Holmer Green Baptist Church MS Minutes of Church Meetings, 1877–1962, Buckinghamshire Record Office (Holmer Green MS).

Ilbert MS Papers of Sir Courtenay Ilbert, Parliamentary Counsel (1899–1902) and Clerk of House of Commons (1902–21), House of Commons Library.

John Clifford Donation Copies of articles, pamphlets and corrected printers' proofs, belonging to John Clifford and given by his Church (containing material not available in the British or Bodleian Libraries), Dr Williams's Library, London.

Liberation Society MS Executive Committee Minutes (1902–3), Party and Electoral Committee Minutes (1902–6), Religious Equality Parliamentary Committee Minutes (1901–3), Greater London Record Office.

Lloyd George MS (Lords) Lloyd George Papers held in the House of Lords Record Office.

Lloyd George MS (Wales) Lloyd George Papers held in the National Library of Wales.

Lower Meeting MS Church Books containing the Records of the Church of Christ assembling at the Lower Meeting House at Amersham, No. 3 (1881–1937), Buckinghamshire Record Office.

Mansfield Road MS Minutes of Church Meetings, Mansfield Road Baptist Church, Nottingham, 1866–1916, University of Nottingham.

Marvin MS Papers of F. S. Marvin, Bodleian Library, Oxford.

McKinnon Wood MS Papers of T. McKinnon Wood MP, Bodleian Library, Oxford.

Milner MS Papers of Alfred, 1st Viscount Milner on deposit in the Bodleian Library, Oxford.

Milton-under-Wychwood Baptist Church MS Minute Book (No. 1: 1844–1928) of Church Meetings, Milton-under-Wychwood Baptist Church, Oxon., by courtesy of Minister and Deacons (Milton MS).

Newbolt MS Papers of Sir Henry Newbolt, Bodleian Library, Oxford.

Newdegate MS Papers of Sir Francis Newdigate-Newdegate MP, Warwickshire Record Office.

Nicoll MS Letters from Lloyd George to W. Robertson Nicoll, 1902–15. Courtesy of Dr K. O. Morgan.

Norwich and District Citizens' League MS Minutes of the League, 1903–14, Norfolk Record Office (Norwich PR MS).

Old Meeting MS Minutes of Church Meetings, Old Meeting [Congregational] Church, Stroud, 1836–1902, Gloucestershire Record Office.

Osborne MS Papers of C. C. Osborne, British Library.

Ponsonby MS Papers of Arthur Ponsonby, Campbell-Bannerman's Private Secretary, Bodleian Library, Oxford.

Prime Ministers' Letters Copies of letters from Prime Ministers to the Sovereign regarding Cabinet meetings, Royal Archives (RA).

Primitive Methodist MS Minutes of Conference of the Primitive Methodist Connexion, John Rylands Library, Manchester (PM Archives).

Protestant Dissenting Deputies MS Minutes of the Finance, General and Parliamentary Committees for 1902–6, Greater London Record Office (Deputies MS).

Protestant Dissenting Ministers MS Minutes of meetings of the General Body of Protestant Dissenting Ministers, 1898–1914, Dr Williams's Library, London (Ministers MS).

Protestant Society MS Minute Books, 1811–57, Dr Williams's Library, London.

Redmond MS Papers of J. E. Redmond, National Library of Ireland; microfilm in Bodleian Library, Oxford.

Ridding MS Papers of George Ridding, 1st Bishop of Southwell, Bodleian Library, Oxford.

Riley MS Papers of Athelstan Riley, Lambeth Palace Library.

Ripon MS Papers of 1st Marquess of Ripon, British Library.

Rosebery MS Papers of 5th Earl of Rosebery, National Library of Scotland.

Runciman MS Papers of Walter Runciman, Newcastle upon Tyne University Library.

Sadler MS Papers of Sir Michael Sadler, Bodleian Library, Oxford.

Salisbury MS Papers of the 3rd Marquess of Salisbury, Hatfield House; formerly at Christ Church College, Oxford.

Samuel MS Papers of Herbert, 1st Viscount Samuel, House of Lords Record Office.

Sandars MS Papers of J. S. Sandars, A. J. Balfour's Private Secretary, Bodleian Library, Oxford.

Selborne MS Papers of the 2nd Earl of Selborne, Bodleian Library, Oxford.

Spender MS Papers of J. A. Spender, editor of the *Westminster Gazette*, British Library.

Stowe MS Papers of Harriet Beecher Stowe, Berg Collection, New York Public Library.

Viscount Gladstone MS Papers of Herbert, 1st Viscount Gladstone, British Library.

Viscount Harcourt MS Papers of Lewis, 1st Viscount Harcourt, Bodleian Library, Oxford.

Wareham Congregational Church MS Minutes of Church meetings, 1902–6, Wareham Congregational Church, Dorset, Dorset Record Office (Wareham MS).

Wesleyan Methodist MS Agendas of Conference, 1890–1902, Journals of Conference, 1902–6 and Minutes of the Committee of Privileges, 1902–6, Wesleyan Methodist Connexion, John Rylands Library (WM Archives).

Wilson MS Papers of H. J. Wilson MP and his family, Sheffield Central Reference Library.

Wotton-under-Edge MS Burial Registers, 1803–91 and Minutes of Church Meetings, Wotton-under-Edge Congregational Tabernacle, Glos., 1803–1911, Gloucestershire Record Office.

NOTES

Abbreviations used in the notes

AHR	*American Historical Review*
BQ	*Baptist Quarterly*
BU	Baptist Union of Great Britain and Ireland
BUHB	*Baptist Union Hand-book*
Bodley	Bodleian Library, Oxford.
BJES	*British Journal of Educational Studies*
BW	*British Weekly*
BN	*Building News and Architectural Review*
BIHR	*Bulletin of the Institute of Historical Research*
Ch.A.	Chairman's Address: Congregational Union.
CH	*Church History*
CQR	*Church Quarterly Review*
Con. Add.	Conference Address.
CQ	*Congregational Quarterly*
CR	*Congregational Review*
CU	Congregational Union of England and Wales
CUYB	*Congregational Union Year Book*
Con. Rev.	*Contemporary Review*
Fort. Rev.	*Fortnightly Review*
FC	Free Church
FCYB	*Free Church Year Book* This term includes all annual reports of meetings of the Free Church Congress (1892, 1894–96) and of the National Council of Evangelical Free Churches (1896 onwards).
HJ	*Historical Journal*
JEH	*Journal of Ecclesiastical History*
LQR	*London Quarterly Review*
Nine. Cen.	*Nineteenth Century [and After]*
P&P	*Past and Present*
Pr. A.	President's Address: Baptist Union or National Council of Evangelical Free Churches.
PM	Primitive Methodist Connexion

PMM	*Primitive Methodist Minutes of Conference*
PP	Parliamentary Papers
QR	*Quarterly Review*
TB	*Temple Bar*
UMFC	United Methodist Free Churches
WM	Wesleyan Methodist Connexion
WMM	*Wesleyan Methodist Minutes of Conference*

Place of publication is London unless stated otherwise. The publisher's name is given for those books in print. References have been grouped together whenever possible for ease of reading.

INTRODUCTION

1 H. F. Lovell Cocks, 'The Nonconformist Conscience', *The Hibbert Journal* xxxviii (1940), p. 472; cf. his book, *The Nonconformist Conscience* (1943).
2 Hugh Walpole, *The Old Ladies* (1924), p. 32.
3 The Rev. William Cuff, Pr. A., Spring 1900, *BUHB*, 1901, p. 96.
4 Anon., 'Some Tendencies of Modern Nonconformity', *CQR*, liv (1902), pp. 113–14.
5 cf. J. E. B. Munson, 'The Oxford Movement by the End of the Nineteenth Century: The Anglo-Catholic Clergy', *CH*, xliv (1975); Anon., 'Recent Changes in Wesleyan Methodism', *CQR*, xix (1885), *passim*; Arnold Bennett, *A Great Man: A Frolic* (1919 edn; 1st publ. 1904), p. 205.

1. THE NONCONFORMIST IMPACT ON VICTORIAN LIFE

1 The Rev. C. H. Kelly, Pr. A., 1900 *FCYB*, 1900, p. 9; *PMM*, 1901, p. 190. For the extraordinary story behind the erection of Cromwell's statue see James Munson, 'Objections Overruled', *Country Life*, 2 November 1989.
2 Anon., 'Some Tendencies', p. 113.
3 Of 3,921,588, 1,946,959 or 49.65% were Nonconformist. *FCYB*, 1902, pp. 320–8.
4 Information taken from the relevant issues of *BUHB*, *CUYB*, *PMM* and *WMM*. The figures for 1871 were: Baptists, 160,978; Wesleyan, 319,794; Primitive Methodists, 148,798. The Rev. Samuel Vincent, Pr. A., Autumn 1898, *BUHB*, 1899, p. 69.
5 R. Mudie-Smith (ed.), *The Religious Life of London* (1904), pp. 15–18. The book was based on a 1902–3 *Daily News*

survey. In 1870 there were 33,679 Baptists; in 1901 there were 62,392, an increase of 28,713 or 85%. In 1870 Baptists constituted 1.2% of London's population which by 1901 had grown to 1.4%. The figures present two problems: the definition of what constituted 'London' changed radically between 1870 and 1901 due to the inclusion of rapidly expanding suburbs, a change which benefited Baptists; second, one must beware that some 'growth' was due to the adherence of some chapels to the BU, chapels which before the 1890s had stood outside it. In Mudie-Smith's survey, however, a chapel was listed as 'Baptist' whether in the Union or not.

6 R. W. Dale, *History of English Congregationalism* (1907), p. 725; H. S. Skeats & C. S. Miall, *History of the Free Churches of England 1688–1891* (n.d. [1891]), p. 644, n. 1; Andrew Mearns, *England for Christ: A Record of the Congregational Church Aid and Home Missionary Society* (1886), pp. 193–6.

7 Information taken from the *BUHB, CUYB, PMM* and *WMM* for the years 1890 to 1902 inclusive.

8 A copy of the appeal brochure may be found in the Gladstone MS, Add. Mss 44188 *ff* 14–15.

9 *FCYB*, 1897, pp. 217–19.

10 Albert Peel, *The Congregational Two Hundred 1530–1948* (1948), pp. 247–8. (This edn includes *A Hundred Eminent Congregationalists*, publ. 1927). A. G. Gardiner, *Pillars of Society* (1913), pp. 201–2. See W. P Jolly, *Lord Leverhulme* (1976); Marina Vaizey, 'The Jewel in Liverpool's Crown', *The Sunday Times*, 19 June 1988.

11 In the author's possession.

12 Edwin Hodder, *The Life of Samuel Morley* (1887, 3rd edn), p. 207; *The Author's Note Book*, 1 February 1877; Agatha Ramm (ed.), *The Political Correspondence of Mr Gladstone and Lord Granville 1868–1876* (1952), p. 43.

13 Joseph Chamberlain to Lord Salisbury, 12 December 1896, Salisbury MS; W. D. Rubenstein, 'British Millionaires, 1809–1949', *BIHR*, 1974 (XLVII), *passim*; B. W. E. Alford, *W.D & H.O. Wills and the Development of the United Kingdom Tobacco Industry 1786–1965* (1973), pp. 98–9 & Rubenstein, 'British Millionaires', *passim*.

14 Anon., *100 Years in Steel* (Sheffield, n.d. [1937]), *passim*. John Brown & Co., originally an Anglican family company, bought a controlling interest in 1903; R. G. Burnett, *The Life of Joseph Rank* (1945), p. 213.

15 A. A. Thomson (ed.), *By Faith and Work: The Autobiography*

of the Rt Hon the First Viscount Mackintosh of Halifax (1966), *passim.*

16 Mark Girouard, *The Victorian Country House* (London, Yale University Press, 1979, rev. and enlarged edn), pp. 205–12.

17 A. S. Peake, *The Life of Sir William Hartley* (1926), pp. 79, 49–51.

18 *The Times*, 8 April and 5 June 1907; *Chemist and Druggist*, 13 April 1907.

19 cf. Tom Jones, *Henry Tate 1819–1899* (1960), R. H. Blackburn, *Sir Henry Tate* (n.d.) and Douglas Cooper (ed.), *The Courtauld Collection* (1954). This contains a memoir of Samuel Courtauld.

20 [F. Rathbone, (ed.)], *Old Wedgwood and Old Wedgwood Ware: Handbook to the Collection* (1885, privately printed), p. v.

21 *Pall Mall Gazette* Extra, *The House of Commons in 1906* (1906), p. 87; *The Times*, 11 November 1912; Viscount Furness to the author, 13 April 1977.

22 *The Times*, 4 April 1910. His estate was proved at £726,356.

23 Roy Douglas, *The History of the Liberal Party 1895–1970* (1971), p. 68; George Cadbury to Herbert Gladstone, 2 June 1905, Viscount Gladstone MS, Add. Mss 46063 *f* 1.

24 H. C. Colman, *Jeremiah James Colman* (1905, priv. printed), p. 443; J. Guinness Rogers, *An Autobiography* (1903), pp. 268ff.; 14 October 1902, Lower Meeting MS, NB/1/3.

25 R. Balgarnie, *Sir Titus Salt* (1877), pp. 131, 145; Gill Charlton, 'Bradford: Weaving a Web of Optimism', *The Sunday Times*, 14 February 1988; see R. W. Suddards (ed.), *Titus of Salts* (Bradford, 1976).

26 Peake, *Hartley*, p. 58; Anne Vernon, *A Quaker Businessman: The Life of Joseph Rowntree 1831–1925* (1958), pp. 146–50.

27 A. G. Gardiner, *Life of George Cadbury* (1923), pp. 141–55.

28 Edmund Swinglehurst, *The Romantic Journey: The Story of Thomas Cook and Victorian Travel* (1974), pp. 35–6; Mona Wilson, 'Travel and Holidays' in G. M. Young (ed.), *Early Victorian England* (1934, 2 vols.), II. pp. 310–13.

29 q. in Balgarnie, *Sir Titus Salt*, p. 129.

30 R. E. Pumphrey, 'The Introduction of Industrialists into the British Peerage', *AHR*, LXV (October 1959), pp. 1–16.

31 Stephen Hobhouse, *Forty Years and An Epilogue: an Autobiography 1881–1951* (1951), p. 132. Hobhouse had the same complaint to make of the Reckitt household.

32 Colman, *Jeremiah James Colman*, p. 443; q. in Eleanor F. Rathbone, *William Rathbone A Memoir* (1905), p. 466;

Samuel Smiles, *George Moore Merchant and Philanthropist* (1879), p. 443.

2. THE SOCIAL NATURE OF NONCONFORMITY

1 Lord George Hamilton, *Parliamentary Reminiscences and Reflections 1868 to 1885* (1916), p. 322; Anon., 'Some Tendencies', p. 108.

2 The Rev. E. G. Gange, Pr. A., Spring 1897, *BUHB*, 1898, p. 103; S. J. Low, 'The Rise of the Suburbs', *Con. Rev.*, LX (1891), p. 553.

3 The Rev. E. Medley, Congress Sermon, 1895, *FCYB*, 1895, p. 113; Margaret Oliphant, *Salem Chapel* (Everyman edn, n.d. [1907], 1st publ. 1863), p. 2; Wotton-under-Edge MS, Burial Register, 2829; Lower Meeting MS, NB/1/3.

4 Con. Add., 1899, *WMM*, 1899, p. 417; Con. Add., 1893, *PMM*, p. 175.

5 The Rev. J. E. Rattenbury, *FCYB*, 1905, p. 52; *Nonconformist and Independent*, 16 March 1882.

6 P. d'A. Jones, *The Christian Socialist Revival* (1968), p. 76. B. R. Mitchell and Phyllis Deane, *Abstract of British Historical Statistics* (Cambridge, 1971), pp. 29–30. The figures were incomplete until well into the 1860s. The decline in the birth rate was noted by Sidney Webb in 'The Decline in the Birth-Rate' (1907, Fabian Tract 131).

7 Richard Lawton, 'Census Data for Urban Areas' in Richard Lawton (ed.), *The Census and Social Structure* . . . (Frank Cass, 1978), pp. 82–4; Mitchell & Deane, *Historical Statistics*, pp. 6–23. The exact figure was 12,327,000 but from 1815 to 1852 the statistics included others than UK subjects; from 1853 onwards the statistics are for UK subjects only. The figures naturally included Irishmen. Mitchell & Deane, *Historical Statistics*, p. 47.

8 Information gathered from relevant annual publications compared with Census returns; John Clifford, *Religious Life in the Rural Districts of England* (1876), p. 5.

9 The percentages by denomination of those urban members who also lived in major urban areas, i.e. above 100,000 were: BU, 69%; CU, 66%; WM, 56%; PM, 49%. Those members living in major urban areas formed the following percentages of their total denominational membership: BU, 46; CU, 44; WM, 34; PM, 23.

10 Clifford, *Religious Life*, p. 5; *CUYB*, 1898, pp. 80–1.

11 W. Tuckwell, 'Village Life and Politics in France and

England, II. England', *Con. Rev.*, LXI (1892), p. 403; Anthony Trollope, *The Vicar of Bullhampton* (1952, World Classic edn, 1st publ. 1869–70), p. 256; *PMM*, 1898, pp. 137–40.

12 *PMM*, 1898, pp. 137–40. The Methodist Archives do not contain a copy of the original report which also showed that of the 24 districts into which the country was divided, only three showed any growth in rural work. There were 1,191 villages with no PM chapel.

13 G. R. Porter (F. W. Hirst, ed.), *The Progress of the Nation* (Methuen & Co., 1912), p. 168. See chs. III and IX; A. L. Bowley, *National Progress in Wealth and Trade* (1904), pp. 11, 13–14; H. E. Stone, *Led from Darkness: The History of a Life Struggle* (1892), p. 21; *BUHB*, 1899, p. 142.

14 The Rev. E. H. Evans, Ch. A., Spring 1892, *CUYB*, 1893, p. 46.

15 *North Wales Observer*, 31 October 1913.

16 W. H. Mallock, *Classes and Masses or Wealth, Wages, and Welfare in the United Kingdom* (1896), pp. 14–16. The number had grown from 1½m. in 1850. To pay for the Crimean War it rose to 1s. 2d. in 1855 and 1s. 4d. in the two following years but then it fell again.

17 W. E. Gladstone, *The Inaugural Address Delivered at the Opening of the Collegiate Institute, Liverpool* (1843), p. 6; Jacob Tonson [Arnold Bennett], 'Middle Class', *New Age*, 4 February 1909; George Jackson, *Collier of Manchester* (n.d. [1923]), p. 58.

18 [Bennett], 'Middle Class', ibid.

19 Lady Bell (Mrs Hugh Bell), *At The Works: A Study of a Manufacturing Town* (2nd ed., 1911), p. 81; Mallock, *Classes and Masses*, pp. 14–16, 10, 28, 31.

20 Anthony Trollope, *Castle Richmond* (1906 edn, 1st publ. 1861), pp. 676–7; *Northamptonshire Nonconformist*, January 1891, p. 6.

21 Mitchell & Deane, *Historical Statistics*, pp. 343–4, 471–3; Bowley, *National Progress*, p. 27; Porter [Hirst], *Progress of the Nation*, p. 170; Anon., 'Rapid Transport in London', *QR*, CLXXV(1892), *passim*: the average fare on the Metropolitan Line was 1¾d. per mile; Masterman in Mudie-Smith, *Religious Life of London*, p. 203; Charles Booth, *Life and Labour of the People in London: Third Series: Religious Influences* (1902, 6 vols.), I, pp. 85, 121; *Booth, Life and Labour*, V, p. 106.

22 G. Laurence Gomme, *London in the Reign of Victoria (1837–1897)* (1898), p. 176; Hugh McLeod, *Class and Religion in the Late Victorian City* (1974), pp. 242, 28; for Reading see

Stephen Yeo, *Religion and Voluntary Organizations in Crisis* (1976), pp. 128–31; Low, 'Rise of the Suburbs', p. 551; Clementina Black, 'Labour and Life in London', *Con. Rev.*, LX (1891), p. 213; Alexander Paterson, *Across the Bridges* (1912, 2nd ed.), p. 117.

23 Masterman in Mudie-Smith, *Religious Life of London*, p. 201; Anon., 'Preachers of the Day', *TB*, LXX (April 1884), pp. 484–502.

24 Henry Cook, *Charles Brown* (1939), pp. 40–9.

25 Wilfrid J. Rowland [Special Commissioner], *The Free Churches and the People: A Report of the Work of the Free Churches in Liverpool* (1908), pp. 21–2, 30, 50, App. C.

26 *FCYB*, 1898, p. 28; McLeod, *Class and Religion*, p. 55; M. Loane, 'The Religion of the Respectable Poor', *Con. Rev.*, LXXXVI (1904), pp. 722–3.

27 *Pall Mall Gazette*, 22 October 1883: the paper featured stories on the tract throughout October; Booth, *Life and Labour*, IV, pp. 85, 57, 85–6, 91; Arthur Sherwell, *Life in West London: A Study and A Contrast* (1897, 2nd edn rev.), p. 150; Booth, *Life and Labour*, IV, p. 14.

28 Rowland, *The Free Churches*, pp. 22, 30, App. C; R. B. Walker, 'Religious Changes in Liverpool in the Nineteenth Century', *JEH*, XIX (1968), pp. 210–11; see Ian Sellers, 'Nonconformist Attitudes in Later Nineteenth-Century Liverpool', *Transactions of the Historic Society of Lancashire and Cheshire*, CXIV (1962), pp. 215–39.

29 Mudie-Smith, *Religious Life of London*, pp. 9–10; J. A. Hobson, *The Crisis of Liberalism* . . . (1909), p. xi.

30 For Garrett see J. W. Broadbent, *A People's Life of Charles Garrett* (1900); Nehemiah Curnock, *Hinde Street Chapel 1810–1910* (1910), p. 76; R. B. Thompson, *Peter Thompson* (1910), pp. 40–1.

31 Booth, *Life and Labour*, II, pp. 189–96: the same negative report was written on the Wesleyans' Victoria Hall in East Greenwich (V, pp. 65–6). The criticisms first came in Robert Currie, *Methodism Divided: A Study in the Sociology of Ecumenicalism* (1968), p. 211. For a differing view see: K. S. Inglis, 'English Nonconformity and Social Reform, 1880–1900', *P&P*, XIII (April 1958); his book, *Churches and the Working Classes in Victorian England* (1964); R. B. Walker, 'The Growth of Methodism in Victorian England and Wales' *JEH*, XXIV (1973), pp. 280–1 and Edward Norman, *The Victorian Christian Socialists* (Cambridge, University Press, 1987).

32 George Jackson, *Collier of Manchester* (n.d. [1923]), pp. 67–

8; W. J. Townsend, H. B. Workman & George Eayrs, *A New History of Methodism* (1909, 2 vols.), I, p. 458.

33 'A Travelling Correspondent', *The Rev. William Cuff in Shoreditch* . . . (1878), *passim*; Henry J. Cowell, *These Forty Years* . . . (1940), p. 4.

34 J. C. Carlile, *My Life's Little Day* (1935), p. 74.

35 *PMM*, 1900, pp. 183, 187–8: £3,300 had been promised; R. W. Russell, *The Life of James Flanagan* (n.d. [1921]), *passim* (cf. James Flanagan, *Scenes From My Life* (1907)); Booth, *Life and Labour*, IV, pp. 111–13.

36 See J. Scott Lidgett, *My Guided Life* (1936), ch. VIII and Booth, *Life and Labour*, IV, pp. 131–4.

37 Booth, *Life and Labour*, IV, pp. 85–7.

38 See Mrs Lockhart, *W. P. Lockhart Merchant and Preacher* (1895).

39 Sir Walter Besant, 'On University Settlements' in Will Reason (ed.), *University and Social Settlements* (1898), pp. 6, 10; [Dorothea Hughes], *The Life of Hugh Price Hughes* (1905), pp. 201–3.

40 Edward Smith, *Three Years in Central London* (1889), pp. 41, 45; (Hughes) *FCYB*, 1897, p. 144; (Walsh) *FCYB*, 1897, p. 59.

41 Reported for *All the Year Round* after visiting Brown's East London Tabernacle and q. in G. H. Pike, *The Life* . . . *of Archibald G. Brown* (1892), p. 115; Booth, *Life and Labour*, I, p. 80, IV, pp. 46–7; cf. McLeod, *Class and Religion*, pp. 71–2.

42 Masterman in Mudie-Smith, *Religious Life of London*, p. 214; The Rev. Thomas Green, Ch. A., Spring 1890, *CUYB*, 1891, p. 46.

43 Porter [Hirst], *Progress of the Nation*, p. 147; Bell, *At The Works*, pp. 205–6 (A MORI poll of 1,053 adults in December 1988 showed that in that year 22% of those questioned, which included all classes, read no books and 25% had not read more than ten, a sad comment on falling standards. *The Sunday Times*, 26 February 1989); A. A. Thomson (ed.), *By Faith and Work: The Autobiography of the Rt Hon. the First Viscount Mackintosh of Halifax* (1966), p. 149 – Viscount Mackintosh's family were Methodist New Connexion; Anon., 'The Self Taught Man' in *CR*, II (October 1890), pp. 333, 335–6.

44 Denis Crane, *John Clifford* (1908), *passim*.

45 Arthur Porritt, *More and More of Memories* (1947), p. 114.

46 John Morley et al., *Books and How to Read Them* (1905), p. v.

47 George Jackson, *A Young Man's Bookshelf* (1898), p. 9; Arnold Bennett, *Literary Taste: How to Form It with Detailed Instructions for Collecting a Complete Library of English Literature* (1912, 4th edn), pp. 3, 125; Sir John Lubbock, Bt, *The 100 Best Books in The World of Literature* (1899), p. 9.

48 W. Robertson Nicoll, *A Library for Five Pounds* (1917), p. 14; Albert Peel, *Thirty-five to Fifty* (1938), p. 60: of these, 5,000 were biography, his favourite reading; T. H. Darlow, *William Robertson Nicoll* (1925), pp. 323–4.

49 Randall T. Davidson, 'The Religious Novel', *Con. Rev.*, LIV (1888), pp. 674, 675; Alexander Mackennal, *Life of John Allison Macfadyen* (1891), p. 109.

50 Albert Peel, *Thirty-five*, p. 49; *Western Daily Press*, 18 February 1904; 17 May 1904, Bristol FC MS.

3. THE NONCONFORMIST CONTRIBUTION TO VICTORIAN CULTURE

1 Matthew Arnold, *Culture and Anarchy: an Essay in Political and Social Criticism* (Nelson classics edn, n.d., 1st publ. 1869), pp. 17, 20, 21, 23, 54, 34, 184, 11; The Rev. Alex Thomson, *Culture and Nonconformity* (1876), p. 12: first given as the Ch. A. to the CU, 12 October 1875; Arnold, *Culture and Anarchy*, p. 85. (To Gladstone the 'narrowness' which Arnold ascribed to Nonconformists could be traced 'not in the absence of State influence, but in what I may call non-veneration of the past, or incapacity, from whatever source, to claim and appropriate our full share of our heritage'. W. E. Gladstone to Matthew Arnold, 30 March 1869, in D. C. Lathbury (ed.), *Correspondence on Church and Religion of William Ewart Gladstone* (2 vols., 1910, I, pp. 167–8).

2 Ralph Waldo Emerson, *English Traits* (1923 World Classics edn, 1st publ. 1856), p. 136.

3 Matthew Arnold, *Literature and Dogma* (Nelson Library edn, n.d., 1st publ. 1873), pp. 16–17.

4 T. G. Selby, *The Theology of Modern Fiction* (1896), p. 1; James Munson, 'Foreign Policy From Fiction: Uncle Tom in England', *Civil War Times*, XXI (1983), *passim*; John Cassell to Lord Brougham, 29 September 1858, Brougham MS, No. 313; W. E. Gladstone, 'Robert Elsmere, and the Battle of Belief', *Nine. Cen.*, XXIII (1888); cf. Davidson, 'The Religious Novel'.

5 Arthur Quiller-Couch, *The Oxford Book of English Verse 1250–1918* (Oxford, University Press, new edn 1968), p. vii.

6 Wyndham Lewis, 'Standing By' in *Bystander*, 28 July 1937, p. 133. cf. Guinevere L. Griest, *Mudie's Circulating Library and the Victorian Novel* (Newton Abbot, Devon, 1970), *passim*, J. A. Sutherland, *Victorian Novelists & Publishers* (Chicago, 1978 edn), p. 25, & Richard Mullen, *Anthony Trollope: A Victorian in his World* (Duckworth, 1990), pp. 153–96.

7 Bell, *At the Works*, pp. 205–6; 'Jacob Tonson' [Arnold Bennett], 'The Potential Public', *New Age*, 18 February 1909.

8 Porritt, *More and More*, p. 76; cf. Darlow, *Nicoll*, pp. 58–9; Harry Jeffs, *Press, Preachers and Politicians: Reminiscences 1874 to 1932* (1933), ch. v; Harry Jeffs, '*J.B.*': *J. Brierley, His Life and Work* (n.d. [1915]), ch. ix; Marianne Farningham, *A Working Woman's Life: An Autobiography* (1907), ch. v.

9 *Daily Chronicle* q. in Darlow, *Nicoll*, p. 210; q. in Porritt, *More and More*, pp. 73ff.; *Punch*, q. in J. D. Jones, *Three Score Years and Ten* (1940), p. 235; Mr Denis Duncan and Mr Edward England to the writer, 18 June and 9 July 1973 respectively. The former was at one time editor of *BW*, while the latter was with Hodder & Stoughton; J. D. Symon, *The Press and Its Story* (1914), p. 274.

10 George H. Doran, *Chronicles of Barabbas 1884–1934* (1935), pp. 79, 75. For an affectionate portrait see Anthony C. Deane, *Time Remembered* (1946 edn, 1st publ. 1945), pp. 152–7.

11 Anon., 'Robertson Nicoll — and Claudius Clear', *The Times*, 8 May 1963; Deane, *Time Remembered*, p. 156.

12 Catherine Robertson Nicoll, *Under the Bay Tree* (n.d., priv. printed), pp. 192ff. See also chs. II, IV, VII; W. R. Nicoll, *My Father: An Aberdeenshire Minister 1812–1891* (1908), pp. ix, 73–4, 79, 100, 99–100.

13 George Blake, *Barrie and the Kailyard School* (1951), p. 27; W. R. Nicoll, '*Ian Maclaren*': *Life of the Rev. John Watson D.D.* (1908), p. 168; Selby, *Theology of Modern Fiction*, p. 131.

14 q. in Catherine Macdonald Maclean, *Mark Rutherford: A Biography of William Hale White* (1955), p. 93.

15 H. W. Massingham, Memorial Introduction to *The Autobiography of Mark Rutherford* (Travellers' Library, 1928), p. 39; Mark Rutherford [W. H. White], *The Autobiography . . .* (1928 edn), p. 45; Selby, *Theology of Modern Fiction*, pp. 175, 191.

16 Mark Rutherford, *Autobiography* (2nd edn), p. x; Arnold Bennett, *A Man from the North* (1898), ch. IV; Arnold Bennett

journal, 29 September 1896 in Frank Swinnerton (ed.), *The Journals of Arnold Bennett* (1954 edn), p. 23; Arnold Bennett, *Anna of the Five Towns* (1902), ch. 1.

17 Arnold Bennett, *The Old Wives' Tale* (1908), ch. v § ii and ch. III § ii; Arnold Bennett, *The Price of Love: A Tale* (n.d. [1913]), ch. x § iii. To be fair, Bennett also had fun with curates in *Buried Alive* published in 1912; Arnold Bennett, *Riceyman Steps*, ch. XIII; Arnold Bennett, *Imperial Palace* (1930), ch. XLVIII § i.

18 James Hilton, 'Goodbye Mr Chips!', *BW*, 7 December 1933; Hilton, *Good-Bye, Mr Chips* (1934), ch. II; Hilton, *To You, Mr Chips* (3rd edn, 1939), pp. 35, 63.

19 *Truth*, 30 March 1882; Richard Mullen & James Munson, *Victoria: Portrait of a Queen* (1987, BBC Books), p. 127.

20 q. in *BW*, 6 March 1902; Col. J. T. Griffin, Pr. A., Spring 1891, *BUHB*, 1892, pp. 40–1; *BW*, 30 January 1902; T. H. Green to R. W. Dale, n.d., q. in A. W. W. Dale, *The Life of R. W. Dale of Birmingham* (1898), p. 496: for Green's opposition to Nonconformists at Oxford see W. B. Selbie, 'Nonconformity at the Universities I: Oxford', *CQ*, I (1923), p. 77. See also V. A. McClelland, *English Roman Catholics and Higher Education* (Oxford, 1973) and J. Derek Holmes, 'English Ultramontanism and Clerical Education', *The Clergy Review*, LXII (1977), pp. 277–8. Nonconformist fears over Oxbridge pre-dated 1854: see the Annual Letter of 1846 in *CUYB*, 1847, p. 39. One famous example was the conductor, Sir Thomas Beecham: at Wadham he was entered on the College books as a 'dissenter' but went down with very little if any religious faith.

21 J. Carvell Williams MP, Ch. A., Spring 1900, *CUYB*, 1901, p. 22; *Crusader*, 7 July 1904; G. W. Gent, 'Religious Life at Oxford', in J. Wells (ed.), *Oxford and Oxford Life* (1892), p. 132; A. M. Fairbairn and James Bryce, 'Nonconformity and the Universities: The Free Churches and a Theological Faculty', *British Quarterly Review*, CLVIII (1884), p. 373; R. W. Macan, 'Religious Changes in Oxford During the Last Fifty Years . . .' (Oxford, 2nd imp., 1917), p. 14; Willis B. Glover, *Evangelical Nonconformists and Higher Criticism in the Nineteenth Century* (1954), p. 140.

22 A. M. Fairbairn, *Mansfield College: Its Idea and Aim* (Oxford, 1886), p. 5; Mansfield College, *Summer School of Theology July 18th to 28th, 1892: Programme* (Oxford, n.d.), *passim*. cf. W. B. Selbie, *The Life of Andrew Martin Fairbairn . . .* (1914), p. 225.

23 Anon., 'Mansfield College', *CR* I (1889), p. 253; *Alden's*

Sixpenny Guide to Oxford (Oxford, 1919), pp. 121–2. The Unitarian college was opened in 1893. The chapel contained windows by Burne-Jones while the library was made possible through the generosity of Sir Henry Tate (*Mowbray's Guide to Oxford* . . . (Oxford, 1919), p. 48; *Alden's Sixpenny Guide*, p. 124). In the twentieth century the Baptists' Regent's Park College followed Springhill to Oxford while the Congregationalists' Cheshunt College migrated to Cambridge. The Wesleyans established Wesley House in Cambridge.

24 J. Wells, 'Expenses of Oxford Life' in Wells (ed.), *Oxford and Oxford Life*, pp. 52, 55.

25 Fairbairn & Bryce, 'Nonconformity and the Universities', pp. 390, 373; Fairbairn, *Mansfield College, passim*.

26 John Morley & Norman Monk-Jones, *Bishop's Stortford College 1868–1968: A Centenary Chronicle* (1969), *passim*.

27 Fairbairn, *Mansfield College, passim*.

28 Fairbairn, *Mansfield College, passim*.

29 Fairbairn & Bryce, 'Nonconformity and the Universities', p. 390; W. B. Selbie, 'Fifty Years at Oxford', *CQ* xiv (1936), p. 282. (See also: Sir Frank Tillyard, 'The Oxford Nonconformists' Union 1883–6', *CQ*, xxv (1947); H. C. Carter, 'Recollections of a Minister', *CQ*, xxvi (1948); Walter Stevens, 'Oxford's Attitude to Dissenters, 1646–1946', *BQ*, xiii (1949); H. W. Strong, 'Modern Oxford and Nonconformity', *LQR*, ii n.s. (1899), p. 281; J. Carvell Williams, Ch. A., Spring 1900, *CUYB*, 1901, p. 22; Albert Peel & J. A. R. Marriott, *Robert Forman Horton* (1937), p. 104; Sir Charles Oman, *Memories of Victorian Oxford* . . . (1941), pp. 235–6. Oman also describes the controversy when Jowett unsuccessfully nominated Horton as an examiner in the 'Rudiments in Faith and Religion' paper. Horton was the first Nonconformist to be nominated. See also Peel & Marriott, *Horton*, pp. 110–13, & Lord Ernle (Rowland Prothero), *Whippingham to Westminster* (1938), pp. 117–18.

30 cf. Nicoll, *'Ian Maclaren'* ch. xiii; Anon., 'Religion in Cambridge', *CQR*, cxvii (1904), p. 13; cf.: B. L. Manning, 'Nonconformity at the Universities ii: Cambridge', *CQ*, i (1923) & H. N. Dixon, 'Religious Life in the Eighties of Last Century', *CQ*, xx (1942). For Manning see F. Brittain, *Bernard Lord Manning: A Memoir* (Cambridge, 1942). For Glover see H. G. Wood, *T. R. Glover* . . . (Cambridge, 1953).

31 *WMM*, 1901, p. 111; Strong, 'Modern Oxford and Nonconformity', p. 287.

32 Joseph Thompson, *Lancashire Independent College 1843–1893* (Manchester, 1893), p. 183. See also: Joseph Thompson,

The Owens College . . . (Manchester, 1886); T. T. James, 'Fifty Years', *CQ*, XXIII (1945); E. Fiddes, *Owens College and Manchester University* (1937). Mr Rayner Unwin to the author, 16 November 1989 and Miss Tabitha Driver, Assistant Librarian, Religious Society of Friends to the same, 28 November 1989. Nonconformists were not the only ones to make use of London: in 1845, one-third of those receiving London BAs were Roman Catholic (*The Tablet*, 25 October 1845).

33 Lord Spencer to his son, C. R. Spencer, 20 July 1892, in Peter Gordon (ed.), *The Red Earl: The Papers of the Fifth Earl Spencer 1835–1910* (Northampton, Northamptonshire Record Office, 1981, 1986, 2 vols.), II, p. 201. cf. pp. 194–206 for the story of the sale.

34 John Grigg, *The Young Lloyd George* (1973), p. 36; Robert Gittings, *Young Thomas Hardy* (Boston, 1975), pp. 25, 45; *Popular Educator*, 1852–4, *passim*.

35 See K. M. Elisabeth Murray, *Caught in the Web of Words: James Murray and the Oxford English Dictionary* (Oxford, 1979 edn, 1st publ. 1977), esp. ch. VI.

4. THE NONCONFORMIST MINISTER

1 Rogers, *Autobiography*, p. 148; Anon., 'Notes on the Action and Pronouncements of Nonconformists with Reference to Public Elementary Education', Board of Education MS, ED 24/13A/8; *The Tablet*, 30 May 1903.

2 *FCYB*, 1902, pp. 323–4. The number for the four leading denominations had increased from 5,682 in 1870. WM, PM & CU had increased the number of their ministers while BU had seen its fall by 14%. Because Baptists were the fastest growing of the four, they obviously made greater use of lay preachers. Figures for the American import, 'Church of Christ' are excluded as no entry for full-time ministers was given but only for lay preachers & comparison is impossible; 'A Travelling Correspondent', *The Rev. William Cuff* (1878), p. 39; Peel & Marriott, *Horton*, p. 206.

3 W. Pedr Williams, *The Devil in Khaki* (1900, Tracts for the Times), pp. 14–15.

4 q. in R. R. James, *Rosebery* (1963), pp. 57–8; for George Eliot quote see Arthur Porritt, *The Best I Remember* (1922), p. 2; Anon., 'Preachers of the Day', *TB*, pp. 500–1; Charles K. Tuckerman, *Personal Recollections of Notable People* . . . (New York, 1895, 2 vols.), II, p. 349; *Truth*, 30 March 1882.

5 Henry Greville diary, 25 November 1858, Countess of

Strafford (ed.), *Leaves from the Diary of Henry Greville* (1883–1904, 4 vols.), III, p. 165; Bishop of Ripon [W. Boyd Carpenter], 'Mr Spurgeon', *Con. Rev.*, LXI (1892), p. 308; Newman Hall, *An Autobiography* (1898), p. 292; *The Times*, 19 June 1884.

6 *CUYB*, 1902, p. 47; Albert Dawson, *Joseph Parker* . . . (1901), p. 140.

7 *The Times*, 26 April 1899.

8 Anon., 'Preachers of the Day', *TB*, p. 502; six years later, when Bottomley stood for Parliament as a Liberal he found that Nonconformists had not let his courtesy to Parker erase his gambling connections. They put up an 'independent liberal', a Congregational minister, who got 804 votes. Bottomley won easily.

9 Augustine Birrell, *Things Past Redress* (1937), p. 178; Frederick W. Macdonald, *As A Tale that is Told: Recollections of Many Years* (1919), p. 232.

10 See correspondence between T. A. Trollope and Henry Allon, Allon MS; cf. L. P. Jacks, *The Confessions of an Octogenarian* (1942), ch. XXV; forgettable novels include: Joseph Parker's, *Paterson's Parish, Weaver Stephen* and *Springdale Abbey*; Silvester Horne's *A Modern Heretic*; John Clifford's *George Mostyn* and Mark Guy Pearse's *Daniel Quorm*; Glover, *Evangelical Nonconformity*, p. 288; A. M. Hunter, *P. T. Forsyth* (1974), p. 13.

11 T. H. S. Escott, *Personal Forces of the Period* (1898), p. 224; J. H. Rigg to Arthur Balfour, ? September 1904, Balfour MS, Add. Mss 49857 *ff* 25–8.

12 *CUYB*, 1905, pp. 157–9.

13 *PMM*, 1932, pp. 330–2; *CUYB*, 1905, p. 188.

14 Maclean, *Rutherford*, p. 50; H. R. Williamson, *The Walled Garden* (1956), pp. 27–30; Kingsley Martin, *Father Figures* (1966), p. 14: the autobiography by his father, Basil Martin, is *An Impossible Parson* (1935); J. W. Dixon, *Pledged to the People: A Sketch of Rev. Richard Westrope* (1896, 2nd edn), *passim*; author's personal knowledge.

15 See C. B. Jewson, 'St Mary's, Norwich', *BQ*, x [n.s.] (1941), pp. 340–52, 398–406; R. J. Owen, 'Wintoun Street Baptist Church, 1870–1895' in *Publications of the Thoresby Society. Miscellany*, LIII Part 2 (1971); Kingsley Martin, *Father Figures*, ch. II & Colman, *Colman*, pp. 137ff. For an example of division over politics cf. J. D. Jones, *Three Score Years and Ten* (1940), p. 224.

16 Joseph Parker, *Paterson's Parish*, p. 16; Tuckerman, *Personal Recollections*, II, p. 349; *The Schoolmaster*, 1 June 1901; J.

A. Hobson, 'Is Poverty Diminishing?', *Con. Rev.*, LXIX (1896), p. 489; J. P. D. Dunbabin, *Rural Discontent in 19th Century Britain* (1974), p. 239.

17 A. C. Whitby, 'Matthew Arnold and the Nonconformists: A Study in Social and Political Attitudes', unpublished B Litt Thesis, University of Oxford, 1954, pp. 101–2; J. J. Moore, *Earlier and Later Nonconformity in Oxford* (Oxford, 1875), *passim*.

18 Of the 30 County Unions four had an average stipend of £60 to £80 p.a.; eight had £80 to £100; twelve had £100 to £120; two had £120 to £140 and four had over £140 p.a.: *CUYB*, 1882, pp. 45–7; Mearns, *England for Christ*, p. 199; Old Meeting MS, 17 March 1897, D. 2569/2/1; Aylesbury Church MS, 1896, NC/1/2; Broad Street Chapel MS, 12 October 1892, Mr/M/a/7.

19 John Angus, 'The Financial Arrangements of Methodism' (n.d. [1901]), *passim*; Mansfield Road MS, Mr/M/b/15.

20 Williamson, *The Walled Garden*, p. 26.

21 Mudie-Smith, *Religious Life of London*, pp. 7, 203; C. F. G. Masterman in Mudie-Smith, ibid., p. 203; Dr J. Edgar Park, q. in Peel & Marriott, *Horton*, p. 341; R. J. Campbell, *A Spiritual Pilgrimage* (1916), p. 37; James A. Newbold, *The Nonconformist Conscience a Persecuting Force* (Manchester, 1908), p. 160; Ernest H. Jeffs, *Princes of the Modern Pulpit* (n.d. [1930]), p. 6.

22 Selbie, *Fairbairn*, p. 209; Mackennal, *Macfadyen*, p. 116; William Adamson, *The Life of the Rev. Joseph Parker* (1902), p. 232; William Wakinshaw, *Gleanings From My Life* (1931), p. 66; W. L. Bradley, *P. T. Forsyth . . .* (1952), p. 38.

23 E. E. Kellett, *As I Remember* (1936), p. 113; Carlile, *My Life's Little Day*, pp. 55–6; A. G. Gardiner, *Prophets Priests and Kings* (n.d., 2nd edn [1914]), p. 268; Peel & Marriott, *Horton*, p. 257; Macdonald, *As A Tale That is Told*, p. 85; Marianne Farningham, *A Story of Fifty Years* (1893), p. 61.

24 J. Compton Rickett, *The Free Churchman of To-Day* (1902), pp. 82–3; W. Robertson Nicoll to A. S. Peake, 4 February 1898 in Darlow, *Nicoll*, p. 345; Anon., 'The Decline of Dissent', *Northamptonshire Nonconformist*, November 1891.

25 Sir James Marchant, *Dr John Clifford* (1924), pp. 81–2 & G. W. Byrt, *John Clifford . . .* (1947), p. 128. Arnold has argued that 'the State is of the religion of all its citizens without the fanaticism of any of them' (p. 302). Clifford's Radical view of the state was close to that of Fascists in the 1920s.

26 T. R. Glover, 'Nonconformity Old and New' in *The Times*,

Fifty Years: Memories and Contrasts . . . 1882–1932 (1932), p. 125.

27 Alexander Maclaren, Pr. A., Autumn 1901, *BUHB*, 1902, pp. 124–5; Thomas Morris, Pr. A., Autumn 1893, *BUHB*, 1894, p. 85.

28 J. Guinness Rogers, 'Ceremonialism v. Experimental Religion', *Con. Rev.*, LXXV (1899), p. 245.

29 Peel, *Thirty-Five to Fifty*, p. 169; 'A Nonconformist Minister', *Nonconformity and Politics* (1909), p. 137; H. Hensley Henson, *Cui Bono?* (1899, 5th edn), p. 17.

30 Darlow, *Nicoll*, pp. 50, 323; Russell, *Flanagan*, pp. 35–6.

31 Gerald France (ed.), *Reminiscences of Thomas Hudson Bainbridge* (1913), p. 156; *PMM*, 1891, pp. 165–6; Anon., 'The Position of Nonconformity', *The Times*, 22 April 1897; *WMM*, 1891, pp. 419, 351.

32 Peel & Marriott, *Horton*, p. 56; Henry Cook, *Charles Brown* (1939), pp. 29–31; William Hale White's strictures on Cheshunt Congregational College in mid-century are well known: cf. Maclean, *Rutherford*, p. 59; Mark Rutherford, *The Autobiography*, esp. ch. II and Kenneth D. Brown, 'College Principals — A Cause of Nonconformist Decay?' *JEH*, XXXVIII (1987), pp. 236–53.

33 Information based on relevant *Year Books* for 1870 & 1900.

34 Anon., 'The Congregational Problem', p. 21.

35 See J. E. B. Munson, 'The Education of Baptist Ministers, 1870–1900', *BQ*, XXVI (1976), pp. 320–27.

36 See *Second Report of the Special Committee on Ministerial Settlements and Removals . . . and Rules Relating to the Recognition of Churches and Ministers*, 16 May 1902 in *CUYB*, 1903, pp. 66–71.

37 Cook, *Brown*, pp. 11–29.

38 Joseph Thompson, *Lancashire Independent College 1843–1893 . . .* (Manchester, 1893), p. 183. See also Joseph Thompson, *The Owens College . . .* (Manchester, 1886) and E. Fiddes, *Owens College and Manchester University* (1937); A. M. Fairbairn to Sir Alfred Dale, 29 April 1902 in Selbie, *Fairbairn*, p. 243.

39 Townsend *et al.*, *New History of Methodism*, I, pp. 475–6.

40 F. Jewell, *Little Abe . . . the Life of Abraham Lockwood* (1880), p. 96.

41 *BW*, 14 August 1902; W. Y. Fullerton, *C. H. Spurgeon* (1920), p. 232; Anon., *Charles Haddon Spurgeon* (1903), pp. 139, 143, 140; *PMM*, 1892, p. 177; *PMM*, 1901, p. 190.

42 [Boyd Carpenter], 'Mr Spurgeon', p. 309; 'A Travelling Correspondent', *Cuff*, p. 2.

43 James Owen, Pr. A., Spring 1890, *BUHB*, 1891, p. 29; John A. Bridges, *Reminiscences of a Country Politician* (1906), p. 86; Anon., 'Some Tendencies . . .', p. 112.

5. THE NONCONFORMISTS' SEARCH FOR DIGNITY

1 Aylesbury Church MS, 31 August 1898, 30 January 1895, NC/1/2.

2 *FCYB*, 1900, pp. 74–5. For the importance of the veteran Nonconformist leader, Jeremiah Colman, see Lord Rendel's diary entry for 2 November 1895 in F. E. Hamer (ed.), *The Personal Papers of Lord Rendel* (1931), p. 126.

3 Maj. J. B. Pond, *Eccentricities of Genius* (1901), pp. 113–14. Pond tried to recruit Spurgeon for his stable of lecturers but failed.

4 The Rev. Arnold Thomas, Ch. A., Spring 1899, *CUYB*, 1900, p. 28.

5 The Rev. Alfred Rowland, Ch. A., Autumn 1898, *CUYB*, 1899, pp. 49–50.

6 *FCYB*, 1901, pp. 105–6.

7 Peel & Marriott, *Horton*, p. 322; Hugh Price Hughes, *FCYB*, 1896, p. 38; the Rev. G. Monro Gibson, *FCYB*, 1897, p. 10.

8 Joseph Parker, *FCYB*, 1896, pp. 107–8; q. in *The Lowestoft Free Press*, 21 July 1888; Marchant, *Clifford*, p. 78.

9 The Rev. Arnold Thomas, Ch. A., Spring 1899, *CUYB*, 1900, p. 28; Balfour to ?, 28 April 1902, Balfour MS, Add. Mss 49854 *ff* 315–16.

10 Albert Peel, *Letters to a Victorian Editor: Henry Allon Editor of the British Quarterly Review* (1929), p. 3.

11 Wotton-under-Edge MS, Church Minutes, 25 May 1892, D 2829/2/1.

12 William Shepherdson, *The Organ: Hints on its Construction, Purchase and Presentation* (1873), p. 5. For advertisements see *CUYB*, 1903, p. 47 & *PMM*, 1902, p. 25.

13 Wotton-under-Edge MS, Church Minutes, November 1893, February 1894, May 1895, D 2829/2/1.

14 John Hunter, *Devotional Services for Public Worship* (Glasgow, 6th edn, 1895), p. x; John Hunter, *A Plea for a Worshipful Church* (1903), pp. 8, 15.

15 R. F. Horton, *The Dissolution of Dissent* (1902), p. 56; Horton's views on liturgy, as on most things, were somewhat confused; Horton Davies, *Worship and Theology in England IV: From Newman to Martineau, 1850–1900* (Princeton, University Press, 1961–65, 5 vols.), IV, p. 64.

16 Booth, *Life and Labour*, IV, pp. 186–7.

17 J. C. Carlile, *C. H. Spurgeon* . . . (1933), p. 155; *BN*, 21 December 1860, 6 April 1860; Anon., 'London: Its Sights, and How to See Them. The Metropolitan Tabernacle', *Cassell's Illustrated Family Paper*, 1 June 1861.

18 G. Holden Pike, *Dr Parker and His Friends* (1904), p. 111; Dawson, *Parker*, pp. 57, 89–95; R. Stanley-Morgan, 'Some Great Victorian Chapel Builders', *CQ*, xxxiii (1955), p. 240; Booth, *Life and Labour*, ii, p. 222; *Truth* article q. in A. L. Drummond, 'A Century of Chapel Architecture 1840–1940', *CQ*, xx (1942), p. 323; Drummond, *The Church Architecture of Protestantism* . . . (Edinburgh, 1934), p. 79, n. 2.

19 Anon., 'Some Tendencies . . .', p. 103; cf. Joseph Hammond, *The Mistakes of Modern Nonconformity* (1895), p. 82 for a similar view.

20 Rev. E. G. Gange, Pr. A., Spring 1897, *BUHB*, 1898, pp. 96–7.

21 *PMM*, 1895, p. 177. The decline in the number of Baptist and Wesleyan churches was 2.5% for the Baptists and 4% for the Wesleyans. Full statistics are not available for the other two major groups. The total number of 'units', which included mission halls, hired rooms, theatres etc. had risen dramatically for BU & CU: 105% and 63% respectively: WM figures dropped by 13% but they had less need to build and one 'unit' could have been a central hall seating thousands.

22 Rev. J. M. Jones, Ch. A., Spring 1896, *CUYB*, 1897, p. 17. Statistics gathered from denominational yearbooks, 1870 to 1901.

23 Joseph Crouch, *Puritanism and Art: An Inquiry into a Popular Fallacy* (1910), pp. 357–8, 364.

24 *CUYB*, 1847, pp. 150–63.

25 F. J. Jobson, *Chapel and School Architecture as appropriate to the Buildings of Nonconformists, particularly to those of the Wesleyan Methodists: with practical directions for the Erection of Chapels and School Houses* (1850), pp. 10, 9, 24, 54; Benjamin Gregory (Elizabeth Jobson, ed.), *The Life of Frederick James Jobson DD* (1884), p. 13.

26 J. C. Gallaway, *Practical Hints on the Erection of Places of Public Worship compiled under the Direction of the Committee of the English Congregational Chapel-Building Society* (1874, 3rd edn), pp. 6, 29, 42, 47; R. P. Pullan, 'Church Architecture in the Nineteenth Century', *BN*, 14 June 1861; John Betjeman, *Ghastly Good Taste* . . . (1970 edn), p. 63.

27 A. W. W. Dale, *Dale*, p. 170; Christopher Stell, *Architects of Dissent: Some Nonconformist Patrons and their Architects*

(1976), p. 25; R.D.W., 'Dissenting Chapels', *BN*, 13 May 1859.

28 Booth, *Life and Labour*, IV, p. 32; *CUYB*, 1897, p. 168.

29 *CUYB*, 1892, p. 217; Peel, *One Hundred Eminent Congregationalists*, pp. 247–8; *CUYB*, 1903, p. 175; Peel, ibid., pp. 186–7; *Church Times*, 10 September 1976.

30 *BUHB*, 1895, pp. 295–300.

31 Alden, *Alden's Oxford Guide*, p. 83. There is perhaps a Nonconformist bias as the Aldens were Baptists.

32 F. S. Clayton, *John Wilson of Woolwich . . .* (n.d. [1927]), p. 348; 'A Travelling Correspondent', *William Cuff*, p. 37; W. T. Whitley, 'Tabernacles: The Evolution of the Title', *BQ*, x (1940), pp. 61–2.

33 K. T. Payne MBE, Hon. Secretary of The Leysian Mission to the author, 15 March 1977.

34 J. A. Tabor, *Nonconformist Protest against the Popery of Modern Dissent as Displayed in Architectural Imitations of Roman Catholic Churches* (Colchester, 1863), pp. 4, 5, 13; James Fergusson (Robert Kerr, ed.), *History of the Modern Styles of Architecture* (1891, 3rd edn, rev., 1st publ. 1862), p. 4; James Fergusson (R. Phene Spiers, ed.), *A History of Architecture in All Countries from the Earliest Times to the Present Day* (1893, 3rd edn, 5 vols., 1st publ. 1865), I, p. xxi.

35 For the building of Union Chapel see Hardy Harwood, *Henry Allon DD . . .* (1894), pp. 56–258; A. L. Drummond, 'A Century of Chapel Architecture 1840–1940' in *CQ*, xx (1942), p. 322; Nicholas Pevsner, *The Buildings of England: London* (1954), p. 230.

36 James Cubitt, *Church Designs for Congregations: Its Developments and Possibilities* (1870), pp. 95, 104, 94; James Cubitt, *A Popular Handbook of Nonconformist Church Building* (1892), pp. 3, 4, 28, 51–3, 74; cf. *The Builder*, 4 March 1876, for Cubitt.

37 J. Compton Rickett, *The Freechurchman of To-Day* (1902), pp. 76–7, 79; cf. Anon., 'Mr Spicer and Congregational Church Policy' in *CR*, I (1889) in which the writer argued that Gothic design was not just a 'great mistake' but a 'distinct hindrance' to preaching because it substituted visual sights for the spoken word; P. T. Forsyth, *Christ on Parnassus: Lectures on Art, Ethic and Theology* (1959 edn, 1st publ. 1911), pp. 191, 176.

38 *CUYB*, 1908, pp. 163–4.

39 Hermann Muthesius, *Die neuere kirlichliche Baukunst in England entwicklung, bedingungen und Grundzuge des*

kirchenbaues der Englischen Staatskirche und der Secten
(Berlin, 1901), p. 151 (author's translation): in a text of 166
pp., one-third is devoted to Nonconformity; A. Elizabeth
Carson, *Union Church Brighton: A Short History* (Brighton,
n.d. [1954]), p. 23, by courtesy of the Rev. Arthur Hughes.
40 Sir Henry Lunn, *Chapters from My Life* (1918), p. 256;
WMM, 1898, p. 344; Currie, *Methodism Divided*, p. 182.
41 W. Y. Fullerton, *F. B. Meyer: A Biography* (n.d.), p. 77.
42 G. W. E. Russell, *Edward King . . . A Memoir* (1912, 2nd
edn), p. 216; Cubitt, *A Popular Handbook*, p. 4; Muthesius,
Die Neurere kirlichiche, pp. 164–5, 156–7.
43 Muthesius, ibid.; *Baptist Times and Freeman*, 23 May 1902.
44 Ronald P. Jones, *Nonconformist Church Architecture: An
Essay* (1914), p. 7. Jones was mainly concerned with
Unitarian architecture.

6. THE MOVE TO UNITY

1 Rogers, 'Dissent in the Victorian Era', pp. 122–3; Townsend
et al., *New History of Methodism*, II, p. 487. Bunting, a
barrister, was the editor of the *Con. Rev.* from 1882 to 1911
and a supporter of Hugh Price Hughes.
2 The Rev. J. G. Greenhough, Pr. A., *FCYB*, 1901, pp. 10–11;
'A Nonconformist Minister', *Home Reunion: A Plea for Unity*
(1899), p. 15.
3 Anon., 'Some Tendencies . . .', p. 100.
4 G. W. E. Russell, 'Individualism and Collectivism', in
Collections and Recollections, (Series II.) (n.d. [1909], 1st
publ. 1902), pp. 67, 72; Joseph Parker, Ch. A., Spring 1901,
CUYB, 1902, p. 33.
5 Edmund Burke, *Letter to Sir Hercules Langrishe in The
Works of the Right Honourable Edmund Burke* (Oxford,
1928 edn, Oxford World Classics edn, 5 vols.), V, pp. 175–6;
C. Silvester Horne, *Nonconformity in the Nineteenth Century*
(1905), p. 148; Alexander Mackennal, *The Story of the
English Separatists . . .* (1893), p. 134; published by the CU.
For a criticism of this see Anon., 'The "Tercentenary"
Literature of the Congregational Union' in *CQR*, XXXVI (1893),
pp. 463–82; Anon., 'The Congregational Problem' in *Tracts
for Congregationalists*: II (1901), pp. 5, 9.
6 Anon., 'Four Letters on Church Membership' in *Tracts for
Congregationalists*: I (1899), p. 6; Mackennal, *Macfadyen*,
pp. 89–90.
7 Holmer Green MS, 4 February, 15 April 1890, 12 January

1897, NB/10/1; Lower Meeting MS, 30 August 1892, 27 April 1897, NB/1/3.

8 Peel & Marriott, *Horton*, p. 196; the Rev. Alfred Rowland, Ch. A., Autumn 1898, *CUYB*, 1899, p. 50; Adamson, *Parker*, p. 30.

9 The Rev. T. M. Morris, Pr. A., Autumn 1893, *BUHB*, 1894, pp. 84–5, 97; the Rev. J. G. Greenhough, Pr. A., Spring 1895, *BUHB*, 1896, p. 68; the Rev. T. V. Tymms, Pr. A., Autumn 1896, *BUHB*, 1897, p. 97.

10 John Clifford, Pr. A., Autumn 1899, *BUHB*, 1900, p. 125; J. C. Carlile, 'Church Organisation', *Baptist Times and Freeman*, 28 August 1903.

11 Conf. Add., 4 August 1896, *WMM*, 1896, p. 391; q. in [Dorothea Hughes], *Hughes*, p. 329.

12 Joseph Parker, Ch. A., Spring 1901, *CUYB*, 1902, p. 19.

13 Ministers MS, RNC, 38, Vol. VII; *The Christian World*, 18 July 1901; Deputies MS, 3083/16: cf. B. L. Manning [Ormerod Greenwood, ed.], *The Protestant Dissenting Deputies* (Cambridge, 1952).

14 See Protestant Society MS, 38.193–38.207 and Herbert S. Skeats & Charles S. Miall, *History of the Free Churches of England 1688–1891* (n.d. [1891]), pp. 450ff.; Liberation Society MS, 1902, A/Lib/9. The suggestion came from the Rev. Charles Aked (Baptist) of Liverpool.

15 Skeats & Miall, *Free Churches*, pp. 471ff.

16 J. L. Paton, *John Brown Paton: A Biography* (1914), pp. 491–2.

17 *BW*, 22 March 1894.

18 *FCYB*, 1895, p. 18; Howard Evans, 'Our Relations to the Press', *FCYB*, 1898, p. 185.

19 C. H. Kelly, Pr. A., 1900, *FCYB*, 1900, p. 19.

20 W. Robertson Nicoll, *FCYB*, 1896, p. 65; John Clifford, *FCYB*, 1898, p. 17.

21 David Heath, *The Free Church Movement in England* . . . (1902), pp. 195, 196, 216; cf. Gardiner, *Cadbury*, pp. 169ff. & *FCYB*, 1895–1900 inclusive.

22 W. J. Townsend, 'Memoir of Thomas Law', *UMFC Minutes of Conference*, 1910, p. 65; Jeffs, *Press, Preachers and Politicians*, p. 146; *The Times*, 4 April 1910; Porritt, *The Best I Remember*, p. 223; Silas K. Hocking, *My Book of Memory* (1923), p. 197.

23 Charles Gore, 'The English Church Union Declaration', *Con. Rev.*, LXXV (1899), p. 459; Horne, *Nonconformity in the Nineteenth Century*, pp. 153–4; E. K. H. Jordan, 'The History of the Free Church Council Movement: 1892–1940', Oxford

D Phil Thesis (1953), p. 117. This was published in 1956 as *Free Church Unity: History of the Free Church Council Movement 1896–1941* but as the thesis is the fuller account it has been used here.

24 Council of the Evangelical Free Churches of Birmingham & District, *Report of the House to House Visitation and Inaugural Meeting of the Council* (Birmingham, 1895), pp. 1–3, 11. Cadbury was Chairman, 1895 to 1898.

25 Information from *FCYB* of the period. For Smith see his autobiography, *Gypsy Smith: His Life and Work* published by the NFCC in 1905. For the mission see *FCYB*, 1901, pp. 185–250. Opinions varied greatly about its value but all agreed it was a good exercise in united work.

26 *FCYB*, 1901, p. 72.

27 Thomas Law, *FCYB*, 1896, p. 130.

28 *BW*, 15 January 1903.

29 Rogers, 'Dissent in the Victorian Era', p. 119; Hugh Price Hughes, 'Free Church Unity: the New Movement', *Con. Rev.*, LXXI (1897), p. 448.

30 *Spectator*, 29 May 1897; *FCYB*, 1897, p. 121.

31 Porritt, *The Best I Remember*, p. 222.

32 q. in *The Tablet*, 30 May 1903; J. Monro Gibson, Pr. A., *FCYB*, 1897, p. 19.

33 C. Silvester Horne, *A Popular History of the Free Churches* (1903, 2nd edn), p. 424; *FCYB*, 1898, p. 144.

34 The Rev. John Smith, *FCYB*, 1896, p. 55.

35 Fairbairn q. in J. R. Diggle, 'The Policy of the Education Bill', *Con. Rev.*, LXX (1896), p. 32; *FCYB*, 1899, p. 95; [Dorothea Hughes], *Hughes*, p. 384.

36 *FCYB*, 1899, p. 94; *WMM*, 1901, p. 7.

37 Hugh Price Hughes, Pr. A., *FCYB*, 1896, pp. 28–9.

38 Anon., 'Some Tendencies . . .', pp. 113–14.

7. NONCONFORMISTS AND THE ANGLO-SAXON WORLD

1 Russell, *Flanagan*, pp. 185, 193, 197.

2 [Dorothea Hughes], *Hughes*, p. 550.

3 *FCYB*, 1902, pp. 126–7.

4 Alexis de Tocqueville (J. P. Mayer, ed. & George Lawrence, tr.), *Journey to America* (New York, 1959), p. 177: the prohibition was only on a national established church and states were free to retain their established colonial churches. Virginia and some of the New England states retained their established churches — Anglican and Congregational respectively — into statehood. In Connecticut the Congregational Church was not disestablished until 1818; Adamson,

Parker, p. 115; W. B. Selbie (ed.), *The Life of Charles Silvester Horne* (n.d. [1920]), p. 110.

5 F. Herbert Stead, 'The English Church of the Future: Its Polity. A Congregational Forecast' (1892), p. 6; the Rev. E. G. Gange, Pr. A., Spring 1897, *BUHB*, 1898, p. 103.

6 Pond, *Eccentricities of Genius*, p. 412; Selbie, *Fairbairn*, p. 337; A. M. Fairbairn, 'The Interestingness of American Life', *The Speaker*, 13 September 1890 & 'The Puritan in America: Parts I and II', *The Speaker*, 1, 8 November 1890; Horton, *The Dissolution of Dissent*, p. 40; Nicoll, *Maclaren*, p. 200.

7 Marchant, *Clifford*, pp. 185–6.

8 A. C. Benson, *The Life of Edward White Benson* (1899, 2 vols), II, p. 133; Alexis de Tocqueville (Henry Reeve tr.), *Democracy in America* (New York, 1961 Schocken edn, 2 vols, 1st publ. 1835, 1838), II, p. 42; Tocqueville (Mayer & Lawrence), *Journey to America*, p. 94; Arnold, *Culture and Anarchy*, Preface, pp. 34, 182; cf. pp. 28–40. In much of what Arnold wrote he repeats what Mrs Trollope argued in 1832.

9 Oliver Wendell Holmes, *Our Hundred Days in Europe* (Boston, 1892 edn, 1st publ. 1887), pp. 203–4.

10 Sir Christopher Furness, *The American Invasion* (n.d. [1902]), p. 29; Mitchell & Deane, *Historical Statistics*, p. 48.

11 See Richard Carwardine, *Trans-atlantic Revivalism: Popular Evangelicalism in Britain and America 1790–1865* (Greenwood Press, 1978); John Kent, *Holding the Fort: Studies in Victorian Revivalism* (1978), p. 155: see chs. IV-VI for an incisive study of Moody and Sankey.

12 Newman Hall, *An Autobiography* (1898), p. 319: see pp. 175, 312–28; *WMM*, 1892, p. 365; *CUYB*, 1901, p. 59.

13 Hall, *Autobiography*, pp. 165–91; Anon., 'Preachers of the Day', *TB*, p. 502.

14 A. W. W. Dale, *Dale*, p. 339: see pp. 331–9 & Dale's articles on American life, 'Impressions of America', *Nine. Cen.*, III (March–May, July, October, 1878).

15 Pond, *Eccentricities of Genius*, pp. 88, 408, 412, 432, 450: cf. pp. 85–9.

16 Michael Slater (ed.), *Dickens on America & the Americans* (The Harvester Press, 1979), pp. 235–6.

17 A. R. C. Grant with Caroline Combe (eds), *Lord Rosebery's North American Journal — 1873* (1967), pp. 91–2; Kellett, *As I Remember*, pp. 144–5.

18 J. M. Richards, *With John Bull and Jonathan* (1905), pp. 91–2.

19 Harriet Beecher Stowe to the Rev. Charles Kingsley, n.d. [1853], Stowe MS, No. 1952/35B; Harriet Beecher Stowe to

Dr Wardlow, 14 December 1852, q. in *The Teetotal Progressionist*, February 1853.

20 'A Publisher's Reader', *Literary Work: Its Ins and Outs* (1883), p. 73; Stowe MS, No. A 923 223691B. This was a play on the 'letter' from 'the women of England', i.e. a committee which collected signatures. The total collected came to .06% of all Englishwomen in 1851. The letter was written by Lord Shaftesbury, and urged America to begin gradual emancipation.

21 Lord Salisbury to Queen Victoria, cypher telegram, 19 December 1895, CAB 41/23/41, R.A.

22 J. S. Drummond, *Charles A. Berry: A Memoir* (1899), pp. 150–6: cf. ch. XIII; W. T. Stead to A. J. Balfour, 6, 25 January 1896, Sandars MS, MS Eng. Hist. c. 728, *ff* 12, 37: cf. *ff* 13–19. Stead called on Balfour later that month (cf. Stead to Balfour, 22 January 1896, ibid., *f* 19); Howard Evans, *Sir Randal Cremer: His Life and Work* (1909), pp. 164–7 (for Venezuela).

23 *BUHB*, 1899, p. 122; *BUHB*, 1900, p. 149; *CUYB*, 1900, p. 59; *WMM*, 1898, p. 429.

8. NONCONFORMISTS AND THEIR PECULIAR CONSCIENCE

1 Lewis Harcourt diary, 15 November 1882, Viscount Harcourt MS, MS Harcourt dep 352 *ff* 66–7; John Morley to Gladstone, 3 November 1890, Gladstone MS, Add. Mss 44256 *ff* 60–1.

2 Gladstone to John Morley, 19 November 1890, Gladstone MS, Add. Mss 44256 *ff* 75–6.

3 *The Star*, 18 November 1890.

4 John Morley to Gladstone, 19 November 1890, Gladstone MS, Add. Mss 44256 *f* 79.

5 Manning to Gladstone, 21 November 1890, Gladstone MS, Add. Mss 44250 *ff* 296–7.

6 *The Times*, 4 December 1890; J. G. Rogers, 'Nonconformists in Political Life', *Con. Rev.*, LXI (1892), pp. 502–3; T. W. Heyck, *The Dimensions of British Radicalism: The Case of Ireland, 1874–1895* (Urbana, Illinois, 1974), pp. 154–6.

7 q. in Frederick Whyte, *The Life of W. T. Stead* (1925, 2 vols.), I. p. 15; Alexander Mackennal, *The Story of the English Separatists* (1893), pp. 138, 130; Horton, *The Dissolution of Dissent*, p. 16; M. S. Aldis, 'Reminiscences of a Church–Rate Struggle', *Con. Rev.*, LVII (1890), p. 427; Horne, *Popular History of the Free Churches*, p. 406.

8 Sydney Smith, 'Methodism' in *The Works of The Rev. Sydney Smith* (1859 edn, 2 vols.), I. pp. 88, 99. See also Valentine Cunningham, *Everywhere Spoken Against Dissent in the*

Victorian Novel (Oxford, 1975), esp. pp. 57–62; Andrew L. Drummond, *The Churches in Literary Fiction: A Literary and Historical Study* (Leicester, 1950), esp. ch. VII and Epilogue; Horne, *Nonconformity in the Nineteenth Century*, ch. V, & Prof. R. E. Welsh, 'The Clergy as Depicted in Fiction', *BW*, 9 August 1934.

9 T. H. S. Escott, *Anthony Trollope* (1913), pp. 111–12; Charles Dickens, *The Old Curiosity Shop* (1977 Everyman edn), p. 297 (ch. XLI).

10 W. M. Thackeray, *Vanity Fair* (1906, 13 vols. edn), I, p. 318. The reference to 'consecrated cobbler' is to Sydney Smith's attack on the Baptist missionary to India, William Carey, who started life as a Northampton cobbler.

11 Margaret Oliphant, *Salem Chapel* (Everyman edn, 1902), p. 2.

12 Anthony Trollope, *The Vicar of Bullhampton* (1952 World Classics edn), pp. 2, 429.

13 George Eliot, *Silas Marner* (Standard edn, n.d.), no vol. [III], pp. 10, 17; *Felix Holt* (Standard edn, n.d.), I, pp. 68–9.

14 G. W. E. Russell, 'Culture' in *Selected Essays on Literary Subjects* (n.d., Dent's Wayfarer's Library), p. 208; Mrs Humphry Ward, *Robert Elsmere* (Leipzig, Tauchnitz edn, 3 vols., 1888), II, p. 19; I, pp. 146–8.

15 Arnold Bennett, *A Great Man: A Frolic* (1904 edn), p. 124; George Gissing, *The Private Papers of Henry Ryecroft* (New York, The Modern Library Edn, 1918), p. 71.

16 James Adderley, *James Mercer* (1897), pp. 10–11.

17 D. W. Bebbington, 'Nonconformity and Electoral Sociology, 1867–1918', *HJ*, XXVII (1984), pp. 640–5.

18 *Methodist Times*, 27 November 1890.

19 *WMM*, 1892, p. 372; *WMM*, 1891, p. 377; Sir George Chubb to Lord Salisbury, 15 June 1885, Salisbury MS.

20 *Methodist Times*, 18 & 25 February 1886.

21 *Northamptonshire Nonconformist*, III (March 1891), p. 27; W. T. Stead to W. Wilkin, 28 December 1891, Bodley, MS Autograph b 9, *f* 383.

22 *WMM*, 1891, p. 333; *WMM*, 1892, p. 306.

23 q. in Anon., *Report of the House to House Visitation and Inaugural Meeting of the Council of the Evangelical Free Churches of Birmingham* (n.d. [1894]), pp. 14ff; *The Times*, 26 April 1899; J. G. Rogers, 'Why do Nonconformists follow Mr. Gladstone?', *Con. Rev.*, LXI (1892), pp. 902, 906.

24 Rogers, 'Nonconformists in Political Life', pp. 505, 498; Birrell, *Things Past Redress*, p. 126; Selbie, *Fairbairn*, p. 241.

25 Joseph Parker to W. E. Gladstone, 1 January 1895, Gladstone MS, Add. Mss 44520 *f* 3. Rogers, 'Nonconformists in Political Life', pp. 506, 498.

26 Ch. A., Spring 1900, *CUYB*, 1901, p. 34; Henry Richard & J. Carvell Williams, *Disestablishment* (1885), pp. 49–50.

27 The Rev. Samuel Vincent, Pr. A., Autumn 1898, *BUHB*, 1899, p. 147. Gladstone's quote became widely known due to an article by G. W. E. Russell, 'Mr Gladstone's Theology' published in the *Con. Rev.*, (LXXIII) in June 1898. There was, of course, rather more to Gladstone's High Church views on Nonconformity than the quote indicated. As Russell added, Gladstone believed that Nonconformity's views on history and theology left 'much to be desired'. In 1914 Robertson Nicoll openly criticized Gladstone as a man who 'regarded Dissenters with something like loathing. He knew that he was mainly indebted to them for his political victories . . . he never made a real friend, so far as I know, of any Dissenter.' (*BW*, 9 July 1914)

28 *PMM*, 1890, pp. 44–7, *passim*.

29 D. W. Bebbington, *The Nonconformist Conscience: Chapel and Politics 1870–1914* (George Allen & Unwin, 1982), p. 24. See also pp. 18–36 and G. I. T. Machin's valuable book, *Politics and the Churches in Great Britain 1869 to 1921* (Oxford, Clarendon Press, 1987), pp. 221ff.

30 Archbishop E. W. Benson to Sir Richard Webster, 15 September 1896, Sandars MS, MS Eng. Hist. c 729 *ff* 114–15; Edmund C. Rawlings, *The Free Churchman's Legal Handbook* (1902), *passim*.

31 A. M. Fairbairn, 'The Genesis of the Puritan Ideal', *Con. Rev.*, LIV (1888), p. 698; Wesleyan Methodist Home Mission Department; *Report for 1886* q. in Currie, *Methodism Divided*, pp. 180–1; Anon., 'Religious Equality: the Bitter Cry of Dissenting Clericalism', in *CQR*, XXXIV (1892), pp. 353–4, 381.

32 *FCYB*, 1897, p. 215; Joseph Parker, *Paterson's Parish* (1898), p. 232; Spring 1890, *CUYB*, 1891, p. 68.

33 The Rev. C. A. Berry, Ch. A., Autumn 1897, *CUYB*, p. 50; Anthony Trollope, *Orley Farm* (1862, 2 vols.), I, p. 64; *Coventry Herald*, 3 July 1903.

34 *CUYB*, 1894, p. 53; CU, *Short Tracts for the Times*, No XI (n.d. [c. 1891–2]), p. 4; the Rev. E. G. Gange, Pr. A., Spring 1897, *BUHB*, 1898, pp. 96–7.

35 *WMM*, 1895, p. 377; *WMM*, 1897, p. 408; *PMM*, 1893, p. 175; *PMM*, 1897, p. 187.

36 Rogers, 'Dissent in the Victorian Era', p. 124.

37 *Primitive Methodist Magazine*, December 1889, p. 764. The 'representatives of the state' were presumably the patrons? For Penzance see Michael Reynolds, *Martyr of Ritualism. Father Mackonochie* . . . (1965), pp. 181–3, and James Bentley, *Ritualism and Politics in Victorian Britain: The Attempt to Legislate for Belief* (Oxford, Clarendon Press, 1978), pp. 82–5 & *passim*, and Thomas Slater SJ, *Cares of Conscience* (1911, 2 vols.).

38 *FCYB*, 1896, pp. 51, 55.

39 Newbold, *The Nonconformist Conscience*, p. 171; *Baptist Times and Freeman*, 21 June 1901; the Rev. William Cuff, Pr. A., Autumn 1900, *BUHB*, 1901, p. 119.

40 Silas K. Hocking, *Reedyford; or, Creed and Character* (1890), pp. 168–9.

41 A. Wilson Fox, 'Agricultural Wages in England and Wales during the last Fifty Years' in W. E. Minchinton, *Essays in Agrarian History* (Newton Abbot, Devon, 1968, 2 vols.), II, *passim* (first read as a paper before the Royal Statistical Society, 21 April 1903); B. Seebohm Rowntree and May Kendall, *How the Labourer Lives: A Study of the Rural Labour Problem* (n.d. [1913]), *passim*; PP, 1901, Cd. Paper No. 849, *Inter-Departmental Committee on the Employment of School Children*, p. 15; E. N. Bennett, *Problems of Village Life* (n.d. [1913]), p. 126; H. H. Mann, 'Life in an Agricultural Village in England', in *Sociological Papers 1904* (1905), pp. 161–93; Flora Thompson, *Lark Rise to Candleford* (1971, World Classics edn), esp. pp. 223–8; Richard Hillyer, *Country Boy* (1966), ch. IV; W. H. Barrett, *A Fenman's Story* (1965), esp. chs. I–III; Alfred Williams, *A Wiltshire Village* (1912), esp. pp. 156–9, 205–6, & Alan Everitt, *The Pattern of Rural Dissent: the Nineteenth Century* (Leicester, Leicester University Press, 1972), *passim*.

42 Bennett, *Problems of Village Life*, p. 126; Rowntree & Kendall, *How the Labourer Lives*, p. 145. (Some surveys of the period 1890 to 1914 do not even mention religion: cf. F. G. Heath, *British Rural Life and Labour* (1911), C. F. G. Masterman, *Condition of England* (1909) & H. H. Mann, *Life in an Agricultural Village* (1905).) Christopher Holdenby, *Folk of the Furrow* (n.d.), p. 267 & Ch. XIII for a standard analysis of religion. M. F. Davies, *Life in an English Village* (1909), p. 283. Holmer Green MS, 14 February 1899, NB/10/1. By non-members the Records did not mean people outside the chapel but those who attended but were not baptized and therefore unable to receive Communion.

43 Harcourt to Fowler, 7 February 1894, Harcourt MS, MS

Harcourt dep. 82, *ff* 44–5; Eliza M. Champness, 'Parish Councils Act' in *The Wesleyan Methodist Year Book for 1895* (1895), pp. 59, 55; Richard Heath, 'The Rural Revolution', *Con. Rev.*, LXVII (1895), *passim*.

44 Townsend *et al.*, *A New History of Methodism*, I, pp. 461–2.

45 *PMM*, 1898, pp. 137–40.

46 The Rev. J. M. Gwynne Owen, *FCYB*, 1897, pp. 227–8; E. C. Pike, *The Heroes of the Meeting-House* (n.d. [1912]), p. 43.

47 *Pall Mall Gazette, House of Commons*, p. 150; H. J. Wilson to his wife, 7 May 1896, Wilson MS, MD 2615/20.

48 R. F. Horton, 'The Free Church in England', *Fort. Rev.*, LXVII (1897), p. 605.

49 J. G. Rogers, 'Liberal Imperialists and the Transvaal War', *Con. Rev.*, LXXVI (1899), p. 408; Hocking, *My Book of Memory*, pp. 183, 185. See J. G. Rogers, 'The Churches and the War', in *Con. Rev.*, LXXVII (1900).

50 *Daily News*, 14 December 1901; *Daily Chronicle*, 24 December 1901. See the *Spectator* of 21 December 1901 for a survey of the controversy.

51 Macdonald, *As A Tale that is Told*, pp. 247–50.

52 *BUHB*, 1900, pp. 147ff; *BUHB*, 1901, p. 132; *BUHB*, 1902, p. 110.

53 *CUYB*, 1897, p. 7; *CUYB*, 1901, pp. 42–3; *CUYB*, 1902, p. 4.

54 *WMM*, 1900, pp. 405, 408–9. Information for military enlistment comes from relevant *Minutes*. The 1880 figures were for the Army: of a total of 100,000, 62,860 were C. of E., 20,872 were Roman Catholic, and 7,125 were Presbyterian. The balance, 8,143, were said to belong 'to the great Nonconforming and other Protestant bodies'. Given the discrepancy between these figures and those Wesleyan statistics for 1890 one assumes that the majority of WM were to be found more in the militia and not in the Royal Navy. (*Pall Mall Gazette*, 9 January 1880)

55 A. H. Wilkerson, *The Rev. R. J. Campbell* (1907), pp. 24–5; *FCYB*, 1900, p. 83.

56 *FCYB*, 1901, p. 62. In 1900 Mackennal had put forward a vision of a 'sacrificial nation': a great power like Britain disarming itself to achieve world peace. He admitted it was only a 'longing' which would not 'command a serious hearing' but without such a vision no nation could be a Christian nation. (*FCYB*, 1900, pp. 6–7)

57 Anon., 'Religious Equality', pp. 376–7; Diggle, 'The Policy of the Education Bill', p. 33; W. E. H. Lecky, *Democracy and Liberty* (1896, 2 vols.), I, pp. 195–6; see p. 435 where Lecky argued that the alleged growth in Nonconformist political

involvement was a means to fill the vacuum caused by the decay in doctrine, especially the old Calvinism of the Baptists & Congregationalists.

58 James Adderley, 'What Do the Nonconformists Teach Us?' in James Adderley (ed.), *Practical Questions: Lectures on Modern Difficulties in Church Life* (1905), pp. 221–2; Anon., 'Musings Without Method', *Blackwood's Magazine* November 1902), pp. 711–13; Anon., *The Nonconformist Conscience Considered as a Social Evil and a Mischief Monger by One Who Has Had It* (1903), *passim*; Newbold, *The Nonconformist Conscience*, pp. 96, 155, 159; Kellett, *As I Remember*, p. 173.

59 A. Tilney Bassett (ed.), *A Victorian Vintage . . . from the Diaries of Sir Mountstuart E. Grant Duff* (1930), p. 205; 'Nonconformist Conscience' in *Oxford English Dictionary* (2nd edn, 1989), x, p. 489; J. B. Foreman (ed.), *Complete Works of Oscar Wilde* (1969), p. 416; the Rev. H. Arnold Thomas, Ch. A., Spring 1899, *CUYB*, 1900, p. 25.

60 W. B. Selbie, *Nonconformity: Its Origin and Progress* (1912), p. 231; Anon., 'Religious Equality', p. 351.

9. PASSIVE RESISTANCE AND NONCONFORMIST POWER, 1902–1914

1 The total for the Parliamentary Liberal Party is for 31 March 1905 and includes Asquith and Haldane as well as the 'Lib–Labs'. There were 9 Nonconformist Conservatives out of 334 and 14 Nonconformist Liberal Unionists out of 68. (*FCYB*, 1905, pp. 285–7).

2 Sir Courtney Ilbert, *Memorandum on the 1896 Education Bill*, Ilbert MS 66, no fol.; *The Times*, 19 January 1895. While Balfour was First Lord his uncle, Lord Salisbury, was Prime Minister as well as Foreign Secretary.

3 *British Weekly* [W. Robertson Nicoll], *The British Weekly Catechism of the Education Bill as it Affects Nonconformists* (1902), p. 5; M. A. Drummond to Joseph Chamberlain, 13 July 1903, Chamberlain MS, JC 18/19/29; *The British Weekly Catechism*, p. 8. RC bishops were not consulted.

4 cf. *BW*, 6 December 1894.

5 cf. J. E. B. Munson, 'The Unionist Coalition and Education, 1895–1902', *HJ*, xx (1977); Gillian Sutherland, *Elementary Education in the Nineteenth Century* (Historical Association General Pamphlet no. 76, 1971) and *Policy-Making in Elementary Education 1870–1895* (Oxford, 1973); G. A. N. Lowndes, *The Silent Social Revolution: An Account of the*

Expansion of Public Education in England and Wales 1895–1965 (Oxford, 1969).

6 *WMM*, 1891, pp. 302–5; *BUHB*, 1894, p. 103; See *CUYB*, 1897, pp. 4, 62–5. It was significant that the CU condemned the 1896 act for 'reopening the whole question of public elementary education' which they saw as 'settled'.

7 Herbert, Cardinal Vaughan to Athelstan Riley, 10 July 1893, Riley MS, 2343 *ff* 200–1.

8 Sir Bernard Mallet, 'Amendments to the Education Bill', 8 June 1896, Balfour MS, Add. Mss 49786 *ff* 226–31; Sir Joshua Fitch q. in J. E. B. Munson, 'The London School Board Election of 1894: A Study in Victorian Religious Controversy', *BJES*, xxiii (1975), p. 7.

9 D. Lloyd George, *Hansard*, 4th Ser., cx (1902), pp. 1282–4; PP, 1901, lvi, Cd. 568, *Statistics of Public Elementary Schools . . . for year ended 31st August 1900*, p. 134.

10 *PMM*, 1896, p. 139.

10 MS note in Lady Laura Ridding's interleafed copy of her biography of her husband, *George Ridding: Schoolmaster and Bishop* (1908, 2 vols.), Ridding MS, MS Eng. Hist. d 186 *f* 124.

11 Michael Sadler, 'Changes in opinion as to the administration of education in England between 1870 and 1896', Sadler MS, MS Eng. Misc. c 551 *ff* 13–54; PP, 1895, lxiii, Cd. 7862, *Royal Commission on Secondary Education*, i, pp. 120–1.

12 *Daily News*, 9 November 1894; R. C. Moberly, *Undenominationalism as a Principle of Primary Education* (1902), pp. 8, 24; cf. Munson, 'The London School Board Election of 1894'; *School Board Chronicle*, 6 January 1894.

13 *BW*, 20 June 1901; for the Halifax controversy see Francis Pigou, *Phases of My Life* (1898), pp. 298–303; London Nonconformist Committee, 'The Conference of Nonconformists at Manchester' (1872), p. 12; Manchester Nonconformist Association, *Report . . . for the Year 1872–1873* (Manchester, 1873), p. 10.

14 J. Guinness Rogers, 'Nonconformist Forebodings', *Nine. Cen.*, xxxvi (1894), p. 793; E. S. Elwell, 'The Elementary Education Question' (1899), p. 9, and cf. George Beach, 'The Work, Disabilities, and Claims of Voluntary Schools' (Manchester, n.d.); *The Vaccination Inquirer and Health Review. Organ of the National Anti-Vaccination League*, 1 January 1903, 1 April 1904.

15 Balfour to Chamberlain, 3 September 1902, Balfour MS, 49744 *ff* 19–25; *Daily News*, 13, 26 August 1902; *BW*, 29 May 1902; A. J. Balfour, 'Dr. Clifford on Religious Education:

A Study in Political Controversy' in *Essays and Addresses* (Edinburgh, 3rd edn, 1905), pp. 442, 428. For a time a new verb was added to the language — 'to Cliffordise', meaning to exaggerate wildly.

16 E. A. Payne to the author, 24 February 1970; Helen Wilson to Gertrude Wilson, 17/18 May 1907. Wilson MS, MD 2466-3, 4.

17 *The Light of Home*, March 1902, n.p.; *BW*, 3, 10 April 1902; q. in Darlow, *Nicoll*, p. 208.

18 *Jackson's Oxford Journal*, 1 August 1903; *BW*, 3 April 1902; Herbert Gladstone to Campbell-Bannerman, 18 January 1904, C-B MS, Add. Mss 41217 *ff* 82-3; *The Times*, 5 April 1902; *Methodist Times*, 15 April 1902.

19 Earl of Selborne, 'Some Memories and Some reflections in my old age', Selborne MS 193 *f* 5; *New Liberal Review*, IV/23 (1902), p. 763; Sir William Harcourt to Campbell-Bannerman, 29 April 1902, C-B MS, Add. Mss 41220 *ff* 60-1.

20 Campbell-Bannerman to Harcourt, 29 April 1902, Harcourt MS, WVH 9/7; Campbell-Bannerman to Gladstone, 28 September 1902, Viscount Gladstone MS, 45988 *ff* 24-5; Campbell-Bannerman to Gladstone, 2 January 1905, Viscount Gladstone MS, Add. Mss 45988 *ff* 139-41; Campbell-Bannerman to Gladstone, 20 November 1905, Viscount Gladstone MS, Add. Mss 45988 *ff* 201-2; *Spectator*, 23 November 1901; Campbell-Bannerman to Gladstone, ? April 1902, C-B MS, Add. Mss 41216 *f* 199; Bryce to Gladstone, 29 September 1902, Viscount Gladstone MS, Add. Mss 46019 *ff* 71-2.

21 Joseph Chamberlain to —?— Dowson, 13 October 1902, Chamberlain MS, JC 11/39/53.

22 Asquith to A. H. D. Acland, 30 October 1901, Acland MS, MS Eng. Lett. d 81 *ff* 107-8; A. H. D. Acland to J. A. Spender, 3 May 1902, Spender MS, Add. Mss 46391 *ff* 105-6; Sir Edward Hamilton diary, 14 October 1902, Hamilton MS, Add. Mss 48680 *f* 33; Rosebery to J. B. Paton, 17 September 1902, Davidson MS; Perks to Rosebery, 1 January 1903, Rosebery MS, Box 40.

23 Sir William Harcourt to Lewis Harcourt, 8 December 1902, Harcourt MS, WVH 1/22; Haldane to his sister, 26 May 1902, Haldane MS, 6010 *ff* 196-7; Grey to Sir Henry Newbolt, 5 January 1903, Newbolt MS, Eng. Lett. d 316 *ff* 23-6; *Hansard*, 4th ser., cxv, p. 1014 (1902).

24 Minutes, Organizing Committee, 12 May 1902, FC Archives. Law reported they had issued 1m. leaflets and 400,000 booklets; *BW*, 19 June 1902.

25 Minutes of the PM Conference, 1902, pp. 174–5, PM Archives; *Methodist Times*, 24 July 1902, 7 August 1902.

26 *BW*, 31 July 1902; Lloyd George to Nicoll, 19 July 1902, Nicoll MS; Augustine Birrell to Herbert Samuel, 28 May 1902, Samuel MS, A/155 (III), *ff* 20–21.

27 Lloyd George *et al.* to Campbell-Bannerman, 31 October 1902, C-B MS, Add. Mss 41237 *ff* 54–5.

28 Morant to Jack Sandars, 23 September 1902, Balfour MS, Add. Mss, 49787 *ff* 84–6; The first song is found in the I.L.P.'s *Sixteen Songs for Sixpence* (n.d.) and was made available by courtesy of the Music Librarian, BBC. By 9 October it had sold 100,000 copies. A copy of Hollowell's song was found in the *Elmsworth Free Church Magazine, 1903–4* (February 1903), n.p. & loaned to the writer by Mr F. Charrett. The third song was found in *Crusader*, 14 April 1904.

29 Silvester Horne diary, 7 October 1902, q. Selbie, *Horne*, p. 130; Minutes, General Purposes Committee, 16 September 1902, BU MS; Minutes, General Committee, 10 October 1902, FC Archives. Some 307 local councils or 37% had not bothered to answer the questionnaire and these, combined with the councils who were neutral or opposed to resistance, came to 384 or 48%.

30 Davidson to Hughes, 7 October 1902, Davidson MS; Lloyd George to Nicoll, 4 November 1902, Nicoll MS; Lloyd George to his wife, 24 March 1902, Lloyd George MS (Wales), Mss 20, 424C, No. 1067.

31 John Clifford, *Ten Years of Protest Against the Intrusion of Churches into State Schools. Passive Resistance June, 1912 — June, 1913* (1913), p. 6, John Clifford Donation; Minutes, General Committee, 1 December 1902, FC Archives; E. A. Payne to the author, 24 February 1970. Of the thirty-eight members whose denomination is known, 14 were Baptists, 10 were Congregationalists, 5 were Primitive Methodists, 3 Wesleyans, 1 Presbyterian and 1 representative from the Quakers and from each of the three minor Methodist groups.

32 Lord Knollys to A. J. Balfour, 5 December 1902, Balfour MS, Add. Mss 49683 *f* 114; Lyttelton to Milner, 27 August 1902, Milner MS, 40, *ff* 154–7; Bryce to Lord Ripon, 22 September 1902, Ripon MS, Add. Mss, 43542 *ff* 17–18; Chamberlain to Balfour, 4 August 1902, Balfour MS, Add. Mss 49774 *ff* 7–12.

33 *Crusader*, 15 May 1903; Minute Book, Norwich PR MS, FC 6/23; Franklin MS.

34 *BW*, 13 November 1902; *The Erith Times*, 2 October 1903; *Crusader*, 15 September 1903.

35 *Crusader*, 30 October 1903, 3 March 1904, 15 February 1903; Minute Book, Executive Committee, Liberation Society, Letter of 21 July 1902 to members of the Executive, Liberation Society MS, A/LIB/9; 3 November 1904.

36 H. J. Wilson to the Chief Assistant Overseer, 30 July 1903, Wilson MS, MD 2608–4; *H. J. Wilson to His Constituents*, 12 February 1906, Wilson MS, MD 2607–3.

37 See, for example, J. G. James, 'The Ethics of Passive Resistance' in *International Journal of Ethics*, xiv (1904).

38 Copies of writs supplied by Mr F. Charrett of Portsmouth and the Franklin MS Collection; J. F. & B. E. Crump, *The Magistrates' Pocket Manual* (1903), p. 14; National Passive Resistance Committee, 'Legal Notes' (Tract No. 14) (1903), n.p., John Clifford Donation.

39 *Western Daily Mercury*, 8 September 1903; *Crusader*, 28 September 1905; *Punch*, 15 November 1905.

40 *Crusader*, 4 August 1904. At the time, 'condescending' did not have the sense of 'patronizing' it now has; it still had its older meaning of being 'gracious' when applied to someone in a superior position, in this case, the magistrate; *Crusader*, 9 October 1903.

41 *Crusader*, 28 July 1904; Mrs Lorna Horstmann to the author, 29 February 1972.

42 *Crusader*, 15 September 1903; Creaton MS, Item 23, telegram dated 13 November 1903; *Crusader*, 21 April 1904.

43 Richard Dalby, 'My Imprisonment for "Passive Resistance"', p. 19. MS loaned to the author by the Rev. J. Dalby; Minutes, 25 May 1907, Bristol FC MS; *Crusader*, 1 June 1905, 15 March 1906.

44 *Crusader*, 21 July 1904.

45 J. C. Carlile, *Story of English Baptists* (1905), p. 312.

46 *The Schoolmaster*, 30 January 1904; *Punch*, 10 August 1904; *Daily News*, 30 January 1904; T. McKinnon Wood, 'London County Council Election, 1904' (Progressive Leaflet No. 2), McKinnon Wood MS, MS Eng. Hist. c. 499 *ff* 92–3; *Report of Proceedings of the Thirty-Fifth Annual Trades Union Congress (London). 1–6 September, 1902* (1902), pp. 71–2; *Report of . . . Thirty-Seventh Annual . . . Congress (Leeds), 5–10 September, 1904* (1904), p. 68; *Labour Leader*, 22 August 1903, 23 May 1903.

47 *Daily News*, 4 June 1903; *Westminster Gazette*, 11 August 1903; *Daily Chronicle*, 27, 26 June 1903; *The Standard*, 10 June 1903; *Pall Mall Gazette* 21 July 1902; *St. James's Gazette*, 8 June 1903; *The Times*, 25 June 1903; J. E. B. Munson, *A Study of Nonconformity in Edwardian England*

as *Revealed by the Passive Resistance Movement Against the 1902 Education Act* (Unpublished Oxford D Phil Thesis, 1973), pp. 321–6.

48 Wareham MS, 25 June 1903, RE 10/1902–18; Minutes of Quarterly Meeting, 25 May 1902, Durham PM MS, M/DU/29; Minutes, Committee of Privileges, 30 January 1903, 4 November 1902, 23 June 1903, WM Archives; *Crusader*, 20, 27 July 1905.

49 Balfour, 'Dr Clifford on Religious Education', *Essays and Addresses*, p. 443; Sydney Smith, 'Methodism', *Works*, I, p. 98.

50 Balfour to Edward VII, 3 May 1905, RA, CAB 41/30/16; Balfour to H. A. Thomas, 22 April 1902, Balfour MS, Add. Mss 49854 *ff* 312–14; Balfour to ?, 19 July 1904, Balfour MS, Add. Mss 49855 *ff* 136–41.

51 Balfour to Devonshire, 4 June 1903, Devonshire MS, 340 *f* 2915; Herbert Gladstone diary, 14 November 1899, Viscount Gladstone MS, Add. Mss 46483 *ff* 47–8 & *f* 31 for 15 July 1899 entry; Campbell, *A Spiritual Pilgrimage*, pp. 135–6; Balfour to Lord Salisbury, 17 November 1904, Balfour MS, Add. Mss 49757 *ff* 366–7.

52 Balfour to Edward VII, 20 November 1903, RA, CAB 41/28/22; Morant to Balfour, 17 September 1904, Balfour MS, Add. Mss 49787 *ff* 97–102; Lloyd George to Nicoll, 15 September 1904, Nicoll MS; Minutes, General Committee, 26 September 1904, FC Archives; *Daily News*, 17 September 1904.

53 Minutes, Education Committee, 10 May 1905, FC Archives; Morant to Balfour, 19 September 1905, Balfour MS, Add. Mss 49787 *ff* 103–109; Thomas Law to Lloyd George, 8 March 1905, Lloyd George MS (Lords), A/1/15/8; Lord Cobham to F. A. Newdegate, 6 December 1903, Newdegate MS, B 6320.

54 C. T. Ritchie, 'Colonial Preference and Corn Duty', 15 November 1902, Sandars MS, MS Eng. Hist. c. 737 *f* 140.

55 Bryce to Campbell-Bannerman, 16 January 1904, C-B MS, Add. Mss 41211 *ff* 169–70; Gladstone to Asquith, 24 December 1903, Asquith MS, Vol. x *ff* 120–1; Campbell-Bannerman to Asquith, 26 December 1903, Asquith MS, Vol. x *ff* 122–3; Campbell-Bannerman to Bryce, 29 December 1903, Bryce MS, UB 32; Herbert Gladstone diary, 29 September 1903, 13 January 1904, Viscount Gladstone MS, Add. Mss 46484 *ff* 53–4, 62; Bryce to Herbert Gladstone, 27 December 1904, Viscount Gladstone MS, Add. Mss 46019 *ff*

94–5; Bryce to Ripon, 4 December 1902, Ripon MS, Add. Mss 43542 *ff* 21–2.

56 *Daily News*, 25 July 1904; *Crusader*, 9 February 1904; W. M. Crook to Herbert Gladstone, 17 September 1903, 7 March 1903, Viscount Gladstone MS, Add. Mss 46024 *ff* 33–4, 19–20.

57 George Cadbury to Gladstone, 29 May 1903, Viscount Gladstone MS, Add. Mss 46060 *f* 201; Gladstone to Campbell-Bannerman, 25 November 1905, C-B MS, Add. Mss 41217 *ff* 279–80.

58 Minutes, Education Committee, 20 December 1905, FC Archives.

59 *Pall Mall Gazette, The House of Commons*, pp. 14–15; Minutes, General Committee, 5 February 1906, FC Archives. The total of 187 comes from *The Crusader* (8 February 1906). The General Committee's total was 176; G. I. T. Machin, *Politics and the Churches*, p. 278, lists 'about 210'. As Nonconformist candidates standing as Liberal Unionists had done badly, it appears the increase came among Labour MPs.

60 For contemporary politicians' views on the election and the importance of education see: undated Memo, Viscount Gladstone MS, Add. Mss 46118 *f* 102 (of 22,521,000 Liberal leaflets sold, only 1,059,000 were on education while 9,096,000 were on tariff reform) and Lord St Aldwyn to Balfour, 25 January 1906, Sandars MS, MS Eng. Hist. c 751 *ff* 121–2; Campbell-Bannerman informed the King that the first Cabinet meeting had appointed committees to 'examine and advise' on education and unemployment. (Campbell-Bannerman to Edward VII, 14 December 1905 (copy), C-B. MS, Add. Mss 42512 no *fol.*)

61 Cecil to Spender, June [?] 1906, Spender MS, Add. Mss 46391 *ff* 191–2; *Crusader*, 8 March 1906. Sears also joined in advocating moderation.

62 Churchill to Charles Dilke, 24 January 1906, Dilke MS, Add. Mss 43877 *f* 53; Arthur Ponsonby diary, 3 July 1906, Ponsonby MS, MS Eng. Hist. c 653, *f* 14; Birrell to R. F. Charles, 17 May 1906 [?], Bodley, MS Eng. Lett. e 94 *ff* 118–19.

63 For difficulties over education bill see Arthur Ponsonby diary, 16 April, 5 August 1906, Ponsonby MS, MS Eng. Hist. c 653, *ff* 11–13, 16; See correspondence between the Irish leader, John Redmond and Cardinal Bourne in Redmond MS, Mss: 15, 168–91; 15, 171–4; 15, 179; 15, 189; 15, 192;

15, 229; 15, 172 and, esp. 15, 229. The most important are
the letters from Bourne to Redmond of 15 June 1906 (MS 15,
172) and Redmond to Birrell, 2 December 1906 (MS 15,
169). This correspondence covers the period 1906–1910 and
1915. Part of Bourne's aim was to put the Duke of Norfolk in
his place; Bourne was to be the spokesman for Roman
Catholics in England, not the Duke.

64 Rector of Bugbrooke to Balfour, n.d. [1906], Sandars MS,
MS Eng. Hist. c 757, *f* 175 n.d. Many clergymen, especially
those in rural parishes, were said to fear 'having their
Schools, on which many of them, and many of the most
evangelical, have bestowed some of the best work of their
lives, taken out of their hands'. (Dean Wace to Lady
Wimborne, 25 April 1906, Osborne MS, Add. Mss 46408 *f*
75. Lady Wimborne, 'Deborah of Dorset' to her enemies,
gave money to the Liberals to ensure appointment of Low
Church bishops wherever possible.)

65 [Walter Runciman], Notes of talk between John Morley and
Walter Runciman, 17 November [1906], Runciman MS, WR
14, no *fol*.

66 Arthur Ponsonby diary, January 1907, Ponsonby MS, MS
Eng. Hist. c 653 *ff* 20a–23; R. L. Morant, largely responsible
for the draughting of the 1902 Act, bemoaned the 'recent lack
of honesty & debasing all our machinery to basely political
purposes'. (Morant to F. S. Marvin, 30 December 1907,
Marvin MS, MS Eng. Lett. d 258 *f* 208); Bryce to J. A.
Spender, 29 May 1908, Spender MS, Add. Mss 46391 *ff* 246–
8. For 1908 Bill the Asquith MS, Vol. xx *ff* 1–80 contain the
various memoranda and letters regarding the bill; also see
Selbie, *Horne*, pp. 198–202 and G. K. A. Bell, *Randall
Davidson* (Oxford, OUP, 3rd edn, 2 vols. in one), pp. 530–40;
Runciman to Asquith, 25 September 1908, Asquith MS, Vol.
X, *ff* 28–31; Silvester Horne diary, 18 November 1908 q. in
Selbie, *Horne*, p. 199; Clifford to Asquith, 23 September
1908, Asquith MS, Vol. x, *ff* 25–7.

67 Lloyd George to Nicoll, 9 September 1909, Nicoll MS.

68 By 1912 only £58,482 had been allocated for the erection of
some 45 schools: rhetoric had once again come up against
reality. (J. A. Pease, Memo, 24 October 1912, Cab. MS, CAB
37/112/117.) For plans on education bills see: Asquith,
Hansard, 5th Ser., xxxi, 19 (13 November 1911); Asquith to
F. B. Meyer, 29 February 1912 in Cabinet MS, CAB
37/112/117; *The Advertiser*, 2 November 1912.

69 *Grantham Journal*, 11 November 1911; John Clifford, *Is
England to be Converted to Rome?* (1910), p. 5, John Clifford

Donation; *Free Church Chronicle*, April, 1912, p. 75; *West Cumberland Times*, 9 December 1911. Also, education was changing: in 1908, for example, in the small Oxfordshire village of Milton-under-Wychwood, the Baptist Chapel agreed to transfer their Sunday school to Oxfordshire LEA in return for a rent of £7 per annum repairs and a 'fair wear and tear' fee. The village's Church school would become the secondary division while the Baptist school would be used for primary classes. Like the church, the chapel was now part of the established order and one 'single school district' had its problem solved peacefully. (Milton MS, 16 June 1907, 29 June, 17 December 1908.)

70 J. A. Pease, Memorandum, 23 May 1913, Cabinet MS, CAB 37/115/32.

71 J. A. Pease, 'A National System of Education for England and Wales', *Con. Rev.*, CXI (1917), pp. 138, 141.

72 Nicoll to Lloyd George, 14 March 1914, Lloyd George MS (Lords), C/11/1/9; J. A. Pease diary, 3 August 1914 q. by him in his MS 'Some Reminiscences', Gainford MS, 47, no *fol.*; Minutes, 14, 21 September 1914, Norwich P.R. MS, FC 6/23. Passive Resistance survived the war: in 1920 an engine-fitter and turner at the Royal Docks, Devonport wrote to John Clifford asking if he and two fellow Resisters should continue their 'feeble protest', especially as 'sometimes it causes a certain amount of ridicule'. Clifford replied: 'We keep on. The patience and persistence of hope upholds us; though it seems of little use. But I am in touch with Mr [H. A. L.] Fisher [President of the Board of Education] and he is considering our case.' The three Devonport Resisters then gave up their protest although Clifford and Robertson Nicoll continued until their deaths in 1923. In Derbyshire, one Bakewell Resister continued until 1926. (Clifford to George H. Brown, 10 January 1920. MS kindly loaned to the writer by Mr Brown's son, Mr L. H. Brown of Galmpton, Brixham, Devon.)

AFTERWORD

1 The Rev. Andrew Clark's War Diary, 11 November 1915, MS Eng. Hist. e 114 *ff* 88–88*v*, Bodleian Library. A typical instance of the older view's survival occurred in the Essex village of Great Leighs when Andrew Clark recorded a rumour that one farm foreman, known as 'an offensive Radical, an offensive "Chapelite", an offensive "Brotherhood"', went about saying 'the authorities are sending out our poor

lads to certain slaughter, and that the Germans are winning all along the line, and will win thoroughly'. (Diary entry for 5 May 1915, MS Eng. Hist. e 103 f 25v.) Nonconformist attitudes were changing before 1914: in 1903 the War Office agreed requests from the BU General Committee and ordered that 'Baptist' and 'Congregationalist' would be included among the religious affiliation blanks in army forms. The two Unions could also now ask local commanders about providing chaplains, none of whom would be appointed without Union agreement and all of whom would be free of the Chaplain General. (19 January 1903, Baptist Union MS)

2 Darlow, *Nicoll*, p. 236; Nicoll to Miss Maud Coe, 18 October 1914 q. in Darlow, *Nicoll*, p. 235.

3 *WMM*, 1920, pp. 358–9; *WMM*, 1892, p. 373.

4 J. M. Winter, *The Great War and the British People* (Macmillan, 1985), pp. 65–6, 71, 92, 266–7.

5 The BU total fell from 164,923 to 255,469, a fall of 9,454 or 3.57%; WM fell from 453,819 to 433,732, a fall of 20,087 or 4.43%; PM fell from 194,908 to 191,709, a fall of 3,208 or 1.64%; CU, however, rose from 289,545 to 295,451, a rise of 5,906 or 2.04%. WM figures include those 'on trial'.

6 WM declined between 1895 and 1896; PM declined between 1891 and 1892; Baptists declined between 1897 and 1898 and again between 1898 and 1899.

7 Between 1901 and 1931 the membership of all four leading denominations grew: WM from 414,049 to 443,786 (7.18%); PM, from 185,000 to 189,843 (2.62%); BU, 243,534 to 254,618 (4.55%); CU, 258,434 to 276,384 (6.95%) although their percentage of the population for England declined by 0.16% (WM); 0.19% (PM); 0.11% (BU); 0.10% (CU) from the 1901 level. In the 60 years between 1871 and 1931 membership and percentage of the English population stood at: PM, 148,798 (.79%) to 189,843 (.51%); WM, 319,714 (1.67%) to 443,786 (1.19%); BU, 160,978 (.85%) to 254,618 (.68%); CU no figures for 1871 to 276,384 (.74%).

8 Stanley Baldwin, 'Religion and Politics' in *On England and other Addresses* (1933 edn, 1st publ. 1926), p. 156. Speech delivered 11 February 1926.

9 Arnold Morley to Sir William Harcourt, 17 November 1896, Harcourt MS, dep 88, ff 240–3.

10 Balfour to Sir Richard Webster, 6 October 1896, Sandars MS, MS Eng. Hist. c 729 ff 128–33. Webster was the Attorney General. *Crusader*, 30 June 1904.

11 Lloyd George to Nicoll, 16 March 1915, Nicoll MS.

12 Machin, *Politics and the Churches*, p. 315; Horton, 'The Free

Church in England', p. 605; Baldwin, 'Religion and Politics', p. 156.

13 *Report of the Census of 1931 (England and Wales)*, p. xv: from 1851 to 1911 the rate of urban growth on a decennial basis never went below 10.3% but by 1921–1931 it was down to 6%.

14 There are no CU statistics for 1871 so BU were used unless other factors made this inappropriate. In addition, both WM and PM based their returns on circuits which could include chapels or 'stations' outside the town being covered; for this reason some comparisons were impossible.

15 David Martin, 'Age and Sex Variations of Church Attenders' in Nationwide Initiative in Evangelism [Peter Brierley, ed.], *Prospects for the Eighties* . . . (Bible Society, 1980), p. 14; the Most Rev. Robert Runcie, Archbishop of Canterbury, 'Address on the Inauguration of the Rev. Bernard Green as Moderator of the Free Church Federal Council, 1988–89: Friday, 18th March 1988'.

16 In this same speech Archbishop Runcie said of the Nonconformist Conscience: 'We in the Church of England deeply need and value your steady support for our maintenance of the ideal of a social consensus and the welfare state. In the Free Churches you have a much longer tradition of being a loyal opposition. If we in the Church of England are sometimes so perceived today, please help us to get used to this prophetic perception.' Whether history will prove Archbishop Runcie's 'prophetic vision' any more lasting than Hugh Price Hughes's 'social purity' only time will tell.

INDEX

The following abbreviations have been used: B. Baptist(s); ch. chapel or church; C. Congregational(ist); L. London; M. mission; N. Nonconformity; Nc. Nonconformist(s); P.M. Primitive Methodist(s); ref. referred to; S. settlement; T. tabernacle; W.M. Wesleyan Methodist(s). Individual churches are listed under chapels, missions and settlements.

350